D0918479

Post-Colonial Studies

Other titles in *The Essential Glossary* series

FRENCH CULTURE AND SOCIETY	Michael Kelly
SPANISH CULTURE AND SOCIETY	Barry Jordan
GERMAN CULTURE AND SOCIETY	Holger Briel
FRANCOPHONE STUDIES	Margaret Majumdar
AMERICAN LITERATURE	Stephen Matterson
IRISH STUDIES	John Goodby
VICTORIAN CULTURE AND SOCIETY	Adam C. Roberts

Forthcoming

SEXUALITY	Jo Eadie

Ref.
325.3
T34

Post-Colonial Studies
The Essential Glossary

John Thieme

A member of the Hodder Headline Group
LONDON
Distributed in the United States of America by
Oxford University Press Inc., New York

Nyack College Library

First published in Great Britain in 2003 by
Arnold, a member of the Hodder Headline Group,
338 Euston Road, London NW1 3BH

http://www.arnoldpublishers.com

Distributed in the United States of America by
Oxford University Press Inc.,
198 Madison Avenue, New York, NY10016

© 2003 John Thieme

All rights reserved. No part of this publication may be reproduced or
transmitted in any form or by any means, electronically or mechanically,
including photocopying, recording or any information storage or retrieval
system, without either prior permission in writing from the publisher or a
licence permitting restricted copying. In the United Kingdom such licences
are issued by the Copyright Licensing Agency: 90 Tottenham Court Road,
London W1T 4LP.

The advice and information in this book are believed to be true and
accurate at the date of going to press, but neither the author nor the publisher
can accept any legal responsibility or liability for any errors or omissions.

British Library Cataloguing in Publication Data
A catalogue record for this book is available from the British Library

Library of Congress Cataloging-in-Publication Data
A catalog record for this book is available from the Library of Congress

ISBN 0 340 76175 X (hb)
ISBN 0 340 76174 1 (pb)

1 2 3 4 5 6 7 8 9 10

Typeset in 10/13pt Minion by Phoenix Photosetting, Chatham, Kent
Printed and bound in Malta

What do you think about this book? Or any other Arnold title?
Please send your comments to feedback.arnold@hodder.co.uk

Contents

Preface   vii

Guide to the Glossary   xiii

Glossary   1

Bibliography   281

Preface

This Glossary is primarily intended as an introduction to post-colonial studies for undergraduates and others new to the subject. It offers an interdisciplinary guide to the various concepts, practices and cultural products that have come to be known as 'post(-)colonial', variously spelt with and without a hyphen (see the entry on the HYPHEN). In addition to providing an orientation map for those beginning courses in post-colonial literature and theory and post-colonial studies more generally, it should serve as a reference tool for those with expertise in particular aspects of the field, who now wish to expand their interest into other areas. It offers entries on major figures, trends and movements, on writers and theorists, on concepts and terms, on historical events and politicians, on music and musicians, on film-makers and artists, on journals and websites, on popular cultural forms and folk artists, on language forms and language usage and on a wide variety of other subjects, such as literary prizes and post-colonial responses to canonical authors.

Post-colonial studies is a comparatively new field, but it has already witnessed a massive expansion, not simply in interest, but also in the areas that are considered to fall within its ambit. The term has come to be used in relation to a diverse range of projects, approaches and subjects that transgress and frequently dismember older disciplinary boundaries. Consequently, to use one of the field's more popular tropes, it has grown haphazardly like a RHIZOME, to a point where its own parameters are becoming distinctly fuzzy and it runs the risk of becoming a colonizing enterprise itself, as it becomes increasingly institutionalized and as it absorbs other subjects into this rhizomatic trajectory. In an endeavour to combat this proliferation, some authorities in the field have, very reasonably, insisted on defining it more narrowly, so as to give it a greater sharpness and urgency. The Glossary itself takes an inclusive approach, so that its users can become acquainted with the various ways in which post-colonial studies are currently being viewed. At the same time it draws attention to some of the problems – and indeed the inherent contradictions – involved in current usages and practices. Insofar as it makes a particular 'intervention' in the subject, it does so by resisting tendencies to homogenize post-colonial experiences and devoting particular attention to cultural specifics. It also places its main emphasis on the experience of those who have been colonized.

The two main formative impulses that came together to shape the genesis of the field (around the time of the publication of Edward Said's landmark study, *Orientalism*, in 1978) both had their origins in literary studies, and the three most famous theorists working in the field, Said, Gayatri Chakravorty Spivak and Homi K. Bhabha all began their careers in 'literature', though in each case their work has engaged with a broad repertory of representational practices. These two impulses were a body of cultural commentary that combined colonial discourse analysis with poststructuralist theory and a revisionist approach to the study of 'world' or 'Commonwealth' literatures (i.e. literatures from outside Europe and the USA), which began to wrest them from their marginalized position in English and other areas of literary studies. Subsequently, the two strands have often existed in an uneasy coalition; sometimes they have completely parted company. The Glossary attempts to bring them together and to demonstrate their intersection with and effect on numerous other practices and fields that have come to be seen as 'post-colonial'. So, while literature (defined in the broadest sense to include ORATURE) and cultural theory are its twin pivots, it also considers the impact of post-colonial thinking on disciplines such as geography, history and ethnography, while stressing its role in eroding traditional academic boundaries.

Until the 1960s, the view that 'culture' was the prerogative of the elite had remained largely unchallenged in the Western academy and Western society more generally for around a century. In the English-speaking world in particular, there was comparatively little dissent from the view most famously expressed in Matthew Arnold's 1873 definition of it as knowledge of 'the best that has been thought and said in the world' (Preface to 'Literature and Dogma', Arnold M. 1954: 537), a construction of 'culture' that usually naturalized it as an activity of the 'civilized' West. It is a view that can be traced back to the Enlightenment era – and in some cases, though usage in previous periods is altogether more erratic, much earlier – but it solidified in the late nineteenth and early twentieth centuries, at a time when academic disciplines such as English studies were taking shape (Palmer, D. 1965; Eagleton 1983). It is no coincidence that such subjects emerged during the late Victorian heyday of British imperialism, a time when several other European nations were pursuing similar expansionist missions. The link between culture, defined in Arnoldian terms, and imperialism has, of course, been discussed by numerous commentators (e.g. Said 1994, *passim*), though several place their emphasis earlier and rather fewer have devoted attention to the correspondence between the rise of modern *academe* and this period of late imperial assertiveness. It is, however, a crucial correspondence, given the extent to which this academic expansion was shaped by the characteristic post-Enlightenment Western practice of defining the self through contradistinction from 'OTHERNESS'.

Such a view of culture continued to underpin most areas of arts and humanities study until the 1960s, when a sea change in the social and political climate, which occurred during the period when the political independences of many of Europe's overseas colonies were being attained, saw major theoretical and ideological challenges being mounted to the liberal humanist study of culture. Around this time the term 'post-colonial' was most frequently used – by historians, sociologists and others – as a synonym for 'post-independent', i.e. to refer to the period *after* colonialism. It is still sometimes used in this way. However, with the conflation of the fields of colonial discourse and post-colonial theory, it has generally been supplanted by a usage that refers to the experience of colonialism shared by pre-independence and post-independence societies. Thus the authors of an influential 1989 study, *The Empire Writes Back*, explain that their usage of the term covers 'all the culture affected by the imperial process from the moment of colonization to the present day', justifying this by saying that 'there is a continuity of preoccupations throughout the historical process initiated by European imperial aggression' and suggesting that it is also 'most appropriate as the term for the new cross-cultural criticism which has emerged in recent years and for the discourse through which this is constituted' (Ashcroft *et al.* 1989: 2).

This summarizes the way in which the term is now most normally used in a *temporal* sense, while also suggesting that something more than a temporal experience is involved. However, others commentators remove 'post-colonial' from any temporal context, by using it as an antonym to 'colonial'. In such a usage, it comes to signify a cultural practice, which can be loosely equated with *anti*-colonialism, without particular reference to a time-frame. This can be justified, at least in part, on the grounds that imperialism operated as a set of discursive practices, as well as through direct political intervention, and on the grounds that it continues to exercise economic, cultural and other forms of control in the NEO-COLONIAL global era. Consequently, *post*-colonialism becomes a necessary COUNTER-DISCURSIVE practice to combat such domination, i.e. it constitutes a political practice that opposes Western HEGEMONY.

However, such a position is at odds with much post-colonial theory and writing, which stresses the intersection of cultures in HYBRID formations (see, e.g. Pratt 1992; Suleri 1992; Bhabha 1994; Young 1995; Thieme 2001) and the AMBIVALENCE of post-colonial discourse, seeing the latter as existing at the porous interface between the colonizer and the colonized. Given the hybrid nature of cultural interventions, adversarial attempts on the part of the (post-)colonized to completely remove themselves from the colonizer's space, the equivalent of a nostalgic return to an ESSENTIALIST Eden, are doomed to failure. Implication in the object of attack is often unavoidable, given the 'intertwined histories' (Said 1994: 1ff.) of colonizer and colonized; at the same time, collusion with the colonizer is altogether less acceptable. So post-colonial discourse habitually finds itself moving along a CONTINUUM between the two poles of oppositional resistance and filial complicity.

So how is one to define 'post-colonial' for working purposes? Helen Gilbert admirably summarizes the various ways in which the term has come to be used in the General Introduction to her anthology *Postcolonial Plays*:

In many contexts, the term indicates a degree of agency, or at least a programme of resistance, against cultural domination; in others, it signals the existence of a particular historical legacy and/or a chronological stage in a culture's transition into a modern nation-state; in yet others, it is used more disapprovingly to suggest a form of co-option into Western cultural economies. What is common to all of these definitions, despite their various implications, is a central concern with cultural power.

For those less interested in staking out disciplinary boundaries, 'postcolonial' has become a convenient (and sometimes useful) portmanteau term to describe any kind of resistance, particularly against class, race and gender oppressions. (Gilbert (ed.) 2001: 1)

Gilbert's own anthology focuses on 'cultural practices which have both a historical *and* a discursive relationship to Western imperialism, whether that phenomenon is treated critically, ambivalently or collusively' (ibid.) and for the most part this glossary has followed the same approach, while recognizing that the term is widely used in numerous other contexts in which resistance to hegemonic power is also operative. However, while sharing Gilbert's view that 'postcolonialism' is best regarded as a set of cultural practices which engage with Western imperialism and placing its main emphasis here, the Glossary endeavours to signal other contexts in which the term is used, through entries that direct readers to further potential sources of information. This said, given the proliferation of senses in which 'post-colonial' is now being deployed and the danger of a work such as this expanding beyond its allotted space, it seemed futile to attempt detailed coverage of related fields, such as African American Studies and Irish Studies, especially since they are the subjects of other Arnold Essential Glossaries, viz. Stephen Matterson's *American Literature* and *Irish Studies*, edited by John Goodby, Alex Davis, Andrew Hadfield and Eve Patten. So here the primary focus is on post-colonial concepts and the post-colonial cultures of Africa, Asia, Australasia and the Americas (where the main emphasis is on the Caribbean and Latin America). Coverage of the cultures of the USA and the UK has for the most part been omitted, but migrant writers have been included, as have entries on movements and theories that have transnational implications. Entries on people have been confined to Africa, Asia, the Caribbean and Latin America, but topic entries on 'SETTLER' cultures have been included, particularly when they relate to aspects of the national metanarratives that shaped their making and when they have questioned the nation's settler 'origins'. Thus, in the case of Canada, there is information on such topics as MULTICULTURALISM, FIRST NATIONS and Margaret Atwood's cultural model of SURVIVAL. The decision to omit person-specific entries on settler cultures inevitably generated some potential anomalies, particularly in the case of South Africa and when I found myself considering omitting Athol Fugard, while planning to include entries on his collaborators, John Kani and Winston Ntshona, and omitting Ruth Prawer Jhabvala, while including Ismail Merchant, it seemed invidious to make ETHNICITY a criterion for exclusion. So those who in any way 'belong' to Africa, Asia, the Caribbean and Latin America have been included, where relevant. Additionally, numerous other people appear in the Glossary in topic entries, which attempt to provide an introduction to the multiplicity of forms, theories, concepts, terms, events and movements that can reasonably be called 'post-colonial'.

Guide to the Glossary

This Glossary has been designed as a handbook that can be used in a number of ways:

Use it as an encyclopedia to look up people, concepts and topics, which are arranged in alphabetical order, beginning with *Abiku* and ending with Zobel.

Use it to find connections with related people, concepts and topics by following up cross-references (marked by capitals in the text) and so gradually build up a broader knowledge of the subject area.

Use it as a guide to further reading by consulting some of the books, articles and websites suggested at the end of the entries. The full publication details for the books and articles are provided in the bibliography at the end of the book.

Abiku   In Yoruba mythology, a spirit child that is born into the world only to die, suffering this fate through a series of incarnations. Several Nigerian writers have introduced the figure into contemporary contexts, without divorcing it from its traditional mythic role, which suggests the interconnectedness of life and death. BEKEDEROMO's (J. P. Clark's) poem, 'Abiku' entreats the child to 'step in and stay'. In Wole SOYINKA's 'Abiku' (in *Idanre and Other Poems*, 1967), powerful imagery associates the figure with a cyclical view of history rooted in traditional Yoruba cosmology. Soyinka's first play, *A Dance of the Forests*, which is centred on an encounter between the living and the dead, contains a variation on the *abiku* in the form of its character of the 'half-child'. The play was first performed as part of Nigeria's Independence celebrations in 1960 and in this context the figure seems to suggest the enigmatic promise of independence for both Nigeria and Africa more generally. Earlier, Derek WALCOTT had included a very similar figure in the character of the Bolom, or foetus, in his play *Ti-Jean and His Brothers* (1958), but in this instance an eventual birth suggests, more optimistically, that a hitherto stifled *Caribbean* consciousness may come into being with independence. The first section of Soyinka's autobiographical *Aké: The Years of Childhood* (1981), also introduces an *abiku* character, Bukola, who is described as 'one of the denizens of that other world where the voice was caught, sieved, re-spun and cast back in diminishing copies'.

The figure is also the central focus of Ben OKRI's 'Abiku trilogy': *The Famished Road* (1992), *Songs of Enchantment* (1993) and *Infinite Riches* (1998). *The Famished Road*, which takes its title from Soyinka's poem 'Death in the Dawn' (also in *Idanre*), departs from the use of the *abiku* motif in Soyinka and Clark by allowing its protagonist, Azaro, to remain alive, albeit in a LIMINAL space between the spirit world and the living world and reference to the country as a spirit-child nation suggests that the *abiku* is being for the purpose of NATIONAL ALLEGORY. More recently, Debo Kotun's *Abiku* (1999), a novel about government corruption by an American-based Nigerian writer, has used the *abiku* in a similar way, for what the author regards as a fictionalized autobiography of the country.

Parallel figures in other West African cultures include the Ibo *ogbanje*. Chinua ACHEBE's first novel, *Things Fall Apart* (1958), includes such a character in Ezinma, the protagonist Okonkwo's favourite child, who, unlike her mother's previous children, survives the traditional fate of her kind. In contexts where the traditional mythic dimensions of the figure have been superseded by a more realistic representation of contemporary social experience, the *abiku* has been associated with

1

other foreshortened lives in African society, particularly the early deaths of so many children as a consequence of famine and the AIDS epidemic.

Further reading

Durosimi-Jones (1998).

Abolitionism, the abolition of slavery   The campaign to bring about the end of first the Slave Trade and then SLAVERY itself gathered force in Britain and the USA in the late eighteenth century. Leaders of the British Movement included William WILBERFORCE, Thomas Clarkson and John Newton, who had earlier been a captain involved in the Slave Trade himself. Their activities led to the abolition of the Trade in 1807. However, slavery continued in the British Empire for another quarter of a century. It was abolished from 1834, but the newly freed slaves were required to undergo a four-year apprenticeship period and therefore EMANCIPATION is more properly dated from 1838. Wilberforce's contribution to the movement is recognized in the Wilberforce Museum in Hull; Newton's in the Cowper-Newton Museum in Olney, Buckinghamshire. Slavery in the Americas continued after 1838: France abolished it in 1848; it continued in Cuba until 1860 and in Brazil until 1888.

In the USA the campaign for abolition was spearheaded by evangelical Protestants and the American Anti-Slavery Society (AASS), which helped many slaves escape to the northern states and Canada through its Underground Railroad, was founded in 1833. The weekly newspaper *The Liberator* (first published 1831) and Harriet Beecher Stowe's novel, *Uncle Tom's Cabin* (1852), which has been criticized for its patronizing representation of African Americans, played an important role in mobilizing white opinion. Slavery was abolished by Abraham Lincoln's Emancipation Proclamation of 1863, but was not enforced until 1865, when the northern Union defeated the Confederate forces of the slaveholding South in the American Civil War.

Aboriginal, Aborigine, Aboriginal writing   'Aboriginal' is a term used both to identify the indigenous or FIRST PEOPLES of a country and more specifically to connote the earliest human inhabitants of Australia. Whereas white settlement of Australia dates back little more than two hundred years, to the landing of the First Fleet in 1788, Aboriginals arrived on the north coast of Australia from South-East Asia approximately 40,000 years ago. Estimates of the size of the pre-CONTACT Aborigine population put its numbers at around 300,000. Within a century, this had decreased to 50,000 as a result of diseases and European genocide. The contemporary Aborigine population numbers about 130,000, of whom approximately 80,000 now have mixed ancestry. Definitions of what constitutes Aboriginality have varied, with 'living black' or self-determination, along with at least a modicum of Aborigine ancestry. being seen as important criteria. The case of the writer Mudrooroo has raised a number of interesting issues relating to such classification.

Australian Aborigines belong to some five hundred different tribal groupings, most of whom speak different languages or DIALECTS. The majority of Aboriginal groups were hunter–gatherers who combined with other communities for the purposes of trade and religious rites. Traditionally such social units were either patrilineal communities that owned and maintained particular sections of land containing sacred sites, or more mobile groupings that moved within specific localities. European settlement in the post-CONTACT period led to the erosion of many Aboriginal groups' semi-nomadic way of life, as the doctrine of TERRA NULLIUS deprived them of lands they had traditionally occupied, though without having the same conceptions of property as the newly established European settler communities. In many cases Aborigines were the victims of genocide. The Tasmanian Aboriginals, a distinct ethnic group, were completely exterminated within a hundred years of European settlement. Written from the viewpoint of one of the last Tasmanian Aborigines, Mudrooroo's *Doctor Wooreddy's Prescription for Enduring the Ending of the World* (1983) focuses on the apocalyptic effect that colonization by white 'ghosts' had on his people. Robert Drewe's novel *The Savage Crows* (1976) is a powerful white Australian response to the genocide of the Tasmanian Aborigines. Jack Davis's historical play *Kullark* (1979) documents the dispossession of the Nyoongah people of south-western Australia, who fared only marginally better.

The land rights campaign gathered momentum in the 1960s and 1970s, with Aboriginal sacred sites such as Uluru (Ayers Rock), one of the most popular destinations for white Australian and international tourism, providing a focal point for the issue of ownership. The commemoration of the bicentennial of white settlement in Australia in 1988 was accompanied by Aboriginal protests at the celebration of such an anniversary, which helped to raise consciousness among white Australians and the 1992 decision of the High Court of Australia in the MABO CASE marked a turning-point for Aboriginal land rights claims.

David Unaipon is generally viewed as the founder of Aboriginal writing in English. His *Native Legends* was published in 1929. More recent Aboriginal writers include: Jack Davis, whose plays other than *Kullark* include *The Dreamers* (1982), in which a naturalistic representation of contemporary Aboriginal suburban dispossession is juxtaposed with the figure of a dancer who suggests the continuing presence of the Aboriginal DREAMTIME in the contemporary world, *No Sugar* (1986) and *In Our Town* (1992); Lionel Fogarty; Kevin Gilbert; Oodgeroo Noonuccal (Kath Walker), whose *We Are Going* (1964) was the first volume of poetry to be published by an Aboriginal writer; and Archie Weller, whose novel *The Day of the Dog* (1981) provides a vivid account of urban part-Aboriginal life. Sally Morgan's autobiography *My Place* (1987) is centred on her discovery of her concealed Aboriginal ancestry. Mudrooroo (a.k.a. Colin Johnson, Mudrooroo Narogin and Mudrooroo Nyoongah), the writer widely credited with having written the first Aboriginal novel, *Wild Cat Falling* (1965) and also well known for *Doctor Wooreddy's Prescription* and the poem cycle, *Dalwurra: The*

Black Bittern (1988), had his claims to Aboriginal identity called into question in the 1990s. The controversy surrounding this matter, which raises a series of issues that are central to debates about what constitutes Aboriginality, are discussed by Maureen Clark in 'Unmasking Mudrooroo' (Clark 2001).

A special double issue of *Kunapipi* includes Wesley Horton's 'Australian Aboriginal Writers', a 'partially annotated bibliography of Australian Aboriginal writing 1924–1987' (Rutherford, 1988: 275–304). See also the DREAMING.

Further reading

Davis and Hodge (eds) (1985); Rutherford (ed.) (1988); Hodge and Mishra (1991); Mudrooroo (1994); Clark (2001).

Acculturation   Originally an anthropological term, referring to the supposed fusion brought about by the interaction of cultures. More recently, acculturation has come to be used in a broad range of social and historical contexts, particularly to describe situations where contact between a dominant and a SUBALTERN group results in the erosion of the latter's culture. Colonial migration invariably results in the acculturation of the immigrant community, e.g. as in the CREOLIZATION of Indo-Caribbeans. Similarly, indigenous communities, e.g. Australian ABORIGINALS, suffer acculturation as a consequence of CONTACT with the West. However, anthropological models that presume the existence of unitary, pre-contact cultures have been called into question as ESSENTIALIST and most contemporary cultural theory prefers models that stress process rather than product, i.e. see cultural change as fluid and dialogic, involving the interaction of discursive formations that are themselves HYBRID. See also SYNCRETISM and ASSIMILATION.

Achebe, Chinua   Born 1930. Nigerian novelist, widely regarded as the finest Sub-Saharan African fiction-writer of his generation. Born in Ogidi in the Eastern region of Nigeria into a Christian family, Achebe attended the University of Ibadan and worked for the Nigerian Broadcasting Corporation, before becoming a Biafran diplomat during the period of the NIGERIAN CIVIL WAR. He later became a Professor of Literature at the University of Nigeria in Nsukka and was the founding editor of *OKIKE: AN AFRICAN JOURNAL OF NEW WRITING*. He was also the founding editor of Heinemann's AFRICAN WRITERS SERIES. In 1990, Achebe was seriously injured in a road accident and since then he has lived in the United States, where he has been a Professor at Bard College, New York. Ezenwa-Ohaeto's *Chinua Achebe* (1997) is a detailed biography.

Achebe's first three novels, *Things Fall Apart* (1958), *No Longer at Ease* (1960) and *Arrow of God* (1964) have been published together as *The African Trilogy* (1988). The 'village' novels, *Things Fall Apart* and *Arrow of God*, depict conflicts in Ibo society partly generated by the impact of European colonialism, but also by tensions within the society itself. In an oft-quoted essay 'The Novelist as Teacher', Achebe has said that he would be content if his work 'did no more than teach my readers that their past – with all its imperfections – was not one long night of savagery from which the first Europeans acting on God's behalf delivered them' (1988: 30) and the two 'village' novels particularly fulfil this purpose by documenting the sophistication of traditional Ibo society, while also providing vivid dramatizations of their protagonists' psychologies. Set in the 1880s, in the period after the Berlin Conference legitimized the 'Scramble for Africa', *Things Fall Apart* shows its protagonist, Okonkwo, wrestling to sustain his belief in his society's codes of manhood and ultimately becoming a tragic figure, destroyed both by internal forces and the advent of the first phase of the British colonization of the region. In *Arrow of God*, set in the 1920s at a time when Britain was trying to introduce a system of indirect rule into Iboland, the hero, Ezeulu, the chief priest of his people, is a more complex and intellectual figure, who finds his traditional role similarly challenged by the incursions of Western society. Both novels make extensive use of Ibo oral tradition and are written in a seemingly transparent English, which in fact subtly refashions the colonizers' language to replicate Ibo patterns of thought and expression. The middle novel in the trilogy, *No Longer at Ease*, is set in the period immediately before Nigerian independence (1960) and deals with the failure of Okonkwo's English-educated grandson to reconcile the seemingly contradictory forces that have determined his identity.

Achebe's other novels are *A Man of the People* (1966), a fierce indictment of corruption in post-independence Nigeria, and the later *Anthills of the Savannah* (1987), set in a fictionalized surrogate for Nigeria, in which democracy has been sacrificed to the interests of a self-serving elite. More complex in mood and structure than *A Man of the People*, *Anthills* shifts its focus between four protagonists, each of whom embodies a different response to the neo-colonial situation and state corruption, and for the first time Achebe includes a fully developed female character. The novel returns to a central concern of all Achebe's work, the African artist's role in helping to create a more just society, particularly emphasizing the importance of storytelling as a shaping force in people's lives.

Although he is best known as a novelist, Achebe has also published the short-story collection, *Girls at War* (1972), children's books and the poetry collections, *Beware, Soul Brother* (1971) (US title *Christmas in Biafra*), which won the 1972 Commonwealth Poetry Prize, and *Another Africa* (1998). His influential essays on African culture and society have been collected in *Morning Yet on Creation Day* (1975) and *Hopes and Impediments* (1988). *Home and Exile* (2000) is a short 'autobiographical' volume, based on three lectures that Achebe gave at Harvard University in 1998. With C. L. Innes, he has edited two collections of African short stories.

Further reading

Achebe (1988); Innes (1990); Petersen and Rutherford (eds) (1990); Ezenwa-Ohaeto (1997).

ACLALS The Association for Commonwealth Literature and Language Studies. ACLALS was founded at the University of Leeds in 1964, with A. N. Jeffares as its first Chairperson. An inaugural conference was held in Leeds in 1964 and the association's first international triennial conference followed in Brisbane in 1968. Supported by funding from the Commonwealth Foundation, ACLALS became the major organization for the worldwide co-ordination of COMMONWEALTH LITERARY studies in the decades that followed and its headquarters has rotated around the Commonwealth on a regular triennial basis. It established numerous regional chapters, e.g. SPACLALS, IACLALS and EACLALS (in the South Pacific, India and Europe respectively) and has recently added an American chapter (USACLALS) to its constituent branches. It holds world triennial conferences and has continued to flourish at a time when the term 'post(-)colonial' has overtaken 'Commonwealth' in popularity as a descriptor for the study of literatures from colonized and ex-colonial countries, playing an important part in bringing scholars and critics from post-colonial communities around the world together.

Details of the first 25 years of ACLALS activities, including a list of its international chairpersons, conferences, conference proceedings and regional chapters, are included in an appendix to Maes-Jelinek *et al.* (eds) (1989). From its beginning until the late 1980s, the Association published the *ACLALS Bulletin*: eight series in all, which varied in format, content and regularity of appearance with the rotation of the international executive.

Further reading

Maes-Jelinek *et al.* (eds) (1989).

Acrolect See CREOLE.

Adams, Grantley (1898–1971). Barbadian politician, who became Prime Minister of the short-lived West Indian FEDERATION in 1958, after having earlier been premier of Barbados from 1954 to 1958. He read classics at Oxford, practised as a barrister and was a prominent trade union leader, prior to his assumption of political office. He received a knighthood in 1957.

Ade, King Sunny Born 1946. Nigerian bandleader, who played an important role in bringing about the international popularity of JUJU music, when he was signed by Island Records in 1982, in the wake of Bob MARLEY's success with the label, and released his albums, *Juju Music* and *Synchro System*. Prior to this, he had enjoyed popularity in Nigeria with his bands, the Green Spots, whose first major hit was the football song 'Challenge Cup' (1962), and the African Beats. His international career subsequently went into decline, but he remained popular in Nigeria and in 1995 once again found success abroad with *E Dide* (*Get Up*). Ade's music treats religious and social themes and his band is notable for the size of its vocal chorus, its mesh of instruments and its innovative use of guitars, particularly the pedal steel guitar.

Affiliation   See FILIATION, AFFILIATION.

African American studies, relationship to post-colonial studies   Opinions on the extent to which African American studies and post-colonial studies overlap vary considerably. Commonalities of interest between the two groupings include shared experiences of discrimination on grounds of 'race', colour and other forms of 'difference', generating analogous needs to retrieve occluded SUBALTERN histories and cultures, and the work of African American theorists such as Henry Louis GATES and bell hooks is often directly relevant to post-colonial practices. Additionally, the case for arguing that African American Studies (and also feminist studies and queer theory) share affinities with post-colonialism can be predicated on the notion that African Americans have been and are victims of *internal* colonization.

Outside North America, 'post-colonialism' has more generally been reserved as a descriptor for the experience of groups that have suffered as a consequence of colonization by an *external* imperial power. The dividing line is, however, a thin one (particularly when one compares the experience of, say, African Americans and ABORIGINAL peoples) and, with so many areas of shared interest, theoretical dialogue between the two fields is frequently very productive. The Emory postcolonial studies website contains a useful introduction to this topic. See also the Preface to this Glossary.

Further reading

hooks (1990); www.emory.edu/ENGLISH/Bahri/AfricanAmerican.html

African Literature Today   Journal/book series founded in 1968 under the editorship of Eldred Durosimi-Jones as a forum for examining African writing. The first four numbers functioned as a journal, including articles on a variety of topics. From its fifth issue onwards, *African Literature Today* has appeared as an annual book, focusing on a particular topic. Durosimi-Jones co-edited the series with Eustace Palmer (Nos 12–19) and his wife, Majorie Jones (No. 12 onwards). Its original publisher was Heinemann Educational Books, but since 1984 it has been published by James Currey in conjunction with Africa World Press. Jones provides a brief history of his experience of editing *African Literature Today* in a valedictory editorial included in issue 23 (2002). Ernest Emenyonu succeeds him as editor.

The African National Congress (ANC)   The major organization in the South African liberation struggle and now the majority party in South Africa's government. The African National Congress was founded in Bloemfontein, South Africa in 1912 with the aim of uniting African groups in defence of their civil rights. This was in the

7

wake of the formation of the union of South Africa (1910), which invested power in local SETTLER groups (Boer and British) that only recognized the rights of whites. See also APARTHEID, Nelson MANDELA.

Further reading

ANC website: www.anc.org.za

The African Writers' Series Pioneering series, launched by Heinemann in 1962, in which many major ANGLOPHONE African writers were first published. Its founding editor was Chinua ACHEBE, whose *Things Fall Apart* (1958) was the first volume to be published in the series. The first work by a woman writer to be included in the series was Flora NWAPA's *Efuru* (1966). Achebe apart, it is notable for having published most of the work of NGUGI wa Thiong'o, Buchi EMECHETA, Bessie HEAD and Ayi Kwei ARMAH. The series has included translations of many of the most significant FRANCOPHONE African texts, including works by Mariama BÂ, Mongo BETI, Ferdinand OYONO and Ousmane SEMBÈNE. Other translations include Tayeb SALIH's *Season of Migration to the North* (from Arabic), Thomas Mofolo's *Chaka* (from Sesotho) and Mia Couto's *Voices Made Night* (from Portuguese). Anthologies include *African Short Stories* (1983) and *Contemporary African Short Stories* (1992), both edited by Achebe and C. L. Innes, *The Heinemann Book of African Women's Writing* (1993), edited by Charlotte H. Bruner and *Opening Spaces: An Anthology of Contemporary African Women's Writing* (1999), edited by Yvonne VERA.

The series underwent a major change in the 1980s, when its hitherto low-cost editions that were widely read in African countries were replaced by 'quality paperbacks', a format that made the books less affordable in Africa itself. Heinemann launched a companion Caribbean Writers' Series in 1970.

Afrobeat A hybrid form of music, which originated in Nigeria. Afrobeat is a fusion of elements from traditional Yoruba music and such 'Western' forms as jazz, funk and big band. The term was coined by Fela Anikulapo KUTI, who became its leading exponent. He developed it in the 1960s, using local krio patois and the call-and-response patterns employed in certain forms of traditional West African music.

Ahimsa A code of living, based on the avoidance of causing harm to any living creature or thing. It is strictly observed in Jainism and also central to Hindu and Buddhist practices. Belief in *ahimsa* underpins the vegetarianism of Jainism and traditional Hinduism. Mahatma GANDHI's political philosophy of SATYAGRAHA was adapted from *ahimsa*. The word derives from the SANSKRIT term for 'non-violence'.

Ahmad, Aijaz Indian cultural theorist, whose best-known work *In Theory: Classes, Nations, Literatures* (1992) is a Marxist critique of the abstract nature of various strands in post-colonial theory. Ahmad attacks the prominent American Marxist, Fredric Jameson for reducing all 'third-world' writing to NATIONAL ALLEGORY, Homi K. BHABHA's use of a poststructuralist critique as an alternative to NATIONALISM, a position which he suggests has little relevance to the lived experience of people in the world's poorer societies, and Edward SAID's 'privileging of literature and philology in the constitution of "Orientalist" knowledge and indeed the human sciences generally' as expressive of a 'will to portray a "West" which has been the same from the dawn of history up to the present' (Ahmad 1992: 163). Ahmad is a Professor of Social Sciences at Jawaharlal Nehru University, Delhi. A fierce critic of the various abstract '-isms' that have dominated contemporary cultural studies in the West, his other publications include *Postcolonialism, Postmodernism, Posthistoire* (1986), *Forms/Figures/Formations: How Nationalisms Are Made* (1996) and *Lineages of the Present: Ideological and Political Genealogies of South Asia* (2002).

Further reading

Ahmad (1992).

Aidoo, Ama Ata   Born 1942. Ghanaian writer, born in the central Fanti-speaking region of Ghana, who has produced work in a wide range of genres. Aidoo's early ambition to become a writer was first realized when she won a newspaper short story writing competition at the age of 19. She was educated at the University of Ghana, Legon, and subsequently taught at various universities in Ghana, elsewhere in Africa and in the USA. A prominent figure in Ghanaian public life, she held office as the nation's Secretary for Education in the early 1980s, but resigned when she found herself unable to implement her policy of universal free education and subsequently went into exile in Zimbabwe and the USA.

Aidoo first achieved widespread recognition as a dramatist. Her play *The Dilemma of a Ghost* (1965) is about a young Ghanaian graduate who brings his African American bride back to Ghana, a situation that provides a focus for a wry examination of tensions between traditional Ghanaian family values and more liberal Western manners. Based on a Ghanaian legend, *Anowa* (1970) also dramatizes a conflict between family expectations and free-thinking individualism. It is a tragic fable about love, in which a young woman defies her parents to marry the man she loves, but fails to find the happiness she seeks. *No Sweetness Here* (1970) is a collection of short stories, which moves between the country and Accra, demonstrating the confusions, and corruption of the post-independence era, but with a more sympathetic angle of vision than that which characterizes Aidoo's fellow-Ghanaian Ayi Kwei ARMAH's treatment of the same theme in his early novels. Like much of her work, the stories of *No Sweetness Here* are particularly notable for their focus on the uncertainties informing the changing roles of women in NEO-COLONIAL society and demonstrate a pragmatic scepticism to both the 'traditional' and 'modern' roles available to women in African society.

Written in both prose and verse, Aidoo's first novel, *Our Sister Killjoy: or Reflections from a Black-Eyed Squint* (1977), is about the process of self-discovery experienced by a Ghanaian student in Europe, who comes to recognize the need to establish links with the African ancestral past, if she is to achieve self-fulfilment in the present. Aidoo is on record as saying that she would never write about love in Accra. Her second novel, *Changes: A Love Story* (1991), which won the Best Book Award for the African section of the COMMONWEALTH WRITERS PRIZE, appears to renege on this by describing the fortunes of a woman who separates from her husband, but struggles to achieve relationships with men on terms that are acceptable to her. However, the perspective renders its sub-title ironic. Aidoo's poetry has been collected in *Someone Talking to Sometime* (1985) and *An Angry Letter in January* (1992), which particularly attacks the neo-colonialism of 'Today's So-Called African Leadership' and is also notable for a number of poems addressed to fellow-writers. She has also published children's books and a second short story collection, *The Girl Who Can and Other Stories* (1997). *The Dilemma of a Ghost* and *Anowa* were republished together in 1996.

Further reading

Brown L. (1981); Davies and Graves (eds) (1986); Azodo and Wilentz (eds) (1999).

Alexander, Meena Born 1951. Diasporic Indian poet, novelist and critic, born in Allahabad into a Syrian Christian family from Kerala. When she was five, Alexander's family moved to the Sudan, where she later studied at Khartoum University. She obtained her doctorate in England at the University of Nottingham and taught at Delhi University before marrying and migrating to the USA, where she was a Professor at Hunter College and the City University of New York. During her early years Alexander found herself repeatedly travelling between the Sudan and India and also experienced a sense of psychic division as a consequence of being educated in English, rather than her native Malayalam. At the same time she felt a conflict between what could be articulated in public discourse and inner feelings, which she only later came to resolve through the writing of poetry. Her sense of split subjectivity is embodied in the geological title of her autobiographical memoir *Fault-Lines* (1993), which serves as a trope for her sense of fractured identity.

Beginning with *The Bird's Bright Ring* (1976), she has published several volumes of poetry, including *Stone Roots* (1980), *House of a Thousand Doors* (1988), *River and Bridge* (1993) and *Illiterate Heart* (2002). The characteristic mode of her poetry is understatement, which nevertheless engages with the social realities of contemporary Indian life, particularly gender roles. Like A. K. RAMANUJAN's 'Small-Scale Reflections on a Great House', Ruth Prawer JHABVALA's *The Householder* (1960) and, from further afield, V. S. NAIPAUL's *A House for Mr Biswas* (1961), the title-poem of *House of a Thousand Doors* responds to the importance of householding as part of the duties of the second ASRAMA of the ideal Hindu life. Alexander's poem appears to redeploy the trope of the house in a feminist context: it depicts a woman, kneeling at each of the house's thousand doors, 'paying her dues' to the 'household gods' who refuse to allow her entry. She has also published the novels *Nampally Road* (1991) and *Manhattan Music* (1997) and *The Shock of Arrival: Reflections on Postcolonial Experience* (1996).

Ali, Agha Shahid   (1949–2001). Indian poet. Ali was born in Delhi and raised in Kashmir. He attended the Universities of Kashmir, Delhi and Penn State, where he obtained his doctorate. He settled in the USA, where he held academic appointments at a number of universities, including Penn State and the University of Utah, but his poetry remained rooted in the Muslim culture of his youth and the conventions of contemporary Urdu verse. A noted exponent of the GHAZAL himself, Ali translated poems by Faiz Ahmed FAIZ and edited *Ravishing DisUnities: Real Ghazals in English* (2000). His technical virtuosity extended into a mastery of various genres of Western verse. His early volumes *Bone-Sculpture* (1972) and *In Memory of Begum Akhtar* (1979) were followed by his first major collection, *The Half-Inch Himalayas* (1987), which includes poems such as 'A Postcard from Kashmir' and 'A Wrong Turn' that intermingle nostalgic memories of Kashmir with a recognition that contemporary communal strife has altered the region's human geography forever. Ali also published *A Nostalgist's Map of America* (1991), *The Beloved Witness: Selected Poems* (1992), *The Country Without a Post Office* (1997), which includes some of his finest work, and *Rooms Are Never Finished* (2001).

Allegory   Traditionally allegory has been seen in Western rhetoric as a mode of expression in which meaning is rendered figuratively, usually through metaphor. Thus a Christian allegory such as John Bunyan's *Pilgrim's Progress* (1678) employs an ono-mastics in which place-names such as the Slough of Despond and personifications such as Worldly Wiseman represent abstract spiritual qualities, in this case function-ing as tropes for the various stages in the protagonist Christian's spiritual journey towards salvation in the Celestial City. However, by the time Bunyan was writing, alle-gorical modes of expression were less dominant than they had been in earlier Western discourse and most commentators see the rise of the novel, with its stress on a cir-cumstantial realism that purports to provide a mirror-like transcription of social experience, as displacing allegory as the dominant mode of representation in Western prose. Nevertheless attempts to draw a binary distinction between allegorical and realistic writing in the Western canon are frequently frustrated by the porousness of these categories: Bunyan's spiritual landscape bears a strong relationship to the terrain of his native Bedfordshire; and his successor Daniel Defoe's *Robinson Crusoe* (1719), which is generally viewed as the *Ur*-text of the realist novel, lends itself to a range of allegorical readings. So the stability of allegory as a category proves to be dependent on the viewpoint of the particular critic or reader. In the twentieth century the debate about allegory and realism resurfaced in a range of contexts, especially with the professional expansion of the study of literature. Thus, in suggesting that metaphor and metonymy represent the twin poles of discourse, the structuralist theorist Roman Jakobson, writing in the middle of the century, provided a reinscription of the binary division between allegory and realism.

In post-colonial contexts the term has been particularly associated with Fredric Jameson's influential 1986 article 'Third-World Literature in the Era of Multinational Capitalism'. Jameson's contention that all third-world writing operates as NATIONAL ALLEGORY relocates allegory as a discursive practice that departs from Western norms, seeing it as the distinctive mode of societies that have not experienced the split between private and public experience that Jameson, writing from a Marxist position, views as a determining aspect of capitalist production. Stephen Slemon commends Jameson's intervention for its 'attempt to call down that professional first-world ethnocentrism which most mainstream programmes of literary study continue to endorse at the level of their methodology' (Slemon 1987: 9) but questions the privileging of a mode of figuration inextricably bound up with 'the tropological technologies of Empire' (ibid.: 9). Slemon's view, which demonstrates an indebtedness to the Yale deconstructionist school of criticism's re-reading of allegory, argues instead for a practice that is attentive to the dialectical relationship involved in the post-colonial use of allegory, seeing post-colonial texts that 'inhabit the site of allegorical figuration' (ibid.: 11) as doing so in order to contest colonialism rather than as expressing a fixed positionality. Thus, such a view wrests allegory from its traditional roots in Western discourse, in which it operates in terms of a stable relationship between a conceptual category and the signifier chosen to represent it, and replaces it with a counter-discursive practice that destabilizes this binary relationship, which is perpetuated in colonial discourse that speaks for 'OTHERNESS'.

Further reading

Jameson (1986); Slemon (1987 and 1988); Ahmad (1992).

Allende, Isabel Born 1942. Peruvian-born novelist, brought up in Chile. Allende fled Chile after the assassination of her uncle, President Salvador Allende and the toppling of his socialist regime in the CIA-backed coup that installed General Augusto Pinochet's right-wing dictatorship. She subsequently lived in Venezuela for several years and is now resident in California. She is arguably the most important feminist voice among Latin American MAGIC REALISTS and her writing combines 'real' and surreal elements in the tradition of Gabriel García MÁRQUEZ. She is best known for her first novel, *La casa de los espíritus* (1982; *The House of the Spirits*, 1985). It spans three generations, offering a microcosmic fictional history of Chile that transmutes harsh political realities though an alternative spiritual vision in which women predominate. Allende writes in Spanish but translations have made her the best-known contemporary Latin American woman writer. Her other novels include *De amor y de sombra* (1984; *Of Love and Shadows*, 1987)

Eva Luna (1987; trans. 1988), *El plan infinitivo* (1991; *The Infinite Plan*, 1993), her first novel with an American setting, and *Retrato en sepia* (2000; *Portrait in Sepia*, 2001). She returned to her picaresque heroine Eva Luna in her short story collection *Cuentos de Eva Luna* (1990; *The Stories of Eva Luna*, 1992). *Paula* (1994; trans. 1995) is an autobiographical memoir that takes the form of a letter to her daughter, who died from a hereditary blood disease after being in a coma for a year.

Alterity   See 'OTHERNESS'.

Amadi, Elechi   Born 1934. Nigerian novelist, who has worked at a range of occupations, including those of teacher, soldier and civil servant. His reputation rests on his trilogy of novels, *The Concubine* (1966), *The Great Ponds* (1969) and *The Slave* (1978). Set in the pre-colonial period in a vividly realized village setting, *The Concubine* tells the story of a woman fated to bring death to all her lovers. *The Great Ponds* is another tragic story, which like Chinua ACHEBE's *Things Fall Apart* (1958) and *Arrow of God* (1964) shows subtle tensions undermining the equilibrium of traditional village life. Amadi has also published a number of plays including *Isiburu* (1973) and *Peppersoup* (1977). *Sunset in Biafra* (1973) is a diary of the NIGERIAN CIVIL WAR, during which he supported the Federal cause. His fourth novel, *Estrangement* (1986), deals with the aftermath of the war.

Further reading

Niven (1981); Booth (1981); Gikandi (1987).

Ambivalence   One of the key terms in Homi K. BHABHA's theoretical lexicon, ambivalence is seen as the characteristic predicament of the colonial subject whose 'double vision' (Bhabha 1994: 88) is split between complicity in and resistance to the colonial project. Bhabha particularly associates this vision with a form of MIMICRY that is parodic rather than straightforwardly imitative and 'in disclosing the ambivalence of colonial discourse also disrupts its authority' (ibid.: 88). He speaks of colonial mimicry as 'the sign of a double articulation', which 'emerges as the representation of a difference that is itself a sign of disavowal' (ibid.: 86). This theory has its roots in Freudian and Lacanian psychoanalytic thinking and the essay in which Bhabha explores this aspect of colonial discourse most fully and from which these quotations are taken, 'Of Mimicry and Man: The Ambivalence of Colonial Discourse', takes Lacan's remarks on mimicry as a form of camouflage as one of its epigraphs and subsequently quotes Freud's comments on the split consciousness of racially mixed individuals (ibid.: 89). See also CULTURAL SCHIZOPHRENIA.

Further reading

Bhabha (1994).

Amerindian   A portmanteau word, formed from 'American' and 'Indian', used to designate the 'indigenous' inhabitants of South, Central and North America, i.e. the descendants of peoples widely, but not universally, believed to have crossed the Bering Strait – from Siberia into Alaska – in three waves of migration, beginning some 30,000 to 40,000 years ago. Recent DNA evidence has identified a strain of Amerindian ancestry that appears to have come from south-western France during the last Ice Age, while confirming the predominance of Asian ancestry in most Amerindian peoples.

The term 'Amerindian' continues to be widely used, but has increasingly been replaced by 'NATIVE American' in the USA and 'FIRST Peoples' or 'First Nations' in Canada. 'Amerindian' is also used as a general term for the 'indigenous' languages of the Americas.

The Amritsar Massacre   A notorious episode in Indian colonial history, which occurred on 13 April 1919, when the British commander General Reginald Dyer ordered 50 troops under his command to fire on a gathering of Indians, who had assembled in the Jallianwallah Bagh (Garden) in the Punjab town of Amritsar to protest against the extension of emergency powers, introduced during World War I, into the post-war period. Dyer issued no prior warning and the soldiers continued firing for ten minutes on the unarmed crowd of approximately 10,000 men, women, and children, many of whom were celebrating a Hindu festival rather than protesting. About 1,650 rounds of ammunition were discharged on the victims, who were trapped within the enclosed space of the Bagh, which had a single exit. Estimates put the number of those killed at nearly 400 and the wounded at 1,200. Dyer was subsequently relieved of his command, but the episode is widely regarded as the most significant event in mobilizing support for the campaign that eventually led to Indian Independence in 1947.

Anancy, Anansi stories   Anancy (spelt in various ways) is a spiderman-hero of Caribbean children's stories. Originally a figure in Ashanti folklore, Anancy was brought to the Caribbean from West Africa by the enslaved Africans of the MIDDLE PASSAGE. In the Ashanti tales, he is a creator-trickster figure, who enjoys mixed fortunes, usually succeeding through his wily cleverness, but sometimes being punished when his deceit and greed transgress the society's moral codes. In the Caribbean he is virtually always celebrated as a hero and one explanation for this shift in attitude is that he personified the slaves' need to resort to subterfuge in a system which denied their common humanity. As a creator-trickster figure, Anancy bears comparison with similar figures in numerous other mythologies, e.g. Coyote in the myths of the North American Plains Indians and Loki in Norse mythology. As a personification of the New World slave (and the dispossessed ordinary West Indian in the post-EMANCIPATION period), he has similarities with such North American figures as Brer Rabbit.

Anancy stories are traditionally told at sunset and, prior to the revival of interest in the Afro-Caribbean heritage in the second half of the twentieth century, had particularly survived in Jamaica. The stories include formulaic elements and traditionally end with the words 'Jack mandora me no choose none', a phrase of uncertain origin, which, it has been suggested, implies the storyteller's straight-faced pose of apparent neutrality with regard to the legitimacy of Anancy's trickery. They sometimes have an aetiological dimension, i.e. they give an account of how certain animal characteristics originated. Thus 'Annancy [sic] and Brother Tiger' (Jekyll 1966: 7–10) explains how it came about that Tiger lives in the woods, while Anancy lives in the 'house-top'. The phrase 'nancy story' is also applied to Caribbean oral tales more generally, as well as being used to refer to fantastic or implausible accounts.

Walter Jekyll's *Jamaican Song and Story* (1907; repr. 1966) is an early collection of Jamaican oral discourse that includes Anancy stories. More recent collections include Sir Phillip Sherlock's *Anansi, the Spider Man* (1954), Louise Bennett's *Anancy and Miss Lou* (1979) and James Berry's *Spiderman Anansi* (1988). More generally, several major Caribbean writers have seen Anancy as a central protagonist for the exploration of Caribbean identity. In his poem 'Ananse' (*Islands*, 1969), (Edward) Kamau BRATHWAITE reclaims the spiderman from the cobwebbed recesses of children's stories and stresses his African roots, his latent potential for artistic creativity and his capacity for political resistance, at one point in the poem linking him with leaders of slave revolts, such as TOUSSAINT L'OUVERTURE. In the novels of Wilson HARRIS, Anancy appears in the guise of the trickster/shaman (e.g. the character of da Silva in *Heartland*, 1964, and the eponymous hero of *Black Marsden*, 1972) who can initiate humankind into new states of awareness. Harris's version of the figure draws on both Amerindian mythology and the Jungian belief in the trickster's capacity for creative transformation. Erna BRODBER's *Jane and Louisa Will Soon Come Home* (1980) includes two ambiguous Anancy tales, which also seem to suggest his importance as a site for creative resistance. Other literary reworkings of Anancy include Gerald McDermott's *Anansi the Spider: A Tale from the Ashanti* (1972) and Andrew Salkey's *Anancy's Score* (1973), which relates the figure to contemporary political practices.

Further reading

Jekyll (comp. and ed.) (1966).

Anand, Mulk Raj   Born 1905. Indian novelist, born in Peshawar (now in Pakistan), the son of a coppersmith. Anand graduated from Punjab University, Lahore, and later studied in Britain, where he had links with members of the Bloomsbury set. He was active in India's struggle for independence and spent time in Mahatma GANDHI's *ashram* at Ahmedabad. Along with R. K. NARAYAN and Raja RAO, Anand came to the fore as a novelist in the 1930s, as one of the 'BIG THREE' of Indian fiction in English. He is best known for his early fiction, particularly his first novel *Untouchable* (1935), a searing indictment of the CASTE system, written in the form of a 'day in the life' of a sweeper. *Coolie* (1936) tells the story of a peasant boy uprooted from the land. In the trilogy,

The Village (1939), *Across the Black Waters* (1940) and *The Sword and the Sickle* (1942), the protagonist's growth into revolutionary awareness mirrors Indian nationalism's movement towards independence. *Private Life of an Indian Prince* (1953; revised edn 1970), the story of a womanizing maharaja's doomed attempt to declare his small kingdom independent, broke new ground for Anand by treating a group at the opposite end of the social spectrum. His other fiction includes *Two Leaves and a Bud* (1937), *Lament on the Death of a Master of Arts* (1938; republished with seven other stories, 1967), *The Big Heart* (1945), *Seven Summers* (1951), *The Road* (1961), *Death of a Hero* (1963), *Morning Face* (1968), *Confessions of a Lover* (1976) and *The Bubble* (1984).

Anand's fictional technique owes more to Western realism than traditional Indian narrative modes and he acknowledges debts to Tolstoy, Joyce and Forster, but he indigenizes imported forms by representing Punjabi and Hindi expressions in English. He began his writing career as an art historian with *Persian Painting* (1930) and *The Hindu View of Art* (1933) and his prolific output of non-fictional writing also spans a vast range of other cultural, social and political topics. It includes *Marx and Engels on India* (1939), *The Indian Theatre* (1950), *The Humanism of M. K. Gandhi* (1967), *The Humanism of Jawaharlal Nehru* (1978) and *Conversations in Bloomsbury* (1981).

Further reading

Cowasjee (1977).

ANC See the African National Congress.

Anglo-Celtic, Anglo-Celtic monoculturalism 'Anglo-Celtic' is a term particularly used in Australia to differentiate the British-descended segment of the population from its other inhabitants. 'Anglo-Celtic monoculturalism' is widely used to suggest the traditional privileging of people of British ancestry over Australians of other descent (see, e.g., the Legend of the Nineties). However, despite its usefulness in distinguishing between older versions of Australianness and more contemporary multicultural conceptions of the nation's identity, this hyphenated version of *monoculturalism* is problematic, since it homogenizes people from heterogeneous British backgrounds and ignores the extent to which divisions between migrants from English and 'Celtic' backgrounds were transplanted into the colonial situation, where they generated local derivatives. Literary representations that help to illustrate such tensions include two recent novels about Ned Kelly – Robert Drewe's *Our Sunshine* (1991) and Peter Carey's Booker Prize-winning novel, *True History of the Kelly Gang* (2000) – both of which locate the bushranger's stand against nineteenth-century Australian authority in the context of his situation as an Irish selector's son.

Anglophone, anglophone English-speaking. The term was introduced into English from French, where it has been employed since the 1960s, along with such terms as

Lusophone and Hispanophone, to categorize particular non-Francophone linguistic communities. Thus it is particularly employed in regions (e.g. the Caribbean) and countries (e.g. Canada), where French and French-based Creoles are widely spoken, but not the only language employed.

Anthony, Michael　Born 1932. Trinidadian novelist and short story writer. Anthony's best work is about children growing up in the Caribbean. It includes *The Games Were Coming* (1963), *The Year in San Fernando* (1965), in which he makes subtle use of his ingenuous child protagonist's point of view, and *Green Days by the River* (1967). He has also published the novels, *Streets of Conflict* (1976), set in Brazil, and *In the Heat of the Day* (1996) and the crime thrillers, *All That Glitters* (1981), which like *The Year in San Fernando* deals with a boy's discoveries about the nature of the adult world, and *High Tide of Conflict* (2002), a story of drugs trafficking. *Cricket in the Road* (1973) is a collection of his short stories.

Aotearoa　Maori name for what British settlers called New Zealand. It means 'land of the long white clouds'.

Apartheid　The policy of 'separate development', involving racial segregation and political and economic discrimination against non-white groups, that prevailed in South Africa until the early 1990s. It affected 'coloured' (mixed) and Indian South Africans, as well as the majority black population. The term, which has also been applied to similar systems in other parts of the world, was coined in the 1930s by the South African Bureau for Racial Affairs (SABRA), but the policy had origins in earlier legislation such as the Natives Land Act of 1913, which established separate areas for European and non-European farms. Apartheid was more fully implemented from 1948, when the Afrikaner National Party came to power and passed a programme of legislation that drastically curtailed the civil liberties of the non-white population. This included the Group Areas Act, which established racially segregated townships such as Soweto (the South West Township of Johannesburg) and the Immorality Act, which banned inter-racial marriages. In the early 1960s the South African government began to establish ten self-governing Bantustans, independent black African 'homelands', which further restricted the freedom and mobility of non-whites. Black opposition to apartheid led to a number of uprisings, such as that at Sharpeville in 1960, when 69 demonstrators against the policy were killed by the police. After this, the government declared a state of emergency and organizations, such as the African National Congress, which opposed apartheid were banned. Internal opposition to the policy in the 1970s and 1980s, together with international sanctions, brought about the repeal of central aspects of the apartheid system such as the Pass Laws, which had limited the movement of non-whites, in the mid-1980s. In 1991 President F. W. de Klerk dismantled most of the remaining legislation. The end of apartheid was assured when, in

1994, the ANC won a majority in South Africa's first elections open to voters of all races and Nelson MANDELA became the country's first black President, heading a Government of National Unity.

Apartheid permeated all areas of South African life during the period when it was in force and virtually all the writing of this era engaged with it in one way or another. Poets of 'the Sharpeville generation' such as Dennis Brutus and Arthur Nortje protested against its iniquities before going into exile; poets of 'the Soweto generation' such as Sipho Sepamla and Wally Mongane Serote produced equally militant verse, which again, on one level, advocated a call to action. White writers expressed their outrage at apartheid in a variety of ways, ranging from Nadine GORDIMER's liberal humanism to J. M. COETZEE's postmodernist interrogation of its linguistic and philosophical foundations. Athol FUGARD's play *Sizwe Bansi Is Dead* (published in *Statements*, 1974), a workshop production, devised in collaboration with the actors John KANI and Winston Ntshona, provides a particularly vivid representation of the dehumanizing effects of pass-book legislation. Fugard's *Statements after an Arrest under the Immorality Act* (also in *Statements*) is a dramatic indictment of the law banning inter-racial sex.

Further reading

Mallaby (1992); Meredith (1988); ANC website: www.anc.org.za.

ARIEL: A Review of International English Literature Calgary-based literary journal, which publishes a considerable amount of post-colonial material, without being exclusively devoted to the field. *ARIEL* was founded by A. Norman Jeffares in 1970 and early issues were jointly edited from the Universities of Leeds and Calgary. *ARIEL* is published four times a year, includes issues on special topics and has been part-funded by a grant from SSHRC (the Social Sciences and Humanities Research Council of Canada). It mainly publishes critical articles, but also includes original poetry and reviews.

Armah, Ayi Kwei Born 1939. Ghanaian novelist. Born in Takoradi into a Fanti-speaking family, Armah was educated at Achimota College, Harvard and Columbia University. He subsequently worked as a translator and as a scriptwriter for Ghana Television. Most of his adult life he has lived outside Ghana. He has worked in various parts of Africa and held academic posts in Dar es Salaam, Lesotho, Massachusetts and Wisconsin. In the 1980s he settled in Senegal.

One of the finest stylists of African fiction in English, Armah has also been seen as one of its most pessimistic writers, especially in his highly acclaimed first two novels, *The Beautyful Ones Are Not Yet Born* (1968) and *Fragments* (1970), which offer searing indictments of the corruption of post-independence Ghana. The most positive elements in his work relate to the past, which he suggests can offer a source of creative renewal for contemporary Africa. *The Beautyful Ones*, a novel about an honest man who finds himself a total misfit amid the venality of the contemporary world, makes remorseless use of imagery of disease, decay, excrement and waste. Its rhetorical tirade against corruption attacks an unnamed West African state, which is a thinly-veiled version of Kwame NKRUMAH's Ghana. *Fragments*, a POLYPHONIC novel that takes an alienated artist, Baako, who returns to Ghana and a job as a television scriptwriter as its protagonist, uses the Melanesian myth of the CARGO CULT as its central trope for commenting on NEO-COLONIAL Ghanaian expectations about the supposedly magical gifts that will be brought home by 'been-to's', returnees from Europe and America. Such bourgeois values are offset by those of Baako's grandmother, whose interior monologues open and close the text, offering a telling contrast to the materialism of the modern world in which Baako is forced to move and which eventually leads to his mental breakdown. Despite their negative view of society, both these novels employ a technique that combines traditional Akan and Modernist forms to suggest that something 'beautyful' may 'be born' through the mediation of the contemporary artist.

Two Thousand Seasons (1973) and *The Healers* (1978) also depict negative aspects of African social life, but, taking a longer historical view, provide a more positive vision by suggesting that the pre-colonial past can be a wellspring for post-colonial reconstruction. *Two Thousand Seasons* is a major departure from Armah's earlier fiction. A historical chronicle that moves across dimly defined periods of time, it is narrated by a communal voice and its structure destabilizes expectations about linear progression. *The Healers* is another historical novel, dealing in this case with the disharmony that led to the fall of the Ashanti Empire. Again its story of the past has an allegorical force, suggesting the restorative potential of unity in the present. Armah has also published the novels *Why Are We So Blest?* (1972) and *Osiris Rising* (1995).

Further reading

Fraser (1980); Wright (1989); Wright (ed.) (1992).

Asramas The four stages of the ideal Hindu life, as laid down in the ancient SANSKRIT text, the laws of Manu, which served as a conduct book, governing and regulating everyday Hindu life and its rituals and validating the belief in BRAHMIN caste superiority. The four *asramas* are those of *brahmacharya*, *grihastya*, *vanaprastha* and *sanyasa*. In the first stage, the young Brahmin becomes a student, who leads a life of devotion. In the *grihastya*, he assumes the secular and spiritual responsibilities of a householder and man of affairs. The *vanaprastha asrama* involves a withdrawal from active life and a retreat into the forest ('*vana*' means 'forest'), where the Brahmin learns about spiritual truth from religious instructors. For some this is followed by the fourth *asrama*, the *sanyasa*, which involves a complete withdrawal from family and worldly pleasures in favour of a contemplative ascetic existence as a mendicant who seeks to achieve oneness with the divine order.

Although the fourth *asrama* is sometimes regarded as the ultimate summation of the ideal life, it is not one which most Hindus are expected to attain and each stage is viewed as equally important in the maintenance of the social order, with the *grihastya*'s role being the lynch-pin of the system. This centrality is reflected in Ruth Prawer JHABVALA's novel, *The Householder* (1960), which, as the title hints, specifically locates the hero's attempts to come to terms with adulthood in relation to the second *asrama*, as does Jhabvala's screenplay for the MERCHANT IVORY film of the novel (1963). The role of the *grihastya* is less obviously foregrounded in V. S. NAIPAUL'S DIASPORIC Hindu novel, *A House for Mr Biswas* (1961), but viewing Biswas's quest to own his own house in Trinidad within this context locates it within a traditional Hindu framework that may not otherwise be apparent. Equally the novel's irony expresses the ACCULTURATION of the Indo-Caribbean situation.

Assimilation　A form of colonialism, which attempts to absorb SUBALTERN subjects into the culture of the colonizing power. Assimilation was particularly practised in French colonies, such as the Caribbean islands of Martinique and Guadeloupe, which remained DOMS (*départements d'outre-mer*), overseas departments of France, when France's former African colonies virtually all attained independence in the 1950s and 1960s. Assimilation was fiercely resisted by the advocates of NEGRITUDE and subsequent FRANCOPHONE post-colonial movements.

The term is also used to refer to a number of other practices, including the process through which members of minority communities are integrated into a dominant culture, e.g. the absorption of immigrant groups into the American MELTING POT. Cf ACCULTURATION, CREOLIZATION, SYNCRETISM.

Aung San Suu Kyi　Born 1945. Burmese (Myanmar) opposition leader, who was awarded the NOBEL PEACE PRIZE in 1991. The daughter of General Aung San (1915–47) who played a leading role in the Burmese struggle to achieve independence from Britain, Aung San Suu Kyi was born in Rangoon and educated in Burma, India and Oxford. After marrying and settling in Britain, she returned to Burma (renamed Myanmar by its military junta) in 1988, when her mother was terminally ill. Her mixture of political acumen, personal charisma and family reputation quickly placed her at the centre of another freedom struggle, as she found herself a rallying point for opposition to the ruling regime. She became co-founder and leader of the NLD (National League for Democracy). She was placed under house arrest in the following year and although she was debarred from standing as a candidate in Myanmar's 1990 elections, the NLD still won 80 per cent of the vote. Suu Kyi continued to campaign for democratic reform through non-violent means. The award of her Nobel Prize heightened her profile and increased international awareness of the junta's repressive policies. She was released from house arrest in 1995 and reappointed General Secretary of the NLD, but had restrictions placed on her movements and activities

She declined to leave the country when her British husband, Michael Aris, whom she had not seen for three years, was dying of cancer in 1999 for fear the authorities would not allow her back to continue the resistance struggle. She was again placed under house arrest in 2000, when she attempted, in defiance of restrictions placed on her personal movement, to travel to Mandalay. She was released unconditionally in May 2002.

The Burmese section of Amitav Ghosh's *Dancing in Cambodia, At Large in Burma* (1998) contains a portrait of her, which depicts her as the personification of Burma's democratic resistance to military rule, by a writer who first met her while he himself was a student in Oxford in 1980 and who now interviews her during two visits in 1995 and 1996. Suu Kyi is the author of *Freedom from Fear* (1991) and can be seen as a figure whose uncompromising resistance to political injustice bears comparison with that of Mahatma Gandhi and Nelson Mandela.

The Australian Legend   See the Legend of the Nineties.

Authenticity, inauthenticity   Although popular usage privileges 'authenticity' over 'inauthenticity', associating the former with truth and genuineness and the latter with falsehood and simulation, contemporary cultural theory has generally reversed this as part of its interrogation of the notion of pure, originary cultures. The move away from essentialism and towards a recognition that all cultural formations are discursively hybrid has been a particularly important facet of most post-colonial practices, since it has challenged the stereotypical and monocultural thinking that characterizes colonial discursive constructs such as the 'Dark Continent' and the Orient. Thus, in a passage which could be read as a rebuttal of Western perspectives, such as that dramatized by E. M. Forster in his representation of Adela Quested's desire to see the 'real India' (in *A Passage to India*, 1924) and which very explicitly associates such thinking with communal exclusiveness, Salman Rushdie itemizes some of the many Indias that invalidate attempts to discover an authentic India:

> One of the most absurd aspects of this quest for national authenticity is that – as far as India is concerned, anyway – it is completely fallacious to suppose that there is such a thing as a pure, unalloyed tradition from which to draw. The only people who seriously believe this are religious extremists. The rest of us understand that the very essence of Indian culture is that we possess a mixed tradition, a *mélange* of elements as disparate as ancient Mughal and contemporary Coca-Cola American. To say nothing of Muslim, Buddhist, Jain, Christian, Jewish, British, French, Portuguese, Marxist, Maoist, Trotskyist, Vietnamese, capitalist, and of course Hindu elements. (Rushdie 1991: 67)

The Bombay talkie-like method of Rushdie's *Midnight's Children* (1981) can be seen as an attempt to represent such a pluralist view of India.

Further reading

Rushdie (1991); Bhabha (1994).

Awoonor, Kofi (Formerly George Awoonor-Williams) Born 1935. Ghanaian writer and critic. Awoonor studied at the Universities of Ghana and London and at the State University of New York, Stony Brook, where he obtained his doctorate and became a Professor. He subsequently worked at the University of Cape Coast in Ghana and as Director of the Ghana Film Corporation and served as Ghana's ambassador to Brazil and Cuba and the nation's representative at the United Nations.

Awoonor has produced notable work in several genres: poetry, fiction, non-fictional prose, drama and translations. His collections of poetry, *Rediscovery* (1964), *Night of My Blood* (1970) and *Ride Me, Memory* (1973), treat a range of mainly autobiographical themes, including the attempt to reconcile the competing influences of local and American traditions. This theme also informs his allegorical novel, *This Earth, My Brother* (1971), which, like Ayi Kwei Armah's *Fragments* (1970), depicts the alienation of a Ghanaian exile who returns home and struggles to come to terms with conditions in post-independence Ghana. In a memorable closing scene, also reminiscent of motifs in *Fragments*, he escapes from the corruption of the contemporary Ghanaian situation, when he is lured 'home' to his death in the apparently pure waters of the Atlantic breakers by a sea woman who seems to symbolize the Africa of his youth. Awoonor has also published two plays, translations of traditional Ewe poetry, the novel, *Come the Voyager at Last* (1992), *Until the Morning After: Collected Poems* (1987) and a number of critical and political studies, including two highly ambitious works that attempt a comprehensive overview of their subjects: *The Breast of This Earth: A Critical Survey of Africa's Literature, Culture and History* (1975) and *Ghana: A Political History from Pre-European to Modern Times* (1990).

B

Bâ, Mariama (1929–81). Senegalese novelist. Brought up as a Muslim, Bâ worked as a schoolteacher and later as a schools inspector and played a prominent part in the Senegalese feminist movement. She was married to a Senegalese Minister of Information, by whom she had nine children and from whom she was later divorced. Her reputation mainly rests on her short first novel, *Une si longue letter* (1979; *Such a Long Letter*, 1981), which won the first Noma Award for publishing in Africa. The novel, which appeared just two years before her death after a long illness, is a pioneering work about the experience of Muslim women in West Africa. It describes the protagonist's sense of betrayal when her husband takes a second wife and her refusal to accept the Islamic practice of polygamy. Written in a brilliantly succinct prose style, *Une si longue letter* also provides a portrait of a society in transition. It is said to be autobiographical, though Bâ herself denied this. Her only other novel, *Un chant écarlate* (1981: *Scarlet Song*, 1986) is about an inter-racial marriage, in which a young Frenchwoman is the victim of her Senegalese husband's traditional attitudes.

Babas   Straits-Chinese men of mixed descent. The baba community of Malacca, Penang and Singapore is believed to have come into existence some five hundred years ago through miscegenation between Chinese merchants and the peoples already living in these areas. It enjoyed a period of economic prosperity during the late colonial era, but this waned after Malaya attained independence in 1957. See also NONYAS.

Babylon   See RASTAFARI.

Bakhtin, Mikhail   (1895–1975). Russian formalist critic, whose work has been influential in various post-colonial contexts. These include his view of CARNIVAL as a time of liberation from established authority and as an alternative discursive system. His ideas on POLYPHONY have also been widely deployed by post-colonial critics to describe the linguistic modes of many non-Western texts, in which conventions of unity are frustrated by a relativistic, dialogic approach that embodies a vision of social and other systems that interrogates the monologic – and by extension monocultural – perspectives engrained in colonial discursive practices. Bakhtin's numerous other contributions to cultural theory include an emphasis on the bodily grotesque, which has proved productive in contesting patriarchal Western 'norms'. His work's stress on the dialogic interaction involved in speech acts, again as opposed to the monologism of traditional Western rhetoric, has influenced African American theorists such as Henry Louis GATES, who have discussed its relevance to the SIGNIFYING processes of African DIASPORA discourses.

Bakhtin's major works include *The Dialogic Imagination: Four Essays* (1975; trans. 1981), *Problems of Dostoevsky's Poetics* (1963; trans. 1984), *Rabelais and His World* (1965; trans. 1984) and *Speech Genres and Other Late Essays* (1979; trans. 1986). *The Bakhtin Reader* (1994) brings together a selection of his most important work and includes a useful glossary of his terminology.

Further reading

Holquist (1990); Bakhtin (1994).

Bandung   Town in Java, where a meeting of African and Asian nations convened by President Sukarno of Indonesia was held in 1955. This conference has been seen as a landmark in the development of non-Western international cooperation to resist colonialism and NEO-COLONIAL economic control of the world's resources. It anticipated the founding of the NON-ALIGNED MOVEMENT in 1961.

It gave its name to *The Bandung File*, a British Channel 4 television programme devoted to MULTICULTURAL issues.

Basilect   See CREOLE.

The Beacon Group   A pioneering group of 1930s' Trinidadian writers, who published their work in *Trinidad* (1929–30) and *The Beacon* (1930–3). The latter magazine was edited by Albert Gomes, who later became Chief Minister in Trinidad and served as an MP in the parliament of the short-lived West Indian FEDERATION. Other notable members included: C. L. R. JAMES; Alfred Mendes, who published the novels *Pitch Lake* (1934) and *Black Fauns* (1935); and Ralph de Boissière, who emigrated to Australia, where his novels *Crown Jewel* (1952) and *Rum and Coca Cola* (1956) were published. Gomes later published an autobiography, *Through a Maze of Colour* (1974), and a novel *All Papa's Children* (1978). Reinhard Sander's *From Trinidad* (1978) is an anthology of writing from *Trinidad* and *The Beacon*. In Gomes's words, '*The Beacon* became more than just a literary magazine and mouthpiece of a clique. Indeed, it became the focus of a movement of enlightenment spearheaded by Trinidad's angry young men of the Thirties' (in Sander 1978: 2). Sander draws a parallel between the group's struggle to create a national literature and the working-class movement that emerged in Trinidad in the years after World War I.

Further reading

Sander (ed.) (1978); Sander (1995).

Bebey, Francis   (1929–2001). Cameroonian musicologist, musician and writer. Born in Douala, Bebey was educated in French and English and was a radio journalist, prior to working for UNESCO as a specialist in charge of music development for 15 years. A guitarist and sanza (thumb piano) player, he composed and sang songs in French, Douala and English. His compositions encompass a wide range of African musical forms and his varied repertory spanned classical and popular styles. He included storytelling and poetry in his concert performances. Bebey played a pioneering role in extending awareness of African music in the West and in 1968 he staged a groundbreaking concert that included Pigmy, Bantu and West African GRIOT forms in Paris. His *Musique de l'Afrique* (1965; *African Music: A People's Art*, 1975) is a succinct illustrated guide to traditional African music. It demonstrates the variety of its forms, musicians and instruments, stresses the centrality of music in African cultures and provides a corrective to mistaken Western notions of the griot. In his later years, Bebey was a notable composer of film music. His discs include *Akwaaba: Music for Sanza* (1984), *La condition masculine* (1991), *Travail au noir* (1997) and *Dibiye* (1998). His novels include *Le fils d'Agatha Moudio* (1968; *Agatha Moudio's Son*, 1971), winner of the Prix Littéraire de l'Afrique Noire, *La poupée Ashanti* (1973; *The African Doll* 1980) and *L'enfant-pluie* (1994), winner of the Prix Saint-Exupéry.

Further reading

Bebey (1975).

Bedwardism   Jamaican millennial cult, whose leader, the pentecostal preacher, Alexander Bedward (1859–1930) prophesied his own ascension to heaven and subsequent apocalyptic return to destroy earth. Although the date on which he had predicted that this would happen, 31 December 1920, passed uneventfully and he was subsequently committed to a mental asylum, his influence on Jamaican revivalist movements was considerable and his ideas anticipated aspects of the teachings of Marcus GARVEY and RASTAFARI.

Bekederomo   (J[ohn] P[epper] Clark) Born 1935. Nigerian dramatist and poet. Bekederomo was educated at the University of Ibadan and subsequently worked as an information officer, editor and academic, becoming a professor at the University of Lagos before relinquishing this post to found a repertory theatre. Like Wole SOYINKA, he has written plays that fuse Greek and West African mythic elements, sometimes suggesting commonalities that transcend cultural barriers, but also foregrounding the distinctiveness of their particular manifestations and his own individual reinscription of them. *Song of a Goat* (1961) and its sequel *The Masquerade* (1964) are tragedies of fate, in which a family curse slowly but inexorably takes its toll. Bekederomo's most ambitious work to date, *Ozidi* (1966), is based on a traditional Ijaw sage of epic proportions, which exists both as a community performance and as an individually told narrative. The Ozidi story fascinated Clark for many years and he has also translated the original saga (as *The Ozidi Saga*, 1977) and filmed a performance of it. His play on the subject can be read as a revenge tragedy or as an allegory about Nigerian political discord and the need for unity. His poetry also brings Western and indigenous forms together, demonstrating a gift for vivid imagery that lends originality to his representation of themes such as political corruption and the impact of colonialism that have been widely treated in post-independence West African writing. His collections of verse include *Causalties* (1970), *A Decade of Tongues* (1981), *Mandela and Other Poems* (1988) and *A Lot from Paradise* (1998). Bekederomo's other work includes the plays, *The Raft* (1964) and *The Boat* (1981) and a controversial travel-book, *Their America* (1964), which attacks the values of American society. Much of his best work has been republished in *Collected Plays and Poems 1958–1988* (1991).

Benegal, Shyam   Born 1934. Indian film-maker, widely regarded as the most significant director of the Indian New Cinema. Born in Hyderabad, Benegal made numerous advertising shorts, prior to directing his first feature *Ankur* (*The Seedling*, 1973),
in which a young man who returns from the city to his ancestral home in Andhra
Pradesh finds himself caught up in the struggle against the feudal system that operates
in the region. It set the agenda for much of Benegal's subsequent work, which repeatedly engages with the situation of oppressed groups and CASTE and gender prejudice.
Like his next film, *Nishant* (*Night's End*, 1975), it links the exploitation of the peasantry by feudal landlords with the mistreatment of women. *Manthan* (*The Churning*,
1976) also deals with an encounter between socially progressive values, here represented by a doctor who comes to a village community and galvanizes the local
UNTOUCHABLES to rebel against their lot, and tradition.

   Kalyug (1981) extended Benegal's range into the realms of myth. Like Shashi
Tharoor's novel, *The Great Indian Novel* (1989), it is a modern-day reworking of the
MAHABHARATA, which in this case transposes the warfare of the original epic into a contemporary business setting. Benegal's more experimental recent films, including *Suraj
Ka Satvan Gora* (*The Seventh Horse of the Sun*, 1993), and *Sardari Begum* (1996), a fictional version of the life of the vocalist Begum Akhtar, have employed a range of narrative modes. He is also a noted documentary film-maker and his work in this genre
includes *Satyajit Ray* (1984), a multi-part television dramatization of Jawaharlal
NEHRU's *Discovery of India* (*Bharat Ek Khoj*, 1988) and *The Making of the Mahatma*
(1996), which tells the story of Mahatma GANDHI's early years in South Africa, offering
a salutary alternative to Richard Attenborough's Western-oriented *Gandhi* (1982).
Benegal's other films include *Bhumika* (*The Role*, 1997), *Junoon* (*Possessed*, 1979),
Samar (*Conflict*, 1988) and *Zubeidaa* (2000).

Further reading

Datta (2002).

Bennett, Louise   Born 1919. Jamaican comedienne, poet, folklorist, actress and
singer. Bennett began composing poetry while still a schoolgirl and first performed
her distinctive Jamaican CREOLE poems at the age of nineteen. She won a scholarship
to study at RADA (the Royal Academy of Dramatic Art) in London in the 1940s and
subsequently worked in English repertory theatre before returning to Jamaica, where
she taught drama to youth and community groups and worked for the Extra-Mural
Department of the University of the West Indies. Bennett was not the first Jamaican
'dialect' poet: she was preceded by Claude McKay and Una Marson, but long before
performance poetry became popular, she pioneered one-woman shows, which
brought together vernacular poetry, storytelling and folksong. Her most famous
poems include: 'Back to Africa', in which she pokes fun at the notion of Caribbean
repatriation to Africa; 'COLONIZATION IN REVERSE', a satire on Jamaican migration to

Britain which moves in two directions by suggesting that this exodus has 'turn[ed] history upside dung', while also poking fun at the economic and entrepreneurial sides of such migration; 'Dear Departed Federation', a comic elegy for the demise of the West Indian FEDERATION; and 'Noh Lickle Twang' ('Not Even a Little Accent'), a poem which generates heavy irony by bemoaning the fact that a Jamaican recently returned from the USA has not picked up any American accent, while the speaker herself is using broad Jamaican CREOLE. Bennett has received numerous accolades and honours, including an OBE in 1961 and the Order of Jamaica in 1974. Her poetry is collected in *Jamaica Labrish* (1966), a work which has gone through numerous editions. Her other books include *Dialect Verse* (1942), *Jamaican Dialect Poems* (1948), *Anancy and Miss Lou* (1979), a collection of ANANCY stories, and *Selected Poems* (1982). Her record albums include *Jamaican Folk Songs* (1954), on which she gives her renditions of such classic Jamaican songs as 'Linstead Market' and 'Cudelia Brown'.

The Berlin Conference A series of meetings held between November 1884 and February 1885 under the chairmanship of Germany's Chancellor Bismarck and attended by representatives of various European nations, the USA and Turkey. It allocated European powers particular 'spheres of influence' in Africa and in so doing both legitimized European appropriations of African territory and provided a framework for the further PARTITIONING of the continent, so that by 1914 most of Africa was under European control. In return for supporting Germany's claim to sovereignty in the Cameroons at the Conference, Britain received Germany's backing against the French in the Niger River area.

Through bilateral agreements with other European powers, King Léopold II of Belgium obtained overall control of the Congo basin, an area that came to be known as the Congo Free State. The region was intended to be a free trade area, in which slavery was forbidden. However, during the succeeding years, Léopold effectively established a private fiefdom, in which slavery was rife, and his economic exploitation of the Congo led to the death of a large proportion of its population. As news of atrocities in the Congo filtered through to Europe, public opinion was outraged. See also the 'SCRAMBLE FOR AFRICA' and CONRAD, POST-COLONIAL RESPONSES TO.

Beti, Mongo (Alexandre Biyidi-Awala) (1932–2001). Cameroonian-born novelist, who spent much of his life in exile in France, where he worked as a schoolteacher in Rouen. Prior to Cameroonian independence, he published a number of satirical anti-colonial novels written in a realist mode. The best-known of these are *Le Pauvre Christ de Bomba* (1956; *The Poor Christ of Bomba*, 1971), in which a white missionary's attendant's ingenuous account of a journey he has undertaken with his master ironically exposes the supposed altruism of the Christian mission in Africa, and *Mission terminée* (1957; *Mission to Kala*, 1964), a critique of Cameroonian villagers' reverence for imported colonial values, which has similarities to Ayi Kwei ARMAH's first two novels. A fierce critic of Cameroonian government policies, Beti went into exile in 1960 and did not return to Cameroon until the early 1990s. Throughout his time abroad, he continued to be a radical critic of post-independence corruption and mismanagement. His review, *Peuples noirs, peuples africains*, which he co-founded with his wife in 1978, was an organ for attacking African NEO-COLONIALISM. His other novels include *Le Roi miraculé* (1958; *King Lazarus*, 1960), *Main basse sur le Cameroun* (1971) and *L'Histoire du fou* (1994; *The Story of the Madman*, 2001).

Bhabha, Homi K. Born 1949. One of the most influential of post-colonial theorists, Bhabha was born into the Parsi community of Mumbai (Bombay) and was educated at the University of Bombay and at Christ Church College, Oxford, where he obtained his doctorate. He has taught at the Universities of Sussex, Chicago and Harvard. Bhabha's work is particularly influenced by French poststructuralist thought, including the deconstructionist philosophy of Jacques Derrida and the psychoanalytic theory of Jacques Lacan. Bhabha repudiates originary notions of culture in favour of a practice grounded in Derrida's emphasis on the decentred subject and *différance* and the more general poststructuralist concern with the moment of enunciation.

His influential essays, which particularly emphasize the intersection of the temporal and the spatial, are collected in *The Location of Culture* (1994). In a sinuous, sometimes opaque prose, arguably justified by the difficulty of the concepts with which he is grappling, he contends that culture is 'located' in the interstitial 'beyond' where meaning is produced and sees the migrant subject as the representative protagonist of the contemporary age. See the Glossary entries on AMBIVALENCE, BORDERS, HYBRIDITY, LIMINALITY, LOCATION, MIMICRY and THIRD SPACE for further information on central aspects of his thinking. He has also edited *Nation and Narration* (1990), a collection of essays that developed Benedict Anderson's work on nations as IMAGINED COMMUNITIES.

Although Bhabha's work has been highly influential, it has had many critics, particularly among Marxist commentators such as Aijaz AHMAD, who have taken issue with its level of abstraction and also dismissed its tendency towards totalizing categorizations, e.g. Ahmad's attack on Bhabha's view that MAGIC REALISM is the distinctive generic mode of post-colonial writing. Bart Moore-Gilbert (1997) provides a discerning analysis of Bhabha's work. John McLeod (2000) offers a valuable introduction to several of his key concepts.

Further reading

Bhabha (ed.) (1990); Bhabha (1994); Moore-Gilbert (1997); McLeod, J. (2000).

The *Bhagavad Gita* One of the most important texts of classical Hinduism, the *Gita* is taken from a central episode in the MAHABHARATA, in which the god Krishna addresses the warrior Arjuna on the eve of the battle of Kurukshetra. Arjuna is horrified to see many of his friends and family among the enemy, but Krishna's spiritual arguments persuade him to go into battle. The *Gita* teaches the power of selfless, detached action, the importance of discriminating between one's lower nature and the soul, in which the godhead is immanent, and the need for devotion to a particular god. Its many translators include Mahatma GANDHI.

The Biafran War   See the NIGERIAN CIVIL WAR.

Biculturalism   See BILINGUALISM.

The 'Big Three'   Name given to three pioneers of Indian fiction in English in the 1930s: Mulk Raj ANAND, R. K. NARAYAN and Raja RAO.

Biko, Steve   (1946–77). South African civil rights activist. Born in King William's Town, Biko studied medicine at the University of Natal, but was expelled for his outspoken criticism of the APARTHEID regime. He was the first President of the South African Students Organization and a founding member of the 1960s' Black Consciousness Movement in South Africa. His murder in suspicious circumstances, while in police custody, provoked an international outcry and he was subsequently seen as a martyr of the freedom struggle. At home, his funeral, at which Bishop Desmond Tutu gave the oration, was attended by 30,000 people. In 1997 five white policemen confessed to having been involved in his death. A selection of his writing, *I Write What I Like* (1979) was published posthumously. Richard Attenborough's *Cry Freedom* (1987) tells the story of his friendship with the white journalist, Donald Woods (1933–2001), as seen through Woods's eyes.

Bilingualism   While in common usage bilingualism connotes the ability to speak two languages, in public policy contexts it means the official recognition of two languages for the conduct of governmental and other public business, as in the cases of Canada and Aotearoa / New Zealand. Bilingualism is frequently separated from biculturalism in such contexts. Thus Canada is officially bilingual, while pursuing MULTICULTURAL policies.

BIM   Pioneering Barbadian little magazine that fulfilled a similar function for 'Bimshire' (Barbados) to that performed by *The BEACON* in Trinidad in the 1930s and *KYK-OVER-AL* in Guyana in the late colonial period. Founded in 1942 and edited by the poet Frank Collymore, *BIM* published both creative and critical work and survived longer than its companion little magazines in other ANGLOPHONE Caribbean countries. In addition to making an important contribution to Barbadian cultural life, *BIM* provided a forum for writers throughout the anglophone Caribbean. Several of (Edward)

Kamau Brathwaite's most important early critical essays were published in the magazine. An index to the first 30 years of *BIM*, compiled by Reinhard Sander, has been published by the University of the West Indies.

Further reading

Sander (comp.) (1973).

The Black Atlantic   A term coined by the sociologist Paul Gilroy to describe the region on both sides of the Atlantic, in which Africans and members of the African DIASPORA live. Gilroy's *The Black Atlantic* (1993) departs from the work of earlier cultural theorists who have traced linkages within the Atlantic region by contending that Africa, America, the Caribbean and Europe constitute a single zone. His thesis avoids black ESSENTIALISM by suggesting that Atlantic space is a configuration shared by blacks and whites, who are mutually interdependent, and by presenting a decentred model of the region, in which Africa remains important, but is no longer envisaged as the sole, originary source of black cultures. Instead Gilroy suggests that the Black Atlantic is a network in which each of the constituent parts can, and does, influence the others. He particularly focuses on the sailing ship, slavery and music as sites in which the transnational nature of the Black Atlantic experience can be seen to operate, arguing that the exchange of ideas among black intellectuals and artists has always transcended national boundaries. In so doing, his work challenges New World/Old World and North/South bifurcations in a similar manner to the way in which theorists such as Edward Said and creative writers such as Amitav Ghosh have dismantled Occidental/Oriental binaries by demonstrating the extent to which trade and other networks have transgressed this discursive duality. Consequently, *The Black Atlantic* played an important role in the late twentieth-century theorization of transnationalism and HYBRIDITY, as well as thinking about black cultures and ethnicities. It has, however, been criticized for placing too much emphasis on abstractions and paying insufficient attention to the specifics of the lived experience of ordinary black people and Africa itself.

Further reading

Gilroy (1993).

The Black Jacobins   See the HAITIAN REVOLUTION and C. L. R. JAMES.

Black Orpheus   Pioneering arts journal founded at the University of Ibadan in 1957 by the German scholars, Jahnheinz Jahn and Ulli Beier, with the aim of fostering African creative arts and writing and with Es'kia MPHAHLELE and Wole SOYINKA as members of the editorial board. Publication ceased in 1967, but the journal was revived at the University of Lagos in 1981.

Bombay Talkies The popular, mainly Hindi-language films produced in India's 'Bollywood', Mumbai (Bombay). Bombay talkies are generally characterized by their use of an eclectic range of elements that confounds Western notions of genre decorum. The *mélange* of forms that typifies the films has implications that extend beyond popular cinema, e.g. Salman Rushdie views his novel *Midnight's Children* (1981), in which cinematic motifs and techniques abound and a broad range of generic elements are fused together, as employing a Bombay Talkie-like mode. In *The Satanic Verses* (1988), Rushdie's character of Gibreel Farishta is a Bollywood film star. In Shashi Tharoor's novel *Show Business* (1991), a critically ill Bollywood film star replays his career in a phantasmagoric fantasy about the illusion of cinema. International interest in Bollywood cinema has grown steadily. In Merchant Ivory's film *Bombay Talkie* (1970), an American novelist travels to Bombay in search of inspiration and becomes involved with the making of one of the movies and its leading man. More recently, 'Bombay chic' reached new heights with the opening of Andrew Lloyd Webber's stage musical, *Bombay Dreams*, in London's West End in 2002.

The Booker Prize Established in 1969, the Booker is the UK's most prestigious prize for a work of fiction. Sponsored by Booker plc (from 2000, after a merger with Iceland, the Big Food Group plc), it is awarded annually for the best full-length novel written in English by a citizen of the UK or the Commonwealth. However, unlike the Commonwealth Writers Prize, the majority of its winners have been from Britain. Winners with broadly defined 'post-colonial' connections include: V. S. Naipaul, *In a Free State* (1971); Nadine Gordimer, *The Conservationist* (1974; joint winner with Stanley Middleton's *Holiday*); Ruth Prawer Jhabvala, *Heat and Dust* (1975); Salman Rushdie, *Midnight's Children* (1981); Thomas Keneally, *Schindler's Ark* (1982); J. M. Coetzee, *Life & Times of Michael K* (1983); Keri Hulme, *The Bone People* (1985); Peter Carey, *Oscar and Lucinda* (1988); Kazuo Ishiguro, *The Remains of the Day* (1989); Ben Okri, *The Famished Road* (1991); Michael Ondaatje, *The English Patient* (1992; joint winner with Barry Unsworth's *Sacred Hunger*); Arundhati Roy, *The God of Small Things* (1997); J. M. Coetzee, *Disgrace* (1999); Margaret Atwood, *The Blind Assassin* (2000); and Peter Carey, *True History of the Kelly Gang* (2001). Peter Carey and J. M. Coetzee share the distinction of being the only two authors to have won the Prize twice. Prior to winning in 2000, Margaret Atwood had been short-listed on three previous occasions. In 1993, Rushdie's *Midnight's Children* was awarded the Booker of Bookers (the 'Best of Twenty-Five Years of the Booker Prize').

In 2002 the organization and administration of the Prize were transferred to a newly registered charity, the Booker Prize Foundation. The financial services conglomerate, the Man Group, became its new sponsor, renaming it the Man Booker Prize and more than doubling the prize money awarded to the winning book to £50,000, so that the Booker once again became Britain's richest literary prize. See

Graham Huggan's *The Postcolonial Exotic* (Huggan 2001: 105–23) for a critical 'short history of the Booker'.

Further reading

Goff (ed.) (1989); Huggan (2001).

Borders, border aesthetics   Recent critical theory has particularly stressed the importance of borderline sites as places where, to adapt Homi K. BHABHA's phrase, culture is located. Challenging fixed views of cultural activity and ESSENTIALIST representational practices, Bhabha privileges migrant, unsettled locations as sites where meaning is produced and cultural formations can be transmuted. Writing specifically about the importance of borders in the context of the colonial encounter, he says:

> A contingent, borderline experience opens up *in-between* colonizer and colonized. This is a space of cultural and interpretive undecidability produced in the 'present' of the colonial moment. . . . The margin of hybridity, where cultural differences 'contingently' and conflictually touch, becomes the moment of panic which reveals the borderline experience. It resists the binary opposition of racial and cultural groups . . . as homogeneous polarized political consciousnesses. (Bhabha 1994: 206–7; italics in original)

Such a line of thinking can be seen as a product of Bhabha's poststructuralist antipathy to the binary modes of classification that Frantz FANON, Abdul R. JanMohamed and others have termed MANICHEAN ALLEGORY. Elsewhere Bhabha extends his thinking on the importance of borders into an attack on both the MELTING POT model of cultural interaction and originary views of cultures, stressing, as is customary in his work, the *temporal* dimension of the location of culture:

> What is at issue is the performative nature of differential identities: the regulation and negotiation of those spaces that are continually, *contingently*, 'opening out', remaking the boundaries, exposing the limits of any claim to a singular or autonomous sign of difference – be it class, gender or race. Such assignations of social differences – where difference is neither One nor the Other, but *something else besides, in-between* – find their agency in a form of the 'future', where the past is not originary, where the present is not simply transitory. (Bhabha 1994: 219; italics in original)

For further discussion of this aspect of Bhabha's work and interstitial spaces more generally, see HYBRIDITY and LIMINALITY.

   In a less abstract sense, the drawing of borders has been one of the major determinants of the lived experience of many inhabitants of post-colonial countries. Geographical demarcations, such as the separation of India and Pakistan at the time of PARTITION, and earlier those brought into being by European nations' imposition of artificial borders at the time of the 'SCRAMBLE FOR AFRICA', have been major factors in the process of colonial dislocation. In this sense, borders may seem to operate in a converse manner to that suggested by Bhabha, as sites that enforce the colonial control over colonized people's lives. However, Bhabha's view of interstitial spaces argues against the colonial binarism of borders that separate, insisting instead on a post-colonial practice that privileges discourses that are situated in borderline regions or traverse frontiers at will. Rarefied though such thinking may seem to many readers, a similar practice finds expression in the work of post-colonial writers such as Wilson HARRIS, Derek WALCOTT and Amitav GHOSH, who even when they resist the abstractions of Bhabha's poststructuralist theorizing, stage similarly transgressive supranational journeys as acts that both physically and discursively resist colonial and NEO-COLONIAL appropriation.

Further reading

Bhabha (1994).

Brahmin, Brahman   The highest in rank of the four Hindu CASTES, Brahmins have traditionally been both the priests and scribes of Hindu India and hence had a particular importance in the evolution of literary traditions in most of the nation's various languages. Thus two of the 'BIG THREE' of Indian writing in English, R. K. NARAYAN and Raja RAO, came from Brahmin backgrounds and dramatize the caste's concerns – in very different ways – in their work. The role of Brahmins was traditionally associated with ritual purity and gave them a monopoly of the scriptures, which extended into scribal discourse more generally. Brahmin caste superiority has persisted in the post-independence period, despite the introduction of government policies to change this situation, regional variations and the challenge of counter-forces such as the DALIT literary movement, which resists any form of caste privilege.

Brand, Dionne   Born 1953. Trinidadian-born writer and film-maker, who moved to Canada in 1970 and has taught at the Universities of Guelph and Toronto and York University in Toronto. Brand came to prominence as a poet, publishing several collections, including the acclaimed *No Language is Neutral* (1990), which particularly reflect on ways in which language shapes women's identities. In her first novel *In Another Place, Not Here* (1996), two women move between the Caribbean and Toronto restively seeking fulfilment 'in another place'. *At the Full and Change of the Moon* (1999), a poetic novel spanning six generations of DIASPORIC African dispossession, is, like much of Caryl PHILLIPS's fiction, made up of a series of interlocking stories. It commences in 1824, with the suicide of a Trinidadian slave, the leader of a secret society, as an act of revolt. This character also poisons her fellow-slaves, but spares her young daughter, whose descendants travel to the USA, Canada and Europe. The accounts of their lives open up a series of lyrical evocations of dispossession, in which dream and historical realities intermingle.

Brand has directed a number of documentary films, mainly concerned with racist and sexist issues, and has also published *Sans Souci and Other Stories* (1988) and several books of non-fiction, including the acclaimed essay collection, *Bread out of Stone: Recollections on Sex, Recognitions, Race, Dreaming and Politics* (1994). Her other collections of poetry include *Earth Magic* (1978), *Primitive Offensive* (1982) and *Land to Light On* (1997), which won Canada's Governor General's Award for Poetry.

Brathwaite, (Edward) Kamau Born 1930. Barbadian poet, historian and literary and social critic. Brathwaite was educated at Barbados's leading school, Harrison College, Cambridge University, where he read History between 1950 and 1953, and the University of Sussex, where he was awarded his PhD in 1968. His doctoral thesis formed the substance of his book, *The Development of Creole Society in Jamaica, 1770–1820* (1971), from which the pamphlet *Folk Culture of the Slaves in Jamaica* (1970; revised 1981) is taken. He worked as an Education Officer in Ghana from 1955 to 1962, a period which he has described as a key formative influence in his self-development, since it led to a realization of the importance of African elements in his own and more generally Caribbean society's make-up. After returning to the Caribbean, he mainly worked as a historian at the Jamaica campus of the University of the West Indies. He has also held posts in North America.

Brathwaite's masterpiece, the trilogy of poems, *Rights of Passage* (1967), *Masks* (1968) and *Islands* (1969) – published together as *The Arrivants* (1973) – is informed by the process of self-discovery he underwent in Africa. The trilogy attempts to create an aesthetic appropriate to the representation of African DIASPORA experience, refashioning Afro-Caribbean, African American and African forms in order to do so. It depicts New World Africans and their ancestors as unceasing travellers, constantly journeying within the Americas, Europe and Africa itself. *Rights of Passage* is particularly notable for its use of a wide range of African diaspora musical forms, including work song, blues and jazz, which it associates with particular phases of the history of the black experience in the Americas. In *Masks*, poet and poem 'return' to Africa, a movement which is accompanied by an account of the migration of a group of Africans, over a period spanning a millennium, from Ethiopia across the Sahara to the very different physical environment of West Africa, where their journey ends in the enslavement that precedes their forcible transportation across the MIDDLE PASSAGE. The poem makes extensive use of Akan rites and music. Brathwaite's representation of Africa is complex: it is both a heartland for the returned traveller and a site riven with internal dissensions, even when the locus is the past golden age of the great eighteenth-century Ashanti kingdom. *Islands* is set in the Caribbean, now seen through the prism of the African experience. In poems such as 'Ananse' and 'Legba', it discovers new creative possibilities in a range of apparently ossified Afro-Caribbean archetypes by uncovering the African retentions latent within them. The trilogy concludes on a characteristically ambivalent note, placing its emphasis on process rather than achievement and suggesting that, while a new consciousness may be evolving, the struggle is ongoing. Brathwaite has also published a second trilogy: *Mother Poem* (1977), *Sun Poem* (1982) and *X-Self* (1987), in which the main focus is on Barbados and, in the first two parts, particularly on the female and male histories of the island. His other volumes of verse include the collections *Other Exiles* (1975), *Black + Blues* (1976), *Soweto* (1979), *Third World Poems* (1983) and *Middle Passages* (1992).

Brathwaite's work as a literary and cultural critic has played an important role in developing Afro-Caribbean cultural awareness. It is particularly concerned with CREOLIZATION, excavating submerged African traces in the Caribbean, the centrality of ORALITY and musical forms in New World African cultures and the importance of what he refers to as NATION LANGUAGE, a concept he develops in his monograph on ANGLOPHONE Caribbean poetry, *History of The Voice* (1984). Several of the best of his often polemical essays have been collected in *Roots* (1993). His late wife, Dorothy Monica Brathwaite, compiled *A Descriptive and Chronological Bibliography of the Work of Edward Kamau Brathwaite* (1988). Brathwaite has often been contrasted with Derek WALCOTT in a binary oppositional pairing, which sees him as an Afrocentric poet and Walcott as EUROCENTRIC, a comparison, which, in its cruder forms, fails to indicate the primarily Caribbean emphases of their respective aesthetic positions and consequently does both writers a disservice.

Further reading

Rohlehr (1981); Brathwaite (1993); Torres-Saillant (1997).

Brodber, Erna   Born 1940. Jamaican novelist and sociologist, who grew up in the St Mary's parish of Jamaica and subsequently studied at the Mona campus of the University of the West Indies, where she obtained her doctorate. She has worked as a civil servant, a teacher and a research fellow of UWI's Institute for Social and Economic Research.

Brodber has written of the Caribbean's 'disvaluing of any other source of knowledge but book learning', saying that 'contrary to what happened in other non-literate societies, a vigorous oral tradition in which the group's history was handed down, did not develop here' and arguing that as a consequence the Caribbean artist must perform the role of the African GRIOT, who was traditionally the oral repository of the tribe's history (Brodber 1983: 7), a position similar to that advanced by writers such as Chinua ACHEBE and Wole SOYINKA in relation to the role of the contemporary African artist. Her fiction represents a major contribution to this project of reclaiming the 'group's' folk culture, in which the 'literary' text accords oral and folk intertexts a central function. Her first novel *Jane and Louisa Will Soon Come Home* (1980) takes its title from a popular children's ring game, which also underpins the text's cyclic structure. It is linked with the enigmatic central symbol of the novel, the *kumbla*, a round calabash-like cocoon, which both protects and stultifies the normal development of the protagonist. Brodber conceived the novel as 'a case study of the dissociative personality for her social work students' (O'Callaghan 1983: 61), but the central figure, Nellie, can be seen to have a more representative significance, since she embodies the injurious psychological effects of colonialism, particularly the extent to which a 'white', middle-class ethic has inculcated black women with guilt feelings about their sexuality. *Myal* (1988) uses the Afro-Jamaican SYNCRETIST religious rites of MYALISM as its central trope for the need to reclaim submerged elements within the Caribbean personality. The novel places particular emphasis on the ways in which religion and education have contributed to the process of infantilizing the colonial subject, while suggesting an approach that transcends 'race'. As in *Jane and Louisa*, the anti-linear fictional technique breaks down many of the assumptions engrained in Western realist fiction. *Louisiana* (1994) takes an African American anthropologist with Caribbean family connections as its protagonist, extending Brodber's attempt to trace community links between past and present by associating Caribbean folk forms such as OBEAH with African American magico-religious practices such as conjure and hoodoo.

Brodber's sociological works include *Abandonment of Children in Jamaica* (1974), *A Study of Yards in the City of Kingston* (1975) and *Perceptions of Caribbean Women: Towards a Documentation of Stereotypes* (1982).

Further reading

O'Callaghan (1983); Cooper (1990).

The Bush Garden   Title of a 1971 essay collection by the Canadian critic Northrop Frye, in which he develops his notion of the 'garrison mentality' of Canadian SETTLER culture that was supposedly formed during its early days as a society attempting to domesticate a 'wilderness' environment. In the final section (originally published as the Conclusion to Carl F. Klinck (ed.), *A Literary History of Canada*, 1965), Frye writes of the 'terror' associated with the 'conquest of nature' and both characterizes and attacks the narrowness of the garrison mentality, saying:

> In the earliest maps of the country the only inhabited centres are forts, and that remains true of the cultural maps for a much later time. Frances Brooke, in her eighteenth-century *Emily Montague*, wrote of what was literally a garrison; novelists of our day studying the impact of Montreal on Westmount write of a psychological one.

> A garrison is a closely knit and beleaguered society, and its moral and social values are unquestionable. . . . The real terror comes when the individual feels himself [sic] becoming an individual, pulling away from the group . . . . It is much easier to multiply garrisons, and when that happens, something

anti-cultural comes into Canadian life, a dominating herd-mind in which nothing original can grow. (Frye 1971: 225–6)

The Bush Garden influenced Margaret Atwood's Survival: *A Thematic Guide to Canadian Literature* (1972), a complementary study of archetypal patterns in Canadian literature.

Further reading

Frye (1971); Atwood (1972).

The Calcutta Writers' Workshop   A publishing house founded in 1958 under the general directorship of the poet and translator, P. Lal. Its early publications particularly championed the need for craftsmanship in Indian poetry, advocating a movement away from the impressionistic romanticism that it saw as having characterized much earlier Indian poetry in English. The Workshop championed the Modernist approach taken by the then-newly emergent generation of poets, of whom Nissim Ezekiel, Dom Moraes and A. K. Ramanujan became the best-known names, while repudiating the supposed mysticism of poets such as Sri Aurobindo Ghose. Under Lal's directorship, it has continued to produce beautifully bound volumes for over forty years.

Caliban   See Prospero and Caliban.

Callaloo   Quarterly journal of African and African-American writing, founded in 1976 and published by The Johns Hopkins University Press. Edited by Charles H. Rowell, it publishes critical studies of and creative work by black writers worldwide. Its title is taken from a popular Creole soup, whose multiple ingredients have made it a synonym for cultural mixing. *Callaloo* includes interviews, photographs and art and publishes special issues, focusing on particular aspects of African diaspora writing.

Calypso, calypsonian   Form of Trinidadian popular song, closely associated with Carnival performance and steelband music. Traditionally, calypsoes were improvised, humorous compositions, in which the calypsonian (originally the 'chantuelle' or 'shantwell', i.e. the male singer/composer) attempted to demonstrate his virtuosity against rivals, often by employing long words in a spirit of oratorical warfare. Calypso has been the most important narrative medium in Trinidad during the last century. More eclectic in orientation than REGGAE, it covers a wide range of topics, including political and social themes, the man–woman relationship and the state of the music itself.

Calypso's origins date from the nineteenth century, when it evolved from the chants of stickfighters. The etymology of the word is uncertain, but it is widely believed to derive from the Hausa '*kaito*', a shout of praise or approbation, and the music is often referred to in Trinidad as '*kaiso*'. In *The Middle Passage* (1962), V. S. Naipaul expresses the widely held view that the music is 'a purely local form. No song composed outside Trinidad is a calypso', adding that 'The calypso deals with local incidents, local attitudes and it does so in a local language' (ibid.: 70). However, calypso's popularity has spread throughout the Eastern Caribbean and the BLACK ATLANTIC region more generally, particularly as a consequence of Caribbean migration. The claims for Trinidadian exclusivity are also undermined by the fact that the most famous of all calypsonians, The Mighty SPARROW was born in Grenada.

In 1939, the first Calypso King, a title that would become a standard annual award, was proclaimed during the festivities of Carnival and this was followed in 1945 by the first people's choice of Road March, another annually awarded accolade. Until the 1970s calypso was an almost exclusively male preserve and the gender ethic implicit in most compositions was distinctly chauvinist. However, during that decade the emergence of female calypsonians such as Calypso Rose (Rose McCartha Sandy-Lewis, born 1940), who won the calypso crown in 1977 and 1978, challenged the male monopoly of the genre and the title of King was subsequently changed to that of Monarch. Debates have raged as to whether the 'purity' of the music should be preserved or whether African American and Latin American elements are admissible. Thus, the 1986 Calypso Monarch, David Rudder (born 1953) attracted controversy for the incorporation of samba elements into his composition, 'Bahia Girl'. The blending of traditional calypso with American soul music gave rise to the related form of soca, which has been popular since the late 1970s. Prize-winning soca compositions have included Calypso Rose's 'Soca Jam' (1978) and 'Soca Baptist' (1980) by Blue Boy (a.k.a. Superblue; Austin Lyons, born 1956).

Literary works that make extensive use of calypso forms or allusions include Naipaul's *Miguel Street* (1959), Earl LOVELACE's *The Dragon Can't Dance* (1979), where the calypsonian Philo's compositions suggest affinities with The Mighty Sparrow, and Derek WALCOTT's *The Joker of Seville* (1974), his Creolized reworking of the original Spanish Don Juan play, Tirso de Molina's *El Burlador de Sevilla*, with music by Galt MacDermot.

See also CARNIVAL.

Further reading

Hill (1972); Warner (1982); Rohlehr (1990).

Camara, Laye   See Laye, Camara.

Cannibalism   While cannibalism is a historically verifiable reality in certain contexts, it attracted a disproportionate and often highly fanciful amount of commentary in Western texts dealing with 'alterity' ('OTHERNESS') and affords one of the most striking instances of the colonial practice of constituting a sense of identity through self-differentiation from the figure of a savage 'other'. As Peter Hulme puts it:

> The modern Cartesian subject . . . depends for its sense of self as an independent identity on an image of a clearly differentiated 'other' who destroys boundaries, the kind of 'other' so powerfully figured in the cannibals who threaten Robinson Crusoe: modernity enters the world's stage attached to its cannibal shadow. (Barker *et al.* 1998: 5–6)

Hulme's comments are interesting not only for their reinforcement of Edward Said's contention that the West has characteristically defined itself through this kind of contradistinction, which has been followed by numerous other post-colonial commentators, but also for locating this process of self-definition in relation to post-Cartesian notions of autonomous subjectivity. This develops a line of thinking initiated by Ian Watt who sees *Robinson Crusoe* as the fictional equivalent of Descartes' *cogito ergo sum* ('I think, therefore I am'), an assertion that has been seen as the founding premise of both modern cognitive philosophy and the post-Enlightenment Western sense of discrete selfhood. In Watt's words:

> Defoe initiated an important new tendency in fiction: his total subordination of the plot to the pattern of the autobiographical memoir is as defiant an assertion of the primacy of individual experience in the novel as Descartes's *cogito ergo sum* was in philosophy. (1963: 15)

Further reading

Watt (1963); Barker *et al.* (eds) (1998).

Cargo cults   Melanesian millenarist movements that have been seen as a metonym for the post-colonial experience more generally. Cargo cults originated shortly after traditional society in New Guinea came into CONTACT with European culture. The cults adapted traditional forms of ancestor-worship to the new colonial situation. Belief-systems in the pre-colonial period viewed the recently departed ancestor as someone who would intercede on behalf of the living in the spirit-world, for example, as Ayi Kwei Armah puts it in his novel *Fragments* (1970), by asking for rain in a period of drought. After colonial intervention, such beliefs were transformed into a more overtly materialistic quest for 'cargo' in the form of Western goods, which the cult's adherents believed might rain down on them from the skies. Armah's *Fragments* redeploys this trope in a Ghanaian context to attack the West African NEO-COLONIAL obsession with consumer goods.

In their original form in New Guinea, the cults have variously been seen as an expression of their followers' dissatisfaction with their status in colonial society (Lawrence 1964: 1) and as an index of the extent to which they were quickly brainwashed with Western values and came to view the colonizer as a godlike figure who could fulfil the traditional ancestral role. Armah's sardonic displacement of the myths into Ghana follows the latter explanation, though his prime targets are the bourgeoisie and new elite of post-independence African society.

Further reading

Worsley (1957); Lawrence (1964).

The Caribbean Artists Movement (CAM) A British-based movement of Caribbean writers, artists and critics, started in London in 1966 by (Edward) Kamau BRATHWAITE. Leading members included the Jamaican novelist, Andrew Salkey, who subsequently migrated to the USA, and the Trinidadian poet and publisher, John La Rose, who founded New Beacon Books, which remained one of the most important small publishers and specialist black bookshops in the UK long after the demise of the Movement. CAM held conferences at the University of Kent in 1967 and 1968 and continued to mount activities until 1972. Other members included Wilson HARRIS, AUBREY WILLIAMS, Louis James and Anne Walmsley, who has written a detailed history of CAM. V. S. NAIPAUL is alleged to have declined to join the Movement.

Further reading

Walmsley (1992).

Caribbean Quarterly Interdisciplinary Caribbean Studies journal published by the University of the West Indies since 1949.

Caribbean Studies Interdisciplinary journal first published by the Institute of Caribbean Studies at the University of Puerto Rico in 1961.

Caribbean Voices BBC radio programme broadcast from London to the Caribbean from 1943 to 1958. The programme was devised by Una MARSON as part of the BBC's Colonial Service and, in the climate of World War II, took the form of readings of published work. Marson was succeeded by *Caribbean Voices*' longest-serving editor, Henry Swanzy, who was responsible for the programme from 1946 to 1954, and V. S. NAIPAUL. Swanzy changed its content to include new work and has been praised by many Caribbean writers of the period for fostering new talent. He solicited previously unpublished material and, at a time when metropolitan outlets for Caribbean writers were comparatively limited, *Caribbean Voices* played a part in helping to establish the careers of major writers such as Sam Selvon, Derek Walcott, George Lamming and (Edward) Kamau Brathwaite. Another regular contributor to the programme, the Jamaican poet and educator John Figueroa, has edited a two-volume anthology of writing from the programme, *Caribbean Voices* (1970). Figueroa's (1989) essay 'The Flaming Faith of These First Years: *Caribbean Voices*' provides an account of the development of the programme and the genesis of his anthology.

Further reading

Figueroa (1989); Nanton (1998); Jarrett-Macauley (1998).

Carnival   Carnival takes varied forms of expression in different parts of the world. Its main types include the traditional Catholic pre-Lenten festivals of southern Europe and New World celebrations, in which African DIASPORA folk forms play a major role. Historically, the world's most famous Carnivals have been those held in Rio de Janeiro, New Orleans and Port of Spain. Europe's largest contemporary Carnival, Notting Hill, began in the early 1960s as a comparatively small celebration of Caribbean arts and culture. It has grown into a MULTICULTURAL event, which today attracts about a million and a half participants and onlookers. Other European Carnivals have evolved from their Catholic origins into celebrations of a range of alternative life-styles, prominent among which are Mardi Gras festivals, in which Carnival's traditional cross-dressing has developed into celebrations of gay identity.

Carnival has its origins in Roman *saturnalia* and the word derives from the Latin *carne vale* ('farewell to the flesh'). The Catholic festivals of medieval Europe, held in the two days before Ash Wednesday, were a brief period of indulgence sanctioned by the Church as a prelude to the abstinence of Lent. In the Americas, Carnival forms emerged as CREOLIZED syntheses of Catholic-derived and New World African folk forms. Thus in Trinidad, the ANGLOPHONE Caribbean country most famed for its Carnival, the island's annual 'bacchanal' developed from the various masquerades and festivals of the early nineteenth-century French PLANTOCRACY *and* aspects of the folk culture of its Afro-Caribbean population, such as *canboulay* (from *cannes brulées*, or 'burnt canes'), a ritual adapted, from the practice of slaves' extinguishing plantation fires, to celebrate EMANCIPATION. Significantly, at one point in the nineteenth century, a period when the festivities of the ex-slaves and their descendants encountered considerable hostility from the colonial authorities, Afro-Caribbean forms of Carnival appear to have been celebrated not in the days immediately before Lent, but on 1 August, Emancipation Day (Hill 1972: 23–4).

In the words of the Russian formalist critic, Mikhail Bakhtin, traditional European Carnival:

celebrated liberation from the prevailing truth and from the established order; it marked the suspension of all hierarchical rank, privileges, norms and prohibitions. Carnival was the true feast of time, the feast of becoming, change and renewal. It was hostile to all that was immortalized and completed. (Bakhtin 1965: 10)

Bakhtin also views Carnival as a system of discourse in which the oral and folk culture of the market-place invades the domain of the scribal. He traces the lineage of such a tradition in European writing from Rabelais, numbering Shakespeare, Cervantes and Dostoevsky among its adherents. His theory is interesting to consider in relation to the use of oral and folk elements in New World literatures, and Caribbean texts such as Sam SELVON s *The Lonely Londoners* (1956) and *Moses Migrating* (1983), Earl LOVELACE's *The Dragon Can't Dance* (1979), Derek WALCOTT's *The Joker of Seville* (1974) and Wilson HARRIS's *Carnival Trilogy* (1993; original parts 1985–90) all engage with Carnival as an alternative discursive system that challenges the HEGEMONY of colonial discourse, albeit in very different ways.

Carnival's various manifestations are, as Bakhtin argues, virtually always associated with a temporary suspension or inversion of the *status quo*, which usually involves comic or parodic elements. Thus the elaborate pageantry of Carnival costumes and floats often MIMICS such establishment targets as royalty, creating an alternative hierarchy in which the people assume positions of rank and privilege, as in Trinidad's crowning of Carnival Queens and CALYPSO Monarchs. The political economies of contemporary Carnival are, however, variable and defy easy categorization, particularly since the commercialization of both older and newer Carnivals, such as that held in Toronto, can be so extensive as to raise questions about whether the festivals are in any meaningful sense egalitarian people's events. *The Dragon Can't Dance* poses the question of whether Carnival is simply a time of licensed escapism or an event that contains genuine revolutionary potential and this is a debate that has raged in Trinidad more generally. Despite this AMBIVALENCE, Carnival remains a site for forms that at least temporarily challenge prevalent social norms as well as offering an opportunity for celebration. Thus in Barcelona, the Carnivals held immediately after the end of the Franco regime provided an outlet for expressing both Catalan nationalism and various forms of individualism that had been suppressed during the years of fascist rule.

With the exception of Notting Hill, which is held at the end of August, the major contemporary Carnivals are now held in the traditional pre-Lenten period: commencing on the Monday before Lent (Trinidad's 'J'Ouvey'/'Jour Ouvert', or 'break of day') and lasting for 48 hours through Shrove Tuesday (New Orleans's Mardi Gras). The numerous musical and other forms associated with Carnival include samba, calypso and STEELBAND.

Further reading

Bakhtin (1965); Hill (1972); Nunley and Bettelheim (eds) (1988).

Carpentier, Alejo (1904–80). Cuban novelist He studied architecture at the University of Havana, but subsequently developed stronger interests in anthropology, music and literature. He was a founding member of the Cuban Minority Group, a faction whose political agenda anticipated many of the concerns of the Cuban Revolution. His early novel *Ecue-Yamba-O* (1933) follows the fortunes of a boy who deserts plantation life and become involved with the underbelly of city life. In 1945 Carpentier left Cuba for Venezuela, which provided the inspiration for his most famous novel *Los pasos perdidos* (1953; *The Lost Steps* 1956). The novel describes a composer's quest to discover primitive musical instruments on an INTE-RIOR JOURNEY into the rainforest, which forces him to interrogate his notion of what constitutes 'civilization'. His initiation into a new vision of consciousness invites comparison with the heartland experience depicted in Wilson HARRIS's later *Palace of the Peacock* (1960). Returning to Cuba after the Revolution, Carpentier played an important part in the nation's cultural life, occupying a number of senior administrative positions, including that of Director of the Cuban State Publishing House. He had lived in Paris in the 1920s and returned there as cultural attaché in 1966.

Carpentier's development of a distinctively Latin American form of surrealism, '*lo real maravilloso*', a mode of writing in which the supposedly real and marvellous co-exist, is widely seen as the beginnings of MAGIC REALISM. His other novels include: *El Reino de Esto Mundo*, (1949; *The Kingdom of this World*, 1989), a short novel about the HAITIAN REVOLUTION, particularly notable for its early use of a magic realist technique; *El Siglo de las Luces* (1962; *Explosion in a Cathedral*, 1963), a historical novel based on the life of the French Revolutionary, Victor Hugues, which follows his political career in the Caribbean; and *El Recurso del Metodo* (1974; *Reasons of State*, 1976), a portrait of the vicissitudes in the career of a Latin American dictator, whose authoritarian and hedonistic life-style is challenged first by liberal rebels and later by Marxist revolutionaries.

Cartography   Although map-making dates back at least as far as the Ptolemaic map of the world (*c.* 2nd century AD), its emergence as a 'modern' science can be dated to the European cartographers of the fifteenth and sixteenth centuries, of whom the Flemish geographer, Gerardus Mercator, famed for his world chart – 'the Mercator Projection' (1569) – is the best known. However, although such cartography has been seen as the beginnings of scientifically accurate depictions of the world's surface, it incorporates elements from classical and other mythologies into its borders to produce an odd amalgam of supposedly objective representation and mythic fabulation. Michael ONDAATJE's description of early European maps of Sri Lanka in *Running in the Family* (1982), which foregrounds the kind of exotic ORIENTALIST mythologizing inherent in this kind of cartography, provides an instance of the characteristic *modus operandi* of this period of European map-making:

At the edge of the map the scrolled mantling depicts ferocious slipper-footed elephants, a white queen offering a necklace to natives who carry tusks and a conch, a Moorish king who stands amidst the power of books and armour. On the south-west corner of some charts are satyrs, hoof deep in foam, listening to the sound of the island, their tails writhing in the waves. (Ondaatje 1982: 63–4)

The same passage is also notable for its focus on the gendered nature of colonial discourse, as Ondaatje goes on to link this kind or cartography with colonial onomastics, drawing an analogy between the exercise of European, and other, HEGEMONIC power in both fields:

The maps reveal rumours of topography, the routes for invasion and trade, and the dark mad minds of travellers' tales appears throughout Arab and Chinese and medieval records. The island seduced all of Europe. The Portuguese. The Dutch. The English. And so its name changed, as well as its shape, – Serendip, Ratnapida ('island of gems'), Taprobane, Zeloan, Zeilan, Seyllan, Ceilon, and Ceylon – the wife of many marriages, courted by invaders who stepped ashore and claimed everything with the power of their sword or bible or language. (ibid.: 64)

Gradually maps became more 'accurate', but as recent work on cartography has increasingly demonstrated, map-making remains an ideologically encoded discourse, involving interpretative strategies on the part of both map-makers and those who read their work. Thus early twentieth-century political maps of the world employed colour coding to indicate which European power 'owned' particular countries and a third of the land surface was shaded pink to signify its presence in the British Empire.

More insidiously, maps such as the Mercator Projection and its many derivatives, which have continued to be used as standard, and supposedly neutral, representations are predicated upon EUROCENTRIC assumptions, engrained in the conventions they employ. A number of maps produced in recent decades have, both playfully and seriously, attempted to correct the biases of Eurocentric cartography. The Peter's Projection, devised by Arno Peters in 1974 (English version, 1983), responds to the distortion in land area that occurs in traditional projections, such as Mercator's, in which the spherical earth is projected onto the flat, two-dimensional surface of a sheet of paper. It does so by shortening the distance between lines of latitude as they approach the north and south poles, thus reducing the size of polar regions such as northern Greenland and Russia. More significantly, since these distortions are readily apparent, it reveals that countries nearer the equator have had their land area reduced by traditional cartography, with the result that Africa, South Asia and equatorial South America occupy a larger proportion of the globe in the Peter's Projection. Overall the Peter's Projection reveals that the land area of the SOUTH is almost exactly double that of the North. The Bligh Revised Map of the World, which circulated in the 1980s, was an Australian response to European cartography. It literally turns the world, as conventionally depicted, upside down, by instating Australia in the centre of the top half of the map, while Western Europe is relegated to the bottom right corner, which, given the way in which books are read in most parts of the world (from top left to bottom right), has the effect of locating it 'last'.

Post-colonial contestations of traditional cartographies have not, however, been solely concerned with combating Eurocentric geographies. Thus, a New Zealand map represents Australia as a small island off the coast of a very large New Zealand. Graham Huggan's *Territorial Disputes* (1994) considers mapping strategies in contemporary Australian and Canadian fiction. See also CENTRE AND PERIPHERY, CULTURAL GEOGRAPHY, GREENWICH, IMAGINATIVE GEOGRAPHY, PARTITION.

Further reading

Jones (1994); Huggan (1994).

Caste   A hierarchically arranged system of social stratification based on heredity, particularly as found in conservative Hinduism. Traditionally, caste determines many aspects of a Hindu person's station in life, including available occupations and eligible marriage partners. Caste is believed to have evolved in ancient India from the earlier *varna* system, which came into being around 1000 BC and has been seen as the bedrock of the social philosophy underpinning Hinduism's emphasis on purity and pollution. Traditional Hinduism identified four main castes, but in practice Hindu society is frequently divided into many more. The four traditional castes are: the BRAHMINS, the class of priest and scribes; the *Kshatriyas*, the warrior class; the *Vaisyas*, the class of farmers and merchants; and the *Sudras*, the peasants and labourers. Below these four classes come those excluded from traditional Hindu society, the UNTOUCHABLES (see also HARIJAN and DALIT). Caste discrimination is less pervasive in contemporary India and legislation to outlaw its practice has been successful in urban areas. It continues to exercise a hold in poorer rural areas and recent atrocities committed in the name of caste include the murder of about 60 villagers in the state of Bihar by a private army, allegedly hired by landowners.

Caste is not confined to sub-continental Hinduism. It is also practised in Sri Lankan Buddhism and also in DIASPORIC Hindu contexts, though usually in a diluted form, since traditionally those Hindus who have crossed the *kala pani* ('black water'), i.e. gone overseas, are considered to be polluted and to have lost all caste. So, insofar as this belief is upheld, migration acts as a leveller that creates a more egalitarian community.

Castro, Fidel   Born 1927. Cuban revolutionary leader and statesman. The son of a wealthy Spanish father, Castro trained as a lawyer and practised in Havana, prior to leading an unsuccessful 1953 uprising against the endemic corruption of Cuba's President Batista's regime. He was sentenced to a fifteen-year term of imprisonment but released as part of a general amnesty in 1955. He left the country to regroup in Mexico and after returning in 1956, along with his brother Raúl and the Argentinian-born Ernesto 'Che' Guevara (1928–67), mounted a guerrilla campaign against Batista's dictatorship from the Sierra Maestra Mountains. Support for his movement grew and Batista was eventually ousted from power in early 1959. Castro became Prime Minister and was later elected as President in 1976.

After abortive attempts at rapprochement with the USA, which had hitherto supported the Cuban economy, he established a Communist regime with the backing of the USSR. The early years of his rule were marked by open confrontations with the USA, but he succeeded in resisting the American-backed invasion of Cuba at the Bay of Pigs in 1961 and survived the Missile Crisis of 1962, when the USSR was forced to withdraw nuclear bases it had established in Cuba. Castro's reforms in areas such as agriculture, welfare, medicine and education made Cuba the most successful socialist state in the Americas despite continued US opposition and a trade embargo. At the height of his power, Castro assisted other countries in the region, such as MICHAEL MANLEY's Jamaica, in the development of their social welfare programmes. Cuba also played an important role in exporting Communism to other parts of the world, sending troops to fight in such causes as the Angolan freedom struggle. Despite his Soviet affiliations, Castro was a leading figure in the NON-ALIGNED MOVEMENT, becoming its President in 1980.

The collapse of the Soviet bloc, and its accompanying financial support for Cuba in the late 1980s led to a dramatic downtown in the nation's economy. However, during a period when other Communist regimes disappeared, Castro's commitment to revolutionary socialism remained firm, though economic necessity led him to make some concessions to free trade. Castro has been excoriated by the many Cuban 'exiles' in the USA and elsewhere, but his place in both the vanguard and rearguard of post-colonial socialism makes him a unique figure in the history of the last half century.

Further reading

Balfour (1995).

Centre and periphery, centre and margins   The binary opposition of the 'centre' and the 'periphery' has been one of the most persistent tropes of COLONIAL and NEO-COLONIAL discourse. Like other such 'MANICHEAN' binaries, it is asymmetrical, since it constructs an unequal relationship between the metropolitan centre of the colonial 'Mother Country' and the colonized margins, which supposedly need the centre to validate their peripheral existence. In his novel *The Doubleman* (1985), the Tasmanian writer, C. J. Koch invokes one of the *Ur*-texts of Western literature, Plato's *Republic*, to convey the sense of cultural exile instilled in the colonial mind by the centre-margins dichotomy:

> Tasmanians, I suppose, were rather like the prisoners in Plato's cave; to guess what the centre of the world was like – that centre we knew to be twelve thousand miles away – we must study shadows on the wall: *Bitter Sweet* at the Hobart Repertory; *Kind Hearts and Coronets* at the Avalon Cinema; the novels of A. J. Cronin and J. B. Priestley and Graham Greene; shadows, all shadows, clues to the other hemisphere we might someday discover. (Koch 1985: 24)

It might be possible to argue that Tasmania – 'twelve thousand miles away' and literally left off the maps drawn by some early European CARTOGRAPHERS – represents a particular instance of isolation, because of 'the tyranny of distance' (the Australian historian Geoffrey Blainey's phrase) separating it from the 'centre', but parallel expressions of psychic exile can be found in post-colonial writing from around the globe. A similar passage about the *shadow*-like predicament of the colonial mentality occurs in George LAMMING's *In the Castle of My Skin* (1953), when a group of Barbadian schoolboys attempts to grasp the notion of a metropolitan essence represented by the figure of the king's head on a penny. After debating whether all pennies are made from a single, quasi-Platonic original, they listen to one of their number telling them that the king is never seen after ascending the throne, his public engagements being undertaken by a shadow: 'The shadow king was a part of the English tradition. The English, the boy said, were fond of shadows. They never did anything in the open' (Lamming 1953: 55). Again, the sense of living in a marginal world where the centre of power is so remote as to be unreal, or at least completely beyond the colonial subject's grasp, is paramount. Superficially, Sam SELVON's *The Lonely Londoners* (1956) frustrates this pattern, since its eponymous Londoners are Caribbean migrants now resident in the 'centre'. Their existence within the former capital of Empire revolves around their romantic conceptions of such London sites as Piccadilly Circus and Trafalgar Square, supposed centres of the 'centre'. This affiliation (see FILIATION) is, however, extremely AMBIVALENT and the novel concludes with a passage in which the narrator, Moses, reflects on the aimlessness of their lives. Throughout the narrative there is the suggestion that they lead centrifugal lives and are as disempowered in London as they were in their former colonial 'homelands', only achieving fulfilment through CARNIVALESQUE subversion of British customs and *mores*.

The centre–periphery binary is not confined to post-colonial formations and also exists in such contexts as contrasts between metropolises and their provinces, though it generally has a less asymmetrical force in such situations. Thus, while the provincial fascination with the metropolis finds expression in such mythologizing as Dick Whittington's belief that the streets of London are paved with gold, this is balanced by an opposite tendency, expressed in pastoral and related discourses, circulating from classical times onwards, which privilege rural simplicity over urban corruption. Some early colonial discourses, e.g. the myth of EL DORADO which saw the New World as a potential Eden, were predicated on such beliefs, but more commonly colonial HEGE-MONY was enforced by educational and cultural conditioning that suggested the primacy of the 'Mother Country'.

Centre–binary oppositions inform numerous colonial discourses, with Renaissance European cartography affording a particularly stark example of a EUROCENTRIC hermeneutic system. Post-colonial attempts to contest them have sometimes taken the form of an oppositional aesthetic or cartographic practice, which endeavours to turn the tables by asserting the centrality of the former 'periphery', e.g. as in the playful Bligh Revised Map of the World or Indonesia's President Sukarno's relocation of the Prime Meridian in Jakarta (see CARTOGRAPHY and GREENWICH). Although such attempts, when undertaken in earnest, can be seen as a necessary form of STRATEGIC ESSENTIALISM, they have the effect of perpetuating dualistic modes of thinking and arguably operate against a practice that dismantles colonial binaries, since they leave Manichean classifications in place. Studies such as Sara SULERI's *The Rhetoric of English India* (1992), which suggests that the cultures of colonizer and colonized were far less discrete than is generally assumed, and CONTINUUM and HYBRID models of culture more generally point in another direction: towards conceptual models and practices which deconstruct centre–periphery binaries by demonstrating the extent to which both the geographical and discursive BORDERS shaped by colonialism are porous boundaries. In Edward SAID's phrase colonizer–colonized relationships are made up of 'overlapping territories, inter-twined histories' (Said 1994: 1ff.)

Further reading

Koch (1987); Suleri (1992); Said (1994); Bhabha (1994).

Césaire, Aimé   Born 1913. Martinican poet, dramatist and politician. Born into a peasant family, he was a staunch opponent of French colonial ASSIMILATIONIST policies. During the 1930s he lived in Paris, where he played an important part in black student movements, invented the term NEGRITUDE and became one of the pioneers of the movement that took its name from his coinage. He wrote the long poem for which he is best known, *Cahier d'un retour au pays natal* (1939; *Return to My Native Country* 1968), while a student in Paris during the period when the ideas of Negritude were taking shape. Using techniques from the then-popular French surrealist movement, the *Cahier* explores the distinctiveness of black cultural identity in a historically grounded manner that prefigures the black consciousness movements of the 1960s, the period when the poem became popular in the English-speaking world. Stylistically varied, it moves between impassioned prose outbursts against injustice and a more lyrical mode that celebrates black ancestry. In 1945 Césaire became Mayor of Martinque's capital, Fort-de-France, and he subsequently represented Martinique in the French National Assembly. He founded the Parti Progressiste Martiniquais in 1958 and remained active in politics into the 1990s.

Césaire's other volumes of poetry include *Les Armes miraculeuses* (1946), *Le Corps perdu* (1950, *Ferrements* (1960) and *Moi, laminaire* (1982). An English edition of his *Collected Poetry* was published in 1983. His plays include *La Tragédie du roi Christophe* (1963), *Une Saison au Congo* (1967), which deals with the death of Patrice LUMUMBA, and *Une Tempête* (1969), an adaptation of Shakespeare's TEMPEST which follows Octave MANNONI and George LAMMING in redeploying the play's archetypes in a critique of colonialism. His *Discours sur le colonialisme* (1955) influenced his younger country-man, Frantz Fanon, whom he taught in school.

Further reading

Arnold, A. .J. (1981); Davis, G. (1997).

Chamoiseau, Patrick   Born 1953. Martinican writer. Chamoiseau studied law in Paris and has spent much of his adult life working with young offenders in Martinique. Édouard GLISSANT is a clear influence on his work, which develops the ideas of CRÉOLITÉ into an aesthetic firmly rooted in the Martinican landscape and Chamoiseau has been a fierce critic of Martinique's status as a DOM, or overseas department of France. Best-know for *Texaco* (1992; trans.1997), which won the prestigious Prix Goncourt, he has also published the novels *Chroniques des septs misères* (1986; *Chronicle of the Seven Sorrows*, 1999) and *Solibo Magnifique* (1988; *Solibo Magnificent*, 1999). *Texaco* is a POLYPHONIC novel, covering 150 years of Caribbean history. It focuses on ordinary Martinicans' struggles from the time of the plantation system to the NEO-COLONIAL present, in which the community is living in a shanty town close to an oil depot, run by the company from which the novel takes its title. *Solibo Magnifique* centres on the death of an old storyteller and the mystery surrounding this, which provides a framework for a complex investigation of the oral tradition. Like much of Chamoiseau's work, it is concerned with the relationship between Caribbean oral narrative and the literary tradition.

His other works include, *Antan d'enfance* (1993; *Childhood*, 1999), an autobiographical account of his early years in Fort-de-France and its sequel, *Chemin d'école* (1994; *School Days* 1998) which is particularly notable for its account of a struggle against the colonial orientation of the Caribbean educational curriculum. Along with Jean Bernabé and Raphaël Confiant, he published *Éloge de la créolité* (1989), a study of Caribbean cultural identity which played an important role in developing the notion of Créolité; and more generally he has tried to move debates about FRANCOPHONE Caribbean identity beyond the long shadow cast by the island's most influential thinker, Aimé CÉSAIRE and the NEGRITUDE movement. Chamoiseau's work became more widely known in Anglo-American circles in the late 1990s, when English translations of several of his books were published in quick succession.

Chandra, Vikram   Born 1961. Indian novelist and short story writer. Born in New Delhi, Chandra moved to the USA to study film at Columbia University. He has subsequently lived in America and India. His fiction demonstrates a *Thousand and One Nights*-like absorption with the processes of storytelling and he has been seen as the most postmodern of the post-Rushdie generation of Indian novelists writing in English. *Red Earth and Pouring Rain* (1995), which won the Commonwealth Writers' Prize for Best First Book, is an epic tale of nineteenth-century India, which intersperses its historical narrative with an account of a young Indian's journey across America by car. Set in contemporary India, Chandra's second book, *Love and Longing in Bombay* (1997), is made up of five stories, dealing with the myths and mysteries of Mumbai and spiralling outwards to encompass a range of other narratives, in which the city itself remains the main protagonist. It won the Commonwealth Writers' Prize for Best Book in the Eurasia region.

Chaudhuri, Nirad   (1897–1999). Indian autobiographer and cultural commentator. Chaudhuri was over 50, when his account of his Bengali upbringing, *Autobiography of an Unknown Indian* was published in 1951. He had previously worked as a clerk and secretary and written books in Bengali. The *Autobiography*'s dedication to 'the memory of the British Empire in India' and its more general pro-British sympathies outraged many of its Indian readers. In fact, its representative significance is broader than the view of Chaudhuri as a colonial anglophile suggests. It is as much an account of his own sense of personal failure – paradoxically now overcome with the book's success – and a tribute to Bengali intellectual life in the early twentieth century as a homage to the Raj.

At the time of the *Autobiography*'s publication, Chaudhuri had never visited England, but when subsequently invited to do so by the British Council, he took a whimsical look at English customs in *A Passage to England* (1960). He subsequently settled in Oxford, where he cultivated an English life-style and died at the age of 101. A second volume of autobiography, *Thy Hand, Great Anarch!* (1987), covering the years 1921 to 1952, ran to over 1,000 pages. His last book, *Three Horsemen of the New Apocalypse* (1997), published when he was 99, was an acerbic attack on what he saw as the decline of Western values.

Chaudhuri has been described by V. S. Naipaul, who regards the *Autobiography* as the one great book to have emerged from the Indo-British encounter, as 'the last of the Aryans' (Naipaul 1972: 61–70), and his individualistic and highly critical history of India, *The Continent of Circe* (1965), supports such a categorization. His other books include *To Live or Not to Live: An Essay on Living Happily with Others* (1971), *Scholar Extraordinary* (1974), a biography of the Sanskrit scholar Max Müller, *Clive of India* (1975) and *Hinduism: A Religion to Live By* (1979). Merchant Ivory's film, *Adventures of a Brown Man in Search of Civilization* (1972), was a BBC television documentary about Chaudhuri, shot during a visit to Oxford to research material for *Scholar Extraordinary*. It took its title from a chapter in *A Passage to England*.

Further reading

Naipaul (1972).

Chinodya, Shimmer   Born 1957. Zimbabwean novelist, educated at a mission school and the Universities of Zimbabwe and Iowa, where he obtained an MA in Creative Writing. Chinodya's autobiographical first novel, *Dew in the Morning* (1982), depicts changes in rural Zimbabwean society in the 1960s and 1970s through the eyes of a boy who spends his summer vacations in his family's country home. *Harvest of Thorns* (1989), which won the Best Book award for the African region of the COMMONWEALTH WRITERS' PRIZE, is a complex, POLYPHONIC novel, depicting the Zimbabwean (then Rhodesian) struggle against white minority rule in a manner sometimes reminiscent of NGUGI's early novels about the MAU MAU movement, in that it refuses to glorify the armed struggle and is delicately sensitive to the impact of such warfare on ordinary people's lives. Chinodya has been seen as the finest stylist of his generation of Zimbabwean novelists. He has also published the novel *Farai's Girls* (1984), the short story collection *Can We Talk* (1998), which moves between different decades, demonstrating the waning of the hopes that came with Zimbabwean independence, and several children's books.

Clark, J(ohn) P(epper)   See BEKEDEROMO.

Cliff, Michelle   Born 1946. Born in Jamaica into a fair-skinned family, Cliff was educated in the USA and the UK, where she obtained her doctorate for work on Italian Renaissance art. She now lives in the USA. Her writing transgresses conventional generic categories and challenges simplistic definitions of ETHNICITY through an approach in which loosely autobiographical investigations raise larger questions about 'RACE', culture and identity and her writing to date represents one of the most probing investigations of the tangled relationship between post-colonial HISTORIOGRAPHY and self-created fictions. Her first novel, *Abeng* (1984), is a coming-of-age story about a mixed-race protagonist, struggling to reconcile the various forces that are shaping her subjectivity. The novels *No Telephone to Heaven* (1987) and *Free Enterprise* (1993) both include transsexual characters who challenge GENDER and sexual norms, along with racial binaries. *No Telephone to Heaven* involves a complex response to the stereotypes of Charlotte Brontë's *Jane Eyre*, informed by Cliff's reading of another classic novel by a 'white CREOLE', Jean Rhys's *Wide Sargasso Sea* (1966), and also reworks intertexts from *The TEMPEST*. Cliff has also published the 'prose poetry', *Claiming an Identity They Taught Me to Despise* (1980) and *The Land of Look*

Behind (1985), and the short story collections, *Bodies of Water* (1990) and *The Store of a Million Items* (1998).

Further reading

Cartelli (1999).

Coetzee, J(ohn) M(axwell)   Born 1940. South African novelist and essayist. Born in Cape Town, Coetzee studied there and at the University of Texas in Austin, where he obtained his doctorate. His training encompassed literature, linguistics and computer science. He subsequently worked as an academic at the State University of New York in Buffalo before returning to the University of Cape Town, where he later became Professor of English Language and Literature. Along with Peter Carey, he is one of only two writers who have won the Booker Prize on two occasions and he is South Africa's most prominent writer of postmodernist fiction. His background in linguistics informs all his writing, which from the outset has been particularly concerned with the discursive construction of subjectivity, the problems facing the artist in a divided society and issues of agency relating to the representation of 'alterity' (see 'otherness'). Although postmodernism has sometimes been seen as an apolitical writing position, since it negates the possibility of definitive signification, in Coetzee's hands it becomes a technique that undermines the essentialism engrained in the segregationist pseudo-philosophy of apartheid.

Coetzee's first book, *Dusklands* (1974), is made up of two seemingly discrete novellas, which share a common concern with ways in which subjects such as historiography and ethnography become implicated in the practice of colonial and neo-colonial oppression. The second of these, 'The Narrative of Jacobus Coetzee', is an interior journey, which destabilizes the very basis of fictional authority. Remote locations, in which received social and cultural values are interrogated along with notions of selfhood, also provide the settings for Coetzee's next novels. *In the Heart of the Country* (1977) focuses on the fantasies of a young woman living on an isolated South African farm. *Waiting for the Barbarians* (1980) is a complex allegory set in a remote outpost of Empire, where a presiding Magistrate contends with the rival claims of power and justice in both personal and public spheres. *Life & Times of Michael K* (1981), whose hero's name appears to invoke that of the protagonist of Franz Kafka's *The Trial*, once again takes a retreat into a rural interior, this time undertaken by a gardener in flight from the civil war raging around him, as a trope for an attempt to escape into an extra-social space beyond the confines of a divided society.

Coetzee's more recent fiction has increasingly engaged with metafictive subjects. *Foe* (1986) is a complex counter-discursive response to Robinson Crusoe, in which 'Cruso' (now spelt without the final 'e') dies shortly after leaving 'his' island, Friday is mute and a female narrator, seemingly displaced from another Defoe novel, *Roxana*, is the main narrator of a quest to get her story told by the fugitive author, Foe. Fiction itself is also central to Coetzee's novel, *The Master of Petersburg* (1994), in which the focus is on Dostoevsky's attempt to discover the truth about the death of his stepson, Pavel. The ostensible subject of *Disgrace* (1999) is the shame and denunciation visited on a middle-aged white academic who has an affair with a student, but this subject conceals layers of possible allegory, which can be related to the white situation in post-apartheid South Africa. Coetzee has also published the novel *Age of Iron* (1990), *Giving Offense: Essays on Censorship* (1996) and *Stranger Shores: Literary Essays, 1986–1999* (2001). *White Writing: On the Culture of Letters in South Africa* (1988) is a notable contribution to critical commentary on the superimposition of European cultural forms on Africa, in this case dealing with the less commonly treated area of *white* African world-views. *Boyhood* (1997) and its sequel *Youth* (2002) are both sub-titled 'Scenes from Provincial Life' and, like much of Coetzee's fiction, deal with the autobiographical aspects of writing, moving between the genres of personal memoir and novel.

Further reading

Coetzee (1988); Attwell (1993); Huggan and Watson (eds) (1995); Head (1998).

Collins, Merle   Born 1950. Grenadian writer, who holds degrees from the University of the West Indies, Jamaica and Georgetown University, Washington. She has worked as a research co-ordinator for the Grenada government, has taught in St Lucia and Britain and now teaches at the University of Maryland. Collins's first novel *Angel* (1987), which deals with the lives of three generations of Grenadian women, has the coming-of-age of a young woman at the time of the American invasion of Grenada in 1983 at its heart. It is notable for its employment of various linguistic registers and its rendition of characters' thought-processes in Grenadian Creole. Collins regards her formative years in Grenada as the central influence on her work and has also published the novel, *The Colour of Forgetting* (1995), the short story collection, *Rain Darling* (1990) and two collections of poems, *Because the Dawn Breaks* (1985) and *Rotten Pomerack* (1992). With Rhonda Cobham, she edited *Watchers and Seekers* (1987), an anthology of creative writing by black women in Britain.

Further reading

Official website: www.geocities.com/merlecollins.

Colonial desire   *Colonial Desire: Hybridity in Theory, Culture and Race* is the title of a 1995 study by Robert Young, which like much other post-colonial theory of the last two decades emphasizes the HYBRID nature of colonial discursive formations. Young, however, puts particular emphasis on miscegenation and the determinants informing transgressive 'inter-racial' sexuality. Taking the view that colonial desire is a social construction, he locates it as a form of exchange produced by colonialism. He traces the provenance of the term 'hybridity' back to the nineteenth-century's use of biologica and botanical vocabulary in cultural, particularly 'racial', contexts. Developing ar argument that has some affinities with Homi K. BHABHA's concept of THIRD SPACE, he explores the problems involved in using 'hybridity' as a term that presupposes two pre-existing 'original' species.

Anne McClintock's *Imperial Leather: Race, Gender and Sexuality in the Coloni* *Contest* (1995) takes a similar approach in arguing that the areas identified in its sub title are overlapping categories and examining such relationships as those betweer gender and violence, race and sexuality and fetishism and money.

Further reading

Young (1995); McClintock (1995).

Colonialism, colonial discourse   'Colonialism' refers to IMPERIALIST expansion int overseas territories and the social and cultural formations that issue from such CON TACT, though the term is sometimes used loosely as a synonym for 'imperialism' Colonialism has taken a variety of forms, ranging from direct military intervention t peaceful co-optation of the subject nation's pre-existing population. Widely practise in most eras of human history, it assumed a new dimension in the nineteenth century as the overseas arm of imperialism. During this period Europe characteristically rep resented it as a 'civilizing' project that would bring enlightenment to less develope parts of the world and their supposedly 'backward' peoples. Such a discourse wa based on racist assumptions of European 'superiority' and frequently masked eco nomic opportunism, but it is mistaken to see all colonialism as operating in the sam way. Although most of its manifestations have entailed economic exploitation, other have involved various kinds of liberal, religious or nationalistic projects. Thus, whil nineteenth-century discourses centred on its 'civilizing' mission have been widely dis credited by Marxist and other commentators, the ways in which colonized people were exploited and the political systems through which colonialism operated varie considerably. The cliché that the colonizer arrived with the Bible in one hand and th sword in the other points up the hypocrisies of colonialism, but also foregrounds th AMBIVALENCE of its practices. Although the phase of colonialism that reached its apoge in the late nineteenth century came to a formal end when the majority of the nation that Europe had colonized attained political independence (mainly in the third quar ter of the twentieth century), NEO-COLONIALISM persists in the era of GLOBALIZATION, par ticularly in the form of economic control by multinational corporations.

Like colonialism itself, colonial discourse is often represented as a uniform phe nomenon. However, although its expression *within* the colonizing nation ofter worked towards producing a homogenizing narrative of Empire, in which Wester culture was bringing enlightenment to the supposedly benighted regions of the worl and such activities as sport, hygiene and boys' adventuring could be seen as domesti correlatives of overseas colonization, in the colonies themselves, practices were more divergent. So, while it is possible to identify a range of commonalities in 'colonial discourse', such as the stereotypical construction of 'alterity' ('OTHERNESS'), such practices were expressed in specific ways in particular contexts and it becomes clumsy, e.g., to speak of ORIENTALISM in relation to the European discursive construction of Sub-Saharan Africa; and post-colonial commentary that homogenizes colonial discourse runs the risk of being viewed as a practice suited to fulfilling the needs of the Western academy, as surely as a discourse such as Orientalism served to consolidate a sense of identity – economic, political and psychic – in *its* exponents.

'Colonization in Reverse'   Title of a poem by Louise BENNETT, in which the speaker suggests that the post-World War II migration of Jamaicans to Britain is having the effect of colonizing the 'Mother Country'. Several works by the WINDRUSH GENERATION, e.g. Sam SELVON's novel *The Lonely Londoners* (1956) also represent Caribbean migrants CREOLIZING aspects of British society and the CARNIVALESQUE narrative method of such texts offers a similar challenge to metropolitan conceptions of literary and cultural authority more generally. Such formal instances of reverse colonization can be seen as a metonym for the destabilization of binary models of cultural authority which is central to most versions of the post-colonial project.

The Commonwealth   An association of over 50 countries, most of which were formerly part of the British Empire. However, a few of its current members such as Namibia and Mozambique were never British colonies. The Commonwealth evolved from the 'British Commonwealth', a term that was introduced after World War I to refer to the relationship between Britain and its dominions, such as Canada and Australia. After World War II, when membership was expanded to include other newly independent countries such as India and Sri Lanka (then Ceylon), it became known as the Commonwealth. English is the official language of many of the governments of the Commonwealth and the language for pan-Commonwealth communication. The 'official' Commonwealth includes a number of organizations, most notably the Commonwealth Secretariat, founded in 1965, and the Commonwealth Foundation, which have their headquarters in London.

The member states of the Commonwealth are: Antigua and Barbuda, Australia, the Bahamas, Bangladesh, Barbados, Belize, Botswana, Brunei Darussalam, Cameroon, Canada, Cyprus, Dominica, the Fiji Islands, the Gambia, Ghana, Grenada, Guyana, India, Jamaica, Kenya, Kiribati, Lesotho, Malawi, Malaysia, Malta, Mauritius, the Maldives, Mozambique, Namibia, Nauru, New Zealand, Nigeria, Pakistan, Papua New Guinea, St Kitts and Nevis, St Lucia, St Vincent and the Grenadines, Samoa, Seychelles, Sierra Leone, Singapore, the Solomon Islands, South Africa, Sri Lanka, Swaziland, Tanzania, Tonga, Trinidad and Tobago, Tuvalu, Uganda, the United Kingdom, Vanuatu, Zambia and Zimbabwe.

Commonwealth Essays and Studies   French Journal of Commonwealth and post-colonial literature. It was founded as the organ of the Société d'Etude des Pays du Commonwealth, which at that time also published *Echos du Commonwealth*, in 1975. Since 1982 it has been edited by Jean-Pierre Durix of the University of Dijon. Published twice a year, *Commonwealth* publishes symposia on particular post-colonial literary topics.

Commonwealth literature   'Commonwealth literature' came to the fore as an academic discipline in the UK in the 1960s, particularly at the University of Leeds, where the JOURNAL OF COMMONWEALTH LITERATURE and ACLALS were founded. In the 1980s and 1990s, the terms NEW LITERATURES IN ENGLISH and 'Post-colonial literature(s)' were often preferred. Problems involved in the use of the term include: its conflation of literatures and cultures that have experienced very different forms of colonialism, most obviously its bringing the literatures of SETTLER and 'DEVELOPING' societies together under a single heading; and its vagaries as a political category, with countries such as South Africa, Pakistan and Fiji having at various periods in their recent history been inside and outside the Commonwealth. 'Commonwealth literature' has, however, continued to be a popular term in some parts of the world, e.g. in India, where it is often seen as a more inclusive term than 'post-colonial'. In contrast, 'post-colonial' has been criticized on the grounds that it defines everything in relation to colonialism, consequently undervaluing the longevity of Indian literary traditions and failing to recognize the extent of their autonomy, particularly in the periods before and after colonization. Thus the novelist Nayantara SAHGAL asks 'is "colonial" the new Anno Domini from which events are to be everlastingly measured?', pointing out that British colonization was 'simply one more layer added to the layer upon layer of Indian consciousness' (Rutherford (ed.) 1992: 30). *A Shaping of Connections: Commonwealth Literature Studies – Then and Now* (Maes-Jelinek *et al.* 1989) is a collection of essays tracing the history and development of the field and the emergence of alternative post-colonial methodologies.

Further reading

Maes-Jelinek *et al.* (eds) (1989); Rutherford (ed.) (1992).

The Commonwealth Writers' Prize   Established in 1987, the Prize is sponsored by the Commonwealth Foundation and is currently administered by the Book Trust in London. Annual prizes are awarded for the best book and the best first book from each of four Commonwealth regions: Africa; the Caribbean and Canada; 'Eurasia'; and Southeast Asia and the South Pacific (which includes Australasia). Regional winners then go forward to the overall final, which is judged by a pan-Commonwealth jury at a venue that rotates around the Commonwealth. Less metropolitan-centred than the BOOKER PRIZE, which also includes Commonwealth, but not American, fiction within its terms of reference, the Commonwealth Writers' Prize has yet to establish as high a profile, though its cosmopolitanism has ensured a greater commitment to the promotion of post-colonial fiction. Winners of the overall prize and best first book award have been:

Best Book: 1987 Olive Senior, *Summer Lightning* (Jamaica); 1988 Festus Iyayi, *Heroes* (Nigeria); 1989 Janet Frame, *The Carpathians* (New Zealand); 1990 Mordecai Richler, *Solomon Gursky Was Here* (Canada); 1991 David Malouf, *The Great World* (Australia); 1992 Rohinton Mistry, *Such a Long Journey* (Canada); 1993 Alex Miller, *The Ancestor Game* (Australia); 1994 Vikram Seth, *A Suitable Boy* (India); 1995 Louis de Bernières, *Captain Corelli's Mandolin* (UK); 1996 Rohinton Mistry, *A Fine Balance* (Canada); 1997 Earl Lovelace, *Salt* (Trinidad); 1998 Peter Carey, *Jack Maggs* (Australia); 1999 Murray Bail, *Eucalyptus* (Australia); 2000 J. M. Coetzee, *Disgrace* (South Africa); 2001 Peter Carey, *True History of the Kelly Gang* (Australia); 2002 Richard Flanagan *Gould's Book of Fish* (Australia).

Best First Book: 1987 Witi Ihimaera, *The Matriarch* (New Zealand); 1988 George Turner, *The Sea and Summer* (Australia); 1989 Bonnie Burnard, *Women of Influence* (Canada); 1990 John Cranna, *Visitors* (New Zealand); 1991 Pauline Melville, *Shape Shifter* (Guyana); 1992 Robert Antoni, *Divina Trace* (the Bahamas); 1993 Githa Hariharan, *The Thousand Faces of Night* (India); 1994 Keith Oatley, *The Case of Emily V* (UK); 1995 Adib Khan, *Seasonal Adjustments* (Pakistan); 1996 Vikram Chandra, *Red Earth and Pouring Rain* (India); 1997 Ann-Marie MacDonald, *Fall on Your Knees* (Canada); 1998 Tim Wynveen, *Angel Falls* (Canada); 1999 Kerri Sakamoto, *The Electrical Field* (Canada); 2000 Jeffrey Moore, *Prisoner in a Red-Rose Chain* (Canada); 2001 Zadie Smith, *White Teeth* (UK); 2002 Manu Herbstein, *Ama: A Story of the Atlantic Slave Trade* (Ghana).

Communalism   In general usage, 'communalism' refers to political systems that are based on collective ownership and/or other forms of co-operative socialism and it is sometimes used as a synonym for 'Communism'. In contemporary post-colonial contexts, it is more often used pejoratively to refer to exclusivist movements that stress a particular community's interests at the expense of those of other groups or those of society at large. It is particularly employed in this way in South Asia to refer to the beliefs and practices of fundamentalist sects that foster *communal* violence against other religious and ethnic groups.

Condé, Maryse   Born 1937. Guadeloupean writer and critic. Condé studied in Paris, where she obtained her doctorate for work on stereotypes of blacks in Caribbean literature and has subsequently lived in France, the Ivory Coast, Guinea, Ghana, the UK and the USA. Since 1995 she has divided her time between Guadeloupe and work as a professor in the USA. She began her writing career as a dramatist, but is best known as a novelist. Condé's historical novel, *Ségou: Les Murailles de terre* (1984; *Segu*, 1987) and its sequel, *Ségou: La Terre en miettes* (1985; *Children of Segu*, 1989), which cover a period from the end of the eighteenth century to around 1860, describe the destruction of the West African kingdom of the title (now part of Mali), as it falls foul of external incursions from both the East and the West, in the form of Islam and the Atlantic slave trade. Her *Moi Tituba, sorcière . . . Noire de Salem* (1986; *I, Tituba, Black Witch of Salem*, 1992), a revisionist HISTORIOGRAPHICAL novel centred on the experience of the Barbados-born slave who was one of the women tried for witchcraft during the Salem trials, has been equally highly acclaimed. It draws on Condé's Caribbean childhood, to offer a compelling account of the tension between Puritan and New World African value-systems. Her other novels include *Hérémakhonon* (1976; trans. 1982) and *Une Saison à Rihata* (1981; *A Season in Rihata*, 1988), which have Guadaloupean women living in Africa as their protagonists and have been read as allegories exploring the Caribbean relationship to Africa; and *La Vie scélérate* (1987; *Tree of Life*, 1994), *Traversée de la mangrove* (1989; *Crossing the Mangrove*, 1995), *La migration des cœurs* (1995) and *Désirada* (1998). *Windward Heights* (1998) relocates aspects of Emily Brontë's *Wuthering Heights* in the Caribbean. Condé's plays include *Dieu nous l'a donnée* (1972; *God Given*) and *Mort d'Oluwémi d'Ajumako* (1973; *Death of a King*) and *Pension Les Ailzés* (1988). Her critical books on FRANCOPHONE Caribbean writing include *La Parole des femmes* (1987) She has also edited a number of anthologies of Caribbean writing and published the short story collection *Pays-mêle* (1985) and the autobiographical *Le Cœur à rire et à pleurer* (1999; *Tales from the Heart: True Stories from My Childhood*, 2001).

Further reading

Pfaff (ed.) (1996); Suk (2001).

Confederation   See FEDERATION.

Congress Party (Indian National Congress)   A political party, founded in 1885, that dominated twentieth-century Indian politics, both during the period of the NATIONALIST struggle for independence and in the post-independence era, when the party was returned to power in successive elections.

Under Mahatma GANDHI's leadership, Congress evolved into a pan-Indian party that led the campaign for self-rule. It achieved considerable electoral success in 1937, but subsequently withdrew from government and many of its leaders were imprisoned during the QUIT INDIA campaign. After the end of World War II, it took the leading role in negotiating independence and its leader Jawaharlal NEHRU became the first Prime Minister of independent India in 1947. After Nehru's death in 1964, Congress split into two factions and his daughter, Indira Gandhi, who had been carefully groomed for succession and was the leader of the more radical wing of the party became Prime Minister in 1966. Controversy surrounded her behaviour during the

1971 elections and she was found guilty of malpractices. She refused to resign and in 1975 declared a state of national 'EMERGENCY'. Congress lost power in 1977, when it was defeated by the Janata Party and Indira Gandhi was replaced as Prime Minister by Morarji Desai, who held office until 1979. Indira Gandhi reconstituted the party as Congress (I) (for Indira) and regained the premiership in 1980. She was assassinated by two of her Sikh bodyguards in 1984, but the Nehru–Gandhi dynasty continued to rule India, when her son Rajiv Gandhi became Prime Minister in 1984. He, too, was assassinated, in 1991. Congress (I) was re-elected under the leadership of P. V. Narasimha Rao, who remained Prime Minister until 1996, when the party was ousted from power at a general election.

Further reading

Ali (1985).

Conrad, post-colonial responses to   Along with *The TEMPEST* and *ROBINSON CRUSOE*, Joseph Conrad's *Heart of Darkness* (1902) has frequently been seen as one three texts central to the canon of English literature, which engage with colonialism in a particularly direct way, and it has been the target of forthright attacks by African commentators such as Chinua ACHEBE. Post-colonial responses to Conrad have not, however, been uniformly hostile: *Heart of Darkness* has also elicited sympathetic reactions, while Conrad's fiction more generally has generated a range of affiliative (see FILIATION) responses from post-colonial writers, who have seen him as a precursor, because of his critical engagement with colonialism and the complexity of his cultural perspectives.

Conrad's early upbringing in a colonial context, as a Pole growing up in the Russian-dominated Ukraine, his career as a merchant sailor who travelled to all the world's continents and gave him first-hand insight into the workings of many forms of colonialism and his ambivalent situation as an émigré in British society all served to distance his narrative persona from those of his English contemporaries. Although he became a naturalized British subject at the age of 29, his representation of societies in Asia, Europe, Africa and the Americas is marked by a sense of the relativism of cultures rare in the English fiction of his period.

On one level, *Heart of Darkness* is a text that overtly criticizes the economic exploitation inherent in the colonial 'idea' and the racism on which it is predicated. Nevertheless, commentators such as Achebe have attacked it as racist because of its dehumanization of Africans as the savage 'alterity' (see 'OTHERNESS') against which 'civilized' European subjectivity can be measured (Achebe 1988: 1–13). Achebe clearly responds to Conrad's view of Africa in his 'village' novels *Things Fall Apart* (1958) and *Arrow of God* (1964), both of which are revisionist fictional histories that attempt to recuperate Africa from Eurocentric construction as the "DARK CONTINENT". Arguably, however, the real heart of darkness in Conrad's novella is located within the European mind, and specifically in the mind, not of Kurtz, the novel's demented bringer of light, but in that of Marlow, its narrator and experiencing consciousness. Marlow's fear of alterity can be related to the various ideologies that had unsettled traditional belief-systems in the late Victorian period, making him a not untypical, albeit more than normally reflective, European man of his age.

Other post-colonial writers, such as V. S. NAIPAUL and NGUGI wa Thiong'o, have taken a very different view of Conrad from Achebe. In a 1974 essay entitled 'Conrad's Darkness', Naipaul talks about how he discovered a kindred-spirit in Conrad, another non-British-born writer whose absorption into the English tradition had done little to dispel his sense of cultural dislocation:

> I found that Conrad . . . had been everywhere before me. Not as a man with a cause, but a man offering, as in *Nostromo*, a vision of the world's half-made societies as places which continually made and unmade themselves, where there was no goal, and where always 'something inherent in the necessities of successful action . . . carried with it the moral degradation of the idea.'
> (Naipaul 1980: 216)

Despite the negative representation of the non-European world as 'half-made', these remarks are perceptive in identifying Conrad's interest in HYBRIDIZATION, specifically the fragmentation and cultural fault-lines generated by colonialism, which could be seen to make him a post-colonial writer *avant la lettre*. Ngugi has taken a similar view of Conrad's representation of morality and in novels such as *A Grain of Wheat* (1967) and *Petals of Blood* (1977), he employs the Conradian techniques of multiple focalizers and time-shifts to suggest the problems of arriving at a definitive version of historical events. In both novels the events in question are recent and relate to the moral and psychological consequences of the MAU MAU freedom struggle against British rule in Kenya. Thus, in *A Grain of Wheat*, a complex study of heroism and betrayal, a character drawn from the inside, with whom many readers sympathize, Mugo, is revealed as the Judas of the action. As such, he is a study in lost honour, comparable with Conrad's Lord Jim.

Heart of Darkness has also provided the departure-point for another major trope in post-colonial fiction, the INTERIOR JOURNEY, a structure particularly employed in novels describing SETTLER encounters with a wilderness environment. Wilson HARRIS's fiction – and particularly his first novel, *Palace of the Peacock* (1960) – provides especially interesting instances of texts that span the settler–indigene divide and elsewhere Harris has described *Heart of Darkness* as a 'frontier novel' which stands on the threshold of transforming 'biases grounded in homogeneous premises' (Harris 1981: 135, 134). Harris's whole *œuvre* has been dedicated to the promotion of communal, cultural and psychic heterogeneity and his *Heart of Darkness* essay takes the view that the African tradition 'tends towards homogeneous imperatives' (ibid.: 135). Francis Ford Coppola's *Apocalypse Now* (1979; re-released longer version, *Apocalypse Now Redux*, 2001) is a cinematic reworking of *Heart of Darkness*, which displaces its action into the NEO-COLONIAL context of the Vietnam War suggesting analogies between its lunacy and that of the European colonial project of the late nineteenth century. See also the BERLIN CONFERENCE, COUNTER-DISCOURSE, the 'SCRAMBLE FOR AFRICA' and Tayeb SALIH.

Further reading

Naipaul (1980); Harris (1981); Achebe (1988); Knowles and Moore (2000); Thieme (2001).

Contact, contact zone   In post-colonial contexts, 'contact' is a term generally used to signify the historical moment when settler and indigenous cultures first met. Thus, in Australia, ABORIGINALS were living a pre-contact existence prior to 1788, when the First Fleet of British settlers landed. Mary Louise Pratt's influential study, *Imperial Eyes: Travel Writing and Transculturation* (1992) defines contact zones as 'social spaces where disparate cultures meet, clash, and grapple with each other' (ibid.: 4), particularly identifying colonial and post-colonial situations that operate in terms of binary asymmetrical relationships (i.e. relationships with dominant and subordinate partners) as such. As a result of her work and the more general movement in cultural studies towards perspectives that emphasize HYBRIDITY, BORDER AESTHETICS, migration and transculturation, contact zones have become one of the key areas of investigation in cultural analysis. Homi K. BHABHA's concept of THIRD SPACE locates the contact zone as the area where meaning is enunciated.

Further reading

Pratt (1992); Bhabha (1994).

Contact language, contact variety   Sociolinguists use the term 'contact variety' to refer to the HYBRID language forms that develop in bicultural and MULTICULTURAL situations. A contact language is a *lingua franca* (see GLOBAL ENGLISH) used in spaces where the speakers have no common language, e.g. bazaar Hindi in Mumbai (Bombay) and historically CREOLE forms of English on Caribbean plantations.

Continuum   In CREOLE and DIALECT language situations, a continuum is a spectrum of variable points along which a language operates. Although the notional opposite ends of Creole and post-Creole continua may be so far removed from one another that speakers whose primary register approximates to one of these notional poles can, in extreme cases, find one another unintelligible, they remain part of the same linguistic system. More commonly, Creole speakers are able to switch registers to suit different contexts, demonstrating a linguistic versatility that approximates towards multilingualism, albeit within a single language continuum. David DeCamp's characterization of the linguistic situation in Jamaica offers an account that typifies how Creole continua operate, while also identifying the linguistic mobility of its users:

> Nearly all speakers of English in Jamaica could be arranged in a sort of linguistic continuum, ranging from the speech of the most backward peasant or labourer all the way to that of the well-educated urban professional. Each speaker represents not a single point but a span on this continuum for he [sic] is usually able to adjust his speech upward or downward for some distance along it. (DeCamp 1961: 82; quoted in Bickerton 1975: 11)

If, as some sociologists suggest, language usage reflects cultural and psychological processes, such adaptability can be seen as a linguistic correlative of dialogic social interaction and thus linguistic continua unsettle monocultural beliefs more generally. Linguistic, social and cultural continua are important to much post-colonial thinking because they challenge the binary separatism engrained in ESSENTIALIST discursive practices such as MANICHEAN ALLEGORY (as popularly understood), ORIENTALISM and the 'DARK CONTINENT', by offering a paradigm that allows for more social mobility and possibilities for cultural interchange.

Further reading

Bickerton (1975).

Convictism   See PENAL COLONY.

Counter-discourse, counter-discursive   A term introduced into discussions of post-colonial writing by Helen Tiffin (1987), who adopted it from Richard Terdiman's *Discourse/Counter-Discourse: The Theory and Practice of Symbolic Resistance in Nineteenth-Century France* (1985), a work which examines the difficulties surrounding putative oppositional discourses, arguing that while dominant discourses may be challenged by counter-discursive practices, counter-discourse cannot ultimately offer 'genuine revolution' (Terdiman 1985: 15–16; quoted in Tiffin 1987: 33), since its engagement with the HEGEMONIC discourse it is attacking involves it in a complicitous relationship with such discourse. Tiffin's adoption of the term for a post-colonial practice suggests an analogy between the efforts of the nineteenth-century French authors discussed by Terdiman to distance themselves from the bourgeoisie and post-colonial writers' need to engage in a similar contestation of the hegemony of a colonially constructed canon of literary texts. She views particular instances of writing back to an English canonical text as metonyms for engaging with 'the whole of the discursive field' within which such a text operated and continues to operate in post-colonial worlds' (ibid.: 23). John Thieme's *Postcolonial Con-Texts* (2001) is a book-length treatment of canonical counter-discourse, which offers case-studies of post-colonial responses to works by CONRAD, the Brontës, Defoe, Dickens and SHAKESPEARE, arguing that such 'contexts' are extremely varied, operating on a CONTINUUM between complicity and oppositionality without ever existing at either extreme. He takes the view that, regardless of whether or not they set out to be combative, such texts characteristically create their own discursive space and in so doing necessitate

a reconsideration of the supposedly hegemonic status of their canonical departure points, opening up fissures in their supposedly solid foundations that undermine [ ] the simplism involved in seeing the relationship between 'source' and con-text in terms of an oppositional model of influence. (Thieme 2001: 2)

Further reading

Terdiman (1985); Slemon (1987); Tiffin (1987); Thieme (2001).

Creative schizophrenia See CULTURAL SCHIZOPHRENIA.

Creole Believed to derive from a Chinese corruption of Spanish 'criollo' ('native'), a Creole is a language generally, but not universally, believed to have evolved from a PIDGIN that has reached a point where it has a fully developed lexis and syntax, so that it becomes the mother tongue of a speech community. Creoles characteristically operate along a CONTINUUM (variously referred to as a Creole continuum and a post-Creole continuum), in which the form closest to 'Standard English' is known as the 'acrolect' and the form furthest from 'Standard' as the 'basilect' and intermediary points on the continuum are referred to as 'mesolect'. In colonial contexts basilect forms have traditionally been the least valued. Most Creoles are based on European languages, but Swahili, the *lingua franca* (see GLOBAL ENGLISH) of parts of East Africa is a notable exception. Loreto Todd provides a listing of pidgin and Creole languages, which indicates where they are most widely used, in an appendix to her *Pidgins and Creoles* (1990). See also DIALECT and NATION LANGUAGE.

In non-linguistic contexts, 'Creole' has a range of other meanings, e.g. it connotes the culture of the Louisiana region of the USA, particularly its cooking and music. In the Caribbean it was used to refer to Caribbean-born people of white ancestry, e.g. as used in Jean RHYS's *Wide Sargasso Sea* (1966).

Further reading

Bickerton (1975); Todd (1990); Balutansky and Sourieau (eds) (1998); Holm (2000).

Créolité A view of Caribbean culture, influenced by the thinking of Édouard GLISSANT and developed by the Martinicans Jean Bernabé, Patrick CHAMOISEAU and Raphaël Confiant, who expounded its aesthetic in *Éloge de la créolité* (1989). Créolité has some similarity to the ANGLOPHONE Caribbean notion of CREOLIZATION and also with more general post-colonial theories of HYBRIDIZATION. It sees Caribbean culture as the distinctive product of the interaction of multiple forms, but in privileging CREOLE as the authentic voice of Caribbean experience has been viewed as promoting a form of

ESSENTIALISM (Suk 2001: 58), a charge which can be refuted by an emphasis on the extent to which Creole forms operate along a linguistic CONTINUUM. Créolité seeks to avoid the pitfalls of asymmetrical power relations, which construct 'alterity' (see 'OTHERNESS') as the inferior partner in a binary relationship, and the erosion of cultural diversity associated with many forms of institutionalized MULTICULTURALISM.

Further reading

Bernabé *et al.* (1989); Suk (2001).

Creolization   The process by which new HYBRID social and linguistic forms are generated through CONTACT between cultures. Creolization is particularly used to refer to the emergence of hybrid forms in the Caribbean and other parts of the Americas, but is also employed to describe the evolution of such forms in Indian Ocean societies such as Mauritius, Oceanian societies such as Fiji and also, less frequently, in parts of Africa and Asia. Some usages suggest that Creolization involves the *adaptation* of pre-existing cultural forms to a new environment and in such cases the suggestion can be that ACCULTURATION simply transforms Old World 'originals' in the New World MELTING POT. This leads to debates over the extent to which particular Creole forms draw on European, African and other elements. However, it is more productive to emphasize the THIRD SPACE dimension of the Creole experience, in which whatever supposedly 'original' elements may be involved, something distinctively new is produced. This said, in the case of New World Creole forms that combined African and European elements, the former were forced underground by colonial policies aimed at eradicating African cultural retentions, so as to lessen the possibility of slave communities' offering resistance to the plantation system. Consequently, a majority of commentators have felt that the need to recuperate buried African survivals has been more imperative than the need to excavate traces of the European folk heritage that have also contributed to and been transformed in the process of Creolization.

(Edward) Kamau BRATHWAITE's *The Development of Creole Society in Jamaica, 1770–1820* (1971), from which his *Folk Culture of the Slaves in Jamaica* (1970; revised 1981) is extracted, is a case study that foregrounds the African aspects of a particular Caribbean culture and Brathwaite's work more generally has attempted to reclaim submerged African traces within the Caribbean. However, his project is conducted within a framework that emphasizes the distinctive *Caribbean* dimension of the folk culture. Erna BRODBER's novels engage in a similar attempt to represent aspects of the folk culture, which may superficially appear to privilege the African heritage, but is once again ultimately more concerned to demonstrate the distinctive Creole nature of the folk heritage, in which African elements have historically been occluded. See also CRÉOLITÉ, MESTIZAJE and MÉTISSAGE.

Further reading

Brathwaite (1971) and (1981); Young (1995); Balutansky and Sourieau (eds) (1998).

Crusoe   See *Robinson Crusoe*.

Cultural geography   A branch of human geography that came to prominence in the last quarter of the twentieth century, cultural geography has interrogated the disciplinary boundaries traditionally drawn between geography and cognate subjects, demonstrated the extent to which supposedly neutral areas of the subject are ideologically encoded and challenged ESSENTIALIST conceptions of LOCATION, by arguing that far from being static, conceptions of 'place' are constituted within time-space CONTINUA.

Cultural geographers such as Edward Soja have argued that space has continued to be the poor relation of time. Soja, who subtitles his influential 1989 study *Postmodern Geographies*, 'the reassertion of *space* in critical social theory' (my italics) takes the view that that 'The nineteenth-century obsession with history did not die in the *fin de siècle*' (Soja 1989: 10); and quotes Michel Foucault's comment that 'space was treated as the dead, the fixed, the immobile. Time on the contrary was richness, fecundity, life, dialectic' (Foucault 1980: 7; quoted in Soja 1989: 10). Doreen Massey argues that 'social relations are never still; they are inherently dynamic' and so it is necessary to 'move beyond a view of place as bounded, as in various ways a site of authenticity, as singular, fixed and unproblematic in its identity' (Massey 1994: 2). In her view, 'the identities of places are always unfixed, contested and multiple' and so 'attempts to institute horizons, to establish boundaries, to secure the identities of places' are no more than 'attempts to get to grips with the unutterable mobility and contingency of space-time' (ibid.: 5). Turning this the other way round, one can argue that attempts to formulate discourses of temporal fixity and linear sequentiality are equally INAUTHENTIC and just as subject to the dynamics of time–space continua. Consequently, an approach that is attentive to the intersection of spatial and temporal discourses is a crucial prerequisite for cultural practices that endeavour to resist the HEGEMONIC binarism of systems such as colonialism. Massey's work also draws attention to the ways in which representations of time and space are engendered, with time usually being 'coded masculine' and space, as 'absence or lack', being seen as 'feminine' (ibid.: 6); and in colonial contexts such engenderings of movement and stasis are often depicted by the trope of active male exploration in passive female territory (see for example the second passage from Michael ONDAATJE's *Running in the Family*, 1982, quoted in the entry on CARTOGRAPHY).

The approach advocated by cultural geographers such as Soja and Massey has particular implications for literary and cultural studies, which have traditionally privileged HISTORIOGRAPHICAL models, since it shifts its axis away from linear historiography – of the kind that informs traditional *histories* of *national* literatures – towards methodologies that grapple with the multiple and fluid discursive constituents of signifying moments and practices and no longer neglect space. Post-colonial theory's emphasis on the discursive construction of location and New Historicism's similar focus on the ways in which the past is constituted have much in common with such approaches by cultural geographers and numerous post-colonial writers and artists have rejected what Derek Walcott refers to as 'The Muse of History' (Walcott 1998: 36–64) in favour of a poetics of migration which transgresses Western temporal and spatial paradigms. Thus in his epic poem, *Omeros* (1990), Walcott presents his Odyssean protagonist as a restive traveller, continually crossing North–SOUTH and East–West binaries. More generally, while writing a poem that appears to employ Homeric intertexts, Walcott insists that he is charting a parallel spatial collocation rather than entering into a derivative temporal relationship. In other words, he is offering a model of literary transmission, which departs from Western culture's usual emphasis on FILIAL lineage, in favour of a practice based on spatial equivalencies, an activity which can be interpreted as a post-colonial equivalent of Soja's project of reasserting space and which could be seen as a metonym for what both post-colonial writing and cultural theory propose more generally. As in Homi K. BHABHA's account of 'How Newness Enters the World' (Bhabha 1994: 212–35) and TRAVEL THEORY such as the work of Mary Louise Pratt, the emphasis is on the CONTACT ZONE in which meaning is constructed rather than replicated from pre-existing discursive systems. See also CARTOGRAPHY, GREENWICH.

Further reading

Foucault (1980); Soja (1989); Massey (1994); Thieme (1997); Walcott (1998).

Cultural schizophrenia Frantz FANON's *Black Skins, White Masks* (1952; trans. 1967) and *The Wretched of the Earth* (1961; trans. 1963) offer an account of colonialism in which the psychology of the 'native' is determined by the MANICHEAN dichotomy of the colonial project and, prior to the emergence of the more recent wave of post-colonial theory that focuses on HYBRIDITY, several creative writers portrayed a similar mentality. Thus Derek WALCOTT's play *Dream on Monkey Mountain* (1967) dramatizes the split between a European and an African consciousness in its protagonist Makak's vision of a White Goddess, who initiates him into an atavistic dream of African chieftainship. This Fanonian view of the double consciousness of the colonial psychology is under-pinned by the epigraphs to the two parts of the play, which are taken from Jean-Paul Sartre's Prologue to *The Wretched of the Earth*. In the second, Walcott quotes a passage from Sartre, in which he emphasizes the inescapability of such a double consciousness, with reference to the dual religious codes that shape colonial subjectivity, seeing these forces as leading to an ever-widening split rather than some form of SYNCRETIC fusion:

> they can't choose; they must have both. Two worlds; that makes two
> bewitchings: they dance all night and at dawn they crowd into the churches to
> hear Mass; each day the split widens. . . . The status of 'native' is a nervous
> condition introduced and maintained by the settler among colonised people
> with their consent. (Fanon 1968a: 20; quoted in Walcott 1970: 277)

However, the conclusion of *Dream on Monkey Mountain* offers a movement beyond such schizophrenia, as Makak awakens from his dream and decides to return to his home on Monkey Mountain, a metonym for a Caribbean natural world that exists outside the twin imperatives of Old World 'origins' and appears to suggest the possibility that a post-colonial consciousness can be achieved through entry into an extra-colonial space. Although the notion that it is possible to evade the legacy of history involves a degree of romanticization (which is typical of Walcott's 'Adamic' poetics), it nevertheless represents an aspirational ideal that moves towards emancipation from both the colonizer's space and a Negritudinist alternative that remains locked into colonial discourse by virtue of its oppositional stance. In an earlier poem, 'Codicil', Walcott represents himself as 'Schizophrenic, wrench'd by two styles' (Walcott 1965: 61), while in his Prologue to the volume of plays in which *Dream on Monkey Mountain* (1970) was collected, 'What the Twilight Says: An Overture', he argues that 'the New World Negro [sic]' can be delivered from 'servitude [by] the forging of a language that went beyond mimicry' and stresses the importance of 'the writer's making creative use of his schizophrenia' (Walcott 1998: 15–16).

Nayantara Sahgal describes the situation of 'educated' Indians in similar terms in her essay 'The Schizophrenic Imagination' (Rutherford (ed.) 1992: 30–6), in which she represents schizophrenia 'as a state of mind and feeling that is firmly rooted in a particular subsoil, but above ground has a more fluid identity that doesn't fit into any single mould'. She argues that, 'A schizophrenic of this description is a migrant who may never have left his people or his [sic] soil' and goes on to refer to her uncle Jawaharlal Nehru's outlook on life as 'a man of two worlds' (ibid.: 30) and her own experience of growing up as instances of such colonial socialization.

Tsitsi Dangarembga's novel *Nervous Conditions* (1988), which provides a more gendered representation of the schizophrenia of the colonial psychology, also takes its title and epigraph from Sartre's Preface to *The Wretched of the Earth*. More generally numerous other post-colonial writers, among them Albert Wendt, V. S. Naipaul and Erna Brodber, have explored the schizophrenic nature of the colonial predicament, variously stressing its debilitating aspects and, as in the case of writers such as Wilson Harris, the creative potential that is latent in such psychic division. Fanon provides a departure-point for some of Homi K. Bhabha's thinking on ambivalence (Bhabha 1994). See also assimilation, hybridity and Kamala Das.

Cumina   See kumina.

Dabydeen, David Born 1956. Guyanese-British poet, novelist and art historian. Born into an Indo-Caribbean family in Guyana, Dabydeen came to Britain, where he later attended the Universities of Cambridge and London, in 1969. He has combined creative writing with an academic career, mainly at the University of Warwick, where he is Director of the Centre for Caribbean Studies. He also serves as a Guyanese ambassador-at-large. Dabydeen's first collection of poetry, *Slave Song* (1984), a volume notable for its use of a combative form of Caribbean CREOLE and a pose of similarly confrontational sexuality won the Commonwealth Poetry Prize. It was followed by *Coolie Odyssey* (1988), which offers a range of viewpoints on the physical and psychic displacements endured by Indo-Guyanese as a consequence of INDENTURESHIP. This experience also provides a central focus for his historical novel, *The Counting House* (1996).

Beginning with *Hogarth's Blacks: Images of Blacks in Eighteenth-Century English Art* (1985), Dabydeen's writing on the pictorial arts has been particularly concerned with the visual representation of Europe's 'OTHERS'. The title-poem of *Turner: New and Selected Poems* (1994), his finest work to date, takes Turner's painting 'The Slave Ship' as its departure-point and he returned to Hogarth for the title of his novel, *A Harlot's Progress* (1999), in which the protagonist, Mungo, London's oldest black inhabitant, is the eighteenth-century 'harlot', who sells his life-story to ABOLITIONISTS in return for their charity. Dabydeen's other novels are *The Intended* (1990) and *Disappearance* (1993), in which a young Caribbean engineer is employed to help save a crumbling English cliff-top village, a metonym for the contemporary condition of England. He has made a notable contribution to the retrieval and dissemination of knowledge about the Indo-Caribbean experience and his work as an editor in this field includes *India in the Caribbean* (1987) and *Across the Dark Waters* (1999) (both with Brinsley Samaroo).

Further reading

Grant (ed.) (1997).

D'Aguiar, Fred Born 1960. Guyanese-British poet and novelist, born in London. Like David DABYDEEN, D'Aguiar spent his early years in Guyana, coming to England, where he later attended the University of Kent, at the age of 12. He now teaches at the University of Miami. Again like Dabydeen, he began his career as a poet, but subsequently turned to writing fiction, particularly historical novels about slavery and the slave trade. In so doing, along with Caryl PHILLIPS, D'Aguiar has helped to bring a subject which had hitherto been largely neglected in Caribbean-British writing to the forefront of 'memory'.

His first collection of poetry, *Mama Dot* (1985), is a sequence centred on the figure of a Guyanese matriarch. It was followed by *Airy Hall* (1989) and *British Subjects* (1993). D'Aguiar's first novel, *The Longest Memory* (1994), tells the tragic story of a slave on a Virginia plantation who violates taboos by falling in love with his owner's daughter. This transgression is accompanied by another, which, the text suggests, represents an even more serious threat to the *status quo*: his lover empowers him by teaching him to read and write. The novel also provides a compelling account of his conflict with his father, who has adopted an Uncle Tom-like persona to combat the suffering and indignity of plantation life. *Feeding the Ghosts* (1997) is based on a particularly infamous episode in the history of the slave trade. After an outbreak of disease on the vessel he commands, a MIDDLE PASSAGE captain instructs his crew to throw sick slaves overboard. One woman survives this ordeal, tries to rally her fellow-slaves and later disputes the captain's insurance claim to be compensated for the loss of his human cargo in London. D'Aguiar's most extended novel to date, *Bethany, Bettany* (2003) takes an abused girl, trying to make sense of the mysteries in her personal and her country's past, as its protagonist. Her dual name suggests the AMBIVALENCE of her situation, while that of the town she lives in, Boundary, hints at the LIMINAL, borderline predicament of her Caribbean world. However, D'Aguiar's poetic prose resists any easy equation of the personal and the national.

D'Aguiar has also published two book-length narrative poems: *Bill of Rights* (1998), which tells the story of another holocaust, the 1978 Jonestown mass suicide, from a highly personal point of view; and *Bloodlines* (2000), a verse-novel written in *ottava rima*, which again takes inter-racial plantation sex as a central focus for a complex exploration of issues of ancestry and imaginative freedom. His other works include the novel *Dear Future* (1996) and the play *A Jamaican Airman Foresees His Death* (1995). *An English Sampler* (2001) is a selection of the best poetry from his earlier collections.

Dalit, dalit literature   *Dalit* is a term now widely used, in preference to UNTOUCHABLE or Gandhi's coinage, HARIJAN ('Children of God'), to identify those Indians who are not members of the Hindu CASTE system and hence have traditionally been required to work at menial occupations and have been excluded from many areas of Indian life. *Dalit* (variously translated as 'depressed' and 'oppressed') keeps the emphasis on the group's social exclusion, as a necessary part of its attempts to achieve equality, since despite legislation that has improved the situation of *dalits* in institutional contexts such as government and education, they continue to be the victims of widespread discrimination. The origin of the term 'dalit' has been traced to the nineteenth-century Marathi social reformer, M. J. Phule; its influence spread through the work of the twentieth-century leader, B. R. Ambdekar, who with his followers turned to Buddhism as an alternative to the discrimination suffered by *dalits* under the caste system.

Recent decades have seen an upsurge of *dalit* writing, initially in Marathi and more recently in other languages, including Telugu. The literature came to prominence in the 1970s, along with the emergence of the revolutionary Dalit Panther Movement. *Dalit* writing frequently expresses social protest, and many of its leading exponents have taken the view that earlier attempts to represent their predicament by outsiders have been woefully inadequate. It has preferred genres such as personal testimony and poetry to fiction, though some *dalit* novels have been published.

Further reading

Mendelsohn and Vicziany (1998).

Damas, Léon-Gontran (1912–78). French Guyanese poet, who was one of the founding figures of the NEGRITUDE movement. Born into a mixed-race family, Damas's education and upbringing typified the ASSIMILATIVE socialization of the French colonial middle classes in the first part of the twentieth century. After receiving his secondary education in Martinique, where he first met Aimé CÉSAIRE, he studied law in Paris, where he met Léopold SENGHOR and was associated with some of the leading figures in the HARLEM RENAISSANCE. Along with Césaire and Senghor, he founded the magazine, *L'étudiant noir*, which promoted ideas that anticipated Negritude, in 1934. His first collection of poems, *Pigments* (1937), is one of the earliest expressions of Negritude and has been seen as the manifesto of the movement. It drew on jazz and blues forms to repudiate stereotypical constructions of blackness, endeavouring through its direct, witty, confrontational style to liberate conceptions of black selfhood from white representational practices. In a poem such as 'S.O.S.', Damas warns that white attitudes to 'the Negro' are a veiled form of fascism, which could culminate in violence equivalent to the Nazis' treatment of Jews. His subsequent volumes of verse, in which he continues to use New World African musical forms to protest against the assimilation and dehumanization of black people, include *Retour de Guyane* (1938), *Graffiti* (1952), *Black-Label* (1956) and *Névralgies* (1966). After World War II, he represented Guyane in the French assembly and subsequently worked for the French Overseas Radio Service and UNESCO. He was a contributing editor to PRÉSENCE AFRICAINE and in the 1970s became a Professor of African Literature at Howard University.

Further reading

Finn (1988); Warner (ed.) (1988).

Dangarembga, Tsitsi Born 1959. Zimbabwean novelist and film-maker, who studied medicine and psychology prior to writing her novel, *Nervous Conditions* (1988). The novel takes its title from Jean-Paul Sartre's comment (in his Preface to Frantz FANON's *The Wretched of the Earth*, 1963) that 'The condition of native is a nervous condition', but moves beyond Fanon's analysis by placing its main emphasis on gendered aspects of the psychology of colonialism. The protagonist, Tambu(dzai), leaves her rural community to receive a mission school education, thanks to the patronage of her wealthy uncle, Babamukuru, but finds this supposed elevation in her status a mixed blessing. *Nervous Conditions* is notable for its characterization of the authoritarian Babamukuru and its portraits of four women, who respond to their socialization in a patrilineal community in varying ways. Babamukuru's putative benevolence is intermingled with the exercise of tyrannical patriarchal attitudes, presented as a product of both his Western education and his Shona upbringing. Tambu is particularly affected by the fate of her English-educated cousin, Nyasha, who finds herself alienated among her own people and resists her father Babamukuru's attempts to control her, but develops a form of *anorexia nervosa* and eventually dies from this 'nervous condition'. Tambu herself is torn between conflicting strands in her upbringing and ultimately becomes disillusioned with Babamukuru's 'great work of developing the family', when he insist that her parents go through the 'charade' of a church wedding.

Dangarembga has also written a number of plays, including *She No Longer Weeps* (1987). After publishing *Nervous Conditions*, she studied film in Germany and wrote the script for the highly popular Zimbabwean film, *Neria* (1992). With *Everyone's Child* (1996), a story of the struggles of four siblings whose parents die from AIDS, she became the first black Zimbabwean woman to direct a feature film.

Further reading

Nnaemeka (ed.) (1997).

The 'Dark Continent'   A Western construction of Africa, which while it has historical origins that date back to antiquity, became the dominant Western stereotype of the continent in the nineteenth century, during the period of European colonial expansion in Africa. Joseph CONRAD's *Heart of Darkness* (1902) represents such IMAGINATIVE GEOGRAPHY in its title and its use of an 'African' setting, which is fairly clearly based on the Congo, but is never named. The novella is as much concerned with 'Africa' as an absence as a malevolent hellish landscape, though Conrad's use of the trope of darkness embodies both aspects. This relates interestingly to the conflict between Frantz FANON's contention that 'The colonial world is a Manichean world', in which 'the settler paints the native as a sort of quintessence of evil' (Fanon 1968a: 41), a reading of MANICHEANISM followed by Abdul R. JanMohamed, and the orthodox Christian usage of the term.

Early on in *Heart of Darkness*, the narrator Marlow talks of his boyhood 'passion for maps' and his particular fascination with an equatorial region that was 'the biggest, the most blank' space on earth, going on to explain that by the time he was actually able to travel there as an adult, 'It had become a place of darkness' through which 'a mighty big river . . . resembling an immense snake uncoiled' flowed. The use of the trope of the snake, reminiscent of the serpent in Eden, suggests that 'Africa' is a benighted region, needing to be redeemed by European 'light'. However, Conrad's representation of the main agency of such light, Kurtz, as demented, interrogates both the morality and the efficacy of Europe's 'civilizing' mission. Nevertheless commentators such as Chinua Achebe have found the novel as a whole racist in its negative stereotyping of Africa.

V. S. Naipaul's redeployment of the trope of darkness in *An Area of Darkness* (1964), a travel book in which he describes his response to his ancestral homeland of India, displaces the stereotype into an Asian location. The text takes an extremely negative view of India, but Naipaul's 'darkness' refers to the focalizer's perception rather than the physical environment of the sub-continent. It becomes interesting to relate this back to the conception of Africa as the 'Dark Continent', since it suggests the extent to which such a usage reveals more about those who employ it than the locations and peoples to whom it is applied. It involves the kind of imaginative geography that occurs when 'we' define 'our' identity through contradistinction with 'our' own invented version of 'alterity' (see 'otherness') (Said 1985: 54–5). In short, constructing Africa as the 'Dark Continent' serves through a binary opposition to define Europeans, and particularly European colonists, as putative harbingers of light.

Further reading

Naipaul (1964); JanMohamed (1983); Said (1985); Achebe (1988).

Das, Kamala (a.k.a. Madhavikkuty and Surayya) Born 1934. Indian poet, painter and journalist, born in Kerala. Married at the age of 15, Das began writing in such time as she had away from family responsibilities. She came to the fore as a poet at the same time as the Modernist generation of Indian poets writing in English. However, her poetry explores very different themes from those of her male contemporaries and she writes about sexuality with a candour rare in their work and almost completely lacking in that of her female contemporaries. Her poem, 'The Freaks', ostensibly a self-dramatization of her questioning, nonconformist outlook, can be seen as having broader significance for Indian women. Several of her best-known poems, such as 'My Grandmother's House' and 'A Hot Noon in Malabar' look back to her Malabar childhood with a nostalgia that is symptomatic of India's journey from country innocence to city experience. 'An Introduction' is an ostensibly autobiographical poem, in which the persona dramatizes herself as a trilingual speaker who has chosen to write in English, asserting that her language is uniquely her own: 'half English, half/Indian, funny perhaps, but it is honest'. The poem goes on to relate such linguistic nonconformity to her 'schizophrenia' and the difficulty she has in conforming to the gender roles traditionally assigned to Hindu women. Other particularly well-known Das poems include 'The Sunshine Cat' and 'The Looking Glass'.

Her volumes of verse include *Summer in Calcutta* (1965), *The Descendants* (1967), *The Old Playhouse and Other Poems* (1973), *Collected Poems, Volume I* (1984) and *Only the Soul Knows How to Sing* (1996). She has also published an autobiography, *My*

Story (1976) and a number of novels in both Malayalam (under the name 'Madhavikkuty') and English. These include *Alphabet of Lust* (1976) and *Palayam* (1990). In the 1970s she engaged in more direct political activity, campaigning for the formation of a green party in Kerala; in the 1980s she caused fresh controversy by painting nudes. In recent years she has deserted poetry for forms, such as a newspaper column, in which her political views can make a more immediate public impact. Her transgression of Indian expectations took a new turn when, in 2000, she assumed the name 'Surayya' and became a convert to Islam on the grounds that purdah provides women with a sense of security lacking in the world's other religions.

Further reading

Harrex and O'Sullivan (eds) (1986).

Decolonization   The process of moving from a dependent colonial situation to an independent condition. Decolonization is often equated with achieving political independence and commentators such as Frantz FANON have argued that revolutionary violence is necessary to its attainment (Fanon 1968a: 35–106). However, decolonization invariably involves a more gradual and thorough-going process of change, entailing economic, cultural and psychological transformations.

At the time when many Sub-Saharan African countries were moving towards independence, Kwame NKRUMAH identified the economic factors that would maintain the West's influence in Africa as NEO-COLONIALISM and half a century of GLOBAL capitalism, based upon the cheap exports of raw materials from 'DEVELOPING COUNTRIES' and the low wages paid to workers in Asia, Africa and Latin America, has perpetuated and sometimes intensified the gap between North and SOUTH. In cultural contexts, the power of the international media has generally resulted in the privileging of Western, or Westernized, globally distributed artistic products over locally produced work. Contesting such cultural HEGEMONY has been a central part of the post-colonial project, but has proved to be fraught with difficulties. Although movements such as NEGRITUDE, which have endeavoured to return to a pure or AUTHENTIC pre-colonial past, have generally failed to address the extent to which colonial CONTACT and neo-colonial economic and cultural factors have generated particularly HYBRID forms, at the opposite extreme approaches that insist on the interstitial location of all cultures run the risk of contesting Western hegemony in such an abstract manner that resistance is effectively depoliticized.

Further reading

Nkrumah (1965); Fanon (1968a); Appiah (1992); Ashcroft *et al.* (1998).

Desai, Anita   Born 1937. Indian novelist and short story writer of mixed Bengali and German parentage. Desai read English at Delhi University and partly came to writing through the inspiration of Ruth Prawer JHABVALA, whom she knew as a young woman in Delhi and with whom she shares German ancestry. Desai is a fellow of Girton College, Cambridge, and has recently taught creative writing at the Massachusetts Institute of Technology.

Speaking of the limited experience available to Indian women writers, Desai said, earlier in her career, that the only training 'the ordinary woman writer receives is in the minute observation of and intense feeling for a very small, seemingly confined and stultifying section of the world' (Butcher, ed., 1983: 57). In her own early fiction such limitations prove to be a strength, since they enable her to depict the inner lives of her middle-class women characters with considerable psychological complexity. Her early works *Cry the Peacock* (1963), *Voices in the City* (1965) and *Where Shall We Go This Summer?* (1975) frequently represent the quiet desperation of Indian women's lives. *Bye-Bye, Blackbird* (1968) explores the situation of Indian immigrants in Britain.

The characteristic mode of Desai's novels is reticence and delicately observed minutiae are conveyed in a subtle, understated prose style. However, in several instances, including *Cry the Peacock, Fire on the Mountain* (1977) and *Baumgartner's Bombay* (1988), restraint and withdrawal give way to outbursts of violence in the closing pages. *Fire on the Mountain* tells of an elderly protagonist's abortive attempt to withdraw from active life in a former British hill-town. Gradually it becomes clear that her apparent detachment is a façade, an attempt to insulate herself from the truth of her own personal past and changes in post-independence Indian society. *Clear Light of Day* (1980) is centred on two sisters, whose different approaches to life provide contrasting perspectives on the possibilities open to women of Desai's generation. The novel is also notable for its observations on the personal consequences of PARTITION. *The Village by the Sea: An Indian Family Story* (1982), a children's novel with an adult theme, attacks the industrialization of India, viewing the proposed destruction of a traditional fishing village by a fertilizer complex through the eyes of two children.

In her fiction of the last two decades, Desai has broadened her social and emotional range to embrace a more varied repertory of situations and characters, including male protagonists and Westerners. It has also been particularly concerned with cross-cultural relationships. The central encounter in *In Custody* (1984) is between a timid college lecturer in Hindi and a volatile Urdu poet, a conflict that enables Desai to contrast the cultural codes attached to two related, but contrasting Indian languages. *Baumgartner's Bombay*, a novel in which Desai moves into new territory by providing a vivid representation of the street life of Bombay, draws on her German heritage. Employing a complex temporal framework, it deals with a different kind of cross-cultural meeting: an elderly German Jew, who has survived the Holocaust many years before and is living out his last years in genteel poverty in Bombay, befriends a young German hippie who eventually murders him. *Journey to Ithaca* (1995) also observes India through foreigners' eyes, this time dealing with various phases of the Western journey to the sub-continent in search of spiritual fulfilment. Like *Clear Light of Day*,

Fasting, Feasting (1999) is built around a contrast between two sisters, one of whom stays on in her close-knit, but sometimes stifling family home in India, while the other lives in the superficially more liberal society of 'feasting' America. Written in Desai's characteristically understated prose, the novel nevertheless points up numerous ironies that reverse the apparent contrast between Indian warmth and repressiveness and Western coolness and tolerance. *Games at Twilight* (1978) and *Diamond Dust* (2001) are collections of Desai's short stories. She wrote the screenplay for MERCHANT IVORY's 1994 film adaptation of *In Custody*. Her daughter, Kiran Desai, made her mark as a novelist with *Hullaballoo in the Guava Orchard* (1998).

Further reading

Lal (1995); Kirpal (ed.) (1996).

Desani, G. V. (1909–2000). Indian novelist, born of Sindhi parents in Kenya. Indian writing in English's most famous one-book novelist, Desani is almost exclusively known for his brilliantly eccentric comic novel, *All About H. Hatterr* (1948). The novel's style anticipates that of later writers such as Salman RUSHDIE and Arundhati ROY in refashioning and subverting the English language through the use of Indian-English neologisms. At the time of *Hatterr*'s publication, its linguistic innovation was compared with that of James Joyce. Subsequently it has come to be seen as a forerunner of Rushdie's *Midnight's Children* (1981). It describes its eponymous Anglo-Indian protagonist's picaresque odyssey to secure wisdom from the seven sages of India. Despite numerous setbacks he remains an irrepressibly ingenuous and optimistic truth-seeker, whose trials and tribulations never dampen his enthusiasm or his odd-ball loquacity. Desani also published *Hali and Collected Stories* (1991).

Deshpande, Shashi Born 1938. Indian novelist and short story writer. The daughter of a renowned Kannada writer and SANSKRIT scholar, Deshpande was born in Karnataka and educated at a Protestant mission school. She studied Economics in Mumbai (Bombay) and Law in Bangalore and later obtained an MA in English Literature. At the end of her novel *That Long Silence* (1988), the protagonist, Jaya, who sees herself as a failed writer, reflects on the fact that, while studying Sanskrit drama, she has learned that 'its rigid rules did not allow women to speak Sanskrit'. Instead they were required to speak the less prestigious language of Prakit. Immediately prior to this, she has reflected on the significance of the final words of Krishna's sermon to Arjuna in the BHAGAVAD GITA, '*Yathecchasi tatha kuru*' ('Do as you desire') and come to the conclusion that they represent the god's conferral of 'humanness' on Arjuna. The novel ends with an affirmation of both Jaya's writing and *her* humanness, as she achieves a state of mind that enables her to transcend the fragmentation that she has hitherto felt has characterized her life. More generally, it suggests an escape from the 'long silence' to which Indian women such as herself have been consigned as a consequence of patriarchal domination and Deshpande's work as a whole is committed to the articulation of feminist concerns, though usually within frameworks that allow for accommodations with traditional family life and marriage.

Her writing career began comparatively late with the publication of the first of her short story collections, *The Legacy*, in 1978. Her first novel, *The Dark Holds No Terrors*, followed in 1980. In *Roots and Shadows* (1983) the protagonist strives to find a *modus vivendi* that will enable her to reconcile the conflicting claims of marriage, career, family and tradition. *That Long Silence* was followed by another silence-breaking novel, *The Binding Vine* (1993), in which the narrator, traumatized by the loss of her young daughter, becomes involved with two cases of rape, a subject that was taboo for a woman writer in Deshpande's youth. She discovers her long-deceased mother-in-law's secretly written poetry and learns from this that she was a victim of marital rape; and in the present of the novel, she encounters a hospitalized young woman, who turns out to be the victim of a violent rape, which *her* mother refuses to acknowledge has taken place. Deshpande's other fiction includes the novels *If I Die Today* (1982), *Come Up and Be Dead* (1982), *A Matter of Time* (1996) and *Small Remedies* (2000) and the short story collections, *The Miracle* (1986), *It Was the Nightingale* (1986) and *The Intrusion* (1994). She is also an acclaimed author of children's books.

De Souza, Eunice   Born 1940. Indian poet from a Goan Catholic background. A teacher of English at St Xavier's College, Mumbai (Bombay), her delicately conceived miniaturist poems often contain layers of rapier-sharp wit. Her first collection *Fix* (1979) immediately established her reputation as a poet who could combine understatement with acerbic expressions of emotion and attacks on social bigotry and narrow-mindedness. In her autobiographical poem 'De Souza Prabhu', the persona reflects on the mixed strands in her 'Catholic Brahmin' ancestry, saying that 'No matter that/ my name is Greek/ my surname Portuguese/ my language alien.// There are ways/ of belonging'. She goes on to comment that she has heard that, when she was born, her parents wanted a boy, but has done her best to meet their expectations, while using 'Words [as] the weapon to crucify'. Other poems in *Fix* attack the hypocrisy of Goan Catholic society. In *Women in Dutch Painting* (1988), De Souza moves between different locations and her irony is more restrained, but she returns to the situations of women who, as in the title-poem, remain silent, but 'are calm, not stupid' and ultimately offer a quietly subversive challenge to conventional perceptions of gender and social expectations more generally. *Ways of Belonging* (1990) reprints poems from *Fix* and *Women in Dutch Painting*, along with a section of new poems, entitled 'Bequest'. De Souza has also published a number of children's stories and *Selected and New Poems* (1994).

'Developing countries'   A term widely used, in preference to 'Third World' or 'underdeveloped', particularly in public policy contexts, to describe countries in part of Africa, Asia and Latin America. While it is dangerous to generalize about 'developing countries' and the term itself is unhelpful when it erodes demographic, economic and other differences between such nations, a majority of 'developing countries' are primarily agricultural economies or producers of raw materials, for which they receive disproportionately low returns. In recent years, they have increasingly been used as sources of cheap labour, as multinational corporations have relocated manufacturing centres and in some cases service industries, such as call centres, within their borders. See also SOUTH.

Dharma   A complex term, originally from SANSKRIT, used in Hinduism, Buddhism and Jainism. In Hinduism it signifies the eternal order of the cosmos and in human affairs, right behaviour: the religious and moral law governing individual conduct, to be followed according to one's CASTE, status and station in life. In Buddhism it continues to be used to refer to universal truth, especially as conveyed through the Buddha's teachings.

Dialect   A variety or sub-branch of a language, generally as used by a group of speakers in a particular region. Unlike CREOLES and PIDGINS, dialects are not languages in their own right, though the borderline can be porous (as in the case of languages such as Dutch and Flemish, where political factors intervene) and popular usage does not always recognize this distinction.

In early literary contexts dialect was often used for comic effect, as in the stereotypical representation of 'Negroes' in much nineteenth-century American fiction written by white authors. In *History of the Voice* (1984), (Edward) Kamau BRATHWAITE argues that dialect is associated with the plantation experience and connotes inferiority. Such a comment typifies contemporary post-colonial attitudes, but dialect continues to be used as a less politically charged term to refer to the speech of particular regional communities in many parts of the world and was the term generally employed by earlier literary exponents of what Brathwaite prefers to call NATION LANGUAGE, e.g. in Jamaica by Claude McKAY, Una MARSON and Louise BENNETT.

Further reading

Brathwaite (1984).

Diaspora   Literally a scattering, the term 'diaspora' derives from Greek and was originally applied to the dispersal of the Jews during the period of their Babylonian captivity. Historically, it continued to be mainly used to refer to the large numbers of Jews living outside Israel, but in recent times it has been applied to the overseas migrant populations of numerous other communities and peoples, e.g. as in the African or Black diaspora, the Armenian diaspora, the South Asian diaspora and the Irish diaspora. Diasporic relocation is the product of widely differing forces, including the enforced movement of Africans across the MIDDLE PASSAGE during the period of the slave trade, religious and political persecution and the voluntary economic migration of members of various communities in different historical periods.

With the challenge to ESSENTIALIST conceptions of identity and culture in the late twentieth century, diasporic studies have assumed a central importance in cultural debates and in the increasingly transnational world brought about by GLOBALIZATION, the diasporic subject has come to be regarded as a representative protagonist rather than a marginalized exile.

Further reading

Chow (1993); Paranjape (ed.) (2001); Nasta (2002).

Divakaruni, Chitra Banerjee   Born 1956. DIASPORIC Indian poet and novelist, who has lived in the USA, mainly in northern California, since 1976. Divakaruni first made her mark as a poet, mainly writing about the experiences of South Asian women in the USA. *The Mistress of Spices* (1997) is a MAGIC REALIST novel in which the heroine is ship-wrecked on a faraway island, where she is initiated into knowledge of the magical powers of spices. She subsequently uses this skill in California in an endeavour to break down boundaries that divide people; and the novel's style replicates her enter-prise by using a mode that blends poetry and prose and introduces fabulist elements into its contemporary American scenes. In *Sister of My Heart* (1999), a novel that employs a similar framework to Anita DESAI's *Fasting, Feasting*, published in the same year, and Desai's earlier *Clear Light of Day* (1980), Divakaruni contrasts the lives of two sisters, one of whom has remained in the family home in Calcutta, while the other has settled in California. Its sequel, *The Vine of Desire* (2002) finds both women in America, facing challenges to their close relationship and assumptions that have hitherto been central to their lives.

Arranged Marriage (1995) and *The Unknown Errors of Our Lives* (2001) are collec-tions of short stories that mainly focus on the lives of Asian-American migrants. Divakaruni's collections of poetry are *The Reason for Nasturtiums* (1990), *Black Candle* (1991) and *Leaving Yuba City* (1997). *Neela: Victory Song* (2002) is a children's novel about a girl caught up in the QUIT INDIA Movement.

Dreaming, Dreamtime   ABORIGINAL Creation myth, referring to the period when spirits created the natural world and humankind. Unlike Western, and most other, Creation myths, the Dreamtime is considered to be simultaneously present in con-temporary time, as well as an account of human origins, especially since the creating spirits are immanent in sacred sites. As the writer Mudrooroo explains it, the Dreamtime is

> the time of Creation [that] symbolizes that all life to the *Aboriginal* peoples is part of one interconnected system, one vast network of relationships which came into

existence with the stirring of the great eternal archetypes, the spirit ancestors who emerged during the Dreamtime. (Mudrooroo 1994: 52; italics in original)

Particular Aboriginal ceremonies function as rites that maintain the connection with the ancestral spirits and the Dreamtime, enabling Aboriginal peoples to rekindle the spiritual energy of the period of Creation, so that analogous processes of cosmogony and transformation can take place in the present. Jack Davis's play *The Dreamers* (1982) provides an interesting dramatic equivalent of this process in scenes where the primarily naturalistic mode of the play, which depicts the contemporary suburban marginalization of Aboriginals, is replaced by expressionist sequences that re-establish contact with the ancestral culture of the Dreamtime.

Drum South African literary journal, first published in 1951 under the name *African Drum*. During its first decade it was the most widely read and influential Sub-Saharan African journal and, although its main office was in Johannesburg, it also published editions in West, East and Central Africa. *Drum*'s recipe for success combined articles that appealed to a popular readership with serious political commentary and literary work. It particularly contributed to the emergence of the short story as a major genre for black and coloured South African writers, publishing work by Richard Rive, Alex La Guma and others. Es'kia Mphahlele and Lewis Nkosi were among the writers who worked on its staff. Although *Drum*'s heyday was during the 1950s, when its readiness to publish challenging proletarian fiction incurred the wrath of the apartheid regime and it was banned for a period in the 1960s, it continued to be published subsequently, becoming something of an institution, albeit one that lacked the social and political urgency of its early days.

Dub poetry A term used loosely to describe a range of Afro-Caribbean and other oral poetry and more specifically to poetry that 'dubs' words onto a reggae-based rhythm. Dub practitioners include Linton Kwesi Johnson, Mutabaruka, 'Mikey' Smith, Oko Onuora, Jean 'Binta' Breeze, Poets in Unity, Benjamin Zephaniah and Levi Tafari. Dub originated from Jamaican disc jockeys' practice of improvising over an instrumental reggae soundtrack, usually the B-side of a 45 single record. Linton Kwesi Johnson, who acknowledges Jamaican DJs as a major influence on his work, is generally credited with having popularized the form in Britain, particularly through his performances of work that appears in *Dread Beat and Blood* (1975). Over the years, dub, which has been compared with rapping, has evolved into and generated a range of other oral forms and become a popular part of youth culture throughout the Black Atlantic region. The international appeal of such forms has demonstrated the porousness of class and colour categories, but their co-optation by the mainstream music industry has defused much of their political force. In the hands of exponents such as Johnson and Smith, dub is a politically charged form of verse that has affinities with the philosophy of Rastafari, articulating resistance to the forces of 'Babylon' through the use of Jamaican Creole and Jamaican-derived forms of nation language.

Further reading

Habekost (ed.) (1986); Habekost (1993); Dawes (1999).

E

Edgell, Zee Born 1940. Belizean novelist. Edgell worked as a journalist, editor, teacher and lecturer, before becoming Director of the Women's Bureau in the Belize Government. She has lived in Jamaica, England, Afghanistan, Nigeria, Bangladesh, Somalia and the USA. Her novel *Beka Lamb* (1982) was a landmark in various ways: it was the first Anglophone Belizean novel, the first original novel to be published in Heinemann's Caribbean Writers Series and, along with works by Erna Brodber and Jamaica Kincaid, a major contribution to the group of Caribbean novels of girlhood published in the 1980s. Set against the backdrop of social and political change in Belize in the late colonial period, it describes its adolescent protagonist's growth into a more mature consciousness. It was followed by *In Times Like These* (1991), in which the adult heroine's struggle to achieve personal independence is parallelled by Belize's crisis-ridden progress towards political independence. Allegedly based on an actual Belizean incident, in which a woman was tried for the murder of her common-law husband, *The Festival of San Joaquin* (1997) deals with domestic violence and a woman's battle to achieve selfhood in a mestizo community, which continues to exploit its women.

Further reading

Patteson (1998).

Ee Tiang Hong (1933–90). Malaysian-born poet of Straits-Chinese descent. Ee was born in Malacca and studied at the University of Malaya, where he subsequently taught. His work frequently returns to the topic of exile: the linguistic exile of the Malaysian writer in English; the more specific exile of the Malaccan baba community, from which he originated, in contemporary Malaysia; and later the physical exile he embraced, after moving to Western Australia in 1975. From his first collection of poetry, *I of the Many Faces* (1960), onwards, his work is characterized by a strong sense of local identity, a belief in ethnic integration and an unflinching, if sometimes cryptic, response to what he saw as social and political injustice. However, his best verse is less concerned with macro-politics than with the evocation of the social world in which he grew up and poems such as 'Tranquerah Road' and 'Heeren Street, Malacca' express a strong sense of elegy for the older baba culture. Ee's collections of poetry include *Myths for a Wilderness* (1976), *Lines Written in Hawaii* (1973), *Tranquerah* (1985) and *Nearing the Horizon* (1994).

Further reading

Quayum and Wicks (eds) (2001).

Ekwensi, Cyprian Born 1921. Nigerian novelist. One of the pioneers of modern West African fiction in English, Ekwensi began his career as a collector of Ibo folk tales and a writer and broadcaster of romantic short stories. His novelette *When Love Whispers* (1948) was one of the earliest works of African fiction in English. Published in Onitsha in Eastern Nigeria, it contributed to the explosion of writing that became known as ONITSHA MARKET LITERATURE. Ekwensi is best known for *Burning Grass* (1961), a novel about Fulani cattlemen, and a number of novels about Nigerian urban life, which chart the pitfalls that the city holds for the unwary, while at the same time demonstrating a fascination for its teeming multifariousness. These include *People of the City* (1954) and *Jagua Nana* (1961).

El Dorado Literally the 'golden one' (Spanish), El Dorado was the name given by early European explorers in the New World to a legendary golden city believed to exist in the interior of the northern part of South America (variously in Colombia, Venezuela or the Guyanas). Explorers such as Gonzalo Pizzaro and Sir Walter Raleigh, who wrote about it his *Discoverie of the Large, Rich and Bewtiful Empyre of Guiana* (1596), mounted unsuccessful expeditions to try to discover its whereabouts. On one level, the quest for El Dorado can be seen as a metonym for early European economic exploitation of the Americas. However, it also had other resonances in the European imagination: in Voltaire's *Candide* (1759), where the protagonist visits El Dorado, it offers the promise of a civic utopia away from the corruption of political life in the Old World; elsewhere, as in the esoteric side of the alchemical quest, the pursuit of gold was complemented by a belief that the attainment of this goal would also bring spiritual fulfilment. In more recent times, the double-sided nature of the quest has been explored by the Guyanese novelist, Wilson HARRIS, initially in his first novel *Palace of the Peacock* (1960), which uses alchemical symbolism to suggest that materialistic obsessions can be transformed by a spiritual vision that brings psychic integration. V. S. NAIPAUL's *The Loss of El Dorado* (1969) is a more prosaic response to the myth of El Dorado, partly devoted to an account of the failure of Raleigh's expedition.

Further reading

Maes-Jelinek (1971); Silverberg (1996); Whitehead (ed.) (1997).

Emancipation   In post-colonial contexts the term is most generally used to refer to liberation from slavery. Elsewhere it relates to other forms of freedom, e.g. as used in the late nineteenth- and early twentieth-century feminist movement's struggle to secure women's rights.

After the British Imperial Act, abolishing slavery in the British Empire was passed in 1833, the Emancipation Proclamation came into force on 1 August 1834, though the ex-slaves were required to serve a four-year 'apprenticeship' before being granted full freedom. In the USA, where slavery continued after this date, Abraham Lincoln issued an Emancipation Proclamation in 1863 during the period of the American Civil War. It was extended by the passing of the Thirteenth Amendment to the American Constitution in 1865. See also ABOLITION.

Emecheta, Buchi   Born 1944. Pioneer Nigerian-British feminist novelist. Born into an Ibo family in Lagos, Emecheta was engaged at the age of 11 and married at 16. She moved, with her husband, to England in 1962. Left alone with five children to support after the break-up of the marriage in 1966, she turned to writing and her semi-auto-biographical first two novels, *In The Ditch* (1972) and its prequel *Second-Class Citizen* (1974), later published together as *Adah's Story* (1983), deal with the struggles of a single mother in London and the events that have brought her to this situation. With *The Bride Price* (1976), a novel in which the protagonist is forced into an arranged marriage by her uncle, Emecheta returned to her Nigerian roots. It was followed by *The Slave Girl* (1977), another novel depicting the treatment of women as property in traditional Ibo society.

The Joys of Motherhood (1979) is Emecheta's finest novel to date. It demonstrates a complex and ambivalent response to local traditions. Initially, its heroine, Nnu Ego, is another victim of the patriarchal gender codes of Ibo village society, which she has internalized. However, she fares no better when she moves to Lagos, where her belief in the fulfilment to be provided by motherhood – the novel's title, and several similar chapter headings, are largely ironic – leaves her particularly vulnerable in a transitional world, which neither accords women the modicum of respect they formerly enjoyed in patriarchal village society, nor the alternative of a meaningful form of emancipation. In *Destination Biafra* (1982), a woman who has hitherto lived a sheltered life undertakes a perilous journey across country at the time of the NIGERIAN CIVIL WAR. *The Rape of Shavi* (1983) is a futuristic novel about the encounter between the residents of the fictional African country of the title and a group of European survivors from a plane crash. Its initial idealization of tribal life gives way to a more complex treatment of its values and the impact of Western technology. Emecheta's other work includes the novels *Gwendolen* (1989; US title, *The Family*), *Kehinde* (1994) and *The New Tribe* (2000) and the 'popular' novels *Naira Power* (1982), *Double Yoke* (1982) and *A Kind of Marriage* (1986). Emecheta has also published *Head Above Water: An Autobiography* (1986) and written television plays. She has a sociology degree from

London University and has served on various British committees, concerned with race relations and issues of equality.

Further reading

Stratton (1994); Sougou (2002).

The 'Emergency' Period from 1975 to 1977, during which the Indian premier, Indira Gandhi (1917–84), who had been found guilty of malpractices in the 1971 electoral campaign, which had returned her to power, suspended the country's Constitution and assumed emergency powers. Her administration imprisoned thousands of its political opponents, imposed press censorship, introduced a policy of sterilization for men to control the birth rate and took control of the legislature. Gandhi's conviction was quashed by the Supreme Court in November 1975, but she was ousted from power, when she called an early election in 1977. The term 'Emergency' is best used in inverted commas, since Indira Gandhi's critics and many neutral commentators disputed the need for her to assume such powers.

Indian novels in English which deal with the period include: Salman RUSHDIE's *Midnight's Children* (1981), in which the magical promise of the 'midnight hour' of independence is finally destroyed by the second 'midnight' of 'the Emergency'; *Rich Like Us* (1985), a work by Indira Gandhi's cousin, Nayantara SAHGAL, who was herself imprisoned at this time; and Rohinton MISTRY's *A Fine Balance* (1996). Sahgal has also written about 'the Emergency' in *Indira Gandhi: Her Rise to Power* (1982).

Further reading

Sahgal (1982); Ali (1985).

The Empire Writes Back An influential 1989 study of 'the theory and practice of post-colonial literatures' by Bill Ashcroft, Gareth Griffiths and Helen Tiffin. It took its title from a *Times* newspaper article by Salman Rushdie, 'The Empire Writes Back with a Vengeance' (Rushdie 1982b), which itself alluded to the then-current film, *The Empire Strikes Back* (1980), the sequel to *Star Wars*. *The Empire Writes Back* is notable for defining post-colonial as referring to 'all the culture affected by the imperial process from the moment of colonization to the present day' (Ashcroft *et al.* 1989: 2) and for according equal prominence to SETTLER COLONIES. See also ENGLISH, ENGLISH.

Further reading

Rushdie (1982b); Ashcroft *et al.* (1989).

English, english A distinction between two kinds of ANGLOPHONE language usage made by the authors of *The EMPIRE WRITES BACK* (1989), who use upper and lower case forms to distinguish between, 'the language of the erstwhile imperial centre [English]' and 'the linguistic code, english, which has been transformed and subverted into several distinctive varieties throughout the world' (Ashcroft *et al.* 1989: 8). While such a distinction may seem to posit a rather reductive conflation of various post-colonial 'englishes', Ashcroft *et al.* remind their readers that 'englishes' vary in different parts of the globe and that 'a continuum exists between the various linguistic practices which constitute english usage in the modern world' (ibid.: 8). In the years since *The Empire Writes Back* was published, the situation has been further problematized by the increasing spread of GLOBAL ENGLISH, in a range of forms which operate on a CONTINUUM between NEO-COLONIAL linguistic dominance and *its* localized 'distinctive varieties'.

Further reading

Ashcroft *et al.* (1989).

Equiano, Olaudah (a.k.a. Gustavus Vassa) (*c.*1745–97). Author of one of the first African scribal autobiographies. The early parts of Equiano's *Interesting Narrative of the Life of Olaudah Equiano or Gustavus Vassa the African* (1789) tell the story of his kidnap on the Guinea Coast of Africa and his experience of the MIDDLE PASSAGE. Doubts have been cast on their reliability and recent scholarship has suggested that he may have been born in Carolina and that these parts of the autobiography may have been taken from other slaves' accounts of their capture and transportation. The later parts of the *Narrative*, which chronicle his time as a slave in the New World and England and his eventual success in buying his freedom, have been considered more reliable. Written in a plain, circumstantial style and published at a time when the ABOLITIONIST movement was at its height, the book quickly became a classic in the struggle to abolish the Slave Trade, with which Equiano had become involved after being befriended by the abolitionist Granville Sharp. Its final sections move beyond autobiography to advance economic and religious arguments against the continuance of the Trade.

Escoffery, Gloria (1923–2002). Jamaican artist and poet of white Haitian, English and Jewish ancestry, whose work particularly celebrates rural values and the folk heritage. Escoffery attended McGill University in Montreal and later the Slade School of Art in London. She was associated with EDNA MANLEY during the period of Jamaican literary and artistic nationalism in the middle of the twentieth century. Her best work was as a painter. It moved from a pastoral portrayal of Jamaican country life to a more abstract and surreal mode in her later years. Her collections of poetry include *Loggerhead* (1988) and *Mother Jackson Murders the Moon* (1998).

Essentialism In general usage essentialism refers to a range of ideas that privilege the notion that objects, identities and concepts have innate characteristics, i.e. unchanging facets that lie behind their apparently different surface manifestations. The origin of essentialism in Western philosophy can be traced back to Plato, who took the view that behind the surface manifestations of things lay the ideal world of the Forms, and Aristotle, who, in a manner characteristic of his more empirical, taxonomical thinking, insisted that in order to be classified as belonging to a particular category, things must share at least one fundamental common attribute.

Ashcroft *et al.* follow the development of essentialism in European thought by referring to its role in Enlightenment philosophy and its displacement by twentieth-century French poststructuralist theory, such as the work of Michel Foucault, Jacques Lacan and Jacques Derrida (Ashcroft *et al.* 1998: 87). Foucault's approach to the discursive constitution of meaning informs Edward SAID's contestation of the signifying practices of ORIENTALISM and other such stereotyping discourses, while Derrida's thinking on the deferral of meaning has influenced the other two members of the 'HOLY TRINITY' of post-colonial theorists, Gayatri Chakravorty SPIVAK and Homi K. BHABHA, whose work is predicated on the belief that meaning is produced in the act of enunciation.

Outside the realms of linguistically oriented theory, the attack on essentialism has been a crucial part of the process of DECOLONIZATION, since it repudiates racist, sexist and other stereotypes, such as 'the African mind', 'feminine intuition', 'the mysterious Orient', 'the wily Pathan' and 'the inscrutable Chinese', and recognizes differences within nations, regions and communities, as well as the HYBRID, discursively constituted nature of subjectivity. Early post-colonial attempts to contest such stereotypes, such as NEGRITUDE, frequently locked themselves into adversarial modes of representation that created alternative essentialist constructions, but at the opposite extreme poststructuralist versions of identity have been criticized for avoiding the lived experience of SUBALTERN peoples. One of the most complex and searching investigations of this representational problem is Gayatri Chakravorty Spivak's essay, 'Can the Subaltern Speak?'(1988b). Spivak advocates the need to practise STRATEGIC ESSENTIALISM in certain contexts, and in so doing effectively justifies the approach taken by movements such as Negritude as a necessary phase in the process of cultural and psychological decolonization.

Tempting as it has been for post-colonial critics to associate the blinkered, monocultural reductiveness of essentialism with COLONIAL DISCOURSE (itself an essentialist category, constructed by post-colonial theoretical perspectives), non-Western discourses offer numerous examples of equivalent approaches, albeit without the same HEGEMONIC authority. Thus, just as Adela Quested's doomed wish to see the 'real India' in E. M. Forster's *A Passage to India* (1924) ignores both the social and discursive hybridity of the country – to which Forster's text is slightly more sensitive than his character's view – so the attempt in Nirad CHAUDHURI's *A Passage to England* (1960) to discover the England he has known from his Bengal reading, when he first visits the country in the 1950s, involves a similar essentialist blindness to differences and distinctions. Extraordinarily, as he himself readily admits, Chaudhuri finds his fantasy becoming real and he claims:

If an Englishman were to find the world described in *Alice in Wonderland* actually presenting itself to his eyes he would have had a feeling broadly resembling mine. In no case was *the idea of England* I had gained from books contradicted by anything I saw, it was on the contrary completed. (Chaudhuri n.d.: 29; my italics)

Chaudhuri sets out to describe what he calls 'Timeless England' through comparison with 'Timeless India' (ibid.: 11) and when he finds his essentialist conception of England's national identity challenged by what actually confronts his eyes, he dismisses the contradictory evidence so as to retain his notion of what constitutes the underlying 'reality' of England. Chaudhuri was a self-declared Anglophile and so it is possible to see this vision as the expression of a colonial psychology, but essentialist thinking is equally present in various forms of Indian discourse that are less obviously tinged with colonial influences. Thus Hindu fundamentalist claims that the country is *essentially* Hindu promote an exclusive form of AUTHENTICITY that ignores the demographic composition of the modern – and the ancient – nation, the extent to which its various communal strands have interacted and the way discourses of identity are themselves shaped. Similarly, the assertion that Raja RAO's *The Serpent and the Rope* (1960) is the Great Indian Novel, founded wholly or partly on the belief that it embodies a SANSKRIT-based Hindu philosophy, is a critical judgement that makes a comparable appeal to a monocultural and sexist view of national identity. This said, post-colonial writing and theory are usually more alert to the reductiveness of essentialism than their Western counterparts, since, irrespective of the extent to which they demonstrate awareness of the AMBIVALENCE of their situation, their authors invariably have more direct experience of cultural relativism and interchange.

Further reading

Spivak (1988b); Ashcroft *et al.* (1998).

Ethnicity, ethnic minorities   'Ethnicity' is a term that has increasingly been preferred to 'race', because it is predicated on less ESSENTIALIST assumptions about supposedly innate characteristics. Nevertheless it is used in widely divergent ways, sometimes to signify the identities of minority elements in a 'host culture', e.g as in 'ethnic group', 'ethnic minority' and even 'ethnic cuisine', and sometimes in a would-be scientific way, though ethnic classifications are often shaped by their subjects' own AFFILIATIVE identifications, as in such contexts as population censuses. Ethnicity can be determined by a group's or an individual's perception of family ancestry, language, originary nationality, culture, religion, customs, or more usually a combination of several of these characteristics.

A sense of ethnic identity is frequently heightened by migration, e.g. members of the WINDRUSH GENERATION frequently saw their country of 'origin' as the primary determinant of their identity until they settled in the UK, at which point, although inter-island rivalries were transplanted, a more general sense of 'West Indian' or 'Caribbean' identity emerged, partly in response to the perceptions of the majority community. Adopted as a tool for bonding and resisting discrimination in the 'host country', ethnicity can be a positive signifier of difference, but at the opposite end of the CONTINUUM on which it is used, it is a negative marker of identity that is little more than a euphemism for 'race'. In non-migratory situations, ethnicity has frequently been a major cause of civil strife, as in a country such as Sri Lanka; at its worst, it leads to ethnic cleansing, of the kind witnessed in former Yugoslavia and Rwanda.

Ethnocentric   Ethnically centred; and thus demonstrating an insensitivity to OTHER cultures. Although ethnocentrism can emerge from any group's thinking, it has been a particular characteristic of Western colonial and NEO-COLONIAL attitudes, which implicitly or explicitly promote a racist belief in the superiority of Western cultures. Thus, discourses which, for example, construct the East as the ORIENT, Africa as the 'DARK CONTINENT' or Australia as the 'down under' antipodes are all inherently ethnocentric. At an opposite extreme, exclusivist post-colonial perspectives, which insist that only those with 'insider' knowledge and experience of cultures can speak with authority about them, as an understandable response to colonial and other forms of cultural appropriation, tend to negate possibilities for dialogue and interchange between cultures, thus perpetuating binary ethnocentric thinking.

Ethnography   The scientific study of peoples and their cultures. As such, it is a supposedly neutral discipline, but since, like cultural anthropology, traditional ethnography often involves the study of 'primitive' peoples by Western 'experts', it lays itself open to the charge that it is a colonial practice, which involves an appropriation of 'alterity' (see 'OTHERNESS') through the apparently superior ethnographic eye of the observer. Such ethnography tends to promote analyses of the 'strange' and the 'different', as in ORIENTALIST discourse. However, as James Clifford points out in *The Predicament of Culture* (1988), when ethnography works to defamiliarize the familiar, it opens up possibilities for more probing cultural analysis. Contemporary ethnographic work increasingly foregrounds the agency involved in its interpretive practices, thereby eroding the asymmetrical binary power relationship (ethnographic expert / 'primitive' subject) of older more static approaches, in which the authority of the ethnographer is unchallenged and the extent to which dialogic interchange with the observed subject has taken place is obscured.

Further reading

Clifford (1988 and 1997); Pratt (1992); Visweswaran (1994).

Eurocentric, Eurocentricity   A form of ETHNOCENTRICITY which sees Europe as the locus from which cognitive understanding issues and which consequently constructs the remainder of the globe as OTHER. Thus, Eurocentricity characteristically produces binary systems of classification, in which a sense of European identity is formed or solidified though differentiation from a European-conceived version of alterity. See the comments on 'them' and 'us' in the entry on ORIENTALISM. See also The 'DARK CONTINENT'.

Exoticism   Rendering 'alterity' (see 'OTHERNESS') as exotic is an aspect of COLONIAL DISCOURSE which particularly, but not exclusively, operated and continues to operate in ORIENTALIST contexts. Edward SAID's discussion of the scope of Orientalism identifies its emergence as part of the cultural chic of the late eighteenth and early nineteenth centuries. Referring to Raymond Schwab's *La Renaissance orientale* (1950), he says:

> Quite aside from the scientific discoveries of things Oriental made by learned professionals during this period in Europe, there was the virtual epidemic of Orientalia affecting every major poet, essayist, and philosopher of the period. Schwab's notion is that 'Oriental' identifies an amateur or professional enthusiasm for everything Asiatic, which was wonderfully synonymous with the exotic, the mysterious, the profound, the seminal. (Said 1985: 51)

Such exoticization persists in the Western popular imagination's construction of Asia, nurtured by advertising and the commercial commodification of products as diverse as food, travel and Asian medicinal treatments.

More recently, as Graham Huggan's study *The Postcolonial Exotic* (2001) convincingly demonstrates, exoticism has become a prominent part of the industry that has grown up around 'postcolonial' studies. Huggan discusses a range of exoticist discourses which he sees as making up 'the global commodification of cultural difference' (2001: vii) and as marketing and domesticating post-colonial products for Western consumption. Huggan includes analyses of anthropological readings of African literary texts such as Chinua ACHEBE's *Things Fall Apart* (1958), the staging of marginality in writers as different from one another in their political agendas as Salman RUSHDIE, V. S. NAIPAUL and Hanif KUREISHI, critiques of Canadian and Australian multiculturalism and transformations of the 'tourist gaze' in recent Australian and Canadian fiction about Asia. His nuanced discussion indicates the extent to which GLOBAL consumer discourses have appropriated the more radically challenging aspects of the post-colonial project, often reshaping it in a manner which, despite its ostensibly very different orientation, is tantamount to a form of NEO-COLONIAL Orientalism. While parts of Huggan's argument seem pessimistic about the possibility of eluding entrapment in such practices and he concludes that 'The language of resistance is entangled, like it or not, in the language of commerce; the anti-colonial in the neo-colonial', he points in a more positive direction when he suggests that 'the postcolonial exotic is both a form of commodity fetishism *and* a revelation of the process by which "exotic" commodities are produced, exchanged, consumed; it is both a mode of consumption *and* an analysis of consumption' (ibid.: 264; italics in original). This leaves the extent to which the Marxist-derived language of such a passage is itself caught in a complicitous relationship with consumer capitalism open to question, but similar objections can, of course, be raised in relation to any commercially published book that attempts a critique of consumerism.

Further reading

Said (1985); Barfoot and D'haen (eds) (1998); Huggan (2001).

Ezekiel, Nissim   Born 1924. Indian poet. Born into a Jewish family in Bombay, Ezekiel became, along with A. K. RAMANUJAN, one of the two most significant figures of his generation of Indian poets. He won a SAHITYA AKADEMI Award in 1983 and has been influential as an academic at Bombay University and as editor of *Poetry India, Quest* and *The Indian P.E.N.* Between 1948 and 1952, he was a student at Birkbeck College in London, and during this period he was influenced by Modernist notions of poetry. On his return to India, he both espoused Modernist forms in his own verse and was influential in encouraging his contemporaries to follow ideas such as T. S. Eliot's stress on the importance of finding objective correlatives to convey emotions and other experiences. This helped initiate a significant shift away from the hitherto predominantly metaphysical, and often mystical, bent of Indian-English poetry, as espoused by a writer such as Sri Aurobindo Ghose, and also exercised a significant influence on the direction of Indian literary criticism. See also the CALCUTTA WRITERS' WORKSHOP.

Ezekiel's early verse is generally conventional in its style and technique, employing forms such as the iambic quatrain. *The Exact Name* (1965) marked a shift in his poetic manner towards a freer mode, more given to personal, lyric expression. It can be seen at its best in a poem such as 'Poet, Lover, Birdwatcher', in which he likens the patience needed for the craft of poetry to the activities of 'those who study birds / Or women'. His reflective verse frequently explores relationships between the external world and the interior life. In much of his writing he adopts the stance of an ironic outsider, as in his semi-autobiographical poem, 'Background Casually', in which he reflects on the travels and choices of his early life, though the persona of a 'poet-rascal-clown'. This figure suffers from anti-Semitic prejudice at school, migrates to England where he finds himself lonely and impoverished, returns to an 'Indian landscape [that] sears my eyes', but finally makes a commitment to his 'backward place'. Ezekiel is also well known for his 'Very Indian Poems in Indian English', which make witty use of the idioms of Indian English. These poems, which employ a range of Indian-English registers, include 'The Professor', 'Soap' and 'Goodbye Party for Miss Pushpa T. S.' and have received a mixed reception. Although they have been among Ezekiel's most popular work, they have also been attacked for what their detractors have seen as comic stereotyping, i.e. their English has been viewed in a manner not dissimilar to the response to the use of DIALECT in some early American and Caribbean fiction. However, at their best, Ezekiel's Indian-English poems represent particular Indian speech patterns and demonstrate an attentiveness to regional nuances. They offer a wry, but not unsympathetic, satirical view of some of the incongruities and pretensions occasioned by HYBRIDITY.

Ezekiel's other volumes of verse include *A Time to Change* (1952), *Sixty Poems* (1953), *The Unfinished Man* (1960), *Hymns in Darkness* (1976) and *Latter-Day Psalms* (1982). Most of his best work is included in *Collected Poems: 1952–1988* (1989). A volume of his *Selected Prose* appeared in 1992 and he has also published *Three Plays* (1969).

Further reading

King (ed.) (1992a); Mishra, S. (1995).

F

Faiz, Faiz Ahmed   (1911–84). Pakistani poet, one of the masters of modern Urdu verse. Born in Sialkot, Faiz is said to have begun learning the QUR'AN at the age of four. He obtained degrees in English and Arabic in Lahore and subsequently pursued a distinguished career as an educator, soldier, arts administrator and journalist. He edited various publications, including the magazine *Adabe-Latif*, the *Pakistan Times* and the Urdu newspaper, *Imroze*. One of the great twentieth-century exponents of the GHAZAL, Faiz blends its conventional romance themes with a socialist commitment, employing a range of registers that vary from demotic speech to an elevated Persianized diction. His challenge to feudal values and elitism led him into conflict with the Pakistan authorities on several occasions and in 1951 he was sentenced to four years' imprisonment. Two of his most important collections, *Dast-e-Saba* (1952) and *Zindan-Nama* (1956), were written during his prison term. Faiz's Marxist sympathies helped secure a considerable audience for Russian translations of his poetry and he received the Lenin Award for Peace. His other collections include *Naqsh-e-Faryadi* (1943), and *Dast-e-Tah-e-Sang* (1965). Faiz's remarkable public popularity gave him the status of a national icon in Pakistan and his influence on contemporary Urdu poetry has been very considerable.

Further reading

Official website: www.faiz.com

Fanon, Frantz (1925–61). Martinican psychologist and writer, whose critique of colonialism draws on a broad range of disciplines, including philosophy, psychology, social anthropology and literature. He was introduced to the ideology of NEGRITUDE by Aimé CÉSAIRE, who was one of his school-teachers in Martinique. His first book, *Peau noire, masques blancs* (1952; *Black Skin, White Masks*, 1968b), a landmark text in the analysis of colonialism, demonstrates the extent to which racist values are internalized by the colonized and attacks the French ASSIMILATIONIST policies that had created what he saw as the MANICHEAN world of the black bourgeoisie. It departs from the ESSENTIAL-IST aspects of Negritude in favour of a political philosophy posited on the possibility of movement between the fixed positioning of peoples inherent in COLONIAL DISCOURSE and colonial policy more generally.

After studying medicine and specializing in psychology in France, Fanon became the Chief of Staff at a psychiatric hospital in Algeria in 1953. His sympathy with the Algerian independence movement found expression in his books, *L'An V de la révolution Algérienne* (1959; *A Dying Colonialism*, 1965) and *Les damnés de la terre* (1961; *The Wretched of the Earth*, 1963), which argued that violence was necessary in the struggle against colonialism, not simply to effect revolutionary change but also as an act of psychic emancipation for the colonized subject. His impact on post-colonial thinking has been considerable and both theorists such as Homi K. BHABHA and writers such as Derek WALCOTT and Tsitsi DANGAREMBGA demonstrate an indebtedness to his work, though Dangarembga's novel *Nervous Conditions* (1988), which takes its epigraph from Jean-Paul Sartre's Preface to *The Wretched of the Earth*, reflects feminist views that Fanon fails to pay sufficient attention to gender difference. More recently, T. Denean Sharpley-Whiting's *Frantz Fanon: Conflicts and Feminisms* (1997) has taken an opposite position in arguing that Fanon's writing contains the kernel of a liberating praxis for women.

Further reading

Caute (1970); Sharpley-Whiting (1997); Macey (2001); Sartre (2001).

Farah, Nuruddin Born 1945. Nomadic Somali novelist, who has spent most of his adult life in exile: in other parts of Africa, Europe and North America. Farah attended the Punjab University in Chandigarh and subsequently worked in secondary schools and at the National University of Somalia, prior to leaving the country more permanently in 1974. His choice of English as the main medium for his fiction was partly determined by the Somali language's lack of an orthography until 1972, but he has also produced work in Somali. Farah's family included a number of oral poets among its members, but unlike some African writers, he values the written word as highly as the oral tradition, taking the view that its role in the development of civilization and power structures is more extensive in Africa than the West. His literary influences include European Modernists and a range of 'Arabic' texts including the QUR'AN and

The Thousand and One Nights. His own multilingualism – he is fluent in five languages – makes for a POLYPHONIC approach, in which political commitment is tempered by a humanist relativism.

Much of Farah's work is concerned with the creation and perpetuation of dictatorships and he has been a fierce critic of abuses of power in Somalia, particularly in his trilogy, *Variations on the Theme of an African Dictatorship: Sweet and Sour Milk* (1979), *Sardines* (1981) and *Close Sesame* (1983). His work is also notable for its representation of the constraints placed on women and his first novel, *From a Crooked Rib* (1970), which was also the first *Somali* novel, depicts a girl's struggles against the gender conventions of the nomadic Somali community into which she is born. In *Sardines*, an educated woman's battle against repressive religious, familial and political forces comes to a head when she has to fight to prevent the circumcision of her young daughter. Farah's work also deals with the abuse of Islamic lore and the predicament of the educated elite in Somali society. His other novels include *A Naked Needle* (1976), and a second trilogy, *Blood in the Sun: Maps* (1986), a fable which lends itself to reading as NATIONAL ALLEGORY, *Gifts* (1992), which examines the ambiguities surrounding international aid, while also suggesting a number of other variations on its title, and *Secrets* (1998), another fabulist novel, which moves restively between modern political situations and the myth-ridden past. Farah won the 1998 Neustadt International Prize for Literature. He has also written a number of plays and non-fictional prose. *Yesterday, Tomorrow: Voices from the Somali Diaspora* (2000) is a book about the experiences of the refugees created by the totalitarian Somali regime, from which Farah himself took flight. It is also fascinating for the insights it offers into his own itinerant life.

Further reading

Wright (1994); Alden and Tremaine (1999).

Fatwa   An edict generally issued by a *mufti*, or Muslim legal expert, under SHARIA law. The most famous *fatwa* of modern times was Iran's Ayatollah Khomeini's pronouncement of a death sentence on the writer Salman RUSHDIE in 1989 on the grounds that his novel *The Satanic Verses* (1988) contained material which blasphemed against the Prophet Muhammad. The *fatwa* provoked considerable criticism in the West and Rushdie went into hiding for a number of years. Iran rescinded its support for the *fatwa* on Rushdie's life in 1998. See also Naguib MAHFOUZ.

Further reading

Ruthven (1990).

Federation   A system of centralized government, in which regions that have previously been separate states or colonies or currently enjoy a degree of administrative autonomy are united in a national or supra-national political structure. In colonial and post-colonial contexts, federations have operated in varying ways. In Britain's SET-TLER COLONIES, they came about when existing colonies were brought together to form more unified political entities. Thus four Canadian provinces, Quebec (formerly Lower Canada) and Ontario (formerly Upper Canada), New Brunswick and Nova Scotia were united at Confederation in 1867, with eight more provinces and territories being added to the Canadian Confederation between 1870 and 1905 and Nunavut in 1999. The Commonwealth of Australia came into being in 1901, when six existing colonies were united to form a federation; and again other territories were subsequently added. The Central African Federation was a short-lived union that linked self-governing Southern Rhodesia (Zimbabwe) and the British protectorates of Northern Rhodesia (Zambia) and Nyasaland (Malawi). It existed from 1953 to 1963, having been formed when the British government acceded to white settlers' economic representations, but collapsed in the wake of African nationalist protests and the acceptance of Nyasaland's right to secede in 1962.

Examples of supra-national federations include the short-lived United Arab Republic, founded by Gamal Abdel NASSER, and the West Indian Federation. The European Union affords an example of a federation that was initially primarily economic, though debate continues on the extent of further future union. In the USA, the threatened break-up of the Union led to the American Civil War and today government is divided between federal authority and state legislatures.

Federal systems introduced in conjunction with the creation of artificially conceived nation-states during periods of colonial rule have generally had troubled histories, as for example in the case of Nigeria, where the creation of the nation ignored traditional demographic divisions. At an opposite extreme, the PARTITION of countries such as India and Ireland has generated communal and sectarian strife.

No two federal systems are quite the same and regional populations' sympathies for moving towards or away from the central authority they represent demonstrate extreme variations. Thus in North America, referenda on Quebec's separation from the rest of Canada have indicated a strong degree of support for such secession within the province, while in the USA, AFFILIATIVE identification with the Union has predominated in most regions and periods, though not in the South at the time of the Civil War. As a sweeping generalization, national formations predicated on what are perceived as 'natural' geographical boundaries, both demographic and physical, have generally elicited more support than those founded on attempts to unite disparate peoples and places. Thus Hungary's borders, drawn at the end of World War I in such a way that some 'ethnic Hungarians' were excluded from the modern nation (while until recently comparatively few members of minority groups lived inside the country), have generated comparatively little dissent. In contrast, the formation of former Yugoslavia, also as part of the peace settlements at the end of World War I, linked a number of disparate ethnic groups in a federation that eroded local identities and culminated in the series of late twentieth-century conflicts that involved ethnic cleansing and other COMMUNALLY motivated atrocities. This generalization is, however, inadequate if it is predicated on a monocultural model of national identity. The notion of nation is itself a shifting discursive formation (Anderson 1983; Bhabha, ed., 1990) and increased popular acceptance of cultural PLURALISM, along with public policy initiatives that promote MULTICULTURALISM, have challenged such thinking.

The situation in the ANGLOPHONE Caribbean offers an interesting case study of a failed federation. The West Indian Federation was formed in 1958 in the years leading up to the attainment of independence by the British colonies in the region. It had ten members, its capital site was located at Chaguaramas in Trinidad and the Barbadian Grantley ADAMS became its Prime Minister. After a Jamaican referendum in 1961 resulted in a vote in favour of Jamaican secession, it collapsed in 1962 amid acrimony and debate as to whether Jamaican interests coincided with those of the Eastern Caribbean states, who were the other main members of the Federation. In retrospect, the failure of full political federation in the region was predictable, given the geographical distances between its members, differences in systems of government that would become more pronounced in the post-independence era and inter-island rivalries. Nevertheless historical links and shared interests have led to continued cooperation in areas such as trade and at the time of writing, CARICOM (the Caribbean Community) promises to be extended into the CSME (Caribbean Single Market and Economy).

Derek WALCOTT's play, *Drums and Colours* (reprinted in his *Haitian Trilogy*, 2001) was commissioned and performed in 1958 at an arts festival held to mark the inauguration of the Federation. Louise BENNETT's poem 'Dear Departed Federation' is a rueful Jamaican response to its demise, while The Mighty SPARROW's 'Federation', one of the two compositions that won him the title of Calypso Monarch in 1962, is a wry Trinidadian reflection on Jamaica's supposed bad faith in leaving the Federation.

Further reading

Lewis (1968).

Feminism and post-colonialism   See GENDER and post-colonialism.

Filiation, affiliation   Terms used by Edward SAID in *The World, the Text and the Critic* (1984) to distinguish two different kinds of literary relationship with tradition. Said takes the 'family metaphor of filial engenderment' (Said 1984: 117) from the eighteenth-century Italian philosopher Giambattista Vico's account of how social institutions such as marriage and community complicate the 'father's place' of 'unassailable eminence' (ibid.: 118) by competing with genealogy for authority. He contrasts *filiative* relationships, the norm in patrilineal societies, with *affiliative* identifications (ibid.: 174) which challenge such eminence. Said is not, in this instance, writing about imperialism or post-colonial societies, but since the cultivation of a parent–child relationship has been an important trope in the discursive constitution of the colonized subject, the terms are particularly useful in considering post-colonial responses to tradition.

In post-colonial texts filiative relationships, such as one supposedly finds in canonical English literature, are replaced by literary genealogies that reject colonial parent figures, or at least only allow such figures to exist as members of an extended, and usually hybrid, ancestral family. Colonial and post-colonial works as different from one another as Marcus Clarke's classic nineteenth-century Australian novel *His Natural Life* (1870) and Salman Rushdie's *Midnight's Children* (1981) employ the trope of the 'violation of the social family' (Elizabeth Perkins on Clarke in Bennett and Strauss (eds) 1998: 62) as a metonym for the ambivalent genealogies generated by colonialism (Thieme 2001).

More generally, various critics have explored writers' relationships with their precursors through the metaphor of 'filial engenderment'. Thus Harold Bloom's (1973) Freudian account of 'the anxiety of influence' discusses individual Romantic writers' endeavours to liberate themselves as an act of patricide, while Sandra M. Gilbert and Susan Gubar's argument that this Oedipal model privileges paternal genealogies displays a feminist scepticism that has parallels with post-colonial affiliative identifications (1984: 3–92).

Further reading

Said (1984); Ashcroft and Ahluwalia (2001); Thieme (2001).

First Nations, First Peoples Terms widely used in Canada, alongside 'indigenous' and 'Native' peoples, and in preference to 'Indians', to identify the country's Aboriginal inhabitants. The use of the plural form in both cases, and the particular emphasis on *nations* in the former, serve to draw attention to the multiplicity of the various peoples that early settler discourse categorized as unitary, thus assisting in the recognition of differences, while also allowing for shared communal affinities. In the USA the term 'Native Americans' is more generally used.

Focus Group A loose coalition of Jamaican artists and intellectuals formed during the late colonial nationalist phase of Jamaican culture. Centred on the sculptress Edna Manley, it was never a tight grouping, but its members included the novelists, V. S. Reid and Roger Mais and the poet George Campbell. It published a number of volumes entitled *Focus*, edited by Edna Manley, between 1943 and 1960 and the title was revived in 1983.

Fourth World Term sometimes used to describe the world's poorest nations and peoples and also, more specifically, indigenous peoples who have suffered from the internal colonization of their countries, e.g. Australian Aborigines and North

American NATIVE PEOPLES. The term is said to have been coined by the French priest, Father Joseph Wresinski (1917–88), founder of the organization ATD (*Aide à Toute Détresse*; 'Aid to All in Distress'), which has endeavoured to eradicate extreme poverty and social exclusion, wherever they may appear, but without specific dedication to indigenous peoples.

Francophone, Francophonie   Originally, Francophone was a term used to describe speakers of French outside France itself. It was coined in 1880 by the French geographer, Onésime Reclus, who attempted to classify the world's population according to linguistic criteria. More recently, it has come to connote not just those who speak French or French-based CREOLES, but also the community of those who share a common French cultural inheritance. This usage became more widespread after the Senegalese President Léopold SENGHOR employed it in this way in an influential 1969 speech, made at a conference of Francophone states held in Niger that led to the establishment of the ACCT (*Agence de Coopération Culturelle Technique*). The early days of this organization were hampered by the complications surrounding Quebec's participation, as a province of FEDERAL Canada, but progress was made after a summit was held at Versailles in 1986 and the organization was subsequently renamed *Agence gouvernmentale de la Francophonie*. Within metropolitan France, the notion of *la Francophonie*, the community of all French speakers around the world, has been seen as a force for maintaining French cultural values and contesting the HEGEMONY of GLOBAL ENGLISH. Francophone regions outside Europe fall into four main groupings: the North African Maghreb; Saharan, Sub-Saharan and Indian Ocean countries; the Caribbean; and North America. Cf. ANGLOPHONE, LUSOPHONE; HISPANOPHONE.

Further reading

Offord *et al.* (2001); Majumdar (ed.) (2002).

Friday and Crusoe   See ROBINSON CRUSOE, POST-COLONIAL RESPONSES TO.

Fugard, Athol   Born 1932. The leading South African dramatist of his generation, Fugard was born to Afrikaans and English-speaking parents and grew up in Port Elizabeth. After working at various occupations connected with the theatre, including those of stage manager, actor and director, he devoted his main attention to writing drama from the early 1960s onwards.

Fugard is best known for political plays dramatizing APARTHEID's effects on individuals, but such plays only form part of his extensive output. His most obviously 'political' plays include *Sizwe Bansi is Dead* (1972) and *The Island* (1973), two 'Open Space' collaborations with the actors John KANI and Winston Ntshona that were published along with Fugard's *Statements after an Arrest under the Immorality Act* (1972) as *Statements* (1974). Influenced by Brechtian 'poor theatre', the *Statements* plays stage situations that are a direct consequence of Apartheid. Thus *Sizwe Bansi* shows how the system can render a black South African a construct of documents, to a point where his 'real' identity is totally erased. Richly humorous in parts, the play nevertheless offers a searing indictment of Apartheid policies, using theatrical role-playing to examine how they generate analogous forms of acting in everyday life. Earlier Fugard plays with township settings include *No-Good Friday* (1958) and *Nongogo* (1959).

Fugard's other early plays are more personal, though they often incidentally dramatize Apartheid's effects, on white and coloured protagonists, usually through a probing representation of family tensions. His *Three Port Elizabeth Plays* (1974) are tightly knit studies of claustrophobic relationships and demonstrate the influence of Samuel Beckett. All three are basically two-handers, though the intense relationship of the couple in *Boesman and Lena* (1969) pivots around the intrusion of an elderly black man. *The Blood Knot* (1961; revised version, 1985) deals with the love–hate relationship of two brothers. *Hello and Goodbye* (1965) examines the Calvinist aspects of the Afrikaner psychology through a study of a brother and sister. *Boesman and Lena* is about a coloured couple who ostensibly occupy the roles of oppressor and oppressed, but emerge as victims of a shared predicament. The later *'Master Harold' . . . and the Boys* (1982), a play about a boy's relationship with his father and the family's servants, deals with similar 'Port Elizabeth' subject-matter. *Dimetos* (1975), a personal allegory which received less acclaim than most of his plays during the politically charged years of Apartheid, has attracted renewed attention in the post-Apartheid era.

Fugard's other plays include *People Are Living There* (1968), *A Lesson from Aloes* (1981), *The Road to Mecca* (1985), *Playland* (1992) and *The Captain's Tiger* (1997). His screenplays include the script for the film of *Boesman and Lena* (1974) and *Marigolds in August* (1980). Fugard has continued to work as an actor throughout his career and he has taken leading roles in productions of several of his plays. He played the part of General Smuts in Richard Attenborough's film, *Gandhi* (1982). His non-dramatic work includes the novel *Tsotsi* (1980), which, like *No-Good Friday* and *Nongogo*, depicts life in the black township of Sophiatown, where Fugard himself worked in his early years, and his *Notebooks 1960–1977* (1983).

Further reading

Blumberg and Walder (eds) (1999); Walder (2002).

Gandhi, Indira   See CONGRESS PARTY and the 'EMERGENCY'.

Gandhi, Mohandas K(aramchand)   (1869–1948). Indian political philosopher and activist. Mahatma (meaning 'Great Soul') Gandhi, as he was generally known, was the single, most important figure in the Indian NATIONALIST struggle against British colonial rule. Born in Porbandar in Gujarat, he trained as a lawyer in London, where he was called to the Bar in 1891. He subsequently practised as a barrister in Mumbai (Bombay), but in 1893 left his Indian practice and settled in South Africa, where he continued to work as a lawyer and later organized an ambulance corps of Indians during the Boer War. He became a fervent opponent of the Natal and Transvaal governments' discrimination against the Indian population that had settled in the two provinces as INDENTURED labourers and served jail terms for his activism. It was during this period that he first employed the distinctive brand of civil protest, SATYAGRAHA (passive resistance), which became central to his later campaign against the British Raj in India and which provided a model for similar struggles against discrimination and social injustice in various parts of the world, e.g. the Civil Rights Movement in the American South under Martin Luther King's leadership in the 1960s.

Gandhi returned to India in 1915 and established his *ashram* (spiritual retreat) at Ahmedabad. He led the Indian National CONGRESS's struggle for *swaraj* (home rule), campaigning against the import of British goods in order to stimulate Indian village production, particularly advocating the use of *khaddar* (homespun cloth). In 1930, he led his famous SALT MARCH as another protest against British economic exploitation. His influence was at its greatest in the years that followed, when he mounted a number of hunger strikes to try to secure his political goals, but his campaign of civil disobedience led to several periods of imprisonment and in 1942 he was once again arrested after the QUIT INDIA RESOLUTION was seen to be undermining the British war effort. Released in 1944, he continued negotiations and played a central role in securing Indian independence in 1947. While the attainment of independence should have represented the fulfilment of Gandhi's goals, it was marred by the PARTITION of the subcontinent, which he had opposed, and COMMUNAL strife between Hindus and Muslims. He once again went on a hunger strike, in an attempt to avert further bloodshed, and is generally believed to have at least partly succeeded in doing so. He was assassinated by a young Hindu in 1948, shortly after India attained independence. Born into the *vaisya* (merchant) CASTE himself, Gandhi was a fierce opponent of discrimination against the group previously known as 'UNTOUCHABLES', whom he rechristened *HARIJANS* (holy ones).

No account of the details of Gandhi's life can do justice to his iconic significance for the modern Indian imagination. His 'Mahatma' persona was a composite of Western, Hindu and other Indian life-styles and, though deeply spiritual, he shrewdly cultivated the persona of an Indian sage, most notably by discarding Western dress in favour of a simple white *dhoti* (loincloth) and by adapting ancient Hindu religious notions to twentieth-century contexts. Gandhi was a prolific author and his best-known writings include *Hind Swaraj* (1910; revised edn. 1939), his manifesto for Indian home rule, and *The Story of My Experiments with Truth* (1927–9), both originally written in Gujarati.

Richard Attenborough's film *Gandhi* (1982), which won nine Academy Awards, including those for best picture, best director and best actor for Ben Kingsley who played Gandhi, is a biopic covering the main events of his life and times from his South African period onwards, albeit in a sentimentalized and understandably hagiographic manner. Shyam Benegal's *The Making of the Mahatma* (1996) is a less Western-oriented account of Gandhi's South African years by a film-maker more concerned with addressing social 'realities'.

Further reading

Iyengar (1973); Parekh (1987).

Gandhism/Gandhianism and Gandhian literature   The philosophical and social movement to which Gandhi's life and teachings gave rise is generally known as 'Gandhism', but is also often referred to as 'Gandhianism'. It is particularly associated with non-violent civil disobedience, which follows the methods he used to combat British colonial rule in India, communal tolerance and the attempt to bring an end to discrimination against those outside the Hindu CASTE system. Gandhi's approach influenced a number of twentieth-century pacifist movements, including those sections of the American Civil Rights Movement led by Martin Luther King and Nelson Mandela's struggle against APARTHEID. 'Neo-Gandhism' is sometimes used to describe more contemporary developments of his political and social philosophy. See also AHIMSA, HARIJANS, the SALT MARCH and SATYAGRAHA.

Gandhi's personality and influence are treated in a vast body of twentieth-century Indian writing. Each of the 'BIG THREE' of Indian fiction in English published a novel in which he figures significantly: Mulk Raj Anand's novel *Untouchable* (1935) was influenced by a period he spent in Gandhi's *ashram* at Ahmedabad and his shadow also looms large in Raja Rao's *Kanthapura* (1938) and R. K. Narayan's *Waiting for the Mahatma* (1955). K. R. Srinivasa Iyengar's *Indian Writing in English* devotes a chapter to 'Gandhi Literature', which demonstrates that 'the Gandhian influence has been a general preference for the mother tongue or the regional language, and occasionally a purposeful bilingualism' (1973: 278), along with a chapter on the writings of the Mahatma himself. While most of the literature devoted to Gandhi is hagiographic, responses such as Bapsi Sidhwa's *Ice-Candy-Man* (1988) present him in a more ambiguous light. When Gandhi visits Lahore, the child-narrator of Sidhwa's novel is struck by the 'ice lurking beneath [his] hypnotic personality'.

Further reading

Iyengar (1973).

Garvey, Marcus (1887–1940). Jamaican-born pan-Africanist, who gave his name to the movement known as Garveyism. After migrating to the USA in 1916, Garvey was associated with the Harlem Renaissance, though his views did not always accord with those of the leading members of the movement. He had founded UNIA (the United Negro Improvement Association) in Jamaica in 1914 and after settling in New York established an American chapter of the Association. UNIA rapidly caught the imagination of African Americans and people of African descent worldwide and one estimate suggests that at its height its membership numbered four million. As the centrepiece of his 'back to Africa' programme, Garvey established the Black Star Line, which promised to repatriate African Americans to their ancestral homeland and the first successful voyage, to Liberia, was undertaken in 1919. However, the project suffered from mismanagement and Garvey was subsequently convicted of mail fraud and sentenced to prison in 1925. After serving nearly three years in jail, he was deported from America in 1927 and lived most of the remainder of his life in Jamaica and England, where he died. Garvey also promoted awareness of African ancestry among New World people of African descent in his newspapers, *Negro World* (first published in the USA in 1918) and *The Blackman* (first published in Jamaica in 1929). Despite the collapse of the Black Star venture, he has remained an important influence on subsequent generations of African Americans and is widely regarded as a 'black Moses'. His play *The Coronation of an African King* (1930) has been seen as a founding document of the Rastafarian movement.

Gates, Henry Louis, Jr Born 1950. African American literary critic, theorist and editor. Gates's work is notable for its movement away from the primarily social concerns of most earlier African American critics and writers. Influenced by the impact of structuralism and post-structuralism on literary studies in the 1980s, Gates attempted to identify the distinctive rhetorical traditions and practices of 'black' writing, stressing the continuities between African and African American oral discourses and placing particular emphasis on the practice of signifying. He established his reputation in the 1980s, with his books, *Figures in Black: Words, Signs and the 'Racial' Self* (1987) and *The Signifying Monkey: A Theory of Afro-American Literary Criticism* (1988). In addition to his writing, he has played an important role in advancing debates about black literary theory as an educator: at Yale and Cornell Universities and more recently as W. E. B. DuBois Professor of the Humanities at Harvard University; and as an editor, whose collections *Black Literature and Literary Theory* (1984) and *'Race', Writing and Difference* (1986) bring together an extensive set of perspectives. Both in his own work and in the collections he has edited, Gates has demonstrated that 'race' (the inverted commas indicate that it is a linguistic categorization) is a social construction rather than a biological 'reality'.

Gates began his career as a textual editor and more recently has been a leading figure in a number of African American literary projects. He is General Editor (with Nellie M. McKay) of the *Norton Anthology of African American Literature* (1st edn., 1997) and the Schomburg Library of Nineteenth-Century Women Writers; and co-editor (with Kwame Anthony Appiah) of *Africana: The Encyclopedia of the African and African American Experience* (1999; also available on CD-ROM as *Encarta African*). He has also co-edited *Identities* (1995) and *The Dictionary of Global Culture* (1997) with Appiah.

Loose Canons: Notes on the Culture Wars (1992) is a collection of Gates's essays on multicultural topics. *Colored People: A Memoir* (1994) is a less academic work: an autobiographical account of Gates's childhood and coming-of-age in segregated West Virginia in the 1950s and 1960s. *Thirteen Ways of Looking at a Black Man* (1997) is a collection of essay interviews which examines how prominent black figures such as Colin Powell, Jesse Jackson, James Baldwin, Harry Belafonte, Sidney Poitier, Louis Farrakhan and O. J. Simpson were shaped by particular class, 'race' and other factors and how they have responded to the dilemmas of contemporary black identity.

Gates's reputation has continued to grow and *Wonders of the African World* (2000), a six-part television documentary series based on his travels in 12 African countries, which attempted to increase awareness of neglected achievements of African civilization, made him a household name in the USA. Increased fame has brought increased criticism, particularly from African American and African commentators, some of whom have seen Gates as a 'Negro', co-opted by the white establishment, while others have disputed claims made in *Wonders of the African World*. Regardless of the validity of such criticism, Gates's contribution to African American causes remains indisputable. His academic achievements, which also include editing several little-known slave narratives, are complemented by his work as an educational activist and he has played a significant role in promoting African American studies at university level and in broadening literary curricula more generally.

Gender and post-colonialism   Gender issues and tropes inform and interact with post-colonial representational practices in numerous ways. This entry indicates *some* of the main areas that have attracted commentary from post-colonial and feminist critics.

Colonial discourse has characteristically personified colonized space as feminine and colonizing incursions as masculine and many post-colonial engenderings of landscape conform to the same pattern, while moving along a CONTINUUM that operates between complicity and oppositionality. Thus discourses as different from one another as the Australian LEGEND OF THE NINETIES, which was shaped around male bonding, and Margaret Atwood's archetypal account of Canadian-American encounters in SURVIVAL (1972) and Surfacing (1972) represent colonial – or in Atwood's case NEOCOLONIAL – incursions into 'native' space as masculine. The trope of the feminized land is, however, frequently employed in an AMBIVALENT way. Thus one of the most famous of Australian poems, 'Australia' by A. D. Hope (1907–2000) represents the land as 'A woman beyond her change of life, a breast / still tender but without the womb is dry', while, in her poem 'Train Journey', his compatriot Judith White (1915–2000) emphasizes the positive potential of the 'delicate dry breasts, country that built my heart'. The second of the passages from Michael Ondaatje's Running in the Family (Ondaatje 1982: 64) quoted in the entry on CARTOGRAPHY provides an instance of an ambivalent usage of the trope of the feminized land that appears to subvert its characteristic association with passivity, by suggesting the active agency of feminized Sri Lanka in seducing its colonial conquerors. See also Doreen Massey's comments on the engendering of space as feminine, quoted in the entry on CULTURAL GEOGRAPHY (Massey 1994: 6).

Western feminist writers and theorists have frequently seen parallels between their struggles and those of post-colonial women and have particularly identified with women who have suffered a 'double colonization'. Nevertheless simple conflation of the two groups as victims of oppression is reductive and many Asian and African women have disputed the relevance of Western perspectives to their situation, particularly when they ignore material realities. At the same time such responses have sometimes acknowledged one form of commonality: the shared experience of being constructed in this way by UNIVERSALIZING Western feminist practices. Third World Women and the Politics of Feminism (1991), edited by C. T. Mohanty et al., is a collection of essays addressing this issue. A text such as Buchi EMECHETA's The Joys of Motherhood (1979) occupies a midway position in attacking the discrimination suffered by women in both traditional Ibo village society and the Westernized urban world of Lagos, but pointing up significant distinctions between the ways in which patriarchy operates in the two contexts.

Various aspects of Gayatri Chakravorty SPIVAK's writing deal with the intersections and divergences of feminist and post-colonial approaches. Her work on attempts to retrieve SUBALTERN experience has particularly addressed the occluded histories of women, a problem she has foregrounded in such contexts as her translations of the work of MAHASWETA Devi. In her discussion of Jane Eyre in 'Three Women's Texts and a Critique of Imperialism', Spivak demonstrates the divergence of feminist and post-colonial viewpoints in arguing that Charlotte Brontë's novel secures Jane's feminist status through the WORLDING of her colonial double, Bertha, whose dispossession legitimates Jane's promotion in English society (Spivak 1985). Similarly, as Helen Carr points out in her account of Jean RHYS's reclamation of 'Bertha' as 'Antoinette' in Wide Sargasso Sea (1966), Brontë becomes something of an embarrassment for critics such as Sandra M. Gilbert and Susan Gubar whose 'celebration of *Jane Eyre* [in *The Madwoman in the Attic*, 1979] as the paradigmatic feminist text ignores Rhys's critique of its chauvinism' (Carr 1996: 93).

NATIONALIST movements have often been personified as masculine, even though, as in the case of India, women frequently played a central role in their struggles, an issue that has been addressed both in revisionist HISTORIOGRAPHY and fiction about the late colonial period, which has drawn attention to the gendered aspects of the nationalist project and the different inflections of the male and female narratives. The prevalence of readings of post-colonial texts that have emphasized the extent to which they operate as NATIONAL ALLEGORY has elicited a response from feminist critics concerned at the lack of gender specificity in such readings and this has been particularly marked in South Asian theoretical and fictional commentary. The Emory post-colonial studies website includes useful entries on both gender and nation and 'third-world' women. See also COLONIAL DESIRE.

Further reading

Spivak (1985); Minh-ha (1989); Mohanty *et al.* (eds) (1991); Massey (1994); Young (1995); Mohanty and Alexander (eds) (1997); McClintock *et al.* (eds) (1997); Ashcroft *et al.* (1998); www.emory.edu/ENG-LISH/Bahri

Ghazal   One of the major forms of Middle Eastern Islamic poetry. A *ghazal* is a short lyric poem ostensibly about subjects such as romantic love and wine, but often dealing, on a deeper, more symbolic plane, with the mystical love of God. The form originated in Persia around the tenth century AD. Notable *ghazals* have also been written in Urdu, Arabic, Hindi and more recently English. The *ghazal* is made up of a series of couplets each of which has a self-contained sense. The traditional *ghazal* employs a complex metrical and rhyme scheme, which may account in part for its status as one of the most prestigious of Islamic verse forms. Among its finest exponents are the eighteenth-century poet Mir Taqi Mir, the nineteenth-century writer Mirza Asadullah Khan Ghalib and more recently Faiz Ahmed FAIZ. In the twentieth century, notable *ghazals* were written in English, though the purity of *ghazals* composed in English has been disputed by traditionalists. Like much Pakistani poetry, the *ghazal* is part of a popular tradition in poetry and readings often attract very large audiences. North American poets who have used the form include Adrienne Rich and the Canadian Phyllis Webb. The late Agha Shahid ALI was a notable American-based Indian writer of *ghazals* in English.

Ghosh, Amitav   Born 1956. Calcutta-born writer who as a boy lived in East Pakistan (later Bangladesh), Sri Lanka and Iran, as well as India. He attended St Stephen's College in Delhi along with fellow-students who later achieved later achieved prominence as novelists or as figures in the SUBALTERN STUDIES movement. After leaving St

Stephen's with a BA in History in 1976, Ghosh obtained an MA in Sociology from the University of Delhi in 1978 and subsequently went to Oxford, obtaining his doctorate in Social Anthropology in 1981 for a study of kinship structures in an Egyptian village community. His 'history in the guise of a traveller's tale', *In an Antique Land* (1992) draws on his experience of living in an Egyptian *fellaheen* village, while doing field-work for this thesis. Ghosh has travelled widely, meticulously researching his novels and non-fiction and now lives in New York, where he became Distinguished Professor at Queens College of the City University.

Ghosh's first novel, *The Circle of Reason* (1986) is centred on a young weaver, who travels from his home village in Bengal to the Gulf and North Africa. Written in a MAGIC REALIST mode, it introduces one of the major tropes of his work, the interweaving of cultures. The central event in *The Shadow Lines* (1988) is the PARTITION of Bengal and the novel suggests that the CARTOGRAPHICAL demarcations of politicians are invisible shadow-lines that generate all-too-real murderous consequences. Shadow lines are, however, much more than this in the novel: they are also the artificial borders that separate colonized and colonizer, present and past and self and image. Ultimately they are the signifying acts that construct notions of discrete identity. Sometimes described as a novel, *In an Antique Land* breaks down conventional generic divisions, moving between a personal memoir that gives an account of a Ghosh persona's time in Egypt engaging in anthropological fieldwork and an investigation of aspects of the medieval trading culture that extended from the Mediterranean to the Malabar coast of India. A section was originally published in *Subaltern Studies* as 'The Slave of MS. H6'. This aspect of *In an Antique Land* demonstrates Ghosh's engagement with the problemat-ics of retrieving subaltern identity from the scant traces to be found in the HISTORIO-GRAPHICAL record, partly remedying this through novelistic invention. The contemporary Egyptian narrative functions in a similar manner, as a parallel investi-gation of subaltern identity in the present.

The Circle of Reason points out that the draw-loom gave rise to the earliest forms of computer and *The Calcutta Chromosome* (1996) moves between futuristic computer technology and events based on the history of late nineteenth-century malaria research to question the authority and independence of Western science. *Dancing in Cambodia, At Large in Burma* (1998) comprises the two longish travel-essays of its title and a shorter Cambodian essay. Like all Ghosh's earlier work, *The Glass Palace* (2000), his most ambitious novel to date, demonstrates the interconnectedness of cultures that are often regarded as separate, this time moving eastwards rather than westwards from India. It is an epic saga, which begins with the fall of Burma's royal family at the hands of the British, follows them into exile in India and also includes sections set in the Malaysian archipelago. Taking its inspiration from his own family connections with Burma (Myanmar), particularly the experience of his uncle, the timber-merchant Jagat Chandra Dutta, it is in some ways Ghosh's most personal novel to date. He has also published *Countdown* (1999) and *The Imam and The Indian: Prose Pieces* (2002).

Further reading

Khair (ed.) (2003); official website: www.amitavghosh.com

Glissant, Édouard   Born 1928. Martinican novelist, poet and cultural theorist. One of the most influential of FRANCOPHONE Caribbean thinkers, Glissant has served as Director of *Le Courier de l'Unesco* and Professor of French Studies at the City University of New York. His theoretical work has moved Francophone debates about Caribbean cultural identity beyond the ESSENTIALISM of the NEGRITUDE phase. His notion of *antillanité* 'denotes a process of relativity, contact, interdependence, and hybridity that the Antilles exemplify. The Creole language becomes the linguistic paradigm of this cultural phenomenon' (Suk 2001: 57). Like such ANGLOPHONE poets as Derek WALCOTT and (Edward) Kamau BRATHWAITE, Glissant promotes an anti-originary Caribbean aesthetic which operates through CRÉOLITÉ and he emphasizes process, crossings and interchange rather than an attempt to retrieve a 'pure' ancestral identity. The trope of the RHIZOME is central to his thinking on this subject. His work has also stressed the importance of 'redefining the relationship to the land, from one of exile from the ancestral soil into a symbiotic ecological unity, in which people and land existed as interdependent elements' (Majumdar (ed.) 2002: 114). *Poétique de la Relation* (1990; *Poetics of Relation*, 1997) develops a view of identity which replaces the notion of the fixed, unitary self with a view of subjectivity that stresses dialogue and collectivity.

Glissant's novels include *La Lézarde* (1958; *The Ripening* 1959), *Le quatrième siècle* (1964), *Malemort* (1975), *Mahogany* (1987), *Tout-Monde* (1993) and *Sartorius* (1999), sub-titled *Le roman des Batoutos*, in which the Batoutos, an imaginary people, inhabiting Africa in the first millennium BC, provide a focus for an exploration of issues of cultural identity and transmission in a context removed from immediate social and political specifics. Glissant's volumes of poetry include *La Terre inquiète* (1954), *Le sel noir* (1959), *Le sang rivé* (1960) and *Boises* (1977). His *Collected Poems* were published in 1994.

Further reading

Dash (1995); Britton (1999); Suk (2001); Majumdar (ed.) (2002).

Global English   Although English was widely disseminated throughout the world through its usage in British colonial territories, its emergence as the global language is a twentieth-century phenomenon and prior to this it was rivalled in international contexts by French, formerly the language of diplomacy, German, formerly the language of science, Arabic and Spanish. Historically, variously other languages have acted as media for communication between speakers of different languages. These include: the language that has come to be used as a synonym for such languages, *lingua franca* (the Italian term for the language of the 'Franks'), which was a compound of Italian and Occitan, the ancient language of the Mediterranean regions of France; Latin in the Roman Empire; Hausa in parts of West Africa; and Swahili, the trading language of East Africa (McArthur (ed.) 1992: 605–6).

The gradual emergence of English as a world second language, which is now the main medium though which non-native speakers communicate with one another, can be dated from the 1930s, when British attempts to counter the Nazi propaganda machinery led to the establishment, in 1934, of the British Council as a culturally focused organization, which was nevertheless founded as a vehicle for combating more overt German propaganda through the inculcation of British values. The BBC's foreign language programmes, which subsequently became the Corporation's World Service, were envisaged as carrying out a similar function, while the Voice of America, first broadcast in 1942, fulfilled a similar role in relation to spreading American values abroad.

American initiatives to combat Communist influence, which gathered momentum when the USA emerged as a superpower after World War II, contributed to the further spread of English as a global language. These included the establishment of the United States Information Agency (USIA), an organization that took a more direct approach to the task of spreading American values than the British Council had been employing in its promotion of British values. Its NEO-COLONIAL promulgation of the American way of life particularly emphasized individualism, democracy and popular culture. Independently of this, American economic power and popular cultural forms, such as Hollywood, made American English an increasingly imitated language.

The need for a common medium of communication in specialist professions, such as navigation, air traffic control, sport and above all trade and commerce, secured the dominance of English, as GLOBALISM and a massive expansion of transnational communications accelerated the volume and range of international contacts in the years that followed. The telecommunications revolution of the late twentieth century further accelerated the worldwide use of English, as it became the main language of the Internet and call centres in the industrialized world were relocated in areas such as the Indian sub-continent, where labour costs were significantly lower than in the West and the level of English spoken by the educated middle classes, for some of whom it had become a first language, compared favourably with that of their metropolitan counterparts.

Concerted policy initiatives had played a crucial role in the promotion of English as the global language from the 1950s onwards, with the USA and Britain collaborating to ensure its pre-eminence. The British Council and the USIA both expanded their work in the language field, developing and promoting forms of English that enabled non-native speakers to acquire a basic fluency in English, sufficient for their everyday needs, in a short time. BASIC – British, American, Scientific, International and Commercial (McArthur (ed.) 1992: 106) – English and Special English, languages with a vocabulary of around a thousand words and a simplified syntax designed to serve international needs, facilitated the ready exchange of ideas and could be supplemented by the technical vocabulary required in specialist fields.

The pre-eminence of English as the global language can be seen to represent a form of American-led neo-colonial cultural HEGEMONY, though such a view becomes reductive, if it ignores the extent to which much of the bilateral communication in English by non-native speakers occurs without any American (or British) involvement. Today global English is beginning to develop a lexis and grammatical forms that bypass standard American and British usage.

Further reading

McArthur (ed.) (1992); Crystal (1997); Rita Raley homepage: www.english.ucsb.edu/faculty/rraley/research/global-English

Globalization, globalism   Although the term has come to prominence in the past two decades, particularly in the context of the impact of multinational capitalism on national, regional and local communities, which has elicited protests from groups at international summits such as G8 meetings, globalization is a phenomenon that has its origins in earlier periods and *can* be dated back to the time when international trade routes first linked continents and cultures. Such globalization is particularly manifest in the mercantilist activities of colonialism which established the basis of the modern world economy and the post-Enlightenment solidification of nation–states, which expanded the basis for *inter*national commerce. However, globalism in the sense of transcontinental trading activity predates Western imperial expansion. Thus, as Amitav GHOSH points out in *In an Antique Land* (1992), there was a flourishing *medieval* trading network that extended from the Eastern Mediterranean to the Malabar coast of India. In Ghosh's view, the centuries-old 'peaceful traditions' of this Indian Ocean trade, built upon 'the rich confusions that accompany a culture of accommodation and compromise' were destroyed by European violence, with the advent of Portuguese colonization, which took control of the trade 'by aggression, pure and distilled' (Ghosh 1994: 287–8), refusing any attempts at co-operation.

In its more recent manifestations, globalization has been particularly associated with the activities of multinational corporations, whose capital and influence frequently exceed those of the nations in which they operate. This aspect of globalization has led to the critique that it operates through American-led Western NEO-COLONIALISM, in which the world's richer nations continue to exploit labour sources and markets in 'DEVELOPING COUNTRIES' and the distinctiveness of local cultures is eroded by the homogenization brought about by the 'McDonaldization' or 'coca-colonization' of the world.

However, globalization also has its supporters among those sympathetic to the amelioration of conditions in the world's poorer nations, who see its benefits as including: networks that facilitate an ecologically responsible attitude to the management of the earth's resources; the creation of markets that benefit *all* the world's inhabitants, even if only through a 'trickle-down' effect; the work performed by globally based aid organizations; and democratic access to such supranational communication systems as the Internet. Certainly the flow of information that has been central to the rapid acceleration of globalization has made for greater social and economic mobility in certain contexts. However, seen from the negative point of view, globalization has done little to reduce the chasm between the worlds 'haves' and 'have-nots' though it has changed the situations of particular countries and groupings. Cases of countries and groupings that have benefited include the 'tiger economies' of South-East Asia, though these have found themselves particularly subject to the volatility of world markets, and 'high-tech' centres, such as the Indian boom city of Bangalore, where a new class of technocrats has been elevated into membership of the world's information elect, while the situation of the majority of their fellow-countryfolk has seen comparatively little change. At the same time, numerous other organizations and networks see their activities as 'global', e.g. GANDHISM sees itself as a religious, moral and social philosophy that promotes a transnational ethic.

Theories of globalization have considerable importance for post-colonial studies, a discipline which has itself variously been seen as a means of resisting the homogenizing practices of Western consumer capitalism and as a subject which colludes in such homogenization by aggregating the cultural productions of markedly different societies and groups together, thereby effectively operating as a kind of latter-day ORIENTALISM that involves an ESSENTIALIST EXOTICIZATION of non-Western experience (Huggan 2001). Certainly international marketing forces have favoured the production and publication of works that combine exotic elements of local colour with an emphasis on a range of fashionable contemporary discourses, such as HYBRIDITY – and globalization itself. In short, like post-colonialism, globalization and globalism are terms that are used in multiple ways, spanning a CONTINUUM that ranges from neo-colonialism to adversarial contestation of Western hegemonic control.

Further reading

Lechner and Boli (eds) (1999); Mittelman (2000); O'Meara et al. (eds) (2000); Hardt and Negri (2000); Huggan (2001); Ilmberger and Robinson (eds) (2002).

Gooneratne, Yasmine   Born 1935. Sri Lankan novelist, poet and critic, resident in Australia since 1972. Educated at what was then the University of Ceylon and Cambridge, Gooneratne subsequently taught at the University of Peradeniya for a decade, before moving to Australia, where has pursued a distinguished academic career at Macquarie University in Sydney. Her father was a member of the eminent Bandaranaike family and she has written about this side of her background in her memoir *Relative Merits* (1986). Her collections of verse include include *Word, Bird, Motif* (1971), *The Lizard's Cry and Other Poems* (1972), *6,000 ft. Death Dive* (1981) and *Celebrations and Departures: Selected Poems 1951–1991* (1991). Her novel *A*

Change of Skies (1992) is a comic account of migrant life in Australia; *The Pleasures of Conquest* (1995) is its sequel. *Masterpiece* (2002) is a collection of her short stories. Gooneratne's academic publications include *English Literature in Ceylon, 1815–1878: The Development of Anglo-Ceylonese Literature* (1968), adapted from her Cambridge doctorate, *Alexander Pope* (1976), *Diverse Inheritance: A Personal Perspective on Commonwealth Literature* (1980) and *Silence, Exile and Cunning: The Fiction of Ruth Prawer Jhabvala* (1983).

Gordimer, Nadine   Born 1923. South African novelist and short story writer, who won the 1991 NOBEL PRIZE FOR LITERATURE. Born in Springs, a mining town in the Transvaaal to a Lithuanian Jewish father and a mother of English descent, Gordimer attended a convent school as a young girl, but had private tutors between the years of 11 and 16 because of ill health. She subsequently spent a year at the University of Witwatersrand in Johannesburg. She began her writing career as a short story writer, publishing *Face to Face* in 1949 and *The Soft Voice of the Serpent* in 1952, and her work in this genre is notable for its economy of effect and its capacity for evoking complex political issues through nuanced accounts of personal relationships. Later short story collections include *Six Feet of the Country* (1956), *Friday's Footprint* (1960), *Livingstone's Companions* (1971), *Selected Stories* (1975), *A Soldier's Embrace* (1980), *Something Out There* (1984) and *Jump* (1991).

Gordimer's fist novel, *The Lying Days* (1953), describes the coming-of-age of a young white woman, whose growth into an awareness of her own sexuality and the possibilities opened up by friendships that transcend class, race and other barriers signalled the emergence of a new cross-cultural consciousness in South African fiction. It also charted territory Gordimer would return to in several subsequent novels, in which the impact of politics on the heroine's private life is again central. These include *Occasion for Loving* (1963), the novella *The Late Bourgeois World* (1966) and *Burger's Daughter* (1979). *The Conservationist* (1974), joint winner of the BOOKER PRIZE, moved her fictional technique into new territory by using Zulu myth to undermine the society's official discourse, while also exposing the obsessiveness of its male protagonist's colonial vision. *July's People* (1981) involves a role reversal that can be seen as allegorically prophetic of changes to come in South Africa, while remaining equally relevant to the time in which it was published: a white liberal family is rescued from a situation of internal warfare by their servant, who assumes responsibility for them by taking them to safety in his ancestral village.

Gordimer's fiction has been centrally concerned with the effects of APARTHEID on the lives of South Africans of all races and from a varied range of backgrounds. Although superficially realistic in form, it frequently employs interrogative elements that challenged the binarism of the status quo by promoting inter-racial dialogue. Characteristically liberal in outlook, her work of the Apartheid years also explores the Marxist contribution to the liberation struggle. On occasions its implied advocacy of more direct political activism led to her books being banned. Her other novels include *A World of Strangers* (1958), *A Guest of Honour* (1970), *A Sport of Nature* (1987) and *My Son's Story* (1990), which explores the compromised private life of a 'coloured' hero of the political struggle and its repercussions on the lives of his family. Gordimer's post-Apartheid novels include *None to Accompany Me* (1994), which probes the troubled personal life of another publicly celebrated figure – on this occasion a woman lawyer, *The House Gun* (1998) and *The Pickup* (2001).

The Black Interpreters (1973) offers critical 'notes' on South African writing; *The Essential Gesture: Writing, Politics and Places* (1988) is a collection of Gordimer's essays. Dorothy Driver *et al.*'s *Nadine Gordimer* (1993) provides an exhaustive listing of primary and secondary sources on her writing up to 1992.

Further reading

Clingman (1986); Newman (1988); Driver *et al.* (1993); Head (1994).

Greenwich   As the place where the zero meridian was established, Greenwich played a pivotal role in the creation of Eurocentric versions of world geography. In parallel with this, the establishment of Greenwich Mean Time accorded Greenwich a similarly central role in the construction of time-zones. These two factors played an important part in the colonial location of the matrix of culture in London and it is no coincidence that the Greenwich Observatory becomes the target for the anarchists' bomb in Joseph Conrad's novel, *The Secret Agent* (1907).

The Observatory was founded in 1675, as a parallel institution to London's Royal Society, England's main seventeenth-century body for the advancement of empirical scientific inquiry. The specific purpose for which the Observatory was set up was the discovery of a means of computing longitude at sea and, although commentators such as Jonathan Swift regarded this as an impossibility, less than a hundred yeas later, in the 1760s, the Board of Longitude awarded John Harrison a prize of £20,000 for a series of chronometers which made this possible. The Greenwich Meridian was used as a reference point for calculating longitude from this time. By 1884, approximately 70 per cent of the world's shipping was using Greenwich as the Prime Meridian and an International Meridian Conference in Washington adopted it as such. During the nineteenth century, Greenwich time came to be used as the standard for Britain's fast developing railways and Greenwich Mean Time became accepted internationally. In 1986 GMT was replaced by Co-ordinated Universal Time, but the world's time-zones are still based on the Greenwich Meridian.

The colonial implications of Greenwich's HEGEMONY have been foregrounded by several post-colonial writers. A central section of Derek Walcott's *Omeros* (1990) asks the question 'Who decrees a great epoch?' and immediately answers it with 'The meridian of Greenwich', thus establishing the Prime Meridian as a metanarrative for the Eurocentric assumption of the right to control global CARTOGRAPHIES. The same section of *Omeros* also refers to the meridian of Pope Alexander VI, who at the end of the fifteenth century decreed the line of demarcation that divided the new world between Spain and Portugal. Frustrating both such impositions, the poem's Odyssean persona crosses his own meridian in a journey to Europe, which reverses the Middle Passage crossing and other similar voyages of Empire and in so doing challenges the hegemonies established by both Pope Alexander's decree and the Greenwich project. A similar relocation is referred to in the Tasmanian-born C. J. Koch's *The Year of Living Dangerously* (1978), which mentions the Indonesian President Sukarno's decision to transfer the zero meridian to Jakarta as part of a more general challenge to Eurocentric versions of world geography.

See CARTOGRAPHY for details of maps such as the Bligh Revised Map of the World, which challenge the hegemony of Greenwich. See also CULTURAL GEOGRAPHY and IMAGINATIVE GEOGRAPHY.

Further reading

Thieme (1997).

Griot   A traditional storyteller in West African communities, who acts as the oral repository of his [sic] people's culture. The term has come to be used more widely in African and African DIASPORA contexts to refer to artists, particularly musicians, who fulfil this role. Thus calypsonians, African novelists, African American poets and reggae singers have all been seen as wordsmiths who perform roles analogous to those of the traditional griot. Stressing the need for the post-independence West African artist to assume social responsibilities akin to those of the griot, Chinua ACHEBE argues that 'The writer cannot expect to be excused from the task of re-education and regeneration that must be done' (1988: 30). Wole SOYINKA advocates a similar griot-like role in the process of DECOLONIZATION, while taking the view that the artist's moral vision should employ an 'eye and ear' attuned to a more UNIVERSAL humanism (Soyinka 1969: 15–16). Caribbean writers such as (Edward) Kamau BRATHWAITE and Erna BRODBER have taken a very similar view of the artist's communal responsibilities, as have African American writers from the period of the HARLEM RENAISSANCE onwards.

In traditional tribal situations, griots acted as counsellors to kings, occupying a position of privilege. They performed a variety of functions, including those of praise-singers, public orators and oral archivists who preserved the memory of the kingdom or community's history and traditions. They characteristically engaged their audiences in dialogic forms, such as call-and-response. Euzhan PALCY's 1983 film of Joseph ZOBEL's novel *Rue Cases Nègres* (1950) includes a vivid sequence in which a Martinican storyteller involves his audience in a typically Caribbean call-and-response dialogue.

Griots' narratives varied from short songs and tales to poems of epic length and scope, such as the thirteenth-century epic of old Mali, *Sundiata*, which has been rendered from traditional griot retellings by D. T. Niane in *Soundjata, ou l'Epopée Mandigue* (1960; *Sundiata*, 1965) and Camara LAYE in *Le Maître de la parole* (1978; *The Guardian of the Word*, 1980). Like such epics as Virgil's *Aeneid* and the RAMAYANA, *Sundiata*, which tells the story of the founding of the Mali Empire, is both a heroic narrative and an aetiological account of a community's origins.

The Group of Seven A Canadian School of painters that flourished from 1920, when it held its first exhibition, to 1933. At a time when 'art' in Canada was mainly associated with imported paintings and locally produced work imitated European conventions, the Group pioneered styles that responded directly to the Canadian landscape in an endeavour to create a national artistic tradition. In order to give a sense of the distinctive beauty of Canadian landscapes, they particularly painted scenes from the Algonquin Park and Georgian Bay 'wilderness' regions of Ontario. The initial reception to their work's challenge to conventional artistic standards was mixed, but like Australia's earlier HEIDELBERG SCHOOL, the Group of Seven gradually came to be seen as a national artistic school. However, although its members shared a commonality of subject-matter, their styles of painting varied between naturalistic and expressionist responses to the landscapes they depicted.

The Group's original members were J. E. H. MacDonald (generally considered to be its founder), Franklin Carmichael, Lawren S. Harris, A. Y. Jackson, Frank Johnston, Arthur Lismer and Fred Varley. Tom Thomson, another important figure in the drive towards the nationalist representational practices that the Group pursued, had drowned in mysterious circumstances in Algonquin Park in 1917, prior to its actual formation. After Frank Johnston resigned from the group in 1924, he was replaced by A. J. Casson, and subsequently Edwin Holgate and Lionel LeMoine FitzGerald were added to its ranks. Through the 1920s the Group sought to disseminate its approach across Canada. After MacDonald's death in 1932, it disbanded to make way for a broader group of artists, called the Canadian School of Painters. The McMichael Collection of Art, situated north of Toronto in Kleinburg, Ontario, in a rural wooded landscape, typical of the many of the subjects of the Group's paintings, has provided a particularly appropriate setting for the exhibition of some of their finest works.

Guillén, Nicolás (1902–89). Cuban poet. Born into a working-class, mixed-race Cuban family, Guillén studied law at the University of Havana, before turning to literary journalism and taking a leading role in the Afro-Cuban literary movement of the late 1920s. His reputation as a pioneering revolutionary poet was established with his collection *Motivos de son* (1930), in which he developed his 'son' poetry, which drew its inspiration from a form of Cuban folk music that synthesizes the traditions of the island's black and white populations. This MULATTO AESTHETIC was in marked contrast to most earlier Cuban writing, which was either ASSIMILATIONIST or, written by white writers, tended to represent Afro-Cuban experience through stereotypical constructions of 'alterity' (see 'OTHERNESS'). Guillén's early poems draw on the rhythmic repetitiveness that characterizes Cuban musical forms such as the *son* and the rumba and the Afro-Cuban vernacular more generally. Such an approach involved a radical break with the dominant trends in the island's poetry of this period and Guillén's use of musical forms to develop an African-based aesthetic has parallels with the work of the writers of the HARLEM RENAISSANCE and more generally the practice of GRIOTS throughout the African and African DIASPORA worlds. In a poem such as 'Balada de los dos abuelos' ('Ballad of My Two Grandfathers') he propounds a view of Cuban identity, which lays claim to *both* the main strands in the nation's ancestry. From *West Indies Ltd.* (1934) onwards, his early lyrical use of Afro-Cuban motifs was complemented by an increasing concern with social and political issues and protests against discrimination on the grounds of race and colour. Guillén's reputation continued to flourish after the Revolution. In 1961 he was proclaimed Cuba's National Poet and became President of the Union of Cuban Writers and Artists. His other volumes include *Primeros Poemas 1920–1930* (1930), *Sóngoro Consongo* (1931), *Cantos para soldados y sones para turistas* (1937), *España* (1937), *El son entero* (1947), *Elegias* (1948–58), *La Paloma de Vuelo Popular* (1958), *Tengo* (1964), *Poemas de Amor* (1964), *El Gran Zoo* (1969) and *En la Guerra de España* (1988).

Man-Making Words: Selected Poems of Nicolás Guillén (1972) is an English translation which offers a representative cross-section of the various periods and themes of his work.

The Haitian Revolution, The San Domingo Revolution   The late eighteenth-century Revolution that established Haiti as the first black republic in the Americas. As such, it occupies a unique place in New World African history and the history of revolutionary class struggle more generally and it has served as an inspiration for many New World African DIASPORA writers, artists and intellectuals, especially during the first part of the twentieth century. Literary treatments include Alejo CARPENTIER's short novel *El Reino de Esto Mundo* (1949; *The Kingdom of this World*, 1989) and three plays by Derek WALCOTT, now collected as *The Haitian Trilogy* (2001). C. L. R. JAMES's classic study of the Revolution, *The Black Jacobins* (1938) has been seen as a model for later works on black revolutionary struggle.

The Revolution is best seen as a series of related revolts that developed in the wake of the French Revolution, which provided an inspiration to the slaves suffering as field workers in Haiti's plantation economy and other oppressed groups. In began in 1791, with a slave uprising led by the VODUN *houngan* (priest), Boukman, and ended 13 years later with Haitian independence secured. The most important leader of the first phase of the Revolution was the former slave, TOUSSAINT L'OUVERTURE, who defeated Spanish and British forces in the island and liberated the slave population. Napoleon sent a French army to San Domingo to re-establish French rule and reintroduce slavery. Toussaint was captured and died in exile in France, but the Revolution continued under the leadership of Jean-Jacques Dessalines and the French were finally defeated in 1804, when Haiti was declared a republic and given its present name.

Further reading

James, C. L. R. (1938).

Hariharan, Githa   Born 1954. Indian novelist and short story writer, educated in Mumbai (Bombay), Manila and the USA. Her reputation was assured with the publication of her first novel, *The Thousand Faces of Night* (1992), in which a complex series of interlocking narratives that draws on traditional legends offers a study of the changing pressures on three generations of women. Hariharan's second novel, *The Ghosts of Vasu Master* (1994) takes a very different direction: the eponymous hero is a retired schoolteacher, whose reflections on his past life raise questions about the reliability of memory. Her third novel, *When Dreams Travel* (1999) changes direction again, while demonstrating a similar absorption in the processes of storytelling. Based on the characters of *The Thousand and One Nights*, it encompasses a broad range of stories and, in a manner reminiscent of the American postmodernist novelist John Barth's *Chimera* (1972), places its main emphasis on the narrative act, while expanding outwards from the main narrator, Sharazad (Scheherazade), to include the stories of her sister, Dunyazad, and their respective husbands. Such an emphasis on storytelling *in extremis* also has affinities with various other postmodernist interrogations of the nature of narrative, including Salman RUSHDIE's *Midnight's Children* (1981), which begins with the narrator, Saleem Sinai, likening *his* narrative situation to that of Scheherezade. Hariharan's collection of short stories, *The Art of Dying* (1993) is particularly notable for the stories, 'Gajjar Halwa', 'The Reprieve' and 'The Remains of the Feast', in which a woman whose death is imminent asserts her individuality by embarking on an eating spree that infringes a range of CASTE, gender and regional taboos.

Harijans, 'children of God'   GANDHI's preferred term for those Indians, formerly referred to as UNTOUCHABLES, who exist outside the four main CASTES of Hindu society and have traditionally suffered from ritual subordination, including marriage taboos and consignment to menial occupations. *Harijan* was introduced by Gandhi as part of his campaign against caste discrimination. Subsequent alternatives include DALITS, the term favoured by the reformer B. R. Ambedkar, and 'scheduled castes', the term generally preferred in Indian public policy contexts.

Further reading

Mendelsohn and Vicziany (1998).

The Harlem Renaissance   African American literary and cultural movement that came to the fore in the 1920s, as its name suggests in the uptown Manhattan district of Harlem. Harlem had seen extensive migration from the rural American South in the second decade of the twentieth century and works such as Claude McKay's novel *Home to Harlem* (1928) reflect the increasingly common perception that it represented an urban homeland for African Americans, as well as those, like the Jamaican-born McKay, who had migrated there from other parts of the New World African DIASPORA. The Renaissance played an important role in asserting African American pride. Its influence lessened during the Depression years of the 1930s, but it had an impact on such later movements as the American Civil Rights Movement, NEGRITUDE, pan-Africanism and African-based elements in post-colonial thinking. Its attempts to develop a distinctive African American aesthetic drew on jazz and other black musical forms, many of which had been brought to the American North by the recently arrived southern migrants. The movement's influence was particularly spread through periodicals, such as *Crisis*, the magazine of the NAACP (National Association for the Advancement of Colored People), which was edited by W. E. B. DuBois, author of *The Souls of Black Folks* (1903), *Opportunity*, the magazine of the National Urban League and Marcus GARVEY's *Negro World*.

Leading figures in the Renaissance included: the writers, Langston Hughes, Zora Neale Hurston, Jean Toomer, James Weldon Johnson, Claude McKay and Countee Cullen; the artists Aaron Douglas, Palmer Hayden, and William H. Johnson; and the sculptor, Augusta Savage.

Further reading

Wintz (ed.) (1996).

Harris, (Theodore) Wilson   Born 1921. Guyanese novelist and critic. Harris attended Guyana's leading secondary school, Queen's College, and later worked as a land surveyor in the Guyanese interior, developing an intimate knowledge of the country's heartland shared by few of his compatriots. He emigrated to England, where he has lived ever since – in London and Chelmsford – in 1959. Prior to this he had published the collections of poetry *Fetish* (1951) and *From Eternity to Season* (1954), in which his life-long concern with the force of the mythic imagination is already apparent, though here the main departure point is Greek mythology and AMERINDIAN legend would subsequently provide a more important wellspring for his imagination, particularly in volumes such as *The Sleepers of Roraima* (1970) and *The Age of the Rainmakers* (1971).

In his essay 'Tradition and the West Indian Novel', Harris expresses the view that 'the novel of the West Indies ... belongs – in the main – to the conventional mode' (Harris 1967: 29–30). He equates the 'conventional mould' with realism and an approach that attempts to persuade readers of the inevitability of received modes of behaviour. Against this he posits the possibility of a mode of fiction that rejects 'apparent common sense' (ibid.: 29) in favour of a dialectical attempt to arrive at a new aesthetic practice and a new view of personality. In the same essay Harris takes the view that most twentieth-century novelists continue to write within 'the framework of the nineteenth-century novel' (ibid.: 29) and sees this as inappropriate in the Caribbean and South America. His own fictional technique has been likened to that of Latin American MAGIC REALISTS and he has always stressed the continuities between Caribbean and South American experience. Yet it remains uniquely his own, a highly individual blend of poetry and prose, of religious and political thinking and of European modernism and post-colonial resistance to categorization.

After moving to England, Harris worked on successive drafts of the novel that became *Palace of the Peacock* (1960), eventually finding a style suited to the expression of his complex cross-cultural vision and non-Western perceptions of culture and society more generally. *Palace of the Peacock* employs a dream-like technique, in which fundamental tenets of post-Cartesian Western thought, such as the autonomy of the individual self, are collapsed: the past and present come together, actual and imagined events are blurred, subject becomes object and vice versa and the dead are resurrected. The novel's central persona has a dual identity: its 'dreaming' first-person narrator's *alter ego*, Donne, is an archetypal imperialist, who represents the fossilized condition of the colonial psyche. Donne leads a mixed crew, representative of the various ancestral strands of the Guyanese people on an INTERIOR JOURNEY into the country's heartland. This journey culminates in a mystical vision of enlarged human possibilities in which deaths usher in a resurrection and Christian symbol is fused with Amerindian myth. *Palace of the Peacock* was followed in quick succession by the novels, *The Far Journey of Oudin* (1961), *The Whole Armour* (1962) and *The Secret Ladder* (1963) and the four works were subsequently published together as *The Guyana Quartet* (1985). Subsequent Harris novels draw extensively on a range of world mythologies and, although many of his influences (which include Blake, Eliot, Yeats and the writings of the medieval alchemists) are European, he has frequently noted the commonalities to be found in the world's various mythologies, has made extensive use of Arawak and Carib mythology and has also on occasions drawn on Afro-Caribbean folk forms such as LIMBO and VODUN.

Harris has increasingly stressed the cross-cultural nature of all experience, writing novels set in a variety of locations, including England, Scotland and Mexico. *Jonestown* (1996) takes the People's Temple Massacre that occurred in the Guyanese interior in 1978, as its departure point and moves between Guyana and California while continuing to occupy characteristically metaphysical terrain and suggesting that psychic regeneration offers the only real hope for human fulfilment. His other novels are *Heartland* (1964), *The Eye of the Scarecrow* (1965), *The Waiting Room* (1967), *Tumatumari* (1968), *Ascent to Omai* (1970), *Black Marsden* (1972), *Companions of the Day and Night* (1975), *Da Silva da Silva's Cultivated Wilderness* and *Genesis of the Clowns* (1977), *The Tree of the Sun* (1978), *The Angel at the Gate* (1982), *Resurrection at Sorrow Hill* (1993) and *The Dark Jester* (2001). His *Carnival Trilogy* (1993) brings together *Carnival* (1985), *The Infinite Rehearsal* (1987) and *The Four Banks of the River of Space* (1990). Harris is also the author of numerous challenging critical essays on literature and culture. These are collected in *Tradition, the Writer and Society* (1967), *Explorations* (1981), *The Womb of Space* (1983), *The Radical Imagination* (1992) and *Selected Essays of Wilson Harris: The Unfinished Genesis of the Imagination* (1999).

Further reading

Harris (1967 and 1999); Gilkes (1975); Maes-Jelinek (1982); Maes-Jelinek (ed.) (1998); Maes-Jelinek and Ledent (eds) (2002).

Head, Bessie (1937–86). South African-born Botswanan novelist and short story writer. Born as the child of an 'illicit' mixed-race union in a Pietermaritzburg psychiatric hospital to which her mother had been committed, Head had a traumatic early life in South Africa before migrating to Botswana in 1964. She spent 15 years as a refugee in her adopted homeland, during which she was fearful of being deported back to South Africa, before being granted citizenship. Although the complex and highly personal nature of her writing resists simplistic classification as NATIONAL ALLEGORY and she suffered a breakdown in Botswana, her migration to an environment that offered release from the mentally divisive binaries of APARTHEID seems ultimately to have assisted her climb back to health.

Her finest novel, *A Question of Power* (1973) can be located within a group of feminist novels about women's experience of supposed 'madness', which includes such works as Charlotte Perkins Gilman's *The Yellow Wallpaper* (1892), Janet Frame's *Faces in the Water* (1961), Jean Rhys's *Wide Sargasso Sea* (1966), Margaret Atwood's *Surfacing* (1972) and Marge Piercy's *Woman on the Edge of Time* (1976). However, with long sections written from inside the protagonist Elizabeth's experience of schizophrenia, it is formally more disturbing than any of these novels. Reputedly autobiographical, it suggests that Elizabeth is a victim of both the dualistic ideology of her South African youth and of black African men. She achieves partial regeneration through her involvement in agricultural work and the inspiration of aspects of Eastern religious thought, which negate the political and gender imbalances engrained in binary power relationships.

Prior to *A Question of Power*, Head had published the novels, *When Rain Clouds Gather* (1968), in which rural Botswanan values are challenged by the advent of a South African political refugee and an English agricultural expert, and *Maru* (1971), the story of a teacher's experience in a remote rural village, in which people are kept as slaves. Her later publications include *The Collector of Treasures* (1977), a collection of Botswanan village tales, and *Serowe: Village of the Rain Winds* (1981), a non-fiction work about the history and myths of the eponymous village. Posthumously published works include: *A Woman Alone* (1990), a volume of autobiographical writings; *Tales of Tenderness and Power* (1989); and *The Cardinals* (1993), a novel written before she left South Africa, which offers a fictionalized version of the hardships of her early years.

Further reading

MacKenzie (1999).

Hegemony   The dominance of one faction in a political entity or grouping; a term widely used in relation to the exercise of imperial power. The word derives from the Greek *hegemonia*, or 'leadership', and was used in classical Greek times in such phrases as 'the Spartan hegemony' to indicate confederations led by a particular section within them. Loosely used, it is simply seen as a synonym for 'domination'. In the twentieth century, the Italian Marxist theorist Antonio Gramsci revived its usage, emphasizing the extent to which 'hegemony' involves a degree of consent on the part of subject peoples. Hence in the narrower Gramscian sense, it refers to the kind of collusion that frequently characterizes colonial subjects' complicity with imperialism and is less concerned with military domination than with social co-optation, in which ASSIMILATIVE linguistic and cultural policies play a central role and SUBALTERN cultural formations are denied significance. Ashcroft *et al.* (1998: 116–17) provide a succinct discussion, which illustrates how the colonized subject is interpellated into imperial discourse.

Further reading

Femia (1981); Ashcroft *et al.* (1998).

The Heidelberg School   A late nineteenth-century Australian school of painters that played a role similar to that of Canada's GROUP OF SEVEN in the development of a national pictorial aesthetic. Influenced by French Impressionism, the School's founding members, Tom Roberts and Frederick McCubbin, deserted the studio for *plein air* paintings that attempted to develop a style suited to the representation of the distinctive qualities of the Australian landscape and Australian light. Roberts and McCubbin originally set up a camp at Box Hill, near Melbourne, but later camps at Heidelberg, Victoria, where they were joined by Arthur Streeton, George Conder and Norman Lindsay, gave the group its name.

   The Heidelberg School's project can be seen as loosely equivalent to what the

Sydney Bulletin writers endeavoured to do for Australian literature in the 1890s: its painters particularly turned their attention to the outback and bush life as the supposedly AUTHENTIC Australia experience, striving to capture the distinctive features of this environment through an approach that favoured a local form of naturalism and the use of pastel colours, but, as with the LEGEND OF THE NINETIES, sometimes inclined towards idealizing outback landscapes and life.

Highlife   A type of West African popular music, which evolved in Ghana in the 1920s from the repertory of dance bands performing for the social elite, or 'highlife'. The Ghanaian, E. T. Mensah, who introduced African, Caribbean and African American elements into European ballroom forms became known as 'the King of highlife', after the release of his first records in 1952. Around 1960, highlife became popular in Nigeria, where it was combined with the music of Ibo palm wine festivals, which had similar guitar traditions, and an eclectic mélange of elements was Africanized through the introduction of local rhythms and lyrics. Bobby Benson, who was influenced by Mensah, was the music's first major Nigerian exponent. Other significant highlife performers who came to the fore before Nigerian Independence (1960) include Cardinal Rex Lawson and Chief Stephen Osita Osadebe. Highlife went into decline in the 1960s at the time of the NIGERIAN CIVIL WAR, but re-emerged in the 1970s, when leading performers included Osadebe, Oliver de Coque and the Oriental Brothers. By the 1970s highlife was regularly being combined with a number of other African musical genres and a proliferation of fusion forms began to emerge. The biggest hit of the decade was the Cameroonian-Nigerian Prince Nico Mbarga's 'Sweet Mother' (1976), which combined highlife with Cameroonian *ashiko* and Zairean rumba. The 1970s also saw the controversial Fela Anikulapo KUTI developing the music into the fusion form of AFROBEAT.

Hindu texts   The classic texts of Hinduism resist comparison with any putative Western counterparts, since they make no significant distinction between the secular and the spiritual. Thus the two great SANSKRIT epics, the *RAMAYANA*, and the *MAHABHARATA*, combine the heroic and nationalist elements of Western epics such as *The Iliad* and *The Aeneid*, with spiritual and devotional elements that are lacking in their Homeric and Virgilian equivalents and have slightly more in common with the Bible. While the major texts of Hinduism are mainly written in Sanskrit, forms frequently exist in other languages and South Indian versions of classic works can differ significantly from those of the North, which in some cases, e.g. the *Ramayana*, have been seen as legitimizing Aryan India's invasion of the Dravidian south.

Other major groups of Hindu texts include the *Vedas*, hymns which predate the classical Sanskrit period and are generally seen as expressing the fundamental tenets of the religion. The *Upanishads*, a collection of mystical texts, which reflect on the nature of ultimate reality and its relationship to individual lives, form the last group of the Vedas The *Puranas* are a later group of 18 epics, which are didactic offshoots of the *Mahabharata*. The tales collected as the *Panchatantra*, which have been compared with Aesop's *Fables* but also demonstrate marked similarities with *The Thousand and One Nights*, also combine narrative and didactic elements.

Hispanophone   Spanish-speaking, especially used to distinguish Spanish speakers in regions where French is also used, e.g. the Caribbean. Cf. Francophone, Anglophone, Lusophone.

Historiography   The writing of history. During the last three decades the study of history has increasingly taken account of the discursive modes through which the past is constituted and the New Historicist approach to literary texts, which had its origins in Renaissance Studies, where the work of Stephen Greenblatt was particularly influential, has emphasized the extent to which history is narrativized. Whereas older forms of historical inquiry had attempted to produce supposedly objective accounts of the past, New Historicism stressed the extent to which history is mediated by the strategies through which it is shaped. In Linda Hutcheon's words,

> The narrativization of past events is not hidden; the events no longer seem to speak for themselves, but are shown to be consciously composed into a narrative, whose constructed – not found – order is imposed upon them, often overtly by the narrating figure. (1989: 66)

Similarly, Hayden White argues,

> *How* a given historical situation is to be configured depends on the historian's subtlety in matching a specific plot-structure with the set of historical events that he wishes to endow with a meaning of a particular kind. This is essentially a literary, that is to say fiction-making, aspiration. (1978: 85)

At the same time, cultural theorists such as Michel Foucault have questioned the primacy of history as a discipline for approaching the past, favouring an archaeological model of investigation, which uncovers layered traces of supposed 'origins' rather than positing a linear explication of causes and effects, as in the mainstream tradition of Western historiographical writing. Central texts that have led to this shift in approach include Foucault's *The Archaeology of Knowledge* (1972) and Hayden White's *Metahistory* (1973) and, with more specific relevance to literary studies, Linda Hutcheon's *The Canadian Postmodern* (1988) and *The Politics of Postmodernism* (1989), in which she uses the term 'historiographic metafiction' to describe self-reflexive fiction that engages with the discursive constitution of history.

Historiography becomes a particularly crucial area for revisionist post-colonial accounts of the past, since the written historical records of the colonial period were almost exclusively those of the colonial authorities and the retrieval of Subaltern histories poses particular difficulties. Hence the significance of oral testimony in post-colonial attempts to recuperate occluded voices. The many post-colonial literary texts that engage with the project of writing revisionist history include Chinua Achebe's *Things Fall Apart* (1958), Ayi Kwei Armah's *The Healers* (1978) and Salman Rushdie's *Midnight's Children* (1981). In his essay 'The Muse of History', Derek Walcott writes of the 'patrician writers' of the New World who 'reject the idea of history as time for its original concept as myth, the partial recall of the race', arguing that for such writers 'history is fiction, subject to a fitful muse, memory' (1998: 36–7). Historiographical metafiction from settler cultures includes: Patrick White's *Voss* (1957), which provides a revisionist perspective on the exploration of the Australian interior, taking as its protagonist a visionary, loosely based on the real-life German explorer Ludwig Leichhardt, whose nonconformist approach challenges the Anglo-Celtic perspectives of the nineteenth-century settler community; Jack Davis's *Kullark* (1982), which tells the story of the Nyoongah people of Western Australia from the Aboriginal point of view; Kate Grenville's *Joan Makes History* (1988), which rewrites the 'story' of Australia from the viewpoint of its missing women; and the Mennonite Rudy Wiebe's *The Temptations of Big Bear* (1973), which incorporates a compendium of documents as part of its project of telling the story of the nineteenth-century Cree leader, who resisted central Canadian authority. Wiebe's 'Where is the Voice Coming From?' (in *The Angel of the Tar Sands and Other Stories*, 1982; and Thieme, ed., 1996) is a metahistorical short story that moves between an account of the last stand of a Cree fugitive, who becomes a personification of his people's dispossession, and a reflection on its narrator's failure to find definitive historical source material, which leads him to adopt a creative fictional approach for the telling his revisionist history.

Further reading

Foucault (1972); White, H. (1973 and 1978); Keith (ed.) (1981); Veeser (ed.) (1989); Hutcheon (1988 and 1989); Walcott (1998).

The 'Holy Trinity'   In post-colonial contexts, Edward Said, Gayatri Chakravorty Spivak and Homi K. Bhabha. Despite its tone of playfully ironic disparagement, the term attests to their pre-eminence in the field.

Hosain, Attia (1913–97). Indian writer, who migrated to England in 1947, the year of India's independence and subsequently enjoyed success as an actress and broadcaster. She is best known for her novel, *Sunlight on a Broken Column* (1961), a classic account of a Muslim woman's struggle against traditional gender codes, which is set in Lucknow in the years leading up to Indian independence. *Phoenix Fled* (1953) is a collection of her short stories.

Hybridity, hybridization   The notion that cultures are inevitably hybrid has become one of the most significant and influential aspects of contemporary post-colonial theorizing. Theories of hybridity challenge notions of authentic or ESSENTIALIST self-hood, nationhood and language by demonstrating the porousness of supposed boundaries and foregrounding the extent of cultural interpenetration. Such theorizing has been particularly associated with Homi K. BHABHA, whose work is concerned with process and the ways in which cultures are enunciated through language. In his Introduction to *The Location of Culture* (1994), Bhabha argues for:

[T]he need to think beyond narratives of originary and initial subjectivities and to focus on those moments or processes that are produced in the articulation of cultural differences. These 'in-between' spaces provide the terrain for elaborating strategies of selfhood – singular or communal – that initiate new signs of identity, and innovative sites of collaboration, and contestation, in the act of defining the idea of society itself. (1994: 1–2)

Such theorizing has had the effect of establishing hybridity as the characteristic predicament of the late twentieth century and early twentieth-first century and making the migrant the representative protagonist. Although it can be argued that all post-colonial writing and culture (and indeed writing and culture more generally) is produced in the interstitial space that Bhabha identifies, there is a clear divide between work that asserts the AUTHENTICITY of particularly cultural formations and work that foregrounds inauthenticity. As an instance, one can contrast V. S. NAIPAUL's emphasis on displacement with that of Salman RUSHDIE. Naipaul's novels, such as *The Mimic Men* (1967), express nostalgia for the 'purity' of lost origins; Rushdie's fiction cele-brates the hybrid nature of 'mongrel' cultures and his essays in *Imaginary Homelands* (1991) embody a similar position to Bhabha's theory, though with a more direct emphasis on social experience and without Bhabha's use of poststructuralist termi-nology and emphasis on enunciation. The passage from *Imaginary Homelands* quoted in the Glossary's entry on 'authenticity' provides a good example of Rushdie's think-ing on hybridity (Rushdie 1991: 67).

One of the many consequences of the acknowledgment that cultural formations are invariably hybrid has been a shift in emphasis away from the study of discrete national literatures and cultures. This has been particularly marked in the study of contempo-rary writing, but it has also informed the study of the literatures and cultures of earlier periods.

Further reading

Rushdie (1991); Bhabha (1994).

Hyphen in 'post(-)colonial'   In an article published in 1996, Bill Ashcroft offered the following guidance on the use of the hyphenated and unhyphenated forms of 'post(-)colonial':

A simple hyphen has come to represent an increasingly diverging set of assumptions, emphases, strategies and practices in post-colonial reading and writing. The hyphen puts an emphasis on the discursive and material effects of the historical 'fact' of colonialism, while the term 'postcolonialism' has come to represent an increasingly indiscriminate attention to cultural difference and marginality of all kinds, whether a consequence of the historical experience of colonialism or not. (Ashcroft 1996: 23)

Useful though such a distinction is, it is so as an ideal, observed by some scholars working in the field, but ignored by or unknown to others, who either use Ashcroft's preferred hyphenated form to refer to what he calls 'an increasingly indiscriminate attention to cultural difference and marginality of all kinds' *or* use the unhyphenated form to identify his more specific set of practices that are grounded in 'the discursive and material effects of the historical "fact" of colonialism'.

As Ashcroft goes on to point out, the problem is further compounded by earlier usages of the term 'post-colonial' to refer to the period 'after colonialism', i.e. as a synonym for 'post-independent' or 'newly independent'. Ashcroft identifies this as a term commonly used by political scientists in the 1960s and 1970s, but has to concede that this 'chronological misapprehension' has endured 'in many people's minds' (ibid.: 24). Along with his fellow-authors of *The Empire Writes Back* (1989), he argues for a different temporal usage of the hyphenated form: 'to cover all the culture affected by the imperial process from the moment of colonization to the present day' (Ashcroft *et al.* 1989: 2). His own analysis of the CONTINUUM of post-colonial practice is precise and very reasonably breaks it down into particular models, and he concludes his article on the hyphen by emphasizing the interventionist aspects of 'post-colonial' discourse:

The hyphen in 'post-colonial' therefore signifies difference, resistance, opposition. But it also carves out a space on the post-colonial continuum which distinguishes it from the relativist exclusivism on one hand [sic] and ironic inclusivism on the other'. (1996: 30)

Again, this usefully describes a specific strategic position and is valuable for identifying a particular post-colonial reading and writing practice, but it fails to correspond to the often indiscriminate ways in which both the hyphenated and non-hyphenated forms of the term have been, and are being, used.

It also fails to take account of the American English tendency to use unhyphenated forms to a greater extent than is the case in so-called Standard ENGLISH or the various post-colonial lower-case 'englishes' used in different parts of the globe. This difference in usage *could* be related to Ashcroft's proposed distinction between hyphenated and unhyphenated forms, since American usage frequently extends the term to signify 'cultural difference and marginality of all kinds', but again the attempt to establish a rigid distinction founders on the inconsistency of the ways in which the term is employed empirically. This Glossary has preferred the hyphenated form, since it endeavours to privilege discursive formations that are 'post-colonial' in the narrower sense of the term (and particularly those that relate to the condition of the *colonized*), but in its desire to be 'inclusive', it attempts, in keeping with the general practice of Arnold glossaries, to provide a smaller-scale route map to all the various usages of the term in question. See also the Preface.

Further reading

Ashcroft (1996).

I

'Imaginary Homelands'   An essay by Salman Rushdie, which propounds an anti-essentialist view of place. It was originally a paper delivered at a seminar on Indian writing in English, held at the Commonwealth Institute in London as part of the 1982 UK Festival of India, and it provided the title for Rushdie's subsequent 1991 collection of essays. The 1991 version of the essay differs in minor respects from the original version of the paper, entitled 'The Indian Writer in English' (Butcher (ed.) 1983: 75–83).

Further reading

Butcher (ed.) (1983); Rushdie (1991).

Imaginative geography   Phrase used by Edward Said in *Orientalism* (1978) to refer to the way in which academic fields are constituted and more specifically to the process of mental mapping that occurs when people 'set up boundaries between . . . a familiar space which is "ours" and an unfamiliar space beyond "ours" which is "theirs"'. Although he does not dispute that 'such things as positive history and positive geography' exist, Said argues that these imaginative configurations '*can be* entirely arbitrary' and that they invariably construct a binary opposition in which the 'other' place occupies an inferior position in a hegemonic power relationship through which societies 'derive a sense of their identities negatively' (Said 1985: 54–5; italics in original). Orientalism apart, examples of such hegemonic imaginative geography include the European myth of Australia as a 'down under' place – and particularly during its pre-colonial phase as a Hell or Purgatory (Gibson 1984), the view of Africa as the 'Dark Continent', and the construction of the Americas as the *New* World (my italics), a place of Edenic promise, as in the myth of El Dorado. Imaginative geography extends into the area of demography in formations such as the Noble Savage and the demo-nization of Zulus such as Shaka. See also CULTURAL GEOGRAPHY.

Further reading

White, R. (1981); Gibson (1984); Said (1985).

Imagined Communities Title of Benedict Anderson's influential 1983 study of the formation of NATIONALISM, sub-titled *Reflections on the Origin and Spread of Nationalism*, in which he advances the view that nations are not natural entities, but narrative constructs that evolved as the shared fictions of the 'imagined communities' of the post-Enlightenment era. Anderson argues that national consciousness, as understood in the modern world, was not only a cultural artefact produced at a par-ticular moment in history from the complex intersection of a range of forces, but also, as a fairly recent arrival on the European scene in the late eighteenth century (though he dates its emergence in 'Creole' Hispanic American societies earlier) something of an anomaly in the longer history of Western culture. In his view, the sea change that ushered in modern nationalism came about as a product of the convergence of the rise of capitalism, the new print technology and the fixity that this technology gave to vernacular languages, which eroded the power of Latin as a scribal lingua franca.

Further reading

Anderson (1983); Gellner (1983); Bhabha (ed.) (1990).

Imperialism In general usage, 'imperialism' is sometimes equated with 'colonialism', but properly speaking it is the totality of the systems and practices of Empire, while colonialism is its overseas manifestation, in which a nation extends its authority into another part of the world through military conquest, political annexation, settlement or other means. The word is derived from the Latin *imperium* ('dominion' or 'supreme authority') and Western imperialism dates back to classical times and earlier. However, the term itself was not widely used until the nineteenth century, when imperialism crystallized as a philosophy that asserted Europe's authority to 'civ-ilize' OTHER parts of the globe, thus legitimizing such appropriations of territory as took place in Africa after the Berlin Conference.

In the twentieth century the positive connotations that 'imperialism' had had during the heyday of the European empires were generally reversed. In the first two decades of the twentieth century, political thinkers such as Rudolf Hilferding, Nicolai Bukharin and Vladimir Ilyich Lenin developed 'the classical Marxist theories of impe-rialism' (Brewer 1980: 79), which linked imperialism with forms of Western monop-oly capitalism that had transformed the world's economy. Around the middle of the twentieth century, equally negative critiques of imperialism were advanced by post-colonial intellectuals such as Kwame Nkrumah and Frantz Fanon, who contested both the legitimacy of colonial occupations and the political philosophy that had sanctioned them.

As Edward SAID and numerous other analysts have pointed out, although imperialism is often associated with military and political coercion, its operation through the supposedly more neutral medium of 'culture' was equally extensive (Said 1994). Thus the 'Victorianization' of the British Empire in the nineteenth century, which can be seen in the naming of post-colonial sites such as the town of Victoria (in *British Columbia*) and the Victoria Falls (in '*Rhodesia*'), peoples – see, e.g. Chinua ACHEBE's comments on his baptismal name of Albert in 'Named for Victoria, Queen of England' (Achebe 1988: 22) – and even plants, such as the Victoria Regia water lily (*Euryale Amazonica*), which became the national flower of Guyana, involved a form of cultural HEGEMONY that interpellated the colonial subject into the discourse of Empire. This was continued in the late colonial period through the implementation of EUROCENTRIC educational curricula, control of the press, the ASSIMILATION of the local elite and other forms of covert cultural co-optation.

Although Western imperialism may seem to have ended when the various occupied territories of Africa, Asia and the Americas attained their independences (mainly in the third quarter of the twentieth century), it has persisted into the NEO-COLONIAL era, particularly through Western nations' continuing control of the global economy. Since the demise of the Soviet bloc, the USA has generally been regarded as the world's sole superpower, but the neo-colonial economic policies of nations such as Japan and of FEDERATIONS such as the European Community can also be seen as latter-day forms of imperialism. Imperialism is also alive and well in such discourses as 'Raj nostalgia', e.g. soft-focus cinema celebrating upper-class Anglo-Indian life, and early twenty-first century New Right revisionist HISTORIOGRAPHY, which emphasizes the positive aspects of the legacy of Empire. Such commentary highlights the benefits of practices like the export of British parliamentary democracy, while turning a blind eye to the narrowness of the franchise in most of Britain's colonies during the imperial era. In most cases, universal suffrage was only achieved in the late colonial period, at a time when, cynics would argue, the countdown to independence had begun and the need to protect the interests of colonial oligarchies was no longer imperative.

Further reading

Brewer (1980); Said (1985 and 1994); Greet *et al.* (eds) (1992).

Inauthenticity   See AUTHENTICITY.

Indentureship   Sometimes referred to as 'the new slavery', indentureship was the system that succeeded slavery in the period after ABOLITION, supplying the PLANTOCRACY with an alternative workforce to replace the emancipated Afro-Caribbean former slaves. Labourers recruited from India and other colonies signed *girmits* (agreements), articles of indenture which committed them to work on overseas plantations for a fixed period of years, at the end of which they were supposed to be repatriated. In practice, although the conditions under which they worked and lived on the plantations were extremely harsh, comparatively few returned home and indentureship significantly changed the demographic make-up of the population of several European colonies. Vigorous recruitment policies were pursued in North India and the new workforce was predominantly male and Hindu, though Muslims (mainly Shia) were also signed up. In the British Empire indentureship was particularly employed in Mauritius, British Guiana (now Guyana), Trinidad, South Africa (particularly Natal) and Fiji. Today all of these countries have significant populations of Indian ancestry. In the late nineteenth century, many Indians also went to work on the rubber plantations in the Straits Settlements (contemporary Malaysia), the tea plantations in Ceylon (Sri Lanka) and the railways in British East Africa, but not as indentured labourers. Indentureship was also used in the Dutch colony of Surinam and in the French colonies of Martinique, Guadeloupe, Guyane (French Guiana) and the Indian Ocean island of Réunion, which became the first colony to receive indentured labourers: in 1829.

In the British Empire the system was first introduced in Mauritius, where between 1834 and 1912 nearly half a million Indians from the sub-continent came to work on the sugar plantations. Chinese labourers were also introduced into Mauritius in the period immediately after Abolition. Indentureship was widely used on the Caribbean sugar plantations, particularly in British Guiana and Trinidad, which together received approximately 400,000 migrants from the Indian sub-continent between 1838 and 1917. Indentured labourers were also brought to the Caribbean from Portugal (specifically Madeira) and China, but members of these communities are generally considered to have adapted to tropical conditions less well.

Indentureship in Fiji commenced in 1879, five years after the country was ceded to Britain and by 1916 approximately 60,000 Indian labourers had come to the Fijian islands. By the middle of the twentieth century Indo-Fijians outnumbered native Fijians and in 1987 an Indian-dominated government was elected, but overthrown shortly afterwards by two ethnic Fijian military coups led by Major General Sitiveni Rabuka. The introduction of a new Constitution, guaranteeing a Melanesian (indigenous Fijian) majority in the country's parliament led to the emigration of many Indo-Fijians. This was amended to give both ethnic groups equal rights in 1997 and Fiji's first Indian Prime Minister, Mahendra Chaudry, was elected to office in 1999. A similar situation occurred in Guyana, in the years before and after the country attained Independence in 1966, with an Indian majority being excluded from power, first by a general strike in 1962, supposedly financed by the CIA, and then by allegedly rigged elections that kept a predominantly Afro-Guyanese government in power. This situation was reversed in 1992, when Cheddi Jagan's People's Progressive Party was elected to office.

Approximately 150,000 indentured labourers travelled to Natal between 1860 and 1911. During his period as a barrister in South Africa, Mahatma Gandhi played a significant role in the campaign to end indentureship and to secure civil rights for Indians in the latter days of the Indentureship system. The Indian nationalist Gopal Krishna Gokhale (1866–1915) was another key figure in the movement to end indentureship. The campaign resembled the earlier struggle to abolish slavery, in that both humanitarian and economic arguments were influential. The British administration in India finally discontinued indentured emigration in 1917.

Caribbean fiction about indentureship and the experience of the diasporic Hindu communities that it brought into being includes: *A House for Mr Biswas* (1961), V. S. Naipaul's epic novel of Hindu ACCULTURATION in Trinidad in the first half of the twentieth century, Sam Selvon's *A Brighter Sun* (1952) and David Dabydeen's *The Counting House* (1996), which chronicles the personal struggles of a young couple who travel from India to plantation life in Guyana. Dabydeen's poem *Coolie Odyssey* (1988) also bears witness to the dislocations occasioned by the passage from India to Guyana. Fijian literary works dealing with the aftermath of indentureship include Subramani's *The Fantasy Eaters* (1988), Satendra Nandan's *The Wounded Sea* (1991) and the short stories of Raymond Pillai.

Further reading

La Guerre (ed.) (1985); Dabydeen and Samaroo (eds) (1987).

The Indian Mutiny   See the Sepoy Mutiny.

Interior journey   Literary and mythological works as different from one another as the RAMAYANA, *The Odyssey*, the Grail Legend and Bunyan's *Pilgrim's Progress* have used physical journeys as correlatives of various kinds of spiritual or psychic quests. This pattern gathered momentum in the Modernist era, when the influence of Freudian and Jungian psychology led to increased interest in inner mental states.

Conrad's novella *Heart of Darkness* (1902) is perhaps the best-known text that uses the journey into the interior of a continent as a trope for the exploration of inner mental states, which are linked with an experience of colonialism. It is a text that has influenced a broad range of post-colonial texts, particularly those which depict settler incursions into 'indigenous' space. Camara Laye's *Le regard du roi* (1954; *The Radiance of the King*, 1956) also takes a white encounter with native space as its subject, but written from the other side of the colonial divide, it provides a complex and powerful riposte to the myth of the 'Dark Continent', in which the European traveller finally appears to be achieving self-knowledge, though the enigmatic conclusion leaves issues open. Other notable African novels depicting interior journeys include Amos Tutuola's *My Life in the Bush of Ghosts* (1964), in which an *African* protagonist encounters a broad range of inner spiritual and psychological forces, and Tayeb Salih's

Season of Migration to the North (1969), which also reverses the pattern of *Heart of Darkness*. Francis Ford Coppola's *Apocalypse Now* (1979; re-released longer version, *Apocalypse Now Redux*, 2001) is a cinematic reworking of *Heart of Darkness*, which displaces it into the NEO-COLONIAL context of the Vietnam War. Post-colonial interior journeys by writers from SETTLER societies include Patrick White's *Voss* (1957) and *A Fringe of Leaves* (1976), Margaret Atwood's *Surfacing* (1972) and Robert Kroetsch's *Badlands* (1975). Wilson Harris's *Palace of the Peacock* (1960) depicts a journey which ultimately transgresses the settler-indigene divide.

Further reading

Thieme (2001).

Interventions   A journal of post-colonial studies, which published its first issue in 1999 with Robert Young as its General Editor. It deals with issues such as contemporary identity politics, histories of imperialism and colonialism, DIASPORA and migrancy, indigenous FOURTH-WORLD cultures, the economics of NEO-COLONIALISM and connections between post-colonialism and postmodernism. It is published by Routledge.

Inuit   NATIVE PEOPLES of Northern Canada and Greenland, formerly often referred to as 'Eskimos' (a pejorative term meaning 'eaters of raw meat'). They traditionally speak Inuktitut (or Inuttituut) and fall into eight main tribal groupings. The Inuit are sometimes identified with the related Native Peoples of Alaska and Siberia, who speak Yupik. In 1999 the Canadian government created the semi-autonomous region of Nunavut, from part of the Northwest Territories, as an Inuit homeland. Although sparsely populated, Nunavut occupies about one-fifth of the land area of Canada.

Jamaica Journal   The quarterly journal of the Institute of Jamaica, first published in 1967. It was set up to develop and promote Jamaican literature, history, science and arts and over the years its coverage of these areas of Jamaican life has been unrivalled. Its first editor was Alexander Gradussov and subsequent editors have included Olive SENIOR.

James, C(yril) L(ionel) R(obert)   (1901–89). Trinidadian-born Marxist historian, cricket writer, novelist and literary critic. One of the most extraordinarily versatile writers and thinkers of the twentieth century, James had a fairly traditional colonial education, attending Trinidad's leading secondary school Queen's Royal College as a scholarship-winner. However, his leftist sympathies were apparent in his first significant work, *The Life of Captain Cipriani* (1932), which offered a critique of colonial government in the Caribbean. James was a member of Trinidad's Beacon Group and his only novel, *Minty Alley* (1936), is a Yard novel, in which a middle-class black Trinidadian, who falls upon hard times financially, goes to live in a poorer part of Port of Spain, an environment that expands both his social consciousness and his awareness of the vagaries of human behaviour. As in other novels by members of the Beacon Group, the use of a middle-class point of view provides an optic through which the novel is able to represent some of the grass-roots realities of the society.

James left Trinidad in 1932 and settled in England, publishing his Trotskyist *World Revolution, 1917–36* in 1937 and the work for which he is best-known, *The Black Jacobins*, in the following year. *The Black Jacobins* has been seen as a forerunner of later post-colonial studies of revolution. It analyses the various phases of the Haitian Revolution in minute detail, particularly concentrating on the complexities of its early leader, Toussaint L'Ouverture. In the UK, James became a friend of the legendary cricketer, Learie Constantine, who played Lancashire league cricket for many years. James became a cricket correspondent for what was then *The Manchester Guardian*, where he worked under Neville Cardus, in 1933. His passionate engagement with the sport and its social and political implications found their finest expression in his book, *Beyond a Boundary* (1963), which is both a classic of cricket literature and a study of the role of the sport in British and British-colonial social evolution. His *Cricket: Collected Writings* was published in 1986.

James's numerous other activities included involvements in the causes of Pan-Africanism, decolonization and international trade unionism. He lived in the USA for fifteen years, before returning to Trinidad in the late 1950s, initially as a close ally of Eric Williams. However, after the two disagreed about the direction in which post-independence Trinidad should be taken, he was briefly imprisoned by Williams. James subsequently taught in the USA and travelled extensively, before once again settling in Britain, in 1981. His best-known work of literary criticism is *Mariners, Renegades and Castaways: The Story of Herman Melville and the World We Live In* (1952). His other writings includes *Modern Politics* (1960), *Nkrumah and the Ghana Revolution* (1977) and the collections *The Future in the Present* (1977), *Spheres of Existence* (1980) and *At the Rendezvous of Victory* (1984). *The C. L. R. James Reader* was published posthumously in 1992.

Jhabvala, Ruth Prawer Born 1927. German-born diasporic novelist and screenwriter. Best known as the writer of the screenplays for most of the films of Merchant Ivory, Jhabvala began her career as a novelist and short story writer. Her early fiction mainly deals with Indian subjects, as does the first phase of her screenplays. She was born in Cologne into a German-Jewish family, who fled to London in 1939. After studying English at London University's Queen Mary College, she moved to India with her architect husband in 1951 and her early writing deals with India, particularly as perceived through Western eyes. Her novels include *The Nature of Passion* (1956), *Esmond in India* (1958), *The Householder* (1960) – the first of her works to be adapted into a Merchant Ivory film – *Get Ready for Battle* (1962), *A New Dominion* (1972; US title *Travelers*), *The Householder*, and her BOOKER PRIZE-winning novel, *Heat and Dust* (1975).

The Householder (1960) is about a young schoolteacher's attempts to come to terms with adulthood and particularly with the second ASRAMA of the ideal Hindu life, referred to in the title. Set in the era of the hippie 'discovery' of India, *Heat and Dust* (1975) is about a young woman who travels to India to try to discover the truth about the life of her grandfather's first wife, who was ostracized by Raj society after her affair with a maharaja. The protagonist's own experience leads to a similar cross-cultural sexual relationship and the novel moves between past and present, employing a complex set of parallels that anticipates the cross-cutting technique of Jhabvala's screenplay for the film version. Both novel and film contrast Western attitudes to India in the pre- and post-independence periods. However, the novel, which emphasizes the *heat and dust* of India, is markedly different from the film, where soft-focus Raj nostalgia preponderates.

From 1975, Jhabvala partly lived in New York. Her more recent novels include her first novel set in the USA, *In Search of Love and Beauty* (1983), *Poet and Dancer* (1993) and *Shards of Memory* (1995). She has also published the short story collections, *Like Birds, Like Fishes* (1963), *How I Became A Holy Mother* (1976) and *East into Upper East: Plain Tales from New York and New Delhi* (1998), which brings together stories of middle-class Indian life in the two metropolises. *Out of India* (1986) is a selection of her short stories. See MERCHANT IVORY for details of her film work, which has mostly treated cross-cultural subjects and is notable for adaptations of novels by Henry James and E. M. Forster that deal with 'the international theme'. Her screenplays for the Merchant Ivory films of Forster's *A Room with a View* (1986) and *Howards End* (1993) both won Academy Awards.

Further reading

Pym (1983).

Jihad, jehad   A holy war undertaken by Muslims. The QUR'AN instructs believers to respond to the call for *jihad* when summoned to defend or help spread Islam. Recent Western portrayals of *jihad* have particularly connected it with militant terrorism. Its origins are, however, more complex and the notion of *jihad* encompasses the need to struggle against impurities within the self as well as external forces. *Jihads* proclaimed against colonialism include those of 'the Mahdi' (Muhammad Ahmed), who defeated the British under General Gordon at Khartoum in 1885 and established a theocratic state in the Sudan, and Mohammad Abdille Hasan Sayyid Hasan (known in the West as the 'Mad Mullah'), who led resistance to Christian colonization in Somaliland in the early years of the twentieth century. More recently, *jihad* has been associated with the call to arms by Islamic revivalists such as the Saudi Osama Bin Laden (born 1957). The related word *mujahidin* refers to those who engage in *jihad*.

Johnson, Linton Kwesi Born 1952. Jamaican-born British performance poet and activist. Johnson is best known as the most significant practitioner of DUB POETRY, though he has sometimes said that he prefers not to be viewed in this light. His work stands at the forefront of a body of Caribbean-British verse that has played a signifi-cant part in redefining notions of what constitutes 'poetry'. Johnson came to Britain when he was eleven and grew up in South London, subsequently studying sociology at Goldsmiths' College, University of London. He first achieved prominence through his concert performances in the 1970s. Touring with Dennis Bovell's Dub Band in the 1980s, he developed an increasingly complex aesthetic, based on performing verse against the backing of a reggae dub track. He numbers Jamaican REGGAE DJs and (Edward) Kamau BRATHWAITE among the major influences on his poetic and political development. Johnson's pop star-like success established him as a leading spokesman for dispossessed black British youth, though from the outset his appeal, like that of much reggae music, has transcended racial binaries. His poetry espouses many of the values of RASTAFARI and throughout his career he has been a forthright critic of English racism. His best-known poems include 'Dread Beat and Blood', 'Bass Culture' and his elegy for his father, 'Reggae fi Dada'.

Recordings of Johnson's work include the albums *Dread Beat and Blood* (1978), *Bass Culture* (1981), *Tings an' Times* (1991) and *LKJ A Capella Live* (1996). His printed collections, which only give a partial sense of the impact that his poetry has in perfor-mance, include *Dread Beat and Blood* (1975) and *Inglan is A Bitch* (1980). *Tings an' Times* (1991) and *Mi Revalueshanary Fren* (2002) provide selections of his poetry. Johnson was a founder member of the Race Today Collective and has been Arts Editor for the collective's magazine. He has also written for popular music magazines, been a reporter for Channel 4 television's *BANDUNG File* and produced a ten-part radio series on Jamaican music for the BBC.

Further reading

Habekost (ed.) (1986); Habekost (1993); Dawes (1999); official website: www.lister.ultrakohl.com

The Journal of Commonwealth and Postcolonial Studies Bi-annual journal which describes its mission as the 'promotion and/or study of the literature, performing arts, history, and politics of nations, which were historically part of the British Commonwealth, and of countries colonized by other European powers in Africa, the

Americas, Asia, and the Caribbean'. It is published from Georgia Southern University in Statesboro, Georgia.

The Journal of Commonwealth Literature (JCL) Founded at the University of Leeds in 1965, the *Journal of Commonwealth Literature* has provided uninterrupted coverage of Commonwealth and post-colonial topics for nearly 40 years. For most of this time it has published three issues a year: two primarily devoted to articles, the third offering an annual bibliography of primary and secondary material from several, but not all, regions of the Commonwealth. The *Journal* publishes critical articles on all aspects of Commonwealth and post-colonial literatures and related areas, such as post-colonial theory, translation studies and colonial discourse. *JCL* does not publish creative writing or book reviews, but its articles issues include a Books Received section, which provides short notices of books sent to the *Journal*. It is now published by Cambridge Scientific Abstracts and from 2003 has moved to four issues a year: three articles issues, with the fourth being devoted to its annual bibliography. Long-serving editors have included Arthur Ravenscroft, Alastair Niven and, currently, John Thieme.

The Journal of West Indian Literature (JWIL) *JWIL* was founded at the University of the West Indies in 1986 as a twice-yearly publication, initially under the editorship of Mark McWatt. Its primary focus has been on the literature of the Anglophone Caribbean, but it also includes articles on non-English speaking Caribbean writing, provided they are of a comparative nature or have a relevance to anglophone Caribbean writing.

Journals See LITERARY AND CULTURAL JOURNALS.

Juju Popular form of Nigerian music which evolved from Yoruba palm-wine festivals. The term is said to have been coined in the late 1920s by Babatunde King. The growth of the music's popularity in Lagos was accompanied by the addition of new instruments, such as the talking drum and the accordion, to the customary palm wine-guitar. The early 1960s saw the emergence of two internationally acclaimed practitioners, Chief Commander Ebenezer Obey and King Sunny ADE, whose rivalry dominated the music during the decades that followed. Other stars of juju music include Segun Adewale and Shina Peters, who developed his own distinctive form of 'Afro-juju' and sparked the phenomenon known as Shina Mania.

Kani, John Born 1943. South African actor, dramatist and director. With Athol FUGARD and Winston Ntshona, he co-devised and wrote two of the *Statements* (1974) workshop plays – *Sizwe Bansi is Dead* (1972) and *The Island* (1973) – which made an important contribution to the struggle against APARTHEID, at home and internationally, both through their themes and their innovative, dialogic theatrical practice. Kani is Managing Trustee of the MARKET THEATRE and Founding Director of the Market's Laboratory. In 2002, he starred in the Market Theatre's production of his own play, *Nothing But the Truth,* a story of the contrasting lives of two brothers during the years of Apartheid. His performance as Othello in Janet Suzman's 1987 Market production of the play was, in the director's own words, a 'politically charged act', challenging the binaries of Apartheid. Kani's film credits include roles in Fugard's *Marigolds in August* (1980), the film version of Doris Lessing's *The Grass is Singing* (1981), *A Dry White Season* (1989) and *The Tichborne Claimant* (1998).

Karma *Karma* is the belief that a person's fate in their present situation has been determined by their behaviour in previous incarnations. Although it is primarily associated with Hinduism, it is also a doctrine of Jainism and Buddhism. It is seen as a causological process that it independent of any divine intervention and hence markedly different from the Christian belief in salvation and damnation. The law of *karma* operates across generations and only those who have achieved spiritual detachment (in the case of Buddhism, nirvana) are exempt from the cycle of rebirth. The *karma yoga*, the Hindu path to such detachment, is outlined in the BHAGAVAD GITA.

A mistaken Western interpretation of *karma* sees it as a fatalistic belief that promotes quietist inertia and social complacency in its adherents. Thus V. S. NAIPAUL describes it as:

[T]he Hindu killer, the Hindu calm, which tells us that we pay in this life for what we have done in past lives: so that everything we see is just and balanced, and the distress we see is to be relished as religious theatre, a reminder of our duty to ourselves, our future lives. (1977: 25)

As a consequence of taking such a view, Naipaul sees *karma* as responsible for post-independence India's immersion in a medieval view of history that maintains the status quo and endorses the CASTE system (Naipaul 1964) and, when he discusses the novels of R. K. NARAYAN, he sees them as embodying a social philosophy, 'compounded of *karma*, nonviolence, and a vision of history as an extended religious fable' (Naipaul 1977: 25; italics in original), that endorses 'the Hindu equilibrium' (ibid.: 27) and negates the novel genre's 'Western concern with the condition of men [sic]' (Naipaul 1964: 226) and with 'social inquiry' (Naipaul 1977: 18). The inadequacy of such a view of *karma* – and such a reading of Narayan – is that it is itself locked into a retrospective vision: it considers how the *past* has influenced the present, without appreciating that *karmic* rebirth is an ongoing process, in which one's action in the present influences one's fate in *future* incarnations, while also allowing for the possibility of liberation from the cycle of continual rebirth.

Further reading

Naipaul (1964 and 1977); Thieme (1987).

Kenyatta, Jomo (*c.*1890–1978). Kenyan politician of mixed Kikuyu and Masai descent, generally regarded as the father of Kenyan nationalism. Like many of the founding figures of African independence movements, Kenyatta was educated in a mission school. He joined what would become the Kikuyu Central Association (at that time the East Africa Association) in 1922 and later became its President. In the 1930s, he attended the London School of Economics, where he studied under Bronislaw Malinowski, the distinguished Polish social anthropologist, and visited Russia on a number of occasions. With Kwame Nkrumah, he founded the Pan African Federation in 1946. In the same year, Kenyatta returned to Kenya after 15 years abroad. He set about building a party of national unity, but was imprisoned in 1953 for allegedly instigating the Mau Mau uprising, a charge which he strenuously denied. He remained in prison throughout most of the remainder of the struggle for independence, only being released in 1961, a year after KANU (the Kenyan African National Union) elected him as its President. He became Prime Minister, when KANU won elections in 1963, shortly before Kenya attained independence, and in the following year he became President of post-independence Kenya. He retained this position until his death in 1978, when he was succeeded by Daniel Arap-Moi, who remained in office until 2002. Kenyatta's writings include *Facing Mount Kenya: The Tribal Life of the Gikuyu* (1938), which examines the impact of colonialism in Kenya.

Kincaid, Jamaica (Elaine Potter Richardson) Born 1949. Antiguan-born writer, who has lived in the USA since she was 17. Kincaid worked as a staff writer for the *New Yorker* from the mid 1970s to the mid 1990s and has taught at Bennington College and Harvard University. Her work frequently blurs the boundaries between fiction and autobiography and is notable for its incantatory, impressionistic style, which has been compared with the prose of Modernist writers such as Virginia Woolf, Gertrude Stein and Jean Rhys.

Beginning with the short-story collection *At the Bottom of the River* (1985), Kincaid's writing has been particularly concerned with women's socialization, usually seen against the backcloth of a vividly realized tropical landscape. Her first novel,

Annie John (1985), depicts a girl's coming-of-age in an Antiguan world that seems paradisal until the onset of her puberty, a time which is accompanied by feelings of loss that are exacerbated by her mother's insistence that she must become an independent 'young lady'. Written in the form of a riposte to European travel-books about the Caribbean, *A Small Place* (1988) is a fierce attack on the forces that have shaped contemporary Antiguan society: colonialism, post-independence corruption and the tourist industry. *Lucy* (1990), a novel which draws on Kincaid's experience of working as an au pair when she was first in America, describes the protagonist's coming to terms with her sexuality and the complexities of her troubled relationship with the mother she has left behind. In her next novel, *The Autobiography of My Mother* (1994), a 70-year-old Caribbean woman, who has never known her mother, looks back over her life and her conscious decision to remain childless after having aborted a child in her early teens. With *My Brother* (1997), a non-fiction account of her response to her younger brother's death from AIDS at the age of 33, Kincaid shifted her characteristic focus on family away from mother-daughter relationships. *Mr. Potter* (2002), a novel in which the narrator tries to create a relationship with her illiterate father whom she has never known, can also be read as a companion-piece to her writing on the matrilineal line in the Caribbean.

Kincaid is also a notable gardening writer. Her work in this genre includes *My Garden (book):* (1999), a collection with pieces on her garden in Bennington, Vermont, the influence of English gardening practices in Antigua and discussions of such gardens as Monet's at Giverny and Vita Sackville-West's at Sissinghurst. She has also edited the anthology, *My Favourite Plant: Writers and Gardeners on the Plants They Love* (1998). *Talk Stories* (2001) is a collection of her *New Yorker* writing.

The *Koran* See the Qur'an.

Kumina, cumina Jamaican religious cult, believed to derive from or to have been inspired by the practices of Bantu migrants, who, unlike most of Jamaica's Afro-Caribbean population, came to the island as 'free Africans' in the mid-nineteenth century. As an ancestor-worship cult, its rites are particularly associated with death and include burials, wakes and memorial ceremonies. Singing, dancing and particularly drumming are central to the practice of kumina and those participating in its rites frequently enter trance-like states of possession. Una Marson's play *Pocomania* (1938) is an early literary treatment of kumina practices. (Edward) Kamau Brathwaite's poem, 'Shepherd' in *Islands* (1969) suggests their potential for cultural and psychic renewal, as gateways for the re-*possession* of African survivals in the Caribbean. Dennis Scott's play, *An Echo in the Bone* (1974), which stages a nine night ceremony, depicts possession rites that are strongly suggestive of kumina or related revivalist practices.

Kumina is regarded as the most 'African' of Jamaica's revivalist cults, which exhibit varying degrees of syncretism. The cognate forms 'pocomania' and 'pukkumina' have been explained in terms of etymologies that reflect differing views on the admixture of elements involved in such revivalist forms: 'pocomania' as deriving from the Spanish for 'a little madness' and 'pukkumina' as partly deriving from the Twi for a possession-dance: hence 'a little possession dance'.

Kunapipi   Bi-annual arts journal publishing creative and critical work, with its main emphasis on 'the new literatures written in English'. Founded by Anna Rutherford at the University of Aarhus in 1979, *Kunapipi* quickly became one of the leading journals in the field, notable for its fine artwork and high production standards. It also served as the journal of EACLALS (the European Association for Commonwealth Literature and Language Studies) and continues to be supported by ACLALS (q.v.). Its name is taken from the Australian Aboriginal myth of the rainbow serpent, an ambisexual symbol of both creation and regeneration. The journal is now edited from the University of Wollongong by Anne Collett.

Kureishi, Hanif   Born 1954. British novelist, screenwriter and dramatist of mixed Pakistani and English parentage. Kureishi was born in Bromley, Kent, and his work in various genres has mainly engaged with the changing mores of London society. He read philosophy at King's College London and subsequently embarked on a career in theatre, working as a stage manager for the dramatist and director Steven Berkoff. During the early 1980s, several of his plays, including *The Mother Country* (1980), *Outskirts* (1981), *Borderline* (1982) and *Birds of Passage* (1983) were performed in a range of venues, including the RSC's (Royal Shakespeare Company's) Warehouse Theatre. They mainly deal with the marginalization of British Asians and the evolving mix of suburban identities that was reshaping aspects of British social life during the 'punk' years of the 1980s. Kureishi's first major success came with his screenplay for the film, *My Beautiful Laundrette* (1985; published 1986), which he saw as a response to the 'Raj Revival' cinema that glorified the British past, while ignoring the realities of contemporary inner-city life that it took as its own subject (Moore-Gilbert 2001: 73ff.). Its main focus was on the gay relationship between an Asian and a white British outsider. It was followed by the film, *Sammy and Rosie Get Laid* (1988; script and diary 1988), which also exposes the ignored 'other' side of life in Thatcherite England.

Kureishi's novel *The Buddha of Suburbia* (1990) won the Whitbread Best First Novel prize and was subsequently filmed as a BBC television series, which he co-wrote (1993). It dramatizes a conflict between traditional Asian values and a generation shaped by the youth culture of the 1970s. His recent film, *My Son, the Fanatic* (1998), based on a story in his collection *Love in a Blue Time* (1997) reverses this situation: set in Bradford it describes the conflict between a Pakistani taxi-driver who willingly transports prostitutes and his son, who is turning to Islamic fundamentalism. Kureishi's other novels include *The Black Album* (1995), in which the protagonist is a young Muslim torn between a range of conflicting cultural forces, *Intimacy* (1998), a story of the failure of a close relationship, in which the protagonist leaves his long-term partner and family, and *Gabriel's Gift* (2001), a coming-of-age novel about an adolescent, beginning to make sense of his troubled family situation though his capacity to paint and draw.

Kureishi's published plays include *Borderline* (1981), *Birds of Passage* (1983), *The King and Me and Tomorrow-Today!* (1983), *Outskirts and Other Plays* (1992) and *Sleep with Me* (1999). With Jon Savage, he co-edited *The Faber Book of Pop* (1995).

Further reading

Moore-Gilbert (2001).

Kuti, Fela Anikulapo (1938–97). Nigerian singer, bandleader and politician, who played keyboards, saxophone and trumpet. Born into a prominent Yoruba family, Kuti studied music in London and on his return to Nigeria in the early 1960s evolved the HYBRID music style known as AFROBEAT. In 1969 he moved to Los Angeles, where he became involved with black consciousness activists and released 'Keep Nigeria One', a single about the NIGERIAN CIVIL WAR. He returned to Lagos and during the 1970s his reputation soared and he became one of Africa's best-loved and most controversial musicians. He established the Kalakatua Republic, a commune which housed his band and an extended family that included some 27 wives, married in the same ceremony in 1978; and his performances were known for their sexually explicit, trance-like gyrations. At the same time, his music attacked a range of social abuses and its uncompromising criticism of political corruption brought him into conflict with the Nigerian establishment, who raided his commune on more than one occasion. In 1979, he founded his own political party, the MOP (Movement of the People) and stood for election as a presidential candidate. After the reinstitution of military government in 1983, he was imprisoned for an alleged currency smuggling offence. He died of an AIDS-related illness. Kuti's best-known songs include 'Zombie', 'Coffin for Head of State', 'Sorrow, Tears and Blood' and 'International Thief Thief'.

Kyk-over-al Pioneering Guyanese little magazine of the late colonial era that provided a forum for publication of most of the country's leading writers and artists of the period. As such, it served a similar function to Trinidad's earlier BEACON and Barbados's *BIM*. Launched in 1945, it was edited by the poet, A. J. Seymour and continued publication until 1961, subsequently being revived in the 1980s under the joint editorship of Seymour and Ian McDonald, since when it has been published intermittently. Its fiftieth anniversary issue (1995) included pieces reprinted from the first issue and articles on the journal's history. Wilson HARRIS, Martin Carter, Edgar Mittelholzer and Jan Carew, as well as Seymour himself, were among the writers published in *Kyk-over-al*. The magazine followed an eclectic publication policy, taking its name, which means 'Look everywhere', from a Dutch fort on a small island at the confluence of Guyana's Mazaruni and Cuyuni rivers.

L

La Guma, Alex (1925–85). Coloured South African novelist, short story writer and political activist, who went into exile in Britain in 1966, after he and his wife had been placed under house arrest and subsequently imprisoned in solitary confinement by the South African authorities. A long-time member of the Communist party, La Guma subsequently moved to Cuba, where he acted as the ANC (q.v.) representative. His fiction is notable for its unsensational depiction of South African urban life during the APARTHEID era. The novella *A Walk in the Night* (1962), which was published together with six of his short stories, takes a night in the life of four coloured South Africans as a focus for providing a picture of life in a Cape Town slum. *And a Threefold Cord* (1964) chronicles the sense of resignation engendered by living in a shantytown. The metonymic dimensions of his work become more obvious in *The Stone Country* (1967), in which a prison serves as a microcosm of the country itself. His most auto-biographical novel, *In the Fog of the Seasons' End* (1972), is an account of the lives of political activists engaged in the struggle against Apartheid, which takes a more radical position than that of his earlier fiction, in suggesting that guerrilla warfare is needed to topple the regime. *Time of the Butcherbird* (1979) deals with the tragedy of a community displaced to live in a tribal homeland. La Guma's other work includes the travel book, *A Soviet Journey* (1978) and a biography of his father, *Jimmy La Guma* (1997).

Further reading

Yousaf (2001).

Lamming, George   Born 1927. Barbadian novelist. Lamming's first novel, *In the Castle of My Skin* (1953), established him as one of the finest Caribbean writers of his generation. Sometimes compared with Richard Wright's autobiographical *Black Boy* (1945), it is on one level a coming-of-age story, in which the young protagonist experiences a gathering sense of loss. It is also an elegiac account of a village's growth into awareness in the late colonial period, as its hitherto feudal loyalty to its English land-lord is transferred to the figure of a local political leader, whose activities bring about the break-up of the community. Written in a POLYPHONIC style that often employs poetic prose and lacks obvious narrative momentum, the novel's technique anticipates that of much of Lamming's subsequent fiction. It was followed by *The Emigrants* (1954), an account of Caribbean migration to Britain, in which the characters form a bond of unity, suggestive of the West Indian FEDERATION, on board ship to England. However, this collapses amid disillusionment, after their arrival in the 'Mother Country' that has shaped their colonial sense of being defined through alterity.

The struggle against being regarded as OTHER is continued in *Of Age and Innocence* (1958), where the protagonists, who include a black artist returning to the Caribbean and a white Englishwoman trying to come to terms with her lesbianism, seek to elude being viewed solely through the prisms of delimiting stereotypes. *Season of Adventure* (1960) focuses on a middle-class Caribbean woman's initiation into an awareness of the African aspects of her personality, when she attends the VODUN-like Afro-Caribbean rite of the Ceremony of Souls, a central trope for the rediscovery of sub-merged African elements in the Caribbean psyche, which Lamming also employs in his non-fiction work, *The Pleasures of Exile* (1960) and his novel, *Water with Berries* (1971). *The Pleasures of Exile* discusses both the exile of Caribbean migrants in Britain and the pervasive sense of existential exile created by colonialism. Following Octave MANNONI, it uses the stereotypes of Shakespeare's TEMPEST as a context for exploring the relationship between colonizer and colonized. However, it goes beyond the obvious opposition between PROSPERO AND CALIBAN to incorporate complex discussion of the roles of Miranda and Ariel in colonial and post-colonial situations. *The Tempest* is also an important intertext in *Water with Berries*, a probing dramatization of a post-colonial psychology of violence that prompts a brutal response to the colonial violence that has provoked it. The novel redeploys the *Tempest* motifs in a fluid and wide-ranging variety of ways to unsettle conventionally held binary assumptions about both 'race' and gender. Set on a seventeenth-century slave ship, *Natives of My Person* (1972) is a complex allegory about colonial guilt, which suggests the possibility of redemption in the New World, personified by women who have been victims of the ship's male crew in the past. Despite its historical setting, it is Lamming's most forward-looking novel, holding out the promise of a post-colonial future in which violence and exploitation may be transcended.

Further reading

Paquet (1982).

Laye, Camara   (*né* Laye Camara) (1928–80). Guinean novelist, who was one of the pioneers of FRANCOPHONE African fiction. The novel which established Laye's fame in both France and his African homeland, *L'Enfant noir* (1953; *The African Child*, 1954) is based on his own upbringing in a village in upper Guinea and the country's capital, Conakry. Its understated account of a boy's discovery of the community and traditions in which he is growing up has a clarity and directness that make it a classic of the literature of childhood. It was followed by a second highly acclaimed novel, *Le Regard du roi* (1954; *The Radiance of the King*, 1956), written in a completely different style, which has been described as Kafkaesque. *Le Regard du roi* is a study of white alienation in Africa, a Conradian INTERIOR JOURNEY, in which a European is gradually divested of his cultural assumptions, finally arriving at a moment of self-discovery, which, as in Wilson HARRIS's *Palace of the Peacock* (1960), suggests the positive potential of the continental heartland. *L'Enfant noir* ends with its protagonist leaving for Paris, where Laye himself studied engineering and worked in Les Halles and a car factory between 1949 and 1956. In the sequel, *Dramous* (1966; *A Dream of Africa*, 1968), he returns to an Africa in which corruption is rife, and the gentle, seemingly apolitical tone of the earlier novel is replaced by a more astringent and disillusioned narrative voice. Laye also published *Le Maître de la parole* (1978; *The Guardian of the Word*, 1980), a rendition of a GRIOT's narration of the thirteenth-century Mali epic, *Sundiata*, but his reputation mainly rests on his first two novels.

Lee Kuan Yew   Born 1923. Singaporean politician, generally seen as the architect of the nation's economic transformation in the post-independence period. The son of wealthy Straits Chinese parents, he was educated at Raffles College in Singapore and Cambridge University, where he obtained a double first, subsequently being called to the Bar in England in 1950. Back in Singapore, he established a reputation as a crusading barrister, fighting for labour rights and anti-racist causes. He founded the progressive PAP (People's Action Party) and became Prime Minister, when the party was elected to power in 1959. In 1963 he took Singapore into the Malaysian Federation, which it left in 1965. He became the first Prime Minister of the independent republic of Singapore in 1965. His economic policies, which encouraged private enterprise and foreign investment, brought about Singapore's metamorphosis into one of Asia's wealthiest nations, with its citizens enjoying the benefits of a standard of living and social services that compare favourably with many Western economies, but his early populism gave way to a more authoritarian style of government. His emphasis on political probity and circumspect public behaviour and his discouragement of alternative political viewpoints led his detractors to see him as the creator of a brave new world, in which individual liberties were sacrificed to his perception of the common economic good. He relinquished the role of Prime Minister in 1990 and assumed that of Senior Minister.

Further reading

Barr (2000).

The Legend of the Nineties   A construction of Australian identity, also known as the Australian Legend, which in the 1890s, developed from a complex of notions about the nation's identity that some commentators (e.g. Ward 1958) have argued had been evolving among its ANGLO-CELTIC population during the second half of the nineteenth century. Opinion has, however, been divided on the issue of whether the Legend emerged from Australian bush workers or whether it developed from transplanted European pastoral notions (Lansbury 1970). It mainly took shape as part of a NATIONALIST endeavour to define what was perceived as unique in the Australian character and experience in contradistinction to Britishness. Its central tenets included egalitarianism, 'mateship', anti-authoritarianism and stoicism in adversity, values that were particularly expounded in the Sydney *Bulletin*, whose slogan 'Australia for Australians' encapsulated its radical nationalist thrust. Though most Australians were already living in the country's urban coastal regions, the Legend identified the bush as the 'real' Australia, viewing it as a hostile environment that could be managed through the male bonding of mateship in much the same way as American popular mythologies of the period saw the Frontier, and the primarily male Western ethic associated with it, as the key site in which American identities were being created.

The two writers most associated with the promulgation of the Legend of the Nineties were A. B. ('Banjo') Paterson (1864–1941) and Henry Lawson (1867–1922), both of whom occupied a particular place in the Australian imagination for several decades. Paterson's contribution particularly took the form of collecting existing bush ballads and writing his own ballads, which celebrated male camaraderie and the outdoor life. His best-known poems include 'The Man from Snowy River', 'Clancy of the Overflow' and 'The Road to Gundagai'. He also wrote Australia's national song, 'Waltzing Matilda'. Lawson's contribution to the Legend is more difficult to summarize, since his representation of the bush is altogether less positive and even in his best-known sketches, such as 'The Drover's Wife', 'The Bush Undertaker' and 'The Union Buries Its Dead', which have frequently been seen as cornerstones of the Legend, he displays an AMBIVALENCE about its ethos, while still continuing to see it as the crucible in which a new Australian identity is to be forged. Other notable contributions to the Legend include those of the writers Joseph Furphy and Bernard O'Dowd. Women writers of the period, such as Barbara Baynton, are even more ambivalent than Lawson in their response to the Legend's androcentric aspects. Thus Baynton's representation of the plight of the bushwoman in her story 'The Chosen Vessel' makes Lawson's disturbing picture in 'The Drover's Wife' seem positively comfortable, while Franklin's *My Brilliant Career* (1901) is torn between FILIAL respect for her male precursors and a feminist impulse that sits awkwardly with their version of Australian nationalism.

The Legend was revivified in the 1950s by works such as Vance Palmer's *The Legend of the Nineties* (1954) and Russel Ward's *The Australian Legend* (1958), but changes in the demographic composition of the country made it harder to sustain its version of Australian national identity. In the late 1960s and 1970s, revisionist accounts of Australian cultural history disputed both its patriarchal and Anglo-Celtic biases, which had produced an ESSENTIALIST account of Australian identity that ignored or discriminated against women, ABORIGINAL Australians and members of other ethnic groups, such as the Chinese who had migrated to the Victorian goldfields in the mid-nineteenth century. Southern European and Asian migration into Australia in the post-World War II period made the Legend's version of Australianness seem increasingly outmoded and several social historians suggested that it had *always* distorted or obscured fundamental aspects of the nation's social life, drawing attention to the overt racism and sexism of some of the early *Bulletin* articles that had played an important role in its shaping. Contemporary accounts of Australian identity and MULTICULTURAL public policy initiatives have recognized the PLURAL, HYBRID nature of the society and more recent versions of Australianness have also turned away from the earlier identification of the bush as the seminal Australian site. Thus a writer such as Robert Drewe, in his short story collection *The Bodysurfers* (1983), ironically sees the beach not the bush as the definitive Australian locus, a place where males experiencing a mid-life crisis (arguably suggestive of the identity crisis experienced by proponents of the Legend) unavailingly seek fulfilment.

Further reading

Palmer, V. (1954); Ward (1958); Lansbury (1970); Serle (1973); White, R. (1981); Senn and Capone (eds) (1992); Bennett and Strauss (eds) (1998).

Limbo   A Caribbean dance-form, in which the dancer has to move his or her body under a bar, which it is gradually lowered. Today it is often regarded as little more than a tourist attraction, but writers such as Wilson HARRIS and (Edward) Kamau BRATHWAITE have linked it with the MIDDLE PASSAGE, where it is said to have evolved as a response to the cramped conditions in which the enslaved Africans were kept. Brathwaite's poem 'Caliban' in *Islands* (1969), the third part of his *Arrivants* trilogy, plays on the various connotations of the word, suggesting the possibility of reclaiming a transformed version of African experience. Harris take a broader cross-cultural view of the regenerative potential of what he calls 'the limbo gateway' in his essay 'History, Fable and Myth in the Caribbean and Guianas', identifying it with the possibilities afforded by the ANANCY syndrome (Harris 1999: 152–66).

The medieval Christian use of 'limbo', to refer to the region on the edge of Hell inhabited by those born before Christ whose righteous lives hold out the promise of salvation at the Second Coming, is ostensibly quite different. However, writers such as Brathwaite play on this meaning to suggest the LIMINAL psychological environment inhabited by the dispossessed Africans of the Atlantic slave trade and their descendants, a threshold or BORDER space that offers the possibility of reversing the legacy of colonialism.

Further reading

Harris (1999).

Liminality, liminal   Term derived from the Latin *limen*, or threshold. Liminal space is the 'in-between' location of cultural action, in which according to various cultural theorists, anthropologists and psychologists meaning is produced. It has particular importance in post-colonial theory, since it identifies the interstitial environment in which cultural transformation can take place and Homi K. Bhabha in particular has stressed the importance of BORDER locations as the threshold environment, where subjectivity finds itself poised between sameness and 'alterity' (see 'OTHERNESS') and new discursive forms are constituted. Ashcroft *et al.*, who provide a useful discussion of liminality in *Key Concepts in Post-Colonial Studies* (1998), refer to it as the 'space in which cultural change *may* occur' (ibid.: 130; my italics), but arguably such change potentially occurs in any form of social or discursive transaction and so in this sense Bhabha's post-colonial theorizing relates to signifying practices more generally, an instance of the way in which post-colonial theory has moved from the margins to unsettle the monocultural assumptions of what was hitherto considered to be the centre.

While Bhabha's theory focuses on signifying practices rather than actual in-between spaces, liminal discourses can be related to a range of physical sites including several which have had particular importance in the post-colonial experience. These include geographical borders, market-places, seashores, ocean crossings, littorals and various other kinds of thresholds, such as those experienced in rites of passage, the context in which the anthropologist Arnold van Gennep, whose work inspired the term's use in a range of other contexts, including art forms such as surrealism, applied it.

In surrealist thinking, the liminal has been seen as the threshold stage between waking and dream, or the conscious and subliminal states of awareness. Van Gennep viewed the liminal or threshold stage as the second phase of a three-fold rite of passage, with separation preceding and reaggregation following it. His thinking was developed by Victor Turner, who identified four phases in such social dramas – breach, crisis, redressive action and reintegration – and identified the second, crisis stage with liminality. Applied to colonial and post-colonial situations, such thinking identifies the colonial experience as a 'crisis' phase and locates (post-)colonial subjectivity, forced to accommodate conflicting value-systems, as an AMBIVALENT predicament that offers the potential for redressive action, though whether complete 'reintegration' is a possibility remains questionable if one follows the kind of approach that Bhabha adopts.

Ultimately, all cultural production can be seen to occur in a liminal environment, since it emerges from the interaction between the individual text and the intertexts to which it responds. Nevertheless the concept of liminality has particular resonance in post-colonial situations, where cross-cultural lines of influence very obviously disturb the possibility of an unquestioned FILIAL approach to tradition. Putting this another way, while all forms of cultural interaction involve cross-fertilization, the post-colonial experience is at the cutting edge of HYBRID encounters. See also BORDER AESTHETICS, CONTACT ZONE and PARTITION.

Further reading

Van Gennep (1960); Turner (1967); Bhabha (1994).

Lingua franca   See GLOBAL ENGLISH.

Literary and cultural journals   The numerous journals that have contributed to the development of post-colonial literary and cultural studies fall into two main categories: those that were founded around the time when ACLALS was first promoting the study of COMMONWEALTH LITERATURE and those that originated as a consequence of the growth of interest in *post-colonial* issues. The former have tended to place their primary emphasis on readings of particular texts; the latter on the theorization of the subject and its relocation as part of the broader field of post-colonial studies. The former include *ARIEL*, COMMONWEALTH ESSAYS AND STUDIES, *The* JOURNAL OF COMMONWEALTH LITERATURE, KUNAPIPI, NEW LITERATURES REVIEW, *SPAN*, WASAFIRI, WORLD LITERATURE TODAY and WORLD LITERATURE WRITTEN IN ENGLISH (*WLWE*). The latter include INTERVENTIONS, POSTCOLONIAL STUDIES, SOCIAL TEXT and THIRD TEXT, some of which are primarily sociological in orientation, but remain invaluable for the study of post-colonial writing. For further information, see the particular entries on these journals. Periodicals concerned with particular literatures and cultures, to which entries are also devoted, include AFRICAN LITERATURE TODAY, *BIM*, CARIBBEAN QUARTERLY, JAMAICA JOURNAL, JOURNAL OF WEST INDIAN LITERATURE, KYK-OVER-AL, *The* LITERARY CRITERION, *The* LITERARY HALF-YEARLY, LITTCRIT, OKIKE and RESEARCH IN AFRICAN LITERATURES. Journals covering broader areas of interest include BLACK ORPHEUS, *MELUS* and STAFFRIDER.

The Literary Criterion   Journal founded by C. D. Narasimhaiah and published from his Dhvanyaloka Centre in Mysore since 1952. The journal has published material on a broad range of Commonwealth writing, as well as more specifically Indian material. Narasimhaiah provides an account of its inception in his autobiography, *N for Nobody* (1991).

Further reading

Narasimhaiah (1991).

The Literary Half-Yearly   Like the LITERARY CRITERION, a Mysore-published literary journal. It was founded in 1960 and has been edited by H. Anniah Gowda.

Littcrit   A half-yearly journal 'reflecting Indian responses to literature', edited by P. K. Rajan of Kannur University from Thiruvananthapuram in Kerala, India.

Liyong, Taban Lo See Taban Lo Liyong.

Location Homi K. Bhabha and others have seen the 'beyond' or interstitial space as the site where culture is located. Bhabha quotes Frantz Fanon's assertion that 'The architecture of this work is rooted in the temporal. Every human problem must be considered from the standpoint of time' (Bhabha 1994: xiv) as one of the epigraphs to *The Location of Culture* (1994), but his own approach argues that 'in the *fin de siècle*, we find ourselves in the moment of transit where space and time cross to produce complex figures of difference and identity, past and present, inside and outside, inclusion and exclusion' (ibid.: 1). This emphasis on the intersection of the spatial and temporal can be seen as a metonym for post-colonial discourse's contestation of HISTORIOGRAPHICAL models of culture and its replacement of such accounts by discourses which follow postmodern geographers such as Edward Soja in arguing for 'the reassertion of space in critical social theory' (Soja 1989: sub-title). Soja says that the 'nineteenth-century obsession with history . . . did not die in the *fin de siècle*', 1989: 10) and quotes Michel Foucault's comment that '[s]pace was treated as the dead, the fixed, the undialectical, the immobile. Time on the other hand was richness, fecundity, life, dialectic' (Foucault 1980: 70; quoted in Soja 1989: 10). The 'reassertion of space' is ubiquitous, either explicitly or implicitly, in post-colonial writing, which characteristically disputes FILIATIVE models of tradition. It can be seen, for example, in Derek Walcott's attempt, in *Omeros* (1990), 'to produce a Caribbean equivalent of [Homer's] epics while trying to resist the complicity implicit in entering into a discursive relationship with them, an endeavour to assert a parallel spatial collocation rather than a linear temporal debt' (Thieme 1999: 154).

Further reading

Foucault (1980); Soja (1989); Bhabha (1994); Massey (1994); Thieme (1997 and 1999).

L'Ouverture, Toussaint See Toussaint L'Ouverture.

Lovelace, Earl Born 1935. Trinidadian writer, who spent his early years in Tobago. He has worked as a proof-reader, journalist and field assistant in Trinidad's Departments of Forestry and Agriculture and taught at universities in the United States. Lovelace's fiction is notable for its use of Carnival and related folk forms, its free-flowing prose and deceptively loose structures, which place their emphasis on communities rather than individuals. His first major novel, *The Dragon Can't Dance* (1979), was preceded by *While Gods Are Falling* (1966) and *The Schoolmaster* (1968). *The Dragon Can't Dance* dramatizes the importance of the island's Carnival culture in the lives of a group of urban Trinidadians, debating whether 'playing mas' (masquerading) can offer genuine release from their situation of deprivation or whether it simply provides licensed escapism and whether their refrain, 'all ah we is one' reflects a genuine sense of community. It is particularly notable for its portrayal of the ways in which its varied characters live their Carnival roles, which include those of dragon, badjohn (a character who poses as a threatening bully), calypsonian and queen, throughout the year and its representation of the contribution of Afro-Caribbean codes of manhood in sustaining a sense of personal worth. Unlike V. S. NAIPAUL's exposure of male codes in *Miguel Street* (1959), *The Dragon Can't Dance* moves between suggesting their limitations and, particularly though the character of the 'dragon', Aldrick, their part in instilling a genuine sense of dignity, which has its origins in notions of African warriorhood.

The Wine of Astonishment (1982) is one of the finest Caribbean novels to be written in CREOLE. Narrated by an ordinary countrywoman, it describes the banning, during the colonial period, of Trinidad's Spiritual Baptist church, a rallying point for the folk culture and a repository of SYNCRETIZED African values in the New World. It also depicts the gradual alienation of two natural leaders of the rural community: a champion stickfighter becomes embittered as he sees the cultural norms that have made him a heroic figure eroded by the forces of modernity; the most educated boy in the village becomes a politician, who only remembers his origins at election time. *Salt* (1996), which won the 1997 COMMONWEALTH WRITERS PRIZE, returns to the subject-matter of *The Dragon Can't Dance*, the struggle of individuals to attain 'selfhood' in a society that has denied their humanity. Its main focus is on two characters: a schoolmaster-turned 'madman'-turned politician and a carnivalesque storyteller, who refuses to surrender to the colonial condition of 'unfreedom'. At first sight, these two figures seem markedly different, but as the novel progresses it becomes clear that they complement one another as representatives of a people's culture which challenges the NATIONALIST politics that dominated Trinidad in the period before and after Independence in 1962. As in *The Dragon Can't Dance*, most of the novel's characters are Afro-Caribbean, but *Salt* promotes an inter-racial vision, which brings together the diverse strands of the island's population, including members of the French Creole and Indo-Caribbean communities. Lovelace's other works include *Jestina's Calypso and Other Plays* (1984), *A Brief Conversion and Other Stories* (1988) and a dramatized version of *The Dragon Can't Dance* (1989).

Lumumba, Patrice   (1925–61). Congolese political leader during one of the most turbulent periods in the country's history. Lumumba was a mission-educated radical nationalist, who was influenced by the ideas of the French Enlightenment and who emphasized the need to overcome tribal divisions in order to oppose colonial rule. He founded the Mouvement National Congolais (MNC; Congolese Nationalist Movement) and made a famous speech demanding Congolese independence and calling for African unity at the first All African People's Congress at Accra in Ghana in 1958. After riots at home, he was imprisoned by the Belgian colonial authorities, but was subsequently elected as Prime Minister of the Congo Republic (later Zaïre and now the Democratic Republic of the Congo), when it attained independence in 1960. An army mutiny and the secession of the mineral-rich province of Katanga under Moise Tshombe led to the return of Belgian troops and Lumumba's seeking support from a United Nations peacekeeping force. After little more than two months as Prime Minister, he was deposed by President Joseph Kasavubu and arrested by Colonel Joseph Mobutu (Mobutu Sese Seko Kuku Ngbendu Wa Za Banga), who was later to become President of Zaire. Lumumba escaped, but was recaptured and was assassinated while in detention in January 1961. His death attracted world attention and Mobutu subsequently declared him a 'national hero'. He is remembered as a founding figure in the movement for African unity and controversy as to who was responsible for his killing has raged for 40 years.

The Ugandan poet, Okot p'Bitek's *Two Songs* (1971) is dedicated to Lumumba. Jean-Paul Sartre's essay on Lumumba's 'political thought' is included in *Colonialism and Neocolonialism* (1964; trans. 2001: 156–200).

Further reading

Sartre (2001).

Lusophone Portuguese-speaking. Derived from 'Lusitania', the Latin name for Portugal. Major Lusophone areas include Brazil, Angola and Mozambique. See also Francophone, Anglophone, Hispanophone.

The Mabo Case A landmark case in the campaign to secure Aboriginal land rights in Australia. Eddie (Koiki) Mabo (1940–92) was a Torres Strait Islander who mounted a legal challenge to the notion of *terra nullius*. In 1982, along with four other people from Mer (Murray Island), he instituted legal proceedings against the Queensland government to secure Meriam ownership of their ancestral island. After a 10-year struggle the High Court of Australia ruled in their favour. For Mabo himself it was a posthumous victory, since he had died five months before, but the case established the principle of Native title.

Macaulay's Minute Thomas Babington Macaulay's influential Minute on Indian Education, presented to the Supreme Council of India in 1835, effectively established English as the official language of Indian education and administration. Macaulay's declared purpose was to create a class that would act as interpreters between the British and the Indian masses and he took the view that this class should be 'Indian in blood and colour, but English in taste, in opinions, in morals, and in intellect'. Prior to 1835, Persian had been the language of Indian diplomacy, while Hindi-Urdu and Sanskrit also acted as link-languages. Subsequently, English became the main medium for education, the law courts and other administrative purposes. It retained this function until just after Indian Independence, when the Constitution established Hindi and English as the two national languages of the country.

Macaulay (1800–59) was a leading British historian and politician, who served as legal adviser to the Supreme Council of India from 1834 to 1838. In addition to his influence on Indian education and language policy, he also played an important role in the drafting of a Westernized penal code.

McKay, Claude   (1890–1948). Jamaican-born poet, novelist and political activist. Born in Jamaica's Clarendon parish, McKay left the island in 1912 and settled in the USA, where he became a prominent figure in the Harlem Renaissance of the 1920s and 1930s. He had been encouraged to write verse by the English folklorist Walter Jekyll and in the year he left Jamaica published two collections of poems, *Songs of Jamaica* (1912) and *Constab Ballads* (1912), notable for their use of Creole (which he himself termed 'dialect') and their intense feeling for the local landscape. In America, McKay briefly studied agronomy at the Tuskegee Institute in Alabama, where he first experienced the blatant American racism, which much of his writing would attack. He subsequently moved to New York, finding Harlem a more congenial environment, and spent much of his later life in Europe and Africa.

In his best novel, *Banana Bottom* (1933), set in the Jamaica of his youth, McKay wrote about the return to Jamaica of a young woman, who has been sent to England for her education by a well-intentioned white missionary couple who have raised her. They see her as 'handiwork' that they have transformed from 'a brown wildling into a decorous cultivated young lady', a theme which evokes the real-life experience of the eighteenth-century Jamaican poet Francis Williams, who was sent to England by the Duke of Montague in an attempt to see whether nurture, not nature was the key factor in black socialization. The novel demonstrates the influence of D. H. Lawrence, a writer whom McKay greatly admired and, like the work of Trinidad's Beacon Group, depicts a middle-class encounter with Caribbean folk society.

McKay's only other Jamaican fiction is the short story collection, *Gingertown* (1932). His other poetry and prose includes the verse collections, *Spring in New Hampshire* (1920) and *Harlem Shadows* (1920), the best-selling novel *Home to Harlem* (1928) and *Banjo: A Story without a Plot* (1929), a novel set in Marseilles. His non-fiction includes the autobiographical *A Long Way From Home* (1937), which contains accounts of his encounters with American race prejudice and a period spent in Russia during a phase of his life when he was strongly influenced by Communism, and

Harlem: Negro Metropolis (1940). In *My Green Hills of Jamaica* (1979), a second volume of autobiography, compiled posthumously from drafts left behind at the time of his death, he reflects nostalgically on his early years.

McKay's poems have been collected in *Selected Poems* (1953). His most famous protest against American racism, the sonnet 'If We Must Die', is an assertion of black pride and resistance, said to have been written in response to a lynching, a subject he also treated his sonnet entitled 'The Lynching'. There is considerable tonal variety in both his poetry and prose, with the Jamaican works generally being more mellow in character than the American works, but some of his best American poems, such as the title-piece of *Harlem Shadows*, are gently lyrical, while others blend protest and lyricism to convey the AMBIVALENCE of his response to life in the USA. Thus, in an early poem entitled 'America' he speaks of his love for this 'cultured hell that tests my youth'. McKay's work was a significant influence on other African American writers of the Harlem Renaissance, including Langston Hughes and Countee Cullen, and the NEGRITUDE movement.

Magic realism   A term originally coined by the critic Franz Roh to describe the style of certain German painters of the 1920s, who depicted fantastic and imaginary subjects in a supposedly 'objective' manner, using clear-cut definition and precisely drawn imagery. The term was subsequently applied to similar work by American artists of the 1940s.

In literary contexts it has been particularly associated with the work of Latin American writers, whose portrayal of the everyday shows how it overlaps with the strange and miraculous. Notable among such writers are the Colombian novelist, Gabriel García MÁRQUEZ, whose *Cien años de soledad* (1967; *One Hundred Years of Solitude*, 1970) has often been seen as the quintessential magic realist novel, the Argentinian writer of gnomic short fictions, Jorge Luis Borges, and the American-based Chilean novelist, Isabel ALLENDE. The use of the term in relation to Latin American writers appears to derive from the Cuban Alejo CARPENTIER, who took the view that the realities of his society could only be expressed through 'lo real maravilloso', a discursive mode in which European divisions between the ordinary and the marvellous no longer exist. Carpentier was influenced by the surrealist movement, but turned away from the Freudian-inspired style of artists like Salvador Dali in favour of a mode that could express the marvellous reality of his own society, which in novels such as *Los pasos perdidos* (1953; *The Lost Steps*, 1956), he saw as a complex and layered formation, shaped by the intermingling of numerous influences and cultures. The term has also been applied to the style of European writers such as Günter Grass, Italo Calvino and Angela Carter and North American regional novels such as the Western Canadian writers Jack Hodgins's *The Invention of the World* (1977) and Robert Kroetsch's *What the Crow Said* (1978), which is clearly influenced by *One Hundred Years of Solitude*.

Magic realism informs the narrative practice of several post-colonial writers, among them Salman Rushdie, whose *Midnight's Children* (1981), a novel which blends a sharp critique of aspects of post-independence Indian political life with a plea for the potential of magical transformation represented by the children of its title, demonstrates a debt to both Márquez and Grass. The term has also been applied to the work of a broad and disparate range of other post-colonial writers, whose style and technique desert European realism for modes that are arguably better suited to the representation of non-Western societies. Among such writers are Amos Tutuola, Wilson Harris, Ben Okri and Pauline Melville. The Guyanese-born Harris sees such realism as closing down possibilities for 'freedom', and consequently argues for a more open form in which 'dialogue' or 'dialectic' replaces 'persuasion' (Harris 1967: 29). However, linking Harris with his South American contemporaries as a magic realist tends to be reductive, since his work is stylistically different in many ways. Elsewhere, too, the term has been used in connection with such a wide range of writers that it has lost much of its force. A writer such as Tutuola, whose reception in the West benefited from his being regarded as a 'naïve' portrayer of his society, seems to draw on the conventions of his own Yoruba culture, with little or no awareness of other fabulist traditions, while his fellow-Nigerian Ben Okri, who also employs Yoruba myth in his fiction, is part of a later writing community that is alert to the international appeal of magic realism.

Homi K. Bhabha takes the view that '"Magical realism", after the Latin American boom, became the literary language of the emergent postcolonial world' (Bhabha (ed.) 1990: 6). However, although magic realism has been the preferred mode of a considerable number of acclaimed extra-territorial post-colonial writers and has also been applied to the work of writers, such as Tutuola, who have 'stayed home', its exponents remain in a minority and many of their contemporaries write closer to the opposite end of a CONTINUUM that has fabulation and magic realism at one end and traditional, or classic, realism at the other. Aijaz Ahmad dismisses Bhabha's claim, bracketing it with Fredric Jameson's view that NATIONAL ALLEGORY 'is the unitary generic form for all Third World narrativities' as examples of 'metropolitan theory's inflationary rhetoric' (Ahmad 1992: 69).

Further reading

Harris (1967); Bhabha (ed.) (1990); Ahmad (1992); Zamora and Faris (eds) (1995).

The *Mahabharata*   Along with the Ramayana, one of the two great Sanskrit epics. the *Mahabharata* is a work of some 110,000 couplets in 18 books and is more than four times the length of the *Ramayana*, which itself is longer than either *The Iliad* or the Bible. The action of the *Mahabharata* centres on the war between two clans of cousins, the Pandavas and the Kauravas, for control of the region of Kurukshetra in North India. It was compiled more than two millennia ago, around 300 BC, and is sometimes said to be the longest poem ever written. Like many other ancient epics, it brings together much of the heroic literature of its period and includes numerous episodes, the most famous of which is the BHAGAVAD GITA, a dialogue in which the god Krishna addresses the warrior Arjuna on the eve of the central battle. *Mahabharata* means 'the great story of Bharat' (India), a title which has been reworked in Shashi Tharoor's satire on twentieth-century Indian politics, *The Great Indian Novel* (1989).

Unlike Western classical epics, such as the works of Homer and Virgil, the *Ramayana* and the *Mahabharata* remain a central part of the living traditions of India, functioning as popular entertainment, which is also revered for its spiritual dimension. Both have been made into highly popular multi-part television series and they continue to be staged in various dramatic forms throughout India and in various other South-East Asian countries, e.g. Java's *wayang kulit* puppet theatre takes its themes from the *Mahabharata*. Contemporary international awareness of the *Mahabharata* was enhanced by Peter Brook's 1985 nine-hour dramatized version of the epic, produced as part of his work with the International Centre for Theatre Research in Paris.

Mahapatra, Jayanta   Born 1928. Indian poet. Mahapatra was born in Cuttack, Orissa, where he has spent virtually his whole life, teaching physics at Ravenshaw College and editing the literary journal, *Chandrabhaga*. His poetry is strongly rooted in the Orissan landscape, its peoples and his own ancestry. Its emphasis on ways in which perception mediates experience appears to be informed by his training as a physicist. Mahapatra's volumes of poetry include *A Rain of Rites* (1976), *The False Start* (1980), *Life Signs* (1983), *Temple* (1989), *A Whiteness of Bone* (1992) and *Bare Face* (2000). His *Selected Poems* appeared in 1978.

Mahasweta Devi   Born 1926. Bengali novelist, short story writer and activist, born in Dhaka. Mahasweta and her family moved to West Bengal, where she attended college, gaining an MA at Calcutta University. Her life-long involvement in campaigns for social justice and the broadening of literary audiences dates from this period of her life, when she was a member of a theatre group that took political drama to villages in Bengal. Throughout her career Mahasweta has been a social activist, particularly campaigning for the advancement of tribal peoples and exploited rural workers. From 1964 to 1984, she taught at a Calcutta college. Her prolific output includes the novels *Jhansir Rani* (1956; *Queen of the Forest*), a fictional account of a nineteenth-century resistance leader, *Amrita Sanchay* (1964), *Andhanmalik* (1967), *Araneyar Adhikar* (1977; *Rights of the Forest*), based on the life of a tribal freedom fighter, and *Hazar Churashir Ma* (1974; *Mother of 1084*, 1997). She won the prestigious Magsaysay Award for journalism, literature and creative communication arts in 1997, with her work on behalf of tribals receiving particular mention in the citation. Mahasweta's work is mainly written in Bengali, but in recent years her short stories have attracted considerable international attention through translations by the Bengali-born theorist, Gayatri Chakravorty SPIVAK: in *Imaginary Maps: Three Stories* (1993) and *Breast Stories* (1997). Spivak's *In Other Worlds: Essays in Cultural Politics* (1988a) includes translations of Mahasweta's stories 'Draupadi' and 'Breast-Giver'. Other works translated into English include *Five Plays* (1986) and *Women, Outcastes, Peasants and Rebels* (1990).

Mahayana One of the two main forms of Buddhism, widely practised in China, Japan and Korea. Unlike the more conservative THERAVADA form of Buddhism it stresses the altruistic idealism of the Boddhisattva, who puts the salvation of others before personal enlightenment.

Mahfouz, Naguib Born 1911. Egyptian novelist and screenwriter, who became the first Arabic writer to be awarded the NOBEL PRIZE FOR LITERATURE in 1988. After studying philosophy at Cairo University, Mahfouz worked in the Egyptian civil service for more than 30 years. He published his first novel in 1939 and during the early phase of his career wrote historical works about ancient Egyptian society. In the mid-1940s he turned to contemporary subjects and subsequently came to be seen as the writer who established the novel form in Egypt, though he was not its originator. He is best known for *Al-Thulahiyya* (*The Cairo Trilogy*): *Bayn Al-Quasrayn* (1956; *Palace Walk*); *Quast Al-Shawq* (1957; *Palace of Desire*) and *Al-Sukkariyah* (1957; *Sugar Street*). The trilogy is a massive saga depicting the experiences of a group of families that reflect transformations in Egyptian social, political and religious life from the time of the First World War until Gamal Abdel NASSER's coup of 1952. Throughout his writing career, Mahfouz has been a trenchant critic of the successive regimes – from the British colonial era onwards – that have exploited ordinary Egyptians and it is only recently that his position as the elder statesman of Egyptian letters has been secured. His controversial novel, *Awlad Haratina* (1959; *Children of the Alley*), was banned throughout most of the Middle East, because of its allegedly blasphemous treatment of Islam.

Although he has been a 'part-time' writer for most of his career and he published no work in the seven years following the revolution of 1952, Mahfouz's output has been prolific. In addition to more than 40 works of fiction, he has written numerous film screenplays; and his achievement in covering a vast range of Egyptian social life has been compared with Honoré de Balzac's *Comédie humaine*. His other major fiction includes: the novels *Al-Liss Wa-Al-Kilab* (1961; *The Thief and the Dogs*), *Al-Summan Wa-Al-Kharif* (1962; *Autumn Quail*), *Al-Shahhadh* (1965; *The Beggar*), *Miramar* (1967), *Malhamat Al-Harafish* (1977; *The Harafish*) and *Layali Alf Laylah* (1982; *Arabian Nights and Days*); and the short story collection *Dunya Allah* (1963; *God's World*). The controversy that had surrounded Mahfouz's treatment of Islam in *Awlad Haratina* resurfaced, when, at the time of the FATWA proclaimed against him, Salman RUSHDIE cited Mahfouz's experience as an instance of the problems facing writers dealing with Islamic issues. Mahfouz responded by distancing himself from both the *fatwa* and Rushdie's treatment of Islam in *The Satanic Verses* (1988), while also arguing for freedom of speech. His status as a Nobel Laureate did not prevent a *fatwa* being proclaimed against him by the fundamentalist *Al-Jihad* group. He survived an attack in 1994, when he was stabbed in the throat.

Further reading

Gordon (1990); Le Gassick (ed.) (1991).

Mais, Roger   (1905–55). Jamaican writer and painter, whose highly individualistic work made an important contribution to the NATIONALIST phase of Jamaican culture in the 1940s and 1950s. Born in Kingston, he spent some of his formative years on plantations in the Blue Mountains area of Jamaica, an experience that informs his vivid representation of rural life in his novel, *Black Lightning* (1955). He is better known as a chronicler of city life. *The Hills Were Joyful Together* (1953) is a vivid picture of Kingston slum life, in the tradition of the Caribbean YARD NOVEL of the 1930s, but offering a more brutally realistic picture of social dispossession. It is also notable for shifting its focus from the middle-class perspective of most earlier Caribbean novels to a concentration on the workings of a community. *Brother Man* (1954), generally regarded as Mais's best novel, takes a prototype RASTAFARIAN figure as its protagonist. It sets his Christ-like persona against a backdrop of deprived urban social life and employs choric elements and a range of shifting viewpoints to explore relationships between individual and community. The rural landscape of *Black Lightning*, a fable about human individualism and the need for interdependency, is an elemental setting that represents a marked departure from the gritty urban realism of Mais's two previous novels.

Mais is also remembered for two famous articles. 'Now We Know', an attack on the new Constitution proposed for Jamaica in 1944, which (in contrast to the attitude of V. S. REID's *New Day*, 1949) he felt preserved the colonial status quo, led to his serving a six-month jail sentence. 'Why I Love and Leave Jamaica', written in 1952 just before his departure for Europe, where he lived for the next two years, expressed his disenchantment with the bourgeois values of the island's middle classes, whom he referred to as 'a moated-tower of mediocrity, close and unassailable'. *Listen the Wind* (1986) is a collection of his short stories. Mais's three novels were published together in 1966 with an Introduction by NORMAN MANLEY. He also wrote numerous plays, of which *George William Gordon* (written late 1940s; published 1976), a work about one of the leading figures in the MORANT BAY REBELLION, is the best known, at least two more unpublished novels and a body of poetry. His work as an artist included the illustrations for *Brother Man*. See also the FOCUS GROUP.

Further reading

D'Costa (1978).

Makeba, Miriam   Born 1932. South African singer. Born in a township outside Johannesburg, as a child she sang in both English and her native Xhosa and she later used the percussive sounds associated with her mother tongue in one of her most famous recordings, 'Qogothwane'/'Click Song' (US release, 1962). After singing with the close harmony Black Manhattan Brothers, she extended her repertory to include Africanized jazz forms. In 1959, she played the role of Joyce, a shebeen owner, in *King Kong*, a jazz opera about a black boxer, which was first performed in Johannesburg, but later transferred to London and New York. In 1960, she was banned from South Africa and spent the next thirty years in exile. She settled in the USA, where Harry Belafonte was influential in promoting her career and the 1967 American release of her hit single, 'Pata Pata', which she had originally written and recorded in 1956, made her an international celebrity.

Although she does not view herself as a politician, Makeba has been involved in various humanitarian causes, most notably the struggle against APARTHEID. Four of her relatives died at SHARPEVILLE and as early as 1958 she had starred in the anti-apartheid film, *Come Back Africa*. In 1968, she was made an honorary citizen of Guinea and she twice addressed the General Assembly of the United Nations on the evils of apartheid as a Guinean delegate. In 1986 she was awarded the Dag-Hammerskjöld Peace Prize. She performed with Paul Simon on his 1987–8 Graceland tour and with Odetta and Nina Simone on the 1990 One Nation tour. In 1999 she was appointed the United Nations FAO (Food and Agriculture Organization) Ambassador in Rome. Her eventful private life has included marriages to Hugh MASEKELA, with whom she left South Africa in 1959, and the American Black Power activist, Stokely Carmichael, with whom she later settled in Guinea, after this marriage had led to her losing favour with the American recording industry shortly after the success of 'Pata Pata'. Her albums include *Forbidden Games* (1962), *The Voice of Africa* (1962), *The World of Miriam Makeba* (1968), *Greatest Hits* (1979), *Sangoma* (1988) and *The Definitive Collection* (2002). Her autobiography *Makeba: My Story* was published in 1988.

The Man Booker Prize   See the BOOKER PRIZE.

Mandela, Nelson (Rolihlahla)   Born 1918. South African nationalist leader and one of the twentieth-century's most respected statesmen. Born in Transkei, Mandela was the son of a tribal chief. He was a pioneering lawyer, who established the first black legal practice in South Africa, before becoming an activist in the struggle against APARTHEID. He joined the ANC (AFRICAN NATIONAL CONGRESS) in 1944 and played a major role in orchestrating the Congress's campaign of defiance against racist state policy. Mandela advocated moderate non-violent resistance to state oppression, but when the ANC was banned in 1960, he became the leading force in the organization of a series of strikes. He was arrested and imprisoned for incitement in 1962 and in 1964, after a trial at which he made a memorable four-hour speech in his own defence, sentenced to life imprisonment for sabotage and treason. He spent the next quarter of a century in jail, initially in the notorious Robben Island prison. Throughout his imprisonment, he remained a powerful symbol of black South African resistance to apartheid and an international campaign to secure his release gained increasing momentum. His eventual release in 1990 was perhaps the single most important event in the process of dismantling apartheid. He assumed the leadership of the ANC, and engaged in talks with President F. W. de Klerk, leader of the ruling National Party, on the introduction of majority rule. The two men were jointly awarded the Nobel Peace Prize in 1993. In 1994, Mandela was elected President of South Africa in the country's first democratic elections, an office which he held until 1997, when he was succeeded by Thabo Mbeki. Throughout his imprisonment his wife, Winnie Mandela, campaigned vigorously for his release and herself became an important figure in the anti-apartheid struggle. However, after her husband's release she was found guilty of kidnapping and being an accessory to assault. The couple separated in 1992 and divorced in 1996. In 1998, Mandela married Graca Machel, widow of Samora Machel, former President of Mozambique. Mandela's autobiography, *Long Walk to Freedom* (1994), begun in 1974 during his imprisonment on Robben Island and completed after his release in 1990, is a moving and dignified account of his personal struggle, which offers insights into the social and political contexts that shaped his early life and an account of his time on Robben Island.

Further reading

Mandela (1994); Meredith (1997).

Manicheanism, Manichean allegory Originally a theological heresy, Manicheanism is a term that has been used by post-colonial theorists to suggest the dualism of European colonial ideology, particularly in contexts which construct binary oppositions between Europe and its racial OTHERS. Frantz FANON introduced the term into post-colonial discourse, arguing, in *The Wretched of the Earth* (1961; trans. 1963), that 'the colonial world is a Manichean world', in which 'the settler paints the native as a sort of quintessence of evil', and seeing this as a practice which dehumanizes the native by 'turn[ing] him into an animal' (Fanon 1968a: 41–2). Fanon had earlier discussed this practice in *Black Skin, White Masks* (1952). In 'What the Twilight Says', his 'Overture' to *Dream on Monkey Mountain and Other Plays* (1970), Derek WALCOTT follows Fanon in referring to his youthful fascination with 'the Manichean conflicts of Haiti's history' and the 'wrestling contradiction of being white in mind and black in body' (Walcott 1998: 10–11), a contradiction which he explores in several of his works, most prominently in the first of his plays about the HAITIAN REVOLUTION, *Henri Christophe* (1950), and his poetic autobiography *Another Life* (1973).

Abdul R. JanMohamed's work on African writing has popularized Fanon's use of the term. JanMohamed argues that Manichean allegory is a form of racial stereotyping which involves the construction of 'interchangeable oppositions between white and black, good and evil, superiority and inferiority, civilization and savagery, intelligence and emotion, rationality and sensuality, self and other, subject and object' (1986: 82). This kind of stereotyping is a discourse that reached its peak in the pseudo-scientific racial binaries of the late Victorian period, though it can be traced back to the 'origins' of Western philosophy. In Plato's *Phaedrus*, for example, the soul is likened to a chariot, pulled in opposite directions by a black and a white horse, which respectively represent compliance to rational instruction and sensual disobedience.

Whether 'Manicheanism' is the most appropriate term to describe such Western binarism is debatable, since to the early Christian Church Manicheanism was a heresy with Eastern origins. Orthodox Augustinian theology was monistic and regarded Manicheanism as heretical precisely because it posited the possibility of a dualistic universe in which Satan struggled against God for supremacy. The Augustinian position asserts that because God is omnipotent, evil is simply an absence, the privation of good; and, in so doing, denies the possible existence of moral alterity. Most post-colonial theorists and writers have, however, chosen to associate Manichean aesthetics with Western rather than Eastern (or other) systems of thought. Amitav GHOSH's novel *The Calcutta Chromosome* (1996) is a notable exception. Its critique of Western thought is more radical, since it views it as denying the very possibility of Manichean alterity, a perspective which accords with the orthodox Christian silencing of Eastern religious discourses.

Further reading

Fanon (1968a and 1968b); JanMohamed (1983 and 1986).

Manley, Edna   (1900–87). Jamaican sculptress and carver. Born in England of mixed Jamaican and English parentage, she played a crucial role in developing a local art consciousness in Jamaica, after marrying NORMAN MANLEY and settling in Jamaica in 1922. Her early Jamaican work was influenced by the work of abstract Modernists such as Constantin Brancusi and Henri Gaudier-Brzeska. Initially she mainly worked in wood and bronze, but from the late 1920s she also began to carve in stone. Depicting scenes from Jamaican life in sculptures and carvings such as 'The Beadseller' and 'Man with Bird', she infused her subjects with a serenity that has been seen as a representation of the stoical mood of some segments of the Jamaican populace at this time. However, carvings such as 'Market Women' and 'Diggers' embody a more assertive attitude to the predicament of ordinary Jamaican people. Her joint exhibition with the Armenian artist, Koren der Harootian in 1932 was the first of its kind to be held in Jamaica.

By the mid-1930s, Manley was turning her attention to more overtly social themes and works such as 'Negro Aroused', which in 1937 became the first modern work to be accepted into the Institute of Jamaica's art collection, can be seen as cultural equivalents of the growing mood of NATIONALISM that informed the political activities of her husband and his associates. She founded the Jamaican School of the Visual Arts (extended into the Edna Manley College of the Visual and Performing Arts in 1970) in the early 1940s and was the driving force behind the FOCUS GROUP, a loose affiliation of artists, which numbered the writers Roger MAIS and V. S. REID among its members. Her subsequent work was produced in the more public context of her role as a political leader and prime minister's wife, and often, but not always, served as a cultural counterpart of the progressive politics of the late colonial and post-independence eras. She continued sculpting and carving into her eighties and the work of her later years is notable for its representation of Jamaican women and religious themes. *Edna Manley: The Diaries* was published in 1989.

Further reading

Brown, W. (1975); Boxer (1985).

Manley, Michael (1924–97). Jamaican political leader, the son of NORMAN and EDNA MANLEY. After serving in the Canadian Air Force in World War II, he studied economics at the London School of Economics and pursued a career in journalism, before becoming more directly involved in politics. He played a central role in the development of Jamaica's trades union movement and became leader of the PNP (People's National Party) in 1969 and Prime Minister in 1972. During this period in office, he pursued socialist policies and received Cuban technical assistance to develop aspects of Jamaica's infrastructure. However, his association with Fidel CASTRO's regime led to the loss of support and funding from the USA and other Western powers and this brought about a decline in the Jamaican economy. Manley lost the general election of 1980, but was returned to power eight years later, pursuing more moderate free-market policies during his second term, which lasted until 1992.

His book *A Voice at the Workplace* (1975) analyses the effect of colonialism on the Jamaican worker and traces the development of the island's trades union movement, demonstrating the divisive nature of the structure of unionism in Jamaica and showing how the split into two major unions, the National Workers Union (NWU), founded by Norman Manley, and the Bustamante Industrial Trade Union (BITU), founded by his rival, Alexander Bustamante, shaped the extreme polarization of Jamaican politics, into progressive and conservative factions, more generally. He also published a number of other books, including *The Politics of Change: A Jamaican Testament* (1974) and *A History of West Indian Cricket* (1988).

Further reading

Manley (1975); Levi (1990); Panton (1993).

Manley, Norman (1893–1969). Jamaican statesman, who played a central role in the country's independence movement and was one of the founders of the PNP (People's National Party). He attended Jamaica College and won a Rhodes Scholarship to Oxford, where he studied law. On his return to Jamaica he pursued a distinguished career as a barrister and in 1932 became a King's Counsel. His involvement in politics began at a time of civil unrest in the late 1930s, when he became leader of the PNP. The party had little success in Jamaica's first election held under full adult suffrage in 1944, but was elected to power in 1955, with Manley as Chief Minister. In 1961 he held a referendum on whether Jamaica should remain within the West Indian FEDERATION, in which the public voted in favour of the country's seeking independence alone; and the following year he lost the election that would have made him the nation's first Prime Minister of the post-independence era.

In addition to his leading role in the independence movement, which had secured full internal self-government for Jamaica in 1959, Manley played a major part in developing social welfare programmes in Jamaica. He is one of the country's National Heroes and the island's international airport and other institutions are named after him. His wife, EDNA, was an important figure in the development of Jamaican culture in the middle decades of the century and his son, MICHAEL, succeeded him as leader of the PNP, becoming Prime Minister in 1972. V. S. REID's *New Day* (1949) contains a thinly-veiled portrait of Norman Manley in the figure of Garth Campbell, who reflects his gradualist approach to political change.

Mannoni, Octave (1899–1989). Corsican-born French psychologist, noted for his work on the psychology of DECOLONIZATION in Madagascar. *Psychologie de la colonisation* (1950; *Prospero and Caliban: The Psychology of Colonization*, 1956) examines the relationship between PROSPERO's inferiority complex and CALIBAN's dependence complex. See also George LAMMING.

Maori, Maori writing The 'original' inhabitants of AOTEAROA / New Zealand, who arrived in the country from Tahiti around the ninth century AD, nearly a thousand years before European settlement. Many Maori were dispossessed of their ancestral lands in the nineteenth century at the time of the TREATY OF WAITANGI. Today the Maori population numbers about 400,000, about a third of whom speak the Maori language. As with Australian ABORIGINALS, land rights issues have been central to the Maori campaign for social and political justice and in the 1990s the New Zealand government acknowledged the claims of two groups of dispossessed Maori by paying them compensation and returning disputed lands to their possession.

Prominent Maori writers include the poet Hone Tuwhare, Witi Ihimaera, whose *Tangi* (1973) was the first Maori novel to be published in English, and Patricia Grace, author of the novels *Potiki* (1986) and *Cousins* (1992). Written by a writer who is herself one-eighth Maori, Keri Hulme's BOOKER PRIZE-winning novel *The Bone People*

(1983), is a complex investigation of issues of New Zealand ancestry, which privileges the Maori genealogical line.

Mapping   See CARTOGRAPHY.

Marechera, Dambudzo   (1952–87). Zimbabwean novelist and short story writer. Educated at a mission boarding school, he later attended the Universities of Rhodesia and Oxford, but was expelled from both institutions: in the former case, after his involvement in a student protest; in the latter, after allegedly refusing to accept psychiatric treatment. His turbulent life came to an untimely end when, after a period of homelessness in Harare, he died of AIDS at the age of 35.

   Marechera's fiction is as tumultuously prodigal as his life appears to have been. It employs a battery of images, intertexts and sensational subjects in a uniquely powerful and imaginative surrealistic style. His iconoclasm made him an inspiration for a younger generation of Zimbabweans and other Africans seeking new forms to express the changing social circumstances of their post-colonial world. The title-piece of his best-known work, *The House of Hunger: A Novella and Short Stories* (1979), winner of the Guardian Fiction Award, depicts chaotic social conditions in a Zimbabwean township, which find a parallel in the protagonist's psyche. Marechera also wrote: the novel *Black Sunlight* (1980), which explores similar correspondences between social and psychic alienation; *Mindblast* (1984), which brings together three plays, a diary, poems and a prose narrative; and the posthumously published, *The Black Insider* (1990), another compendium of his fictional and poetic work, and *Cemetery of Mind* (1992), a collection of poems.

Further reading

Veit-Wild and Chennels (eds) (1999).

Margins and centre   See CENTRE AND MARGINS.

The Market Theatre   Johannesburg theatre, which achieved fame in the 1970s as a multi-racial venue, staging a broad cross-section of plays and particularly nurturing local theatrical work during the years of APARTHEID. The Market opened in 1976 – with a production of Chekhov's *The Seagull* – as the home of a company founded in 1974 by writer/director Barney Simon and producer Mannie Manim. It is a complex consisting of three theatres and two galleries, to which a theatre laboratory, directed by John KANI, has been added in recent years. During the apartheid years it was a self-financing organization, supported by private donations; more recently, it has received state funding. The Market has sometimes had its institutional positioning questioned (e.g. see Fuchs 2002) and certainly walked a tightrope during the late 1970s and 1980s, when its commitment to political theatre had to contend with the constrictions of state censorship. Despite this AMBIVALENCE, it played a major role in nurturing work that had an important impact on South African theatre at large, helping to foster the development of workshop productions that subsequently toured the townships. *Woza Albert!* (1981), a play about the Second Coming of Jesus Christ into apartheid-divided South Africa, is one of its best-known achievements. Developed at the Market by Barney Simon, and the actors Percy Mtwa and Mbongeni Ngema, it was subsequently a major success in both township performances and when it toured internationally. Simon's workshop production, *Born in the RSA* (1985) enjoyed similar success, both at home and abroad. Janet Suzman's 1987 production of OTHELLO, with John Kani in the title-role, was another notable landmark in the theatre's history. Other leading South African dramatists whose work has been premiered or showcased at the Market include Gibson Kente, Matsemela Manaka, Maishe Maponya, Zakes Mda, Paul Slabolepszy and Bartho Smit. Athol FUGARD plays performed at the Market included *A Lesson from Aloes* (1978), *Master Harold . . . and the Boys* (1982), *The Road to Mecca* (1984) and *Playland* (1993). Today the Market is a South African institution, though it has had to contend with the problem of a rising crime-rate that has deterred some theatre-goers from attending productions in its inner-city location.

Further reading

Blumberg and Walder (eds) (1999); Fuchs (2002).

Marley, Bob (Nesta Robert Marley; 1945–81). Jamaican singer-composer, who became the first REGGAE superstar. Of mixed-race parentage, Marley was born in the St Ann parish of Jamaica, but in 1957 he moved with his black mother to the Trenchtown area of Kingston, a ghetto which he would later immortalize in song. With 'Bunny' Livingston, Peter Tosh and Junior Brathwaite he formed the Wailing Wailers in 1960. Their first single, 'Judge Not' was recorded in 1962. Initially they imitated popular African American groups such as the Drifters, often adapting their musical styles into locally inflected SKA versions. The Wailers, as they became known, set up their own record label in 1967 and gradually developed a rawer musical style that responded to urban Jamaican social conditions and their recording 'Trenchtown Rock' enjoyed enormous popularity in Jamaica in 1971.

A move to the UK Island label, which produced their 1972 album *Catch a Fire*, propelled reggae into the international mainstream of pop music. However, Marley's work remained committed to a politics that had its roots in RASTAFARIANISM and his cult status subsequently did much to popularize and promote the movement's beliefs internationally. His increasing involvement in politics led to an attempt on his life during the Jamaican election campaign of 1976. He was wounded, but survived and continued working to heal the divisions in Jamaican political and social life, on one occasion bringing Prime Minister MICHAEL MANLEY and opposition leader (later Prime Minister) Edward Seaga together. By the time of his tragically young death from cancer in 1981, Marley was a living legend and he was given a state funeral. The songs for which he is best known include: 'Get Up, Stand Up' and 'I Shot the Sheriff' from his 1973 album *Burnin*'; 'No Woman, No Cry' from *Natty Dread* (1974); 'Jamming' from *Exodus* (1977) and 'Zimbabwe' from *Survival* (1979).

Further reading

White, T. (1998).

Maroons   Term, from the French 'marron', used to describe escaped slaves and their free descendants, particularly in Jamaica and other parts of the Caribbean. *Marronage* also occurred in other regions of the Americas and, in addition to being a social and historical reality, became a symbol for New World African freedom. Hispanic 'maroons' were known as 'cimarróns'.

Afro-Jamaicans runaway slaves established settlements in the interior of Jamaica during the first phase of the era of slavery. The earliest Maroons escaped from the Spanish in the seventeenth century. Subsequently, their settlements attracted further escapees – from the plantations established by the island's English colonizers. Maroon communities retained more (CREOLIZED) African practices and forms than mainstream Jamaican society and were organized along complex military lines. Under a 1739 treaty with the British, negotiated by their leader Kojo (Cudjoe), the Maroons living in western Jamaica were granted land and others rights. They enjoyed variable relationships with the English PLANTOCRACY, sometimes acting in concert with the colonial authorities, sometimes opposing them. Such AMBIVALENT interaction continued after EMANCIPATION. Thus, as depicted in V. S. REID's novel *New Day* (1949), they were allies of the colonial 'Redcoats' in their attempt to put down the 1865 MORANT BAY REBELLION.

Other creative works about Jamaican Maroons include Namba Roy's *Black Albino* (1961), a historical novel set in an eighteenth-century Maroon community, and Reid's *Nanny-Town* (1983), a novel about the eighteenth-century leader who led her people in the struggle against English rule. Milton McFarlane's *Cudjoe the Maroon* (1977; US title *Cudjoe of Jamaica*) is an account of Cudjoe and his sister, Nanny, by an American-based Jamaican Maroon, which draws on both the documentary record and oral history. It presents Cudjoe as a 'pioneer for black freedom in the New World', and, as such, a Jamaican forerunner of TOUSSAINT L'OUVERTURE. Olive SENIOR's *A-Z of Jamaican Heritage* contains a succinct summary of Jamaican Maroon history (Senior 1983: 103–5). Richard Price's *Maroon Societies: Rebel Slave Communities in the Americas* (1996) covers a broad range of New World Maroon communities.

Further reading

Senior (1983); Price (ed.) (1996).

Márquez, Gabriel García Born 1928. Colombian novelist, born in the tropical northern town of Aratacara. He studied in Bogotá and worked as a journalist, before leaving Colombia in 1955. He has subsequently lived in Venezuela, France, Mexico and Spain. Márquez was awarded the NOBEL PRIZE FOR LITERATURE in 1982 and his influence on world literature – including post-colonial writing seeking to find alternative modes of expression – has been very considerable. Sometimes wrongly credited with having founded MAGIC REALISM, Márquez is nevertheless its most famous exponent and his fiction conflates the mundane and the supernatural in ways that challenge his readers' conceptions of what constitutes normality. His early literary influences included Franz Kafka and William Faulkner, whose Yoknapatawpha County is said to have provided a literary inspiration for his own highly localized world of Macondo, a setting that provides a microcosm for investigating larger concerns, including the political 'realities' of Latin American society.

Márquez's early work includes the short story collections *La hojarasca* (1955; *Leaf Storm*, 1972) and *El coronel no tiene quien le escriba* (1961; *No One Writes to the Colonel*, 1971) and the novel *La mala hora* (1962; *In Evil Hour*, 1979). It culminated in his masterpiece, *Cien años de soledad* (1967; *One Hundred Years of Solitude*, 1970). The novel is set in the remote village of Macondo, a locale where the ordinary and the extraordinary intersect and the world is discovered anew by its inhabitants, who from the first paragraph find it 'so recent that many things lacked names'.

Márquez's later work includes: the novels *El otoño del patriarca* (1975; *The Autumn of the Patriarch* 1976), which depicts the ambiguities in the life of a corrupt dictator in his characteristically hyperbolic and sometimes humorous manner; *El amor en los tiempo de cólera* (1985; *Love in the Time of Cholera*, 1988) and *El general en su laberinto* (1989; *The General in his Labyrinth*, 1990), a fictional account of the last months in the life of Simon Bolívar, the South American revolutionary who dreamt of unifying the countries for whose liberation he had fought; the short story collection, *La increíble y triste historia de la candida Eréndira y de su abuela desamalada* (1972; *Innocent Eréndira*, 1978); and the novella *Crónica de una muerte anunciada* (1981; *Chronicle of a Death Foretold* 1982). *Vivir para contarla* (2002) is the first volume of a projected trilogy of autobiographical memoirs in which Márquez begins from the premise that the past is a creation of memory and takes the story of his early life – and the Columbian society in which he grew up – as far as the year 1957, when he first travelled abroad.

Further reading

Williams, R. (1984); Bell-Villada (1990); Bell-Villada (ed.) (2001).

Marson, Una (1905–65). Jamaican poet, dramatist, social activist and broadcaster. One of the most extraordinary Jamaican women of her generation, Marson made a distinctive contribution to Jamaican poetry in the years immediately before and during the NATIONALIST phase of the late colonial period, but is best remembered for her involvements in a broad range of egalitarian causes outside Jamaica. Born into a rural Jamaican environment, the daughter of a Baptist parson, she worked as a journalist and published two collections of poetry, *Tropic Reveries* (1930) and *Heights and Depths* (1931), prior to leaving for England in 1932. In Europe, her involvement in anti-racist and feminist causes brought her into contact with numerous famous figures, including Haile Selassie, Paul Robeson and Winifred Holtby. She was the founding editor of the BBC's CARIBBEAN VOICES programme, which was first broadcast in 1943, and throughout her life remained a tireless campaigner for social justice, creating many of the contexts in which she operated. Recent scholarship, particularly a detailed 1998 biography by Delia Jarrett-Macauley, has demonstrated the variety of her achievements in a male-dominated society and has paved the way for a re-evaluation of her writing.

Marson's other writing includes the poetry collections *The Moth and the Star* (1937) and *Towards the Stars* (1945) and her best work, the play *Pocomania*, which remained unpublished during her life-time. *Pocomania* anticipates the work of such later writers as Erna BRODBER in its investigation of the alternative spiritual possibilities afforded by KUMINA and its depiction of a NINE NIGHT ceremony, though it finally rejects revivalist practices in favour of a conclusion that reaffirms the values of the colonial society.

Further reading

Jarrett-Macauley (1998).

Masekela, Hugh Born 1939. South African jazz trumpeter and composer, whose work has fused jazz with popular African musical forms, such as AFROBEAT. Masekela became a trumpeter after being inspired by *Young Man with a Horn* (1950), a film about the life of Bix Beiderbecke, and during the first phase of his career was also influenced by other American jazz musicians, including Louis Armstrong and Count Basie. He left APARTHEID-divided South Africa after the SHARPEVILLE Massacre with his then-wife Miriam MAKEBA and his international career was furthered by John Dankworth and Cleo Laine in the UK and Harry Belafonte in the USA. His music has sometime been criticized for its mellow, middle-of-the-road style, but at its finest, in singles such as the best-selling 'Grazing in the Grass' (1968) and albums such as *Technobrush* (1984), it represents a highly distinctive fusion of Western jazz and African forms, such as the dance music *mbaqanga*. Masekela continued to play a part in the anti-apartheid struggle and his 1987 album *Tomorrow* included 'Bring Him Back Home', a plea for the release of Nelson MANDELA. Makeba apart, he has worked with several of Africa's leading musicians, including his fellow-countryman Abdullah Ibrahim and the Nigerian Fela Anikulapo KUTI. He appeared at the Monterey Pop Festival in 1967 and was part of Paul Simon's 1987–8 Graceland tour. More recent albums include *The Lasting Impressions of Ooga Booga* (1996) and *Sixty* (2000).

Mau Mau   A secret Gikuyu freedom organization, active in Kenya in the late colonial period, between 1952 and 1956. The term appears to have been a European coinage and certainly the movement was demonized in the Western media, where it was represented as a terrorist organization that drew its members from various tribes. Equally, its violent attempts to coerce Gikuyu non-participants into the movement lent some credence to such Western representation. Mau Mau administered oaths that committed its members to the struggle to expel white settlers from Kenya. The British declared a State of Emergency in 1953 and this was not lifted until 1960, by which time many Mau Mau leaders had been captured and executed. Kenya attained independence in 1963, when the NATIONALIST leader Jomo KENYATTA, who had been imprisoned during the insurgency, despite having denounced Mau Mau activities, became Prime Minister.

Western reaction to the supposed atrocities of Mau Mau are referred to in Derek WALCOTT's poem 'A Far Cry from Africa' (in *In a Green Night*, 1962) and V. S. REID's *The Leopard* (1958) was also partly written as a corrective to Western media misrepresentation. NGUGI wa Thiong'o's novels *A Grain of Wheat* (1967; revised edn. 1986) and *Petals of Blood* (1977) portray the Mau Mau struggle from the inside, placing as much emphasis on its injurious consequences, both physical and psychological, for the Kenyan villagers affected by its activities as on the iniquities of colonial rule.

Melting pot   Term used to describe the process, through which the various originary identities of the constituent communities of a nation, or social grouping, are ASSIMILATED to produce a supposedly unified cultural character that erodes traces of OTHER subjectivities. It is particularly used of the USA and contrasts with the Canadian model of the MOSAIC, in which a range of communal strands supposedly co-exist without being brought together in the New World crucible. Whether and, if so, how such discourses relate to the lived experiences of a nation's population is, of course, questionable, since perceptions vary and frequently bear little relationship to the national rhetoric. Equally, they play a part in shaping responses and in the case of the USA the ideal of the melting pot has helped to promote the belief in egalitarianism and democratic opportunity on which the American Dream has traditionally been based. It is a model of American cultural identity which held sway for most of the twentieth century, but which has begun to look increasingly dated in recent years.

The term 'melting pot' was popularized by an English Jewish author, Israel Zangwill, who used it, in the title of a 1908 play, to refer to the experience of migrating to America. It had previously been used by Ralph Waldo Emerson and St Jean de Crèvecœur, who had put forward the idea that individuals of different ethnicities 'melted' together to create a new American identity. German immigrants, appear to have used the term '*Schmelztiegel*' ('melting pot') from the mid-nineteenth century onwards.

MELUS Journal of the Society for the Study of the Multi-Ethnic Literature of the United States. First published in 1974, *MELUS* appears four times a year and publishes articles, interviews and reviews relating to multi-ethnic American literature, past and present. Currently based at the University of Connecticut, it is supported by the University of Massachusetts at Amherst.

Melville, Pauline Born 1948. British novelist and short story writer of part-Guyanese ancestry. After working as an actress for many years, Melville received instant recognition as a fiction writer with the publication of her collection of short stories, *Shape Shifter* (1990), which won a number of prizes including the Commonwealth Writers Prize Best First Book Award. It was followed by the novel, *The Ventriloquist's Tale* (1997), which won the Whitbread First Novel award, and a second collection of short stories, *The Migration of Ghosts* (1998). Melville's short stories move between Guyana and Britain, employing a polyphonic variety of techniques to consider issues of identity. Several are written in a magic realist mode that suggests the influence of novelists such as Gabriel García Márquez and Wilson Harris. Set in Guyana, *The Ventriloquist's Tale*, her most ambitious work to date, particularly considers the issue of cultural appropriation by outside commentators. Its main story is a tale of mythic incest, which draws on the anthropologist Claude Lévi-Strauss's work on Amerindian cultures. This is introduced by a 'ventriloquist' frame-narrator, who claims the shamanistic ability to assume any kind of voice, but the main tale is told in a primarily realistic mode, which lends plausibility to what might otherwise seem an incredible story.

Memmi, Albert Born 1920. Tunisian Jewish sociologist, novelist and commentator on the psychology of colonialism. He is best known for *Portrait du Colonisé précédé du Portrait du Colonisateur* (1957; *The Colonizer and the Colonized*, 1965), which like the work of Octave Mannoni and Frantz Fanon, has come to be regarded as a classic account of the psychological factors that shape colonial oppression. Written before the Algerian war of independence, it predicted the course and aftermath of that war. Memmi's other books include the novel, *Le Statue de sel* (1953; *Pillar of Salt*), a semi-autobiographical account of a boy coming of age in the Jewish quarter of Tunis who gradually sheds the various identities – Jewish, Arab and African – which he has inherited.

Mento A traditional form of Jamaican folk music, which uses a 2/4 rhythm. The term also refers to the words and the dance steps accompanying the music. Mento lyrics resemble those of Trinidadian calypso in that they treat topical subjects and are often humorous. Although mento's popularity declined with the advent of such forms as ska and reggae, it has exercised an influence on these forms.

Merchant Ivory   A film company noted for its art-house movies about India and cross-cultural themes. Formed by the American director, James Ivory (born 1928) and the Indian producer, Ismail Merchant (born 1936), most of its scripts have been written by the novelist Ruth Prawer JHABVALA, who adapted two of her own novels for Merchant Ivory productions: the Hindi-language film of *The Householder* (1963) and *Heat and Dust* (1983). Early Merchant Ivory films mainly treat Indian subjects. They include an adaptation of Geoffrey Kendall's *Shakespeare Wallah* (1965), the story of a travelling theatre company, in which the author's daughter, the actress Felicity Kendall, received her first major role. In addition to her adaptations, Jhabvala also wrote original screenplays for *The Guru* (1969) and *Bombay Talkie* (1970), in which Merchant Ivory ventured into the world of Indian popular entertainment and focused on then-fashionable East–West encounters for their themes. The lower-budget *Autobiography of a Princess* (1974) and *Hullabaloo over Georgie and Bonnie's Pictures* (1978) were subtler films dealing with the changing fortunes of upper-class Indians in the post-independence era.

As its reputation developed, the company increasingly turned its attention to adaptations of a broader range of classic and contemporary novels concerned with cultural interaction. These included versions of: Henry James's *The Europeans* (1979), *The Bostonians* (1984) and *The Golden Bowl* (2000); Jean RHYS's *Quartet* (1981); E. M. Forster's *A Room with a View* (1986), *Maurice* (1987) and *Howards End* (1992); and Kazuo Ishiguro's BOOKER PRIZE-winning Condition of England novel, *The Remains of the Day* (1993). Other notable Merchant Ivory films include: *Adventures of a Brown Man in Search of Civilisation* (1972), a documentary about the writer Nirad CHAUDHURI; *Helen, Queen of the Nautch Girls* (1973); the New York-set *Roseland* (1977) and *Jane Austen in Manhattan* (1980); *The Courtesans of Bombay* (1983); *Mr and Mrs Bridge* (1990); *Jefferson in Paris* (1995); *Surviving Picasso* (1996); and *Le Divorce* (2003).

Merchant Ivory have received numerous accolades and awards, including three Academy Awards for *A Room with a View*, a film that was nominated for eight in all, and have been particularly praised for their attention to period detail. However, some of their detractors have attacked their work for glossing over harsher social 'realities'. In many ways, these strengths and weaknesses go hand-in-hand. Thus, in a film such as *Heat and Dust*, the use of soft-focus photography has the effect of creating a visually compelling picture of India, past and present, but encourages a mood of Raj nostalgia that is at odds with the version of India suggested by its title, which is more prominent in Jhabvala's original novel.

Books that relate to Merchant Ivory productions include *Autobiography of a Princess* (1975), which contains the screenplay for the film of the same name and a pot-pourri of material on the India of the Maharajas collected by Ivory, John Pym's *The Wandering Company* (1983), which offers an account of the first 21 years of their films, and Robert Emmet Long's *The Films of Merchant Ivory* (1991; revised edn.

1997). Ismail Merchant has also directed a number of films, including adaptations of Anita Desai's *In Custody* (1993) and V. S. Naipaul's first novel, *The Mystic Masseur* (2001), with a screenplay by Caryl Phillips.

Further reading

Ivory (comp.) (1975); Pym (1983); Long (1997).

Mesolect   See Creole.

Mestizo, mestizaje   *Mestizo* is a term used in Latin America for a person of mixed Spanish (or Portuguese) and Amerindian ancestry. *Mestiza* is sometimes used as the feminine. Like mulatto, the term has come to carry pejorative connotations, but as with mulatto aesthetics and the Francophone notion of *métissage*, the concept of *mestizaje* has been used by artists and intellectuals in a more positive way to identify the distinctive Creolized formations that characterize New World Hispanophone cultures. However, the ethnic strands that have gone into its making have meant that *mestizaje* has generally stressed different aspects of New World cultural interaction (viz. the importance of the Amerindian legacy) to those emphasized by Anglophone and Francophone artists and intellectuals, though the approach of the Guyanese writer Wilson Harris can reasonably be linked with it. The Cuban writer, Alejo Carpentier's *Los pasos perdidos* (1953; *The Lost Steps* 1956) can be read as a *mestizo* interior journey, in which the protagonist discovers the traces of a supposedly vanished culture and comes to understand its residual importance in his own identity.

Mestizaje promotes an aesthetic approach that transcends 'race' in favour of a broader-based notion of the fusions that have shaped contemporary Latin American cultural identities. The Venezuelan writer, Arturo Uslar Pietri locates the origins of *mestizaje* in the hybrid culture Spaniards brought *to* the New World and discusses its historical development in the Americas with reference to Simon Bolívar's 1819 statement, 'We are not Europeans, we are not Indians, but something intermediate between the natives and the Spanish. . . . [T]hus our situation is most extraordinary and complicated' (1972: 176).

Further reading

Uslar Pietri (1972).

Métis, métissage   In Canada and elsewhere, Métis is the term used for people of mixed French and Native descent. In 1869–70, the Métis community of the Red River settlements of Manitoba, who by this time constituted a distinct ethnic group, resisted the imposition of central Canadian authority under the leadership of the controversial figure of Louis Riel (1844–85). Riel later led a second Métis rebellion – further West in Saskatchewan in 1885 – before being captured, found guilty of treason and hanged. The title of an essay by the Mennonite writer Rudy Wiebe, 'In the West, Sir John A. [Macdonald, Canada's first Prime Minister] is a Bastard and Riel a Saint. Ever Ask Why?' (Keith, ed. 1981: 209–11) sums up Riel's iconic significance as a REGIONAL hero. Wiebe has also written an epic novel about the nineteenth-century Métis, *The Scorched-Wood People* (1977).

In both Canada and the Caribbean *métissage* has been used to describe an aesthetic practice in which two ancestral strands (European and AMERINDIAN in Canada; more usually European and African in the Caribbean) are fused together to form a new cultural entity. Consequently, *métissage* is roughly equivalent to the ANGLOPHONE Caribbean advocacy of MULATTO AESTHETICS and the HISPANOPHONE emphasis on MESTIZAJE, though it remains crucially important to be attentive to the specific ingredients that shape the new form in each case.

The Middle Passage   The second leg of the TRIANGULAR TRADE, i.e. the crossing made by the ships of the Atlantic Slave Trade. Also the title of a 1962 travel book by V. S. NAIPAUL, subtitled 'The Caribbean Revisited'.

The Mighty Sparrow   See SPARROW, The Mighty.

Mimicry   Mimicry is a term that has been employed to describe a range of post-colonial attitudes and practices and, while its usage in theoretical contexts has come to be associated with the position taken by Homi K. BHABHA in his account of the AMBIVALENT site occupied by colonial discourse and the colonial subject, earlier usages, which can of course be subjected to the kind of analysis that Bhabha proposes, often carry more straightforwardly negative, and very occasionally positive, connotations. Thus V. S. NAIPAUL's representation of mimesis in his novel that most obviously addresses this issue, *The Mimic Men* (1967), dramatizes the extent to which the colonial mentality is the product of a sense of inferiority instilled by cultural indoctrination. In the passage from which the novel takes its title, its Indo-Caribbean narrator/protagonist Ralph Singh (né Kripalsingh, with the first element of this name playing on the English 'Cripple') expresses the predicament of the INAUTHENTIC colonial, who feels cut off from the 'purity' of the colonial 'CENTRE', as follows:

> There, in Liège, in a traffic jam, on the snow slopes of the Laurentians, was the true, pure world. We, here on our island, handling books printed in this world, and using its goods, had been abandoned and forgotten. We pretended to be real, to be learning, to be preparing ourselves for life, we mimic men of the New World, one unknown corner of it, with all its reminders of the corruption that came so quickly to the new. (Naipaul 1967: 175)

Bhabha's account develops and contests ideas explored by Frantz FANON (1968b), as well as being more generally indebted to Freudian and post-Freudian psychoanalytic thinking. His position on mimicry is expressed most succinctly in 'Of Mimicry and Man: The Ambivalence of Colonial Discourse' (Bhabha 1994: 85–92), which cites part of the Naipaul passage quoted above, but other essays in *The Location of Culture* (1994) also deal with the condition.

Some of the most striking examples of cultural forms committed to LIMINAL mimicry that operates on the a borderline between complicity and subversion are to be found in the parodic performances of CARNIVAL, both in its 'doubling' of the life-styles of colonizers and more recently of authority figures more generally. Equally, Carnival's potential as a force for social change remains questionable, suggesting the continuing post-colonial ambivalence of mimicry.

Further reading

Naipaul (1967); Fanon (1968b); Hill (1972); Bhabha (1994).

Mistry, Rohinton Born 1952. Indian-born novelist and short story writer, who migrated to Canada in 1975. Mistry's fiction is primarily concerned with the group into which he was born, the Parsi community of Mumbai (Bombay). *Tales from Firozsha Baag* (1987) is a short story collection which mainly focuses on the residents of a Parsi apartment building. Superficially comic in tone, most of the stories combine a despairing humanism with a strong sense of emotional attachment to Bombay. Mistry's first novel, *Such A Long Journey* (1991), which won the COMMONWEALTH WRITERS PRIZE, is also centred on the enclosed world of a Parsi apartment building and, though complex in tone, is ultimately similarly pessimistic. It follows the fortunes of Gustad Noble, a bank clerk who becomes caught up in a tragic-comic web of intrigue and espionage at the time of the 1971 war that led to the creation of Bangladesh. As his surname seems to suggest, Gustad represents the heroism of an ordinary 'little' man, but the novel is less sanguine about society at large, offering a scatological vision of Bombay; and, despite hints at the need for PLURALISM, Gustad's moral struggle revolves around attempts to preserve his insulated community from outside encroachments. *A Fine Balance* (1995) also takes a negative view of Indian society, while rendering the stories it tells with impressively realized local detail. Set in an unnamed city by the sea at the time of the 'EMERGENCY' declared by Indira Gandhi in 1975, it throws together four protagonists – two tailors, a middle-aged widow and a young student – whose histories expand outwards to provide a panoramic view of Indian society in crisis.

Mistry is generally regarded as a realist writer and his technique has been compared with that of Dickens. Nevertheless, as with Dickens, his supposed realism frequently hovers on the edge of sentimentalism and the intertwining of public and private events in his fiction lends itself to allegorical readings, in which the personal can be seen as a microcosm of the national. His most recent novel, *Family Matters* (2002) focuses on a single Parsi family and is superficially about its close-knit relationships, particularly the King Lear/Cordelia-like interaction between the family patriarch and his daughter, but again Mistry uses an apparently narrow vantage point to examine wider social issues, particularly COMMUNALISM. Set in the 'present' of the 1990s, the novel demonstrates the writer's distance from the subject-matter about which he writes, a problem Mistry had previously avoided by locating his fundamentally elegiac fiction in the Bombay of his youth and early manhood.

Mobutu Sese Seko Kuku Ngbendu Wa Za Banga (Joseph Mobutu; 1930–97). Former President of Zaïre (now the Democratic Republic of the Congo). Mobutu joined the Belgian Congolese army and rose through the ranks to become its Commander. He was a member of Patrice LUMUMBA's Congolese Nationalist Movement, when Lumumba became President of the newly independent Congo in 1960. During the turbulent events of that year, he arrested Lumumba and was instrumental in Joseph Kasavubu's installation as President. He remained Commander-in-Chief of the army and in 1965 removed Kasavubu from office and assumed the Presidency himself. He ruled dictatorially for the next quarter of a century and in the early 1970s introduced a programme of Africanization, changing the country's name to Zaïre and his own to Mobutu Sese Seko Kuku Ngbendu Wa Za Banga ('The mighty warrior who, because of his endurance and unbending will to conquer, will move from victory to victory, leaving fire in his wake'). Corrupt government and economic mismanagement made Zaïre increasingly impoverished, while he amassed one of Africa's largest fortunes and resisted coups that attempted to replace him. Seen as a counter-force to leftist regimes in the region, he continued to attract Western support until the end of the Cold War. In 1991 he was forced to agree to a form of power-sharing with opposition leaders and he was finally replaced as President by Laurent Kabila, in 1997. He died shortly afterwards in exile in Morocco.

Moraes, Dom Born 1938. Indian poet and autobiographer born in Mumbai (Bombay) into a Catholic family. Widely travelled as a boy, he achieved early recognition as a poet, when his first volume, *A Beginning* (1958), published while he was an undergraduate at Oxford, made him the youngest-ever and the first non-English winner of the Hawthornden Prize. It was followed by *Poems* (1960) and *John Nobody* (1965). During his early years Moraes was widely regarded as one of the finest talents writing poetry in English, but he produced very little work in the middle of his career and some commentators have felt his later output has failed to realize his early promise. It includes *Absences* (1983), *Collected Poems* (1987), *Serendip* (1990) and *Cinnamon Shade: New and Selected Poems* (2001). However, at its best, his poetry demonstrates a capacity to write about personal, social and topographical subjects in a deceptively simple style that achieves both intellectual and emotional depth. Moraes has edited magazines in London, Hong Kong and New York and written numerous prose works, including the autobiographical *Gone Away* (1960), *My Son's Father* (1969) and *Never at Home* (1992). His other books include a 1980 biography of Indira Gandhi.

The Morant Bay Rebellion   A Jamaican uprising at a time of famine in 1865, when a force of some 250 local men, led by the Baptist pastor Paul Bogle, challenged the authority of the ruling PLANTOCRACY by marching on the town of Morant Bay in Jamaica's St Thomas parish, allegedly with the intention of fomenting a larger rebellion in the island. The uprising was ruthlessly crushed by Governor Edward Eyre, who had earlier enjoyed a rather different colonial reputation, as a heroic explorer in Australia. In the ensuing events more than four hundred 'rebels' were killed and more than three hundred, including Bogle himself, summarily executed. Jamaica's elective assembly was subsequently suspended and Eyre's actions led to his being recalled from his post, on the grounds that he had used unnecessary force. Coming shortly after the SEPOY MUTINY in India, the events in Jamaica alarmed many in England, where the 'Eyre Controversy' divided public opinion. Meanwhile Jamaicans continued to suffer from the poverty and economic discrimination that had occasioned the rebellion. V. S. REID's historical novel *New Day* (1949) devotes its first half to a vivid boy's-eye view of the rebellion.

Morris, Mervyn   Born 1937. Jamaican poet and critic. Morris was a Rhodes Scholar at Oxford and subsequently pursued a highly successful academic career at the Jamaica campus of the University of the West Indies. His collections include *The Pond* (1973; revised edn. 1987), *Shadowboxing* (1979) and *Examination Centre* (1992). His poems are notable for their spare, understated treatment of large themes. Morris is also a notable critic, who has played an important role in encouraging younger Jamaican poets, among them the late 'Mikey' SMITH, whose oral work he prepared for publication in *It a Come* (1986). He has edited several anthologies including *The Faber Book of Contemporary Caribbean Short Stories* (1990).

Mosaic   Term formerly widely used to describe the Canadian model of social interaction, in which particular ethnic and cultural groups work together, but (like the small individual stones that make up the totality of a mosaic) retain their characteristic distinctiveness as juxtaposed pieces in the larger national design. In Canadian public policy contexts the mosaic can be seen as the forerunner of the MULTICULTURAL initiatives pioneered in Canada in the early 1970s. It is in marked contrast to the ASSIMILATIVE model of the MELTING POT that is particularly associated with the USA. As with the melting pot, the mosaic model is best seen as a rhetorical aspiration rather than a description of a social reality. Equally, such national discourses play a significant part in shaping policy at a grass-roots level and in influencing individual perceptions. See also PATCHWORK.

Mphahlele, Es'kia (Ezekiel Mphahlele) Born 1919. South African writer. Born in Pretoria, Mphahlele describes his impoverished upbringing in a ghetto in his autobiography, *Down Second Avenue* (1959). He worked as a teacher, but was dismissed from his post because of his opposition to segregationist policies and became a reporter for Drum during the magazine's early days of publication. Also falling foul of the authorities in this capacity, because of his continued opposition to the APARTHEID regime, he left South Africa in 1957 and subsequently lived in Nigeria, Kenya, France and the USA, where he worked at the Universities of Denver and Pennsylvania. After his return to Africa in 1977, he became a Professor of African Studies at the University of Witwatersrand.

Mphahlele is best-known for *Down Second Avenue* and *The African Image* (1962; revised edn. 1974), a pioneering work on African literature which contests European modes of representation and has been influential throughout Africa. Mphahlele has also published the novels *The Wanderers* (1971) and *Chirundu* (1979), and the short story collections, *Man Must Live* (1947), *The Living and the Dead* (1961) and *In Corner B* (1967). *Voices in the Whirlwind* (1972) is a collection of his essays and *Afrika My Music* (1984) is a second volume of autobiography. Mphahlele's work as an editor includes the Penguin anthology, *African Writing Today* (1967).

Further reading

Mphahlele (1974); Barnett (1976).

Mujahidin See JIHAD.

Mukherjee, Bharati Born 1940. Indian-born novelist and short story writer. Mukherjee was born in Calcutta and educated at the Universities of Calcutta, Baroda and Iowa. She has lived most of her adult life in North America: from 1966 to 1980 in Canada, where she says she felt an exiled member of a 'visible minority' and subsequently in the USA. Her short story collections, *Darkness* (1985) and *The Middleman* (1988) mainly focus on the lives of migrants into North America, encompassing a varied range of transcultural encounters that offer probing interrogations of American values. Her novel *Jasmine* (1989) tells the story of an Indian woman, who is widowed in her teens and whose life undergoes a radical transformation when she moves to the USA and, instead of 'Jasmine', becomes the assertive 'Jane Ripplemeyer'. Her most ambitious novel to date, *The Holder of the World* (1993), is centred on a contemporary American woman's involvement with the history of a seventeenth-century New England precursor whose travels took her to the India of the Moghul court. It blends Mukherjee's characteristic concern with cross-cultural themes, which some have seen as particularly directed towards her American readership, with a contrasting study of the lives of independent women across the centuries. She has also published the novels *The Tiger's Daughter* (1971), *Wife* (1975), *Leave It to Me* (1997) and

Desirable Daughters (2002) and the travel memoir, *Days and Night in Calcutta* (1977), which she co-wrote with her husband, the Canadian novelist Clark Blaise.

Further reading

Alam (1996).

Mulatto, mulatto aesthetics   Literally a mulatto is a person of mixed (usually black and white) parentage. 'Mulatta' is sometimes used as the feminine form. Historically, the term identified people who were half-white and half-black, distinguishing them from quadroons, who were one-quarter black, and octoroons, who were one-eighth. None of these terms is widely used today. 'Mulatto' developed pejorative overtones in the late colonial period, when attempts at precise scientific classification of people's supposed racial origins, which frequently entailed racism, fell into disfavour. The term has, however, been used in a more positive way by writers such as Derek WALCOTT, who is himself of mixed origins, to identify an aesthetic practice, which combines various ancestral strands. Thus, in the Caribbean a mulatto aesthetic opposes the privileging of African ancestry in accounts of Caribbean identity, preferring to emphasize the process of CREOLIZATION and the variety of 'originary' elements that have shaped the region's culture. MESTIZO and MESTIZAJE are used in broadly similar ways in Hispanic American contexts, though *mestizo* connotes a different form of ethnic admixture, and *MÉTISSAGE* is a roughly analogous French term. See also HYBRIDITY and CULTURAL SCHIZOPHRENIA.

Multiculturalism   A term variously used to describe the demographic make-up of a country's population, as an expression of an ideal of cross-cultural inter-ethnic and inter-communal harmony *and* to describe public policy initiatives that promote such an ideal. Multicultural policies were pioneered in Canada, at both national and provincial level, in the early 1970s; and Australia introduced similar policies shortly afterwards. Canadian policies have been attacked by those who have see them as funding cosmetic manifestations of cultural PLURALISM, such as ethnic street festivals and cuisine, while ignoring the realities of discrimination against minorities. Neil Bissoondath's *Selling Illusions: The Cult of Multiculturalism in Canada* (1994) is a fierce indictment of such policies and fiction such as Joy Kogawa's novel *Obasan* (1981), which exposes the Canadian government's treatment of Japanese-Canadians during World War II and the subsequent cover-up, and Rohinton MISTRY's satire of multiculturalism in his story 'Squatter' (in *Tales from Firozsha Baag*, 1987) takes a similar view.

In the UK, the Swann report of 1985 led to the introduction of multicultural educational polices to combat racial disadvantage. However, critics such as Salman RUSHDIE took a similar view to Bissoondath's view of Canadian multiculturalism, when, in 'The New Empire within Britain', a talk originally delivered on Britain's

Channel 4 television station in the 1980s, he said:

> In our schools, [multiculturalism] means little more than teaching the kids a
> few bongo rhythms, how to tie a sari and so forth. In the police training
> programme, it means telling cadets that black people are so 'culturally
> different' that they can't help making trouble. Multiculturalism is the latest
> token gesture towards Britain's blacks, and it ought to be exposed, like
> 'integration' and 'racial harmony', for the sham it is. (Rushdie 1991: 137)

Bhikhu Parekh's *Rethinking Multiculturalism* (2000) offers a particularly wide-ranging account of multiculturalism, beginning with the plurality contained within Christian monism and including case-studies of such controversial practices as female circumcision and the Rushdie affair. Parekh argues that the deep-rooted emphasis on homogeneity in Western thought needs to be replaced by a broad-based humanism, which recognizes cultural difference. Comparatively unusually, he develops this thesis along theoretical lines *and* also examines public policy practices.

Further reading

Rushdie (1991); Bissoondath (1994); Parekh (2000).

Myal, myalism Syncretist Jamaican magico-religious cult, in which the devotees supposedly possessed the spirits of ancestors. Like OBEAH, myal was declared illegal by the colonial authorities and consequently functioned as a secret African-based, anti-colonial social network; unlike obeah, it was generally regarded by its adherents as a positive force for transformation. According to Olive SENIOR (1983: 113), myalism probably no longer exists, but some of its practices have been subsumed into other Jamaican revivalist forms such as KUMINA. In Erna BRODBER's novel, *Myal* (1988), an inter-racial group of myal acolytes finds an alternative to the spirit-theft of colonialism in the cult's emphasis on repossession of submerged aspects of the Caribbean psyche.

Further reading

Senior (1983).

N

Naipaul, V(idiadhar) S(urajprasad)   Born 1932. Trinidadian-born writer, who has mainly lived in England since 1950. Naipaul was born into a Brahmin family in rural Trinidad and, unlike many other Indo-Caribbean descendants of the labourers who came from the sub-continent during the period of INDENTURESHIP, received a fairly traditional Hindu upbringing. He satirizes the attempt to preserve Hindu forms in Trinidad, particularly in his first novel, *The Mystic Masseur* (1957) and the novel that many regard as his masterpiece, *A House for Mr Biswas* (1961). His family moved to Trinidad's capital Port of Spain where Naipaul attended the country's leading secondary school, Queen's Royal College, from which he won a scholarship to Oxford, where he read English. He subsequently edited the BBC's CARIBBEAN VOICES programme. His early novels are written in a broad comic vein, as is his first-written book, *Miguel Street* (1959), a collection of interlinked short stories about the inhabitants of a fictional Port of Spain street, which draws on CALYPSO narrative modes and themes. *A House for Mr Biswas* is based on the life of his father Seepersad Naipaul (1906–53), a journalist and author, who himself published a collection of short stories, *Gurudeva and Other Indian Tales* (1943) and provided Naipaul with the inspiration to be a writer. While highly personal, it is a novel that can also be read as an allegory of the attenuation of Hindu culture in the Caribbean and it also demonstrates an obvious indebtedness to H. G. Wells's *A History of Mr Polly* (1910).

In *Mr Biswas*, Naipaul blends comedy with pathos. Subsequently the tone of his writing became more sombre and his next two novels, *Mr Stone and the Knights Companion* (1963), set in England, and *The Mimic Men* (1967), which takes the form of an exiled Caribbean politician's memoirs, are both powerful studies of displacement, a theme that has been a major preoccupation of Naipaul's writing throughout his career. During the 1960s he published his first travel books, *The Middle Passage* (1962), a scathing indictment of Caribbean societies, and *An Area of Darkness* (1964), which took a similarly disillusioned view of his ancestral homeland of India, as did the later *India: A Wounded Civilization* (1977). Naipaul has increasingly moved from fiction to non-fiction and his later work has frequently conflated the two modes. He was awarded the BOOKER PRIZE for *In a Free State* (1971), a work in which the title-novella, about two English expatriates in East Africa, is accompanied by two shorter fictions and excerpts from an otherwise unwritten Egyptian travel-journal. *Guerrillas* (1975) helped secure Naipaul's reputation in the USA, where it was widely read as an attack on the black radicalism of the late 1960s and early 1970s. From *The Mimic Men* onwards, Naipaul's fiction had been strongly influenced by CONRAD and *A Bend in the River* (1979), another study of a displaced DIASPORA Indian, is set in the same terrain as *Heart of Darkness*.

Naipaul continued to receive numerous accolades. He was knighted in 1990 and became the first winner of the David Cohen Prize for 'lifetime achievement by a living British writer' in 1993. Meanwhile he had lost some of his appeal in academic circles, as a consequence of his sweepingly dismissive remarks about post-colonial societies and the increasing popularity of the post-RUSHDIE generation of writers, whose stress on the positive aspects of HYBRIDITY found more favour than Naipaul's emphasis on the negative consequences of migration in the last two decades of the twentieth century. His 'novel', *The Enigma of Arrival* (1987) is a thinly-veiled autobiography which, like the earlier *Mr Stone*, can also be read as a 'Condition of England' novel. It is also a powerful and moving elegy for the unsustainability of an older, homogeneous view of England, which lends credence to Derek WALCOTT's view of Naipaul as an 'elegiac pastoralist' (Walcott 1998: 122). When Naipaul was awarded the NOBEL PRIZE FOR LITERATURE in 2001, *The Enigma of Arrival* was referred to as his masterpiece in the Swedish Academy's citation.

Naipaul's later writing demonstrates some softening of his acerbic attitude towards post-colonial societies, though he continues to write in a polemical vein. His third book about India, *India: A Million Mutinies Now* (1990), takes a more positive view of contemporary Indian culture, albeit while radically reversing his earlier position with scant acknowledgement of the change; *A Way in the World* (1994) is more sympathetic to the cultures of the Caribbean past than his earlier dismissive views of Caribbean history, expressed in *The Middle Passage* and *The Loss of El Dorado* (1969); and his second book about Islam, *Beyond Belief* (1998), is less caustic than the earlier *Among the Believers* (1981).

His other books are *The Suffrage of Elvira* (1958), *A Flag on the Island* (1967), *The Overcrowded Barracoon* (1972), *The Return of Eva Perón with the Killings in Trinidad* (1980), *Finding the Centre* (1984), *A Turn in the South* (1989), *Letters between a Father and Son* (1999), *Half a Life* (2001) and *The Writer and the World* (2002). His brother Shiva (1945–85), whose novels include *Fireflies* (1970) and *The Chip-Chip Gatherers* (1973), was also a writer, as is his nephew, the Canadian-based Neil Bissoondath (born 1955), whose books include the novel *A Casual Brutality* (1988) and *Selling Illusions* (1994), a critique of MULTICULTURALISM.

Further reading

White, L. (1975); Hamner (ed.) (1977); Thieme (1987); Nixon (1992); Weiss (1992); King (1993); Theroux (1998); Hayward (2002).

Nair, Mira   Born 1957. Indian film director. Born in Orissa, Nair studied sociology in Delhi and at Harvard and her films show the influence of this background. After making a number of documentary shorts, she achieved international fame, when her first feature *Salaam Bombay* (1988) won the award for Best New Director at Cannes. It deals with the life of Mumbai street children, focusing on the errand-boy of a teashop and employing a style which compounds grittily realistic observation of the slum life it depicts with moments of pathos. Since *Salaam Bombay*, Nair has directed *Mississippi Masala* (1991), a film about an Asian family expelled from Uganda, whose daughter falls in love with an African American, *Kama Sutra: A Tale of Love* (1997), set in sixteenth-century India, and *Monsoon Wedding* (2001), which takes the contemporary subject of an arranged marriage in upper-class New Delhi society as a focus for juxtaposing and contrasting globalized Indian culture and traditional Hindu customs. *Monsoon Wedding* won the Golden Lion award at the Venice film festival. Nair's early shorts include *Jama Masjid Street Journal* (1979), a film about a Muslim community in Old Delhi, and *India Cabaret* (1985), in which her camera dispassionately observes the ageing strippers of a Mumbai (then Bombay) club.

Narayan, R. K. (Rasipuram Krishnaswami Narayan Swami; 1906–2001). Indian novelist and short story writer. Along with Mulk Raj ANAND and Raja RAO, Narayan came to the fore in the 1930s, as one of the 'BIG THREE' of Indian fiction in English, after Graham Greene, who was to become his life-long friend and mentor, assisted in the English publication of his first novel *Swami and Friends* (1935). He was brought up in Chennai (Madras) and Mysore, where his father was a headmaster and where he lived most of his subsequent life, though his final years were spent in Chennai. *Swami and Friends* depicts an education and childhood in which Tamil and English are equally powerful influences on the young protagonist and Narayan himself was trilingual, also speaking Kannada. *Swami* forms a loose trilogy with *The Bachelor of Arts* (1937) and *The English Teacher* (1945), which also focus on the development of a young man experiencing different roles in the educational system. Narayan was deeply affected by the early death of his wife in 1939 and the latter half of *The English Teacher* (US title *Grateful to Life and Death*) contains an autobiographically based account of the hero's attempts to make contact with his recently deceased wife through the intercession of a medium. Published in the middle of this sequence, *The Dark Room* (1938), in which a sensitive independently minded woman finds herself unable to escape from a loveless marriage, has been seen as an early feminist text.

All Narayan's fiction has been set in the imaginary small South Indian town of Malgudi, a composite creation drawing on aspects of Mysore, Chennai and Coimbatore. He has said Malgudi is 'nowhere', but it remains a site that enables him to explore his recurrent preoccupation with the intersection of tradition and modernity in a very specific *South* Indian milieu. His finest novels are those of his middle period: *Mr. Sampath* (1949), *The Financial Expert* (1952), *The Guide* (1958), *The Man-Eater of Malgudi* (1961), *The Sweet-Vendor* (1967) and *The Painter of Signs* (1976). They explore the conflicts that occur when seemingly settled Hindu values, personified by a small Malgudi businessman, engaged in a BRAHMINICAL profession such as printing, are challenged by the incursions of an alien force. By the end the protagonist has usually managed to re-establish the order that characterized his life at the outset, but in the later novels Narayan's vision is less sanguine about Malgudi's ability to withstand the encroachments of the outside world, as the pace of social change accelerates. Formally, these novels follow ostensibly the same pattern, subtly mixing social comedy and mythic fable and in so doing staging a dialectic similar to that expressed in their thematic conflicts. *Waiting for the Mahatma* (1955), in which the GANDHIAN freedom struggle plays a part, has been seen as his most political novel, but as in the other novels of this period, public issues are played out through the microcosm of personal relationships.

During the second half of his life, Narayan spent several periods as a visiting professor at American universities and he talks, in the title-essay of *Reluctant Guru* (1973), about the American attempt to cast him in the role of a mystical Indian to fit Western stereotypes of Indians that flourished in the late 1960s and 1970s. Despite his detachment from this role, his writing of this period tilts the balance of his perennially HYBRID fiction towards the Tamil side of his temperament. His novel *The Guide*, regarded by some as his masterpiece, is about the transformation of a tourist guide into a holy man. The equally impressive *Man-Eater of Malgudi* is a conscious reworking of a story from the *puranas*, albeit in a form that demonstrates Narayan's characteristic comic irony. During this period he produced *Gods, Demons and Others* (1964), a retelling of Hindu myths and his own retellings of Tamil versions of the two great Indian epics, the RAMAYANA (in 1972) and the MAHABHARATA (in 1978).

Narayan's later novels were *A Tiger for Malgudi* (1983), *Talkative Man* (1986) and *The World of Nagaraj* (1990). In the novella *Grandmother's Tale* (1992), he returned to a story from his youth in a work that appears to mix fact and fiction. He was also a prolific writer in genres other than the novel. His collections of short fiction, in which stories are often repeated, include *An Astrologer's Day* (1947), *Lawley Road* (1956), *A Horse and Two Goats* (1970), *Malgudi Days* (1972), *Old and New* (1981) and *Under the Banyan Tree* (1985). His non-fiction includes the travel books *Mysore* (1939) and *The Emerald Route* (1977) and the autobiographical *My Days* (1974). His essays are collected in *A Writer's Nightmare* (1988), *Salt and Sawdust* (1993) and *A Storyteller's World* (1989). *Indian Thought* (1997) is a 'miscellany' of pieces from a journal he edited during World War II, which includes his play *Watchman of the Lake*.

Further reading

Harrex (1978); Naik (1983); Kain (ed.) (1993); McLeod, A. L. (ed.) (1994); Ram and Ram (1996).

Nasser, Gamal Abdel (1918–70). Egyptian politician, who played a major role in the DECOLONIZATION of his country and the Middle East more generally. Born in Alexandria at a time when Egypt was under British rule, he founded a nationalist movement, while being trained as an officer at Cairo's military academy. After serving as a major in the Arab-Israeli War of 1948, in which he was wounded, he led a coup that toppled the pro-Western regime of Egypt's King Farouk in 1952. He became

Prime Minister in 1954 and President in 1956, the year in which he nationalized the Suez Canal, a crucial artery for European interests in Asia. The 'SUEZ CRISIS', which weakened British and French influence in the Middle East and led to the resignation of British Prime Minister, Anthony Eden, was a defining moment in the history of the region. An alliance between England, France and Israel quickly restored Western control of the canal, but American and Russian intervention forced Britain and France to withdraw and Nasser became a hero in the Arab world. He subsequently sought to establish an Arab FEDERATION, founding the United Arab Republic (UAR) with Syria in early 1958 and the United Arab States, a union between the UAR and Yemen a month later. Syria withdrew in 1961, but Nasser's reputation as an Arab leader grew and he also became a central figure in the NON-ALIGNED MOVEMENT. His policies led to the Six-Day War with Israel in 1967, in which Egypt suffered heavy losses. He temporarily resigned the Presidency, but returned to office and remained in power until his death. At home he established a one-party state and introduced reforms that brought about a wide-ranging socialist revolution, with land redistribution and increased access to education transforming the situation of the hitherto disempowered *fellaheen* (peasantry) and industrial projects such as the Aswan Dam, financed with Soviet Aid, helping to secure economic modernization.

Further reading

Jankowski (2001).

National allegory Term particularly associated with the American Marxist critic Fredric Jameson's contention that all 'third-world' writing operates as national allegory, since it has not experienced the split between private and public experience that Jameson sees as a determining aspect of capitalist societies (Jameson 1986). This view has been disputed by Aijaz AHMAD, who, writing from a Marxist position himself, argues against the reductiveness of seeing all third-world writing as belonging to this generic mode, and by Stephen Slemon, who questions the privileging of a mode of figuration inextricably bound up with the discursive practices of Empire, positing as an alternative a dialectical practice which recognizes the extent to which contestatory meanings emerge in the interstitial space of the colonial encounter. Arguably such approaches make insufficient allowance for the interpretive participation of readers, who *may* choose to see particular post-colonial texts, e.g. Wole SOYINKA's *A Dance of the Forests* (1960), Earl LOVELACE's *Salt* (1996) or Fred D'AGUIAR's *Bethany, Bettany* (2003), as national allegory. Also works such as Salman RUSHDIE's *Midnight's Children* (1981) and Bapsi SIDHWA's *Ice-Candy Man* (1988), which foreground the extent to which they are operating as national allegory, support Jameson's contention, but it is debatable whether their self-consciousness in this respect is markedly different from, say, Condition of England novels such as Elizabeth Gaskell's *North and South* (1855) or E. M. Forster's *Howards End* (1910) or more recent texts from 'SETTLER' COLONIES, such as

Margaret Atwood's *Surfacing* (1972) and Keri Hulme's *The Bone People* (1983), which invite similar interpretations. In short, national allegory *can* be a useful term for describing particular 'third-world' texts or the readings they promote, but it is dubious whether it is more specifically applicable to such texts than to works from Western cultures. Consequently, the attempt to categorize all non-Western literary production with such a label can easily become a restrictive form of ESSENTIALISM, analogous to the signifying practices of ORIENTALISM, which appropriate a myriad range of forms of 'alterity' ('OTHERNESS') into a reductive, unitary category. See also ALLEGORY.

Further reading

Jameson (1986); Slemon (1987 and 1988); Ahmad (1992).

Nationalism   An ideology which affirms the autonomy of the nation–state and is usually represented by political movements that seek to achieve national unity or, as in the case of colonialism, independence from external rule. While nationalism invariably has connotations that involve the assertion of some form of national unity or aspiration towards such a goal, it has markedly different associations in varying social contexts. In colonial situations, it played a particularly prominent role in the independence movements of the late colonial period, in which the struggle to attain political freedom was often accompanied by similar impulses towards DECOLONIZATION in the arts and culture.

According to Ernest Gellner (1983), nationalism arose in response to the economic needs of industrializing societies, which demanded a degree of homogeneity not present in pre-modern cultures. Benedict Anderson (1983) locates the origins of modern-day nationalism in the eighteenth century, when the notion of 'nation' solidified. In nineteenth-century Europe, movements to unify France and Italy and the quests for independence in such countries as Ireland, Belgium and Bohemia can be seen as products of nationalist ideology. In the twentieth century, the Indian nationalist movement provided a model for the struggles of various other Asian, African and Caribbean countries to free themselves from British colonial rule. In Africa, nationalist movements came into being shortly after the 'SCRAMBLE FOR AFRICA' apportioned most of the continent's land mass to various European powers and by the outbreak of World War II, nationalist movements had emerged in virtually every African colony. More recently, nationalist ideology has underpinned the attempts by putative nation–states that have been subsumed into larger political entities to achieve autonomy from what is often regarded as an artificially constructed nation. In twentieth-century Europe this has been manifest in the near-total disintegration of the FEDERATION that was Yugoslavia, the Republican movement in Northern Ireland and the Basque separatist movement in Spain. Asian nationalist movements have included the Tamil Tigers in Sri Lanka and the struggles of various minority communities in Myanmar (Burma).

While anti-colonial nationalism is generally regarded as a positive force, since it asserts people's rights to self-determination and freedom from oppression, other forms of nationalism have much more negative connotations, especially in situations where national pride becomes tainted with supremacist beliefs, as in the case of the Nazi discourse of Aryan purity. So, although nationalisms operate along a continuum – African freedom movements underpinned by nationalist ideology often became corrupt in themselves; European colonial exploitation was often accompanied by well-intentioned missionary zeal – it is tempting to make a moral distinction between 'good' and 'bad' nationalisms, in which the former involves a justifiable resistance struggle or a healthy iteration of national pride, while the latter seek to impose the interests of one nation or group on another. See also DECOLONIZATION and the 'WINDS OF CHANGE'.

Further reading

Anderson (1983); Gellner (1983); Sethi (1999).

Nation language   Term coined by (Edward) Kamau Brathwaite in *History of the Voice* (1984; repr. in Brathwaite 1993: 259–304) to identify 'the kind of English spoken by the people who were brought to the Caribbean, not the official English now, but the language of slaves and labourers, the servants who were brought in by the conquistadors' (Brathwaite 1984: 5–6). Brathwaite sees nation language as strongly influenced by the African aspect of the Caribbean heritage and uses the term in preference to 'dialect', which he argues has pejorative connotations, since it suggests inferiority and in literature has often been associated with caricature. He says dialect has 'a long history coming from the plantation where people's dignity is distorted through their language and the descriptions which the dialect gave to them' and argues that the languages of the Caribbean region are African offshoots which despite English 'lexical features' have an underlying African 'rhythm and timbre' (ibid.: 13). Originally delivered as an 'electronic lecture' at Harvard University in 1979, *History of the Voice* traces 'the development of nation language in anglophone Caribbean poetry' (the work's sub-title) with reference to poets from Claude MCKAY to 'Mikey' SMITH and performers such as Louise BENNETT and calypsonians such as The Mighty SPARROW, whom he argues employ the distinctive dactylic metres of Caribbean speech. Although Brathwaite's advocacy of the African-derived aspects of Caribbean language – as opposed to its operation through one of the many CREOLE CONTINUA that most linguists identify as its main distinguishing feature – is polemical, *History of the Voice* remains a powerful manifesto, arguing for recognition of the submerged African elements in Caribbean speech, the unity of the language used in the region and the primacy of the ORAL in Caribbean discourse.

Further reading

Brathwaite (1984 and 1993).

Native Peoples, Nativism 'Native Peoples' is a term widely used to identify the ABORIGINAL peoples of a country, as in 'Native Americans' in the USA. It is problematic for various reasons, particularly its pejorative connotations, which have tended to equate the 'native' with the 'primitive' and 'savage'. 'Aboriginal' and 'FIRST PEOPLES' (a term favoured in Canada) more accurately describe the situation of SETTLER societies' earliest migrants. Both terms support their claims to primacy in issues of land ownership, without asserting an originary indigeneity.

'Nativism' is sometimes used to describe post-colonial subjects' attempts to return to a 'pure' pre-colonial past. Like NEGRITUDE, it is best seen as a form of STRATEGIC ESSENTIALISM, employed to counter the dislocations occasioned by colonization rather than as an atavistic attempt to deny the HYBRID social conditions of the post-colonial experience.

Negritude A black consciousness movement which originated among African and African DIASPORA students in Paris in the 1930s. Negritude sought to assert pride in African cultural values to counterbalance the inferior status accorded to them in European colonial, particularly French, cultural discourses. The movement's most important figures were the Senegalese Léopold SENGHOR, the Martinican Aimé CÉSAIRE, who coined the term in his poem *Cahier d'un retour au pays natal* (1939), and the French Guyanese, Léon-Gontran DAMAS. They drew inspiration from the HARLEM RENAISSANCE's efforts to promote the richness of African cultural identity and particularly opposed French ASSIMILATIONIST policies, which threatened to erode African and African diaspora identities. The coming together of the founding figures of Negritude in Paris has parallels with the formation of other NATIONALIST movements, whose origins can also be traced to assimilationist policies that attempted to brainwash post-colonial intellectuals and co-opt them into the ranks of the colonial elite. Such policies backfired, both by bringing such intellectuals together in the metropolis and by making them intimately familiar with colonial discourse and consequently equipping them to contest its practices.

Senghor argued that African consciousness is innately different from European, since it functions through an intuitive form of cognition, in which the analytical faculties are less important than the emotional. Later African intellectuals have seen Negritude as a problematic response to European constructions of 'alterity' (see 'OTHERNESS'), because its opposition to Western stereotypes of African and African diaspora peoples has led to the creation of its own alternative form of ESSENTIALISM. How far such a charge is valid is debatable, particularly since even the original founders of the movement saw it in different ways. Whereas Senghor's promotion of negritudinist ideals was based on the assumption that all persons of African descent share certain common characteristics, Césaire saw Negritude as a historical phenomenon that had evolved from commonalities in the post-colonial history of African peoples, such as the MIDDLE PASSAGE and the experience of plantation slavery. Insofar as the charge is valid, the Negritudinist position can still be defended as a form of STRATEGIC ESSENTIAL-ISM that was a necessary phase in the development of black consciousness movements.

Nehru, Jawaharlal (1889–1964). Indian statesman and writer, who was the first Prime Minister of post-independence India and is widely regarded as the father of the modern nation. Born in Allahabad, he was educated at Harrow and Cambridge and subsequently admitted to the English Bar. He returned to India in 1912 and, after the AMRITSAR MASSACRE, joined the Indian National CONGRESS, working in collaboration with Mahatma GANDHI, and becoming the Congress's President in 1929. His opposition to British rule led to his being imprisoned on numerous occasions during the period of the freedom struggle and in all he spent some 18 years in jail. He was instrumental in the QUIT INDIA RESOLUTION of 1942 and in the negotiations that secured India's independence in 1947. He became the first Prime Minister of a COMMONWEALTH republic, when India attained independence and subsequently pursued policies that made him a leading figure in the NON-ALIGNED MOVEMENT.

Known as Pandit ('Teacher') Nehru, he was the main architect of the establishment of India as a modern secular, democratic state. His policies blended technological advancement with attempts to eradicate poverty and CASTE and gender discrimination. His best-known books are his *Autobiography* (1936), which was mainly written while he was in prison in 1934 and 1935, and *Discovery of India* (1946). His writing is notable for its capacity to synthesize a Western style with a non-EUROCENTRIC view of world history and culture. His other works, several of which were also written during periods in prison, include *Letters from a Father to His Daughter* (1930), *Glimpses of World History* (1934–5), *The Unity of India* (1941) and *Independence and After* (1950).

Nehru is often regarded as having founded a dynasty. He was succeeded by his daughter Indira Gandhi (1917–84), whose leadership style attracted considerable controversy and led to the 'EMERGENCY' she declared in 1975. After her assassination, her son, Rajiv Gandhi (1944–91), who was also assassinated, served as India's Prime Minister.

Further reading

Ali (1985).

Neo-colonialism A surrogate form of colonialism operating in the post-independence era, mainly but not exclusively through economic control, either by a former colonial power or another nation–state, most prominently the USA, or by a multinational corporation. Kwame NKRUMAH identified and analysed the operation of the phenomenon in the period shortly after many African countries had attained their independences in *Neo-Colonialism: The Last Stage of Imperialism* (1965).

Further reading

Nkrumah (1965).

Nettleford, Rex   Born 1933. Jamaican choreographer, cultural historian and educator. Nettleford's achievement is difficult to summarize under conventional headings, since he has worked in numerous areas of arts and education, but he has made particularly significant contributions in the fields of dance and educational policy aimed at eroding the gap between middle-class and ordinary Jamaicans. He was born in the parish of Trelawny and his early experience of rural Jamaican folk culture was a formative influence that has informed all his work in the arts. He studied history at the Jamaica campus of the University of the West Indies (UWI) and was subsequently a Rhodes Scholar at Oxford University. Along with Eddy Thomas, he co-founded Jamaica's National Dance Theatre Company (NDTC) in 1962, the year of Jamaican independence. The NDTC's work has demonstrated the centrality of dance in Caribbean culture, promoted such folk forms as KUMINA and taken performance standards for Caribbean dance to new levels. It has become a highly significant repository for Afro-Jamaican cultural forms and has toured extensively throughout the world.

As Director of UWI's Extra-Mural programmes, Nettleford played a major role in increasing access to higher education in Jamaica and elsewhere in the ANGLOPHONE Caribbean. In 1998 he was appointed as Vice Chancellor of UWI. His publications include *Mirror, Mirror: Race, Identity and Protest in Jamaica* (1970) and *Caribbean Cultural Identity* (1978) and he has edited CARIBBEAN QUARTERLY. Along with figures such as (Edward) Kamau BRATHWAITE, Nettleford has particularly promoted awareness of the African contribution to the Caribbean's CREOLIZED culture, taking the view that several models of the region's identity that acknowledge its HYBRID constitution, have nevertheless continued to privilege the European dimension. Nettleford was one of the earliest academic champions of RASTAFARI and, along with M. G. Smith and Roy Augier, he co-authored the influential 1960 UWI *Report on the Rastafari Movement in Kingston Jamaica*, a monograph that helped to change popular Jamaican perceptions of Rastafarianism, which had hitherto been mainly negative. Albertina Jefferson's *Rex Nettleford and His Works* (1998) is an annotated bibliography, compiled by UWI librarians.

Further reading

Nettleford (1970); Jefferson (ed.) (1998).

New Historicism   See HISTORIOGRAPHY.

New Literatures in English   A term used to describe post-colonial literatures in English, which has been particularly popular in mainland Europe, where it continues to be used. Its advantages over 'COMMONWEALTH LITERATURE' include an avoidance of the political associations inherent in 'Commonwealth', which have been seen to contain vestigial connotations of Empire – particularly since the contemporary COMMONWEALTH evolved from the British Commonwealth – and the vagaries of the

Commonwealth as a geographical category. 'New Literatures' also allows for the inclusion of ANGLOPHONE writing unconnected with the Commonwealth, such as Filipino literature in English and the work of individual writers such as the Somalian-born Nuruddin FARAH, who have chosen English as a medium for reaching an international readership. Its advantages over 'post-colonial literature' include an avoidance of locating everything in relation to the colonial era and the confusions occasioned by different interpretations of the 'post-' prefix. Its main drawbacks lie in its use of 'new' to categorize literatures, such as Australian, Indian and Canadian, which have histories that date back some two hundred years, its privileging of English and the lack of clear definition as to what its project comprises.

New Literatures Review Australian-published journal, devoted to post-colonial literatures and particularly emphasizing comparative approaches and the application of literary theory to the field. Founded in 1975 and edited by a collective, it is currently based at the University of Wollongong under the executive editorship of Paul Sharrad.

Ngugi waThiong'o (James Ngugi) Born 1938. Kenyan novelist, dramatist and critic. Ngugi received a mission education and attended Makerere University College in Kampala and the University of Leeds, prior to working as a lecturer at the University of Nairobi, where he chaired the Literature Department for several years in the 1970s. More recently he has held academic appointments in the USA.

Beginning with *Weep Not, Child* (1964), generally considered to be the first East African novel in English, his early fiction is mainly concerned with the effects of the MAU MAU freedom struggle on the lives of ordinary Gikuyu villagers. It particularly focuses on the destruction of personal and family relationships, offering a complex consideration of issues of heroism and betrayal. In contrast to several other African novelists, Ngugi has spoken of his admiration for Joseph CONRAD and novels such as *A Grain of Wheat* (1967; revised edn. 1986) and *Petals of Blood* (1977) employ a POLYPHONIC Conradian technique, in which shifting points of view and disrupted chronologies create a relativistic ambience that problematizes issues of moral authority. *Petals of Blood* adopts a Marxist stance in relation to its representation of the exploitation of the Kenyan peasantry by the NEO-COLONIAL elite. All Ngugi's fiction engages with the difficulties inherent in HISTORIOGRAPHY, but he has increasingly moved away from social realism and towards forms that allow for a more allegorical expression of his political concerns. In *Caitaani Mutharaba-ini* (1980; *Devil on the Cross*, 1982), a novel originally published in Gikuyu, he draws on the conventions of traditional ballad singing to describe a woman's return to her home-town to attend a feast of thieves organized by the Devil. The thieves are former businessmen who have exploited the poor and gradually the protagonist comes to acknowledge her own complicity in corruption.

Ngugi's plays include *The Black Hermit* (1968) and *The Trial of Dedan Kimathi* (with Micere Mugo, 1976). His attempts to take political drama to Kenya's villages led to his arrest and detention without trial for a year, an experience he has written about in *Detained: A Writer's Prison Diary* (1981). He has expressed the view that African literature written in English is really an 'Afro-European' literature and from *Caitaani Mutharaba-ini/Devil on the Cross* onwards he has favoured initial publication in Gikuyu and Kiswahili, the lingua franca of East Africa. His ideas on language are most fully expressed in *Decolonising the Mind: The Politics of Language in African Literature* (1986). His second novel to be written in Gikuyu, *Matigari ma Niruungi* (1987; *Matigari*, 1989) deals with a former freedom fighter in an unnamed African country who returns from the mountains to find his family and settle down to a peaceful life, only to discover that the need to fight for liberation is as urgent as ever in the post-independence era.

Ngugi's other work includes his earliest written novel, *The River Between* (1965), which depicts the impact of Western value-systems on traditional Kenyan society and several volumes of essays: *Homecoming* (1972), a study of African and Caribbean writing; *Writers in Politics* (1981; revised edn. 1997); *Moving the Centre* (1993); and *Penpoints, Gunpoints and Dreams* (1998). *Secret Lives* (1975) is a collection of his short stories.

Further reading

Ogude (1999); Williams, P. (1999).

The Nigerian Civil War, The Biafran War   In 1967, seven years after Nigeria attained independence, civil war broke out, when, after a coup and counter-coup in the previous year, the Ibo-dominated eastern region of the country seceded from the Federal Government and proclaimed itself independent as the Republic of Biafra. Federal forces, led by General Yakubu Gowon, sought to regain control of the region and in the three-year war that ensued, it is estimated that a million people died: 100,000 soldiers and many more civilians who were the victims of famine and disease. Eventually the outnumbered Biafran troops, led by Lt Col Chukwuemeka Odumegwu-Ojukwu, were defeated and Biafra ceased to exist. Prior to the war international opinion had generally regarded Nigeria as politically stable and exempt from the conflicts that had emerged in some other newly independent African states, as the Western-conceived multi-ethnic FEDERATIONS, introduced at the time of the 'SCRAMBLE FOR AFRICA', began to unravel. However, its post-independence Constitution was potentially flawed from the outset and disputes as to the representation of particular groupings quickly emerged.

The Civil War also proved a defining moment for the development of Nigerian writing, not simply because it led to the production of a considerable and impressive body of writing, but also because it was crucially 'important in both the periodization and the aesthetic development of Nigerian literature' (Killam and Rowe (eds) 2000:

178). It signalled the end of the NATIONALIST phase of Nigerian writing and the beginning of a more sombre chapter, which recognized the persistent problems facing an artificially created multi-ethnic nation–state. The bulk of writing about the war, most of which was written after it ended, was by 'Biafran' authors. It includes Flora NWAPA's *Never Again* (1975), Isidore Okpewho's *The Last Duty* (1976), a fictionalized allegory of the ethnic divisions that caused the war, and Buchi EMECHETA's *Destination Biafra* (1982). The most highly acclaimed Nigerian poet of his generation, Christopher Okigbo (1932–67), whose poems are collected in *Labyrinths* (1971), was tragically killed in the first phase of the war. Chinua ACHEBE served as a Biafran diplomat during the war and responded to it in poems in *Beware Soul Brother* (1971) and stories in *Girls at War* (1972). Yoruba responses to the war include Wole SOYINKA's, *The Man Died* (1972), a journal which documents his experience of imprisonment at the hands of the Gowon regime. Soyinka spent 27 months, mostly in solitary confinement, without being charged or brought to trial. His collection of poems, *A Shuttle in the Crypt* (1972) is a slightly more oblique response to his imprisonment, in which the eponymous shuttle is his creative imagination. He deals with events leading up to the war in his novel *Season of Anomy* (1973).

Further reading

St Jorre (1972); Saro-Wiwa (1989); Killam and Rowe (eds) (2000).

Nine night   A Jamaican ceremony commemorating a person's death, which is believed to originate from Africa and is linked with the syncretist spirit-possession religion of KUMINA. The ceremony is held at the deceased's home nine nights after they have passed away and has some similarities with the wakes held in Ireland and other parts of the world. Olive SENIOR points out that the rituals associated with the nine night make it a repository of folk customs more generally, noting that it has 'served as the means of preserving a great deal of Jamaican folk culture as this is manifested in songs, games, riddles, stories, etc.' (Senior 1983: 118). It provides the central focus for Dennis Scott's play *An Echo in the Bone* (1974), in which spirit-possession enables the characters, each of whom plays a number of roles, to revisit various episodes in the Caribbean's traumatic history of SLAVERY and thereby re-*possess* aspects of Jamaica's African heritage. Other plays about the nine night ceremony include Edgar White's *The Nine Night* (1983), a domestic drama, in which a Jamaican exile, resident in England for two decades, proposes to travel, not to Africa, but back to Jamaica, in the hope of healing the rifts in his family, and Glenville Lovell's *When the Eagle Screams* (1992). Una MARSON's play *Pocomania* (1938) includes an early representation of a NINE NIGHT ceremony.

Further reading

Senior (1983).

Nkrumah, Kwame (1909–72). Ghanaian politician and political philosopher, who played a leading role in the independence movement and PAN-AFRICANISM. He was educated at mission schools, Lincoln University in Pennsylvania and the London School of Economics, where he became involved in African NATIONALIST politics, first meeting such figures as Jomo KENYATTA and Hastings Kamuzu Banda, and helped organize the Sixth Pan-African Congress in 1945. He returned to what was then the Gold Coast in 1947 and founded the nationalist Convention People's Party (CPP), which campaigned for self-government. He was imprisoned for sedition in 1950, but when the CPP won the 1951 election, he was released to become 'Leader of Government Business'. He became the first post-independence Prime Minister of a Sub-Saharan nation, when Ghana was formed from the Gold Coast and British Togoland in 1957. The new country was heralded as a model for other African states. Nkrumah's opposition to colonialism continued into the post-independence era, particularly since he was one of the first to identify the continuing exploitation of African countries through economic NEO-COLONIALISM. He was one of the main architects of the 1961 Charter of African Nations. His belief in pan-Africanism led to the forging of political links with Guinea and Mali.

The introduction of socialist education and healthcare policies and the Africanization of the new state's institutions brought his administration considerable popularity in the years immediately after independence, but mounting debt led to such policies being replaced by a more autocratic style of government. Nkrumah declared Ghana a republic in 1960, proclaimed himself President for Life in 1964 and established a one-party state, which suppressed political dissent by interfering with the judiciary and introducing imprisonment without trial. He was increasingly seen as the dictatorial leader of a corrupt and repressive regime, which was squandering the country's economic resources and denying basic human rights. Ayi Kwei ARMAH's indictments of post-independence corruption in his first two novels, *The Beautyful Ones Are Not Yet Born* (1968) and *Fragments* (1970), are fictionalized portraits of Ghana during the period of Nkrumah's rule. He was overthrown by an army coup, while he was away in China in 1966 and subsequently went into exile in Guinea.

Nkrumah has remained a controversial figure, but is more generally remembered as one of the founding figures of pan-Africanism than as a politician who abused power and destroyed the promise of independence. His publications include *The Autobiography of Kwame Nkrumah* (1957), *Why Africa Must Unite* (1963), *Consciencism: Philosophy and Ideology for De-Colonization* (1964), *Neo-Colonialism: The Last Stage of Imperialism* (1965), *Handbook for Revolutionary Warfare* (1968) and *Class Struggle in Africa* (1970).

Further reading

Nkrumah (1965); Davidson (1973); Birmingham (1999).

The Nobel Peace Prize   One of the five annual prizes awarded since 1901 under the terms of the will of Alfred Nobel (1833–96), the Swedish chemist who invented dynamite, but was a noted pacifist. Nobel's will stipulated that one of the prizes he had endowed should be given to the person who 'shall have done the most or the best work for fraternity between nations, for the abolition or reduction of standing armies and for the holding and promotion of peace congresses'. The other four prizes are for physics, literature, chemistry and medicine. Unlike the awards for the other prizes, which are made by juries of the Swedish Academy, the Peace Prize is conferred by a committee of the Norwegian Parliament. A sixth prize, for economics, which is funded by the Swedish National Bank, was instituted in 1969.

Notable winners of the Peace Prize in recent decades have included Mohamed Anwar al-Sadat and Menachem Begin (1978), Mother Teresa (1979), Bishop Desmond Tutu (1984), Aung San Suu Kyi (1991), Nelson Mandela and F. W. de Klerk (1993), Yasser Arafat, Shimon Peres and Yitzhak Rabin (1994), John Hume and David Trimble (1998) and the United Nations and its Secretary-General, Kofi Annan (2001).

The Nobel Prize for Literature   Another of the annual prizes endowed by Alfred Nobel and awarded by the Swedish Academy. Nobel's will stipulated that one of the prizes should be given to the person who 'in the field of literature shall have produced the most outstanding work in an ideal direction'. Consequently, humanitarian considerations, as well as literary excellence, have informed the Academy's juries' award of the Prize, which has, on occasions, been given to authors whose work is not strictly literary, e.g. the historian, Theodor Mommsen (1902), the philosophers Henri Bergson (1927) and Bertrand Russell (1950) and the statesman Winston Churchill (1953). In recent years the Prize has been awarded to more non-Western writers.

Nobel Literature laureates with colonial or post-colonial connections include Rudyard Kipling (1907), Rabindranath Tagore (1913), Saint-John Perse (Alexis Léger) (1960), Miguel Angel Asturias (1967), Pablo Neruda (1971), Patrick White (1973), Gabriel García Márquez (1982), Wole Soyinka (1986), Naguib Mahfouz (1988), Ocatavio Paz (1990), Nadine Gordimer (1991), Derek Walcott (1992), Seamus Heaney (1995) and V. S. Naipaul (2001). When Derek Walcott won the 1992 Prize, he became St Lucia's second Nobel laureate: Sir Arthur Lewis had preceded him as joint winner of the Prize for Economics in 1979.

The 'Noble Savage'   A European Enlightenment stereotype of the supposed innocence of 'primitive' people, popularized by Jean Jacques Rousseau (1712–78), who saw such innocence as the 'natural state' of humanity prior to civilization. Aphra Behn's novel *Oroonoko* (1688), in which an African prince leads a slave revolt in Surinam, is often seen as the earliest instance of the stereotype in English fiction. Behn's novel was adapted in Thomas Southerne's tragedy of the same name (1695).

In the New World, the concept was associated with the supposed Edenic innocence of uncontaminated Nature and in America it was specifically linked with the Frontier ethic. James Fenimore Cooper's 'Leatherstocking Novels' use the stereotype in their representations of NATIVE Americans, particularly in their portrayal of Chingachgook, the 'Indian' counterpart of Cooper's frontiersman hero, Natty Bumppo, a character who has his origins in the Romantic vogue for primitivism. Although the Noble Savage has been associated with the more progressive, anti-colonial strains in eighteenth- and nineteenth-century thought, it remains a simplistic idealization of the virtues of indigenous peoples, which still embodies an ESSENTIALIST construction of 'alterity' ('OTHERNESS') and reveals more about its authors than those it purports to describe. See also SHAKA.

The Noma Award for Publishing in Africa   A literary prize, established in 1979, which is awarded annually for a work in one of three categories: scholarly or academic work, children's writing; and literature or creative writing. The Award was founded by the Japanese publisher, Shoichi Noma, with the aims of promoting African publishing and bridging the divide between North and SOUTH. It is given for work in any of the languages of Africa, whether indigenous or European, and is administered by the journal, *The African Book Publishing Record*. It is open to all African writers and scholars, but only work published in Africa itself is eligible. Recent winners have been: Peter Adwok Nyaba's *The Politics of Liberation in South Sudan: An Insider's View* (1998), Djibril Samb's *L'interprétation des rêves dans la région Senegambienne* (1999), Kimani Njogu and Rocha Chimerah's *Ufundishaji wa Fasihi: Nadharia na Mbinu* (2000) and Abosede Emanuel's *Odun Ifa/Ifa Festival* (2001).

Non-alignment, The Non-Aligned Movement (NAM)   After a partially successful earlier attempt led by President Sukarno of Indonesia to establish a 'neutral' bloc of countries at BANDUNG in Java in 1955, the Non-Aligned Movement was founded in 1961, in an endeavour to combat the superpowers' NEO-COLONIAL influence over non-Western countries. NAM is a loose confederation, mainly made up of 'DEVELOPING COUNTRIES' opposed to all forms of IMPERIALISM. Its main principles include respect for the internal sovereignty of nations, peaceful co-existence, the resolution of disputes through negotiation and a more equitable distribution of wealth. Its first conference was convened in Belgrade in 1961 by Yugoslavia's President Tito, with 29 Heads of State in attendance. Since then the movement has generally held triennial conferences and it now has over a hundred members states. Its uniquely decentred form of administration has a rotating Chair (the Head of State of the country hosting its summit) and its multilateral, transnational composition is reflected in its lack of a formal constitution or secretariat. It aims to be non-hierarchical, allowing its members to present a concerted front, when they share common positions, while recognizing the diversity of the aims and ideologies of its component nations.

In late 2001 its member states were: Afghanistan, Algeria, Angola, the Bahamas,

Bahrain, Bangladesh, Barbados, Belize, Benin, Bhutan, Bolivia, Botswana, Brunei Darussalam, Burkina Faso, Burundi, Cambodia, Cameroon, Cape Verde, the Central African Republic, Chad, Chile, Colombia, Comoros, Congo, the Democratic Republic of the Congo, Côte d'Ivoire, Cuba, Cyprus, Djibouti, Ecuador, Egypt, Equatorial Guinea, Eritrea, Ethiopia, Gabon, Gambia, Ghana, Grenada, Guatemala, Guinea, Guinea-Bissau, Guyana, Honduras, India, Indonesia, Iran, Iraq, Jamaica, Jordan, Kenya, the Democratic People's Republic of Korea, Kuwait, Lao, Lebanon, Lesotho, Liberia, Libya, Madagascar, Malawi, Malaysia, Maldives, Mali, Malta, Mauritania, Mauritius, Mongolia, Morocco, Mozambique, Myanmar (Burma), Namibia, Nepal, Nicaragua, Niger, Nigeria, Oman, Pakistan, Palestine, Panama, Papua New Guinea, Peru, the Philippines, Qatar, Rwanda, St. Lucia, Sao Tome and Principe, Saudi Arabia, Senegal, Seychelles, Sierra Leone, Singapore, Somalia, South Africa, Sri Lanka, Sudan, Surinam, Swaziland, Syria, Thailand, Togo, Trinidad and Tobago, Tunisia, Turkmenistan, Uganda, the United Arab Emirates, Tanzania, Uzbekistan, Vanuatu, Venezuela, Vietnam, Yemen, Yugoslavia (suspended), Zambia and Zimbabwe.

While the relevance of non-alignment in the post-Cold War world has been questioned, NAM remains an important forum for the evolution of a non-Western form of GLOBALISM. Non-alignment has been seen by various commentators as an ideology that predates the Bandung Conference and Indian commentators have traced its origins to a speech made by Jawaharlal NEHRU at the Haripura Congress in 1938 (Srivastava (ed.) 2001). In addition to Nehru, Sukarno and Tito, leading figures in the movement have included Tanzania's Julius NYERERE, Egypt's Gamal Abdel NASSER and Cuba's Fidel CASTRO.

Further reading

Srivastava (ed.) (2001).

Non-violence   See *AHIMSA*, GANDHI, Mohandas K. and *SATYAGRAHA*.

Nonyas   Straits-Chinese women of mixed descent. See also BABAS.

Nwapa, Flora   (1931–93). Nigerian novelist, short story writer and publisher, generally credited with having been the first Nigerian woman to publish novels. Nwapa is best known for her novels *Efuru* (1966) and *Idu* (1970), which anticipate the work of Buchi EMECHETA in their depiction of the problems facing women in Ibo society. Her novels draw on oral storytelling traditions and their use of Ibo proverbial lore particularly invites comparison with the village novels of Chinua ACHEBE. Both *Efuru* and Achebe's *Things Fall Apart* (1958) are centrally concerned with gender roles in traditional Ibo society and the impact of colonialism on such codes. However, Nwapa reverses Achebe's concentration on how codes of manhood shape individuals' subjectivities by placing her main emphasis on the socialization of women, a focus which led to hostile and dismissive reviews of *Efuru* by male critics who saw it as too woman-centred (Stratton 1994: 81ff.).

A prototype feminist, though she resisted the label herself, Nwapa established her own publishing companies, Tana Press and Flora Nwapa Books as part of her project of giving voice to Nigerian women's experiences. She also published the novels *Never Again* (1975), *One is Enough* (1981) and *Women Are Different* (1986), the short story collections, *This is Lagos* (1971) and *Wives at War* (1980) and several collections of stories for children.

Further reading

Stratton (1994).

Nyerere, Julius (1922–99). Tanzanian statesman, widely regarded as the father of independent Tanzania, where he was known as '*mwalimu*' ('teacher') and one of the most highly respected of post-independence African leaders. Educated at a government school, Makerere University College, Uganda and Edinburgh University, he was a teacher prior to becoming involved in politics in the early 1950s. During the period when many of the leading African nationalist movements emerged, he founded TANU (the Tanganyika African National Union) in 1954. Nyerere became Chief Minister of Tanzania in 1960 and President in 1964. A committed leader of the NON-ALIGNED MOVEMENT, he established a one-party state and a regime that championed the values of self-help and agrarian socialism. His policy of *ujamaa* ('familyhood'), which sought to relocate large sections of the nation's population in agricultural collectives, is generally considered to have been a failure. A war with Uganda during the period of Idi Amin's rule, which culminated in his successfully invading Uganda and capturing Kampala, seriously affected Tanzania's economy and prevented the attainment of many of his idealistic political goals. Nyerere relinquished the presidency in 1985, but continued as Chairman of his party until 1990. His scholarly pursuits included translating Shakespeare into Swahili.

OAU   See the ORGANISATION OF AFRICAN UNITY.

Obeah, obeahman   Obeah is an Afro-Caribbean magico-religious practice, brought from West Africa by Asante (Ashanti) slaves. It is particularly practised for medical purposes, with the obeahman (sometimes called the 'man of science'), or obeahwoman usually dispensing herbal remedies, particularly in cases where the patients believe that their illnesses have supernatural causes. It is also used to 'work' various kinds of spells: to bring harm to enemies, to secure secret information and to influence the outcome of events, particularly in romantic situations. The word is said to derive from the Akan word, 'obayi' or sorcerer. Obeah has links with SHAMANISM and Haitian VODUN. It is practised in most parts of the ANGLOPHONE Caribbean, from Jamaica to Guyana, though the forms in which it is expressed vary and SYNCRETIC versions influenced by similar North American practices have developed.

Literary treatments of obeah occur in texts as varied as the sensation novels of the early Jamaican writer, H. G. de Lisser, most famously *The White Witch of Rosehall* (1929), a historical novel based on the exploits of a nineteenth-century plantation owner, which was one of the most popular novels in Jamaica in the first half of the century, and the first stories in Pauline MELVILLE's *Shape-Shifter* (1990), which leave the question of obeah's efficacy open, while attesting to its continuing importance in the Guyanese folk imagination. Obeah also plays a significant role in the middle sections of Jean RHYS's *Wide Sargasso Sea* (1966), where the Creole protagonist Antoinette (Rhys's reworking of 'the first Mrs Rochester') tries to regain her husband's affections through the use of a love potion, provided by her childhood nurse Christophine, who warns her that obeah is not for her, because she is *béké* ('white').

Okike: An African Journal of New Writing Nigerian periodical founded by Chinua ACHEBE in Nsukka in 1971. In the troubled climate of post-independence West African publishing, *Okike* has demonstrated greater longevity than most of its competitors. Originally published three times a year, it has not sustained this regularity over the decades. *Okike* is pan-African in approach and has published work by many of the continent's leading writers, including Achebe, Nadine GORDIMER, Arthur Nortje and Kole Omotoso. It expanded its activities in the 1980s to include the publication of an educational supplement and the bilingual *Uwa Ndí Ibo: A Journal of Ibo Life and Culture*.

Okot p'Bitek (1931–82). Ugandan poet, who wrote in Luo and English and whose inspiration mainly derived from Acoli traditional songs. He travelled to Britain in 1956 as a member of the Ugandan national soccer team and stayed on to become a student, studying law at the University of Wales in Aberystwyth and social anthropology at Oxford, where he wrote a thesis on traditional Acoli and Lango songs. He subsequently returned to Uganda, where he was appointed Director of the National Theatre and Cultural Centre in Kampala in 1966. He went into exile during the period of Idi Amin's rule in Uganda and held academic appointments in Kenya, Nigeria and the USA. After returning to Uganda, he became a Professor of Creative Writing at Makerere University.

Okot attempted to recapture what he saw as the AUTHENTIC spirit of traditional

African ORATURE in his *Song of Lawino* (1956), which was originally written in Acoli. When its English translation appeared in 1966, it was hailed as the first major modern African poem to show no traces of European influence and, while such an estimate fails to take account of the implications of TRANSLATION and the extent to which the poem's subject-matter treats the interpenetration of cultures, the *Song* nevertheless represents a highly distinctive formal departure from Western conventions. The poem takes the form of a lament by an Acoli wife who has been rejected by her husband in favour of his westernized girlfriend. It was followed by a companion-piece, *Song of Ocol* (1970), in which the husband gives his response. Taken together, the two poems provide a satirical dialogue on the relative merits of traditional Acoli and Western values.

'Song of a Prisoner' and 'Song of Malaya', both written in the same vein as Okot's earlier poems, were published together as *Two Songs* (1971). Okot's commitment to Acoli oral forms is also to be seen in *The Horn of My Love* (1974), a collection of songs, and *Hare and Hornbill* (1978), a collection of folktales. Much earlier, he had published the novel, *Lak Tar Miyo Kinyero Wi Lobo* (1953; *White Teeth*,1989). His non-fictional works include *African Religions in Western Scholarship* (1971) and *Africa's Cultural Revolution* (1973), in which he called for a total repudiation of Western cultural standards and their replacement by African values. His championing of traditional folkloric discourse and his own reworking of such genres, which introduced a generation of African poets to the possibilities of non-Western forms, made him one of the most influential African writers of his era.

Further reading

Heron (1976); Lindfors (1993).

Okri, Ben   Born 1959. Nigerian-British novelist and short story writer. Born in Nigeria, Okri spent his early years moving between Nigeria and Britain. He eventually settled in England, studying at Essex University, where he read philosophy and English, and publishing his first novel, *Flowers and Shadows* (1980), while still an undergraduate. He was awarded an OBE in 2001. *Flowers and Shadows* and *The Landscapes Within* (1981) are *Bildungsromane*, in which young protagonists struggle to come to terms with the realities of contemporary Nigerian urban life. Okri's next two books, the short story collections, *Incidents at the Shrine* (1986) and *Stars of the New Curfew* (1988), demonstrate a movement towards traditional Yoruba forms and his more mature fiction has favoured MAGIC REALIST modes that make use of elements from Yoruba traditional culture. Consequently, he can be seen, on one level, as an heir to the tradition of Nigerian writing in English founded by Amos TUTUOLA, but his self-conscious awareness of cosmopolitan literary trends makes him an altogether more knowing exponent of fabulist modes.

Okri's BOOKER PRIZE-winning novel, *The Famished Road* (1992) takes an ABIKU, a figure already popular in Nigerian writing in English, on an imaginative journey that comments on the present state of the nation. It forms a trilogy with *Songs of Enchantment* (1993) and *Infinite Riches* (1998). *In Arcadia* (2002) replaces the African journeying of Okri's trilogy with a European search for spiritual fulfilment that critics have felt lacks the same degree of imaginative depth. Okri has also published the novels *Astonishing the Gods* (1995) and *Dangerous Love* (1996). *An African Elegy* (1992) is a collection of his poetry; and *A Way of Being Free* (1997) is a collection of his essays, which ranges across subjects as diverse as Shakespeare, Picasso, Chinua ACHEBE and Salman RUSHDIE.

Ondaatje, Michael   Born 1943. Sri Lankan-born Canadian writer. Like much of his work, Ondaatje's origins and upbringing confound attempts at neat national categorization. Of mixed Sri Lankan Dutch burgher and Tamil ancestry, he was educated at an English public school, before migrating to Canada. He began his writing career as a poet and his prose work also uses highly charged, sensuous poetic language. His early volumes of poetry, *The Dainty Monsters* (1967), *The Man with Seven Toes* (1969) and *Rat Jelly* (1973), display a surrealist vision in which images are juxtaposed in startling and unexpected ways. His subsequent volumes of poetry include *There's A Trick with a Knife I'm Learning to Do* (1979), *The Cinnamon Peeler* (1989), a collection which includes work from his earlier volumes, and *Handwriting* (1998), a series of poems about Sri Lanka.

Ondaatje's early work owes a debt to postmodernism, particularly in its erosion of traditional generic boundaries. *The Collected Works of Billy the Kid* (1970) and *Running in the Family* (1982) are both discontinuous mixed-mode narratives that move between history and fiction and incorporate poetry, photographs and documentary collage. The fascination with American mythologies demonstrated in *Billy the Kid*, which explores the outlaw's eccentricities and psychopathic tendencies, is also prominent in *Coming through Slaughter* (1976), a fictional treatment of the life of the legendary New Orleans Jazz pioneer, Buddy Bolden, who spent his later years in a mental hospital. *Running in the Family* is Ondaatje's most personal work to date: it describes the author's return to Sri Lanka to try to make sense of the 'historical relations', both familial and narrative, that have shaped him, while also reflecting on various aspects of Sri Lankan identity and its representation by outsiders.

With *In the Skin of a Lion* (1987), a novel about the lives of migrants in Toronto in the years between the two world wars, which can be read as an alternative SUBALTERN history of the growth of the modern city, Ondaatje entered the distinctive terrain of his later work. The novel demonstrates a recurrent concern with both the inescapability and the inadequacy of ESSENTIALIST definitions of identity. His best-known work, *The English Patient* (1992), winner of a Canadian Governor General's Award and joint winner of the 1992 BOOKER PRIZE, is set in a semi-ruined Tuscan villa at the end of World War II. It brings together four characters of different nationalities, whose lives, despite their apparent isolation, are indelibly marked by larger public forces, among them the militaristic nationalism of the war and British imperialism in India. At the centre of the narrative lies the dying 'English' patient, a mysterious bedridden victim of a plane crash in the North African desert. In memory he revisits the desert where he has been an explorer, engaging in necrophiliac recollections of his lost love. The Tuscan and North African sections of the novel are linked by an emphasis on the ways in which political CARTOGRAPHY affects the lives of even those whose desires seem to transcend national categories – the four inhabitants of the villa *seem* to form a supra-national micro-community; the English patient is a Hungarian count – and the closing sections are played out against the background of news of the bombing of Hiroshima. The popularity of the novel was further enhanced by the success of Anthony Minghella's 1996 film adaptation, which won nine Oscars, including that of best director for Minghella, but shifted its main emphasis from the Tuscan villa to the love story in the desert.

In *Anil's Ghost* (2000) a forensic anthropologist working for an international human rights group returns to her native Sri Lanka, to try to discover the truth about murder campaigns in the country's civil war. Her attempt to identify a particular skeleton becomes a metonym for a more general archaeological investigation into issues of history, culture and identity. Again Ondaatje intermingles public and private fates and, as in *Running in the Family*, the representation of Sri Lanka is complicated by the juxtaposition of ancient and modern perspectives on the island's identity.

Further reading

Smythe (ed.) (1994).

Onitsha Market Literature   A popular form of Nigerian pamphlet writing, which emerged in the late 1940s, taking its name from the town of Onitsha in Eastern Nigeria, a uniquely individual CONTACT ZONE for various segments of Nigerian society until the outbreak of the NIGERIAN CIVIL WAR. Onitsha pamphlets run from just a few pages to nearly a hundred and are usually written in mixed registers that are easily accessible to ordinary, literate Nigerians and bring together language forms ranging from PIDGIN to heightened archaic English. The rapid growth in popularity of the writing has been attributed to a change in the economics of local printing that arose, when cheap army surplus presses became available in the post-World War II period. Cyprian EKWENSI's romantic novelette, *Where Love Whispers* (1948) is an early example of one of the leading forms of Onitsha writing.

Romantic fiction apart, Onitsha chapbooks span a wide variety of popular genres, including the moral homily, the instruction manual (offering advice on such subjects as how to write love letters) and the compendium of facts. The genre's romantic works can be seen as West African equivalents of North American Harlequins or English Mills and Boon fiction. Emmanuel Obiechina (1973) suggests that they have been influenced by the impact of Western notions of romantic love and certainly Hollywood intertexts can often be discerned. Notable examples of Onitsha literature include Ogali Ogali's play *Veronica My Daughter*, Okenwa Olisah's *No Condition is Permanent* and J. O. Nnadozie's *What Women Are Thinking about Men*. Ekwensi is the most famous writer to have begun his career as a writer of Onitsha pamphlets, but the genre has also been credited with facilitating the emergence of major Ibo writers such as Chinua ACHEBE. Obiechina's AFRICAN WRITERS SERIES collection of Onitsha writing (1972) is a useful introduction.

While Onitsha Market Literature is the best-known form of West African popular writing, it is by no means the only one. Stephanie Newell's *Ghanaian Popular Fiction* (2000) is a study of similar writing from Ghana, which also includes comparative discussion.

Further reading

Obiechina (ed.) (1972); Obiechina (1973); Newell (2000).

Orality   Orality occupies a particular place in the study of post-colonial literatures and cultures, since many colonized societies had highly developed oral (and also pictorial and plastic) traditions that were not matched by their scribal equivalents in the society. Indeed, in some cases, e.g. Somali (see Nuruddin FARAH), languages that had strong oral traditions lacked an orthography. Consequently, work such as OKOT p'Bitek's rendition of traditional Luo material into English and Chinua ACHEBE's attempts to capture the idioms of Ibo oral expression in a carefully adapted cognate form of English, have played a significant role in disseminating knowledge of cultures that would otherwise be under-represented in written discourse as a consequence of colonialism and the more general Western privileging of the scribal.

It is, however, mistaken to propose a simple opposition between scribal and oral forms, since the two frequently intersect, e.g. in the case of oral poetry which is transcribed for literary consumption. Also many societies with highly developed oral traditions, e.g. ancient India, had equally advanced literary traditions. Thus, the *RAMAYANA* and the *MAHABHARATA* exist in various written forms as well as having been transmitted across the generations through oral performance. Nevertheless the reclamation of oral histories has been an important aspect of many post-colonial projects, as they remain one of the most significant sources for the retrieval of occluded subaltern experience, especially since the official HISTORIOGRAPHY of colonial societies is almost exclusively maintained in the written record. Such work includes the SUBALTERN STUDIES project and ranges from the recording of slave narratives in North America to the chronicling of migrant experiences in such undertakings as Mike and Trevor Phillips's documentation of the personal testimony of WINDRUSH GENERATION migrants to Britain.

The commitment to oral forms is frequently a political act offering resistance to HEGEMONIC language norms, as in the language of RASTAFARI and DUB POETRY. The Mighty

Sparrow's calypso 'Dan is the Man in the Van' (Thieme (ed.) 1996: 543–5), a brilliant exercise in colonial MIMICRY, is a classic rebuttal of the scribal, in which the song's persona protests against the colonial educational curriculum's attempts to brainwash him by indoctrinating him with English nursery rhymes, expressed in the calypso as so much nonsense-verse. It concludes with the calypsonian explaining that he has escaped this injurious legacy as a result of having remained illiterate, despite the best efforts of his colonial educators: 'They beat me like a dog to learn that in school/ If me head was bright I woulda be a damn fool' (ibid.: 545). See also (Edward) Kamau BRATHWAITE and NATION LANGUAGE.

Further reading

Finnegan (1970); Ong (1982); Brathwaite (1984); Olson and Torrance (eds) (1991); Phillips and Phillips (1998); Ashcroft *et al.* (1998).

Orature   A term that has been used to invest oral forms with the same degree of cultural status as their scribal equivalents. It has, however, been criticized by various experts on orality on the grounds that it implies the primacy of the written word, e.g. Walter Ong's view that it involves regarding oral discourses as variants of the written, rather than seeing them as self-sufficient forms.

Further reading

Ong (1982); Olson and Torrance (eds) (1991).

The Organisation of African Unity (OAU)   An organization, founded in Addis Ababa in 1963, which has given practical shape to the ideals of PAN-AFRICANISM. It has sought to further African co-operation and to counter economic NEO-COLONIALISM. Its pressure on the South African government helped bring about the dismantling of APARTHEID and the nation was admitted as a member of the Organization in 1994. The OAU also opposed white minority rule in Zimbabwe and Namibia. It made considerable advances after Salim Ahmed Salim of Tanzania was elected as its Secretary-General in 1989.

Orientalism   A Western discursive practice, now particularly associated with Edward SAID's highly influential 1978 study, *Orientalism: Western Conceptions of the Orient*, which has sometimes been seen as a founding text for post-colonial theory, though the work of Frantz FANON and his contemporaries predates Said by a generation. Said uses the term to describe the discursive construction of Asia and North Africa by the Western imagination. It was, of course, in general use, without negative connotations, prior to the appearance of his study, e.g. in the titles of many Western institutions and academic departments. Subsequently, it has also been used loosely to refer to other forms of European constructions of 'alterity' (see 'OTHERNESS'), but in such contexts it is arguably inappropriate, since Orientalism, as used by Said, identifies a set of signify-ing practices that are peculiar to the European imagination's invention of its versions of Asia and North Africa.

Using a form of discourse analysis that is indebted to the work of Michel Foucault, Said starts from the premise that the 'Orient' is 'man-made', not given, and that the 'relationship between Occident and Orient is a relationship of power, of domination, of varying degrees of a complex hegemony' (Said 1985: 5). Throughout the work he traces relationships between the exercise of overt political power, such as Napoleon's invasion of Egypt, and discursive projects that manifest themselves in a range of con-texts, including the academic creation of Orientalism as a field of study. He takes the view that:

> Orientalism is not a mere political subject matter or field that is reflected passively by culture, scholarship, or institutions; nor is it a large and diffuse collection of texts about the Orient; nor is it representative and expressive of some 'nefarious' Western imperialist plot to hold down the 'Oriental' world. It is rather a *distribution* of geopolitical awareness into aesthetic, scholarly, economic, sociological, historical and philological texts; it is an *elaboration* not only of a basic geographical distinction (the world is made up of two unequal halves, Orient and Occident) but also of a whole series of 'interests' which, by such means as scholarly discovery, philological reconstruction, psychological analysis, landscape and sociological description, it not only creates but also maintains; . . . it is, above all, a discourse that is by no means in direct, corresponding relationship with political power in the raw, but rather is produced and exists in an uneven exchange with various kinds of power. (ibid.: 12; italics in original)

Said distinguishes between different aspects of Orientalism, but throughout his study argues that the West invariably renders the East a passive partner in their asymmetri-cal power relationship – 'the former *writes* about, whereas the latter is *written* about' (ibid.: 308; italics in original) – and sees the totalizing tendencies of such sub-sets of Orientalism as '*an* Islamic society, *an* Arab mind, *an* Oriental psyche' (ibid.: 301; ital-ics in original) as having the effect of eradicating a 'plurality of differences' (ibid.: 309). See also CARTOGRAPHY, IMAGINATIVE GEOGRAPHY.

Further reading

Said (1985); Barfoot and D'Haen (eds) (1998); Ashcroft and Ahluwalia (2001).

Osofisan, Femi   Born 1946. Nigerian dramatist, poet and literary theorist. Born in a Yoruba village, Osofisan attended Government College, Ibadan, and the University of Ibadan, where he studied French, was active in student drama productions and worked with Wole SOYINKA's Orisun Theatre Company. He subsequently did postgraduate work in Dakar, Paris and Ibadan, where he later lectured before becoming a professor at the University of Benin. Osofisan is the most successful Nigerian dramatist since Soyinka and his plays have been particularly popular with local audiences. From the outset they demonstrate disillusionment with the politics of the independence generation of Nigerian leaders and the abstract mythic approach adopted by their artistic counterparts, such as Soyinka and BEKEDEROMO. When he has used myth, in plays such as *Esu and the Vagabond Minstrels* (1991), in which the god Esu tests the motivation of a group of musicians, he has related it to contemporary political issues. His early plays such as *A Restless Run of Locusts* (1975) and *You Have Lost Your Fine Face* (1969; republished as *Red is the Freedom Road*, 1982) are critiques of social injustice, informed by a socialist concern with class issues.

Osofisan's subsequent drama has been extremely varied in genre and theme, but frequently demonstrates a concern with historical revisionism. Two of his best-known plays *The Chattering and the Song* (1976) and *Morountodun* (1979) deal with the Agbekoya Framer's Rebellion of 1968–9, seeing this as a moment when a people's struggle to unsettle middle-class HEGEMONIES might have succeeded. In addition to drawing on Yoruba folklore and recent and not-so-recent Nigerian historical events, Osofisan has also used European dramatic intertexts. *The Oriki of a Grasshopper* (1986), a play about a university professor waiting to be arrested by secret service agents show the influence of Beckett's *Waiting for Godot. Who's Afraid of Solarin?* (1978) adapted Gogol's *The Government Inspector* to satirize Nigerian political leaders. His other plays include *Once upon Four Robbers* (1980), *Farewell to a Cannibal Rage* (1986), *Aringindin and the Night Watchmen* (1991) and *Many Colours Make the Thunder King* (1997). Collections include *Morountodun and Other Plays* (1982), *Birthdays Are Not for Dying and Other Plays* (1990) and *The Oriki of a Grasshopper and Other Plays* (1995). He has also published the novel, *Kolera Kolej* (1975).

Further reading

Dunton (1992).

Othello, post-colonial responses to   Although it is less obviously concerned with colonialism than *The* TEMPEST, *Othello* is the Shakespeare play that deals most overtly with 'race' and, as Caryl PHILLIPS makes clear in both his travel-book *The European Tribe* (1987) and his novel *The Nature of Blood* (1997), it is no coincidence that, like *The Merchant of Venice*, where the plot turns upon the behaviour of another ethnic outsider, Shylock, it is set in the trading capital of Renaissance Europe, Venice. As Phillips sees it, Venice 'was the New York of the Renaissance, controlling the whole of the Western world, dedicated to capitalism and an unthinking exploitative trade' (1993: 45). As such, its colonial sphere of influence offered a model for the capitalist-imperialist ventures on which Britain was embarking, ventures that increasingly involved contacts with 'OTHER races' and peoples. Quoting the play, Phillips refers to

Othello as an 'extravagant and wheeling stranger' (*Othello*, I.i.136), who has been co-opted into white society and finds himself 'a sad black man, first in a long line of so-called achievers' (Phillips 1998: 182).

Ania Loomba takes a similar position in pointing out that 'the play is not just about race in general but about a black man isolated from other black people. His loneliness is an integral feature of the play's racial politics' (Loomba 1998b: 148); and in recent years, post-colonial commentators have particularly focused on *Othello*. This possibly reflects the extent to which '"First World" societies find themselves compelled to address the inequities of internal colonization and the imperatives of multicultural-ism' (Cartelli 1999: 124) and the fact that, unlike Caliban, who is

> locked into his island kingdom where he must sink or swim, Othello has functioned from his moment of production as the exotic outsider, licensed, from the early modern period to the present, to move freely about the metropolitan 'First World' and to interact, on a privileged basis, with its movers and shakers. (ibid.: 124)

Clearly, there are differences between Caliban and Othello that have to do with both the geopolitical situations in which they find themselves and the ways in which their ethnicity is staged.

Recent productions of *Othello* such as Yvonne Brewster's at the Drill Hall, London (1997), which drew a parallel with the then-contemporary O. J. Simpson case, have emphasized the play's treatment of relationships between black men and white women and the responses these have elicited (see too Djanet Sears's *Harlem Duet*, mentioned below). Most notably, Janet Suzman's production for the Market Theatre in Johannesburg (1987) with John Kani in the title role moved the play a world away from classic renditions such as Laurence Olivier's performance in black-face. Earlier famous Othellos by black actors included those of Ira Aldridge (1833), the so-called 'African Roscius', and Paul Robeson (1930), whose partnering with Peggy Ashcroft as Desdemona also caused considerable controversy.

Phillips's work apart, recent post-colonial texts that specifically respond to *Othello* include the British-born Afro-Canadian dramatist Djanet Sears's *Harlem Duet* (1997), which foregrounds the omission of representations of black *women* in canon-ical Western texts by making the figure of 'Billie', Othello's first wife, its protagonist, while also addressing the emotions aroused by contemporary inter-racial sexual rela-tionship. George Lamming's *Water with Berries* (1971) also takes black male–white female relationship as a particular focus. Although the novel subordinates *Othello* ref-erences to its pervasive *Tempest* intertexts, its violent conclusion has a Caribbean-born actor, who has earlier achieved a limited degree of fame in Britain by playing Othello at Stratford, appearing to achieve a dubious liberation from English society's stereotyping by raping a white actress on stage. Other notable post-colonial responses to *Othello* include Salman Rushdie's *The Moor's Last Sigh* (1995) and a 1996 *kathakali* dance-theatre adaptation of the play, both of which are discussed by Loomba (1998b). However, such listings represent little more than the tip of an iceberg.

Cartelli provides details of some of the critical work on the play that appeared between 1987 and 1994 (Cartelli 1999: 204, Note 2 and bibliography).

Further reading

Phillips (1993); Loomba (1998b); Cartelli (1999); Thieme (2001).

'Otherness', alterity   Representational practices, such as ORIENTALISM, which see non-Western peoples as 'other' have been central to much colonial discourse. They characteristically involve the West's definition of a sense of self through differentiation from supposed 'otherness', or alterity. George LAMMING's phrase 'the Other's other', used to describe the predicament of a colonial Barbadian in his novel *In the Castle of My Skin* (1953), both identifies the extent to which such external definition denies colonial subjectivity the right to shape its own sense of selfhood and neatly contests this by foregrounding the extent to which it is the product of a figure who, from the colonized subject's point of view, is at least as alien. Much of Lamming's other work, most notably *The Pleasures of Exile* (1960), involves a similar contestation of this form of appropriation, as does Jamaica KINCAID's *A Small Place* (1988).

Instances of constructing non-Western peoples and places as 'other' are widespread in colonial writing, relating both to the representation of colonized peoples and places. Orientalism apart, examples of such practices discussed in this Glossary include CANNIBALISM, the 'DARK CONTINENT', post-colonial responses to CONRAD and SHAKA. See COUNTER-DISCOURSE and the SUBALTERN STUDIES project for examples of 'writing back' to such representation.

Further reading

Lamming (1960); Said (1985).

Ousmane Sembène   See SEMBÈNE, Ousmane.

Oyono, Ferdinand   Born 1929. Cameroonian novelist. Educated in Cameroon and France, Oyono later served as a Cameroonian diplomat and UN representative and at home as Minister for Foreign Affairs and Minister of Culture. His first novel, *Une Vie de boy* (1956; *Houseboy*, 1966) was an early fictional indictment of the injustices of colonialism. Using the form of a diary, it details the experiences of a Cameroonian teenager who becomes a houseboy for hypocritical white missionaries. *Le Vieux nègre et la médaille* (1956; *The Old Man and the Medal*, 1969) also foregrounds links between Christianity and colonial exploitation, this time through a focus on an ingenuous older protagonist, who suffers humiliation at the hands of the French administration that is ostensibly rewarding him for his services to the regime. Heavy irony lightens the mood of the novel without diminishing its critique of colonialism. A third novel, *Chemin d'Europe* (1960; *Road to Europe*, 1989) deals with the disenchantment suffered by a young Cameroonian who fulfils his dream of going to France.

P

Pakeha   Maori term for the white inhabitants of Aotearoa/New Zealand.

Palcy, Euzhan   Born 1958. Martinican film director. She first attracted international attention, when her 1983 film of Joseph Zobel's novel, *Rue Cases Nègres* won numerous international awards. It was made with the encouragement of François Truffaut, whom she had met in Paris after having gone there to study film-making in the 1970s. Her adaptation of André Brink's novel, *A Dry White Season* (1989) made her the first black woman to direct a Hollywood feature. Her other films include *Siméon* (1992), *Aimé Césaire: A Voice for History* (1994), a tribute to Martinique's most famous poet and the television films, *Ruby Bridges* (1998) and *The Killing Yard* (2001).

Pan-Africanism   Pan-Africanism is both a belief in the innate unity of all Africans and usually also people of African descent overseas and a political movement that seeks a united Africa. The movement was founded at the first Pan-African Congress convened in London in 1900 by H. Sylvester Williams. Subsequent congresses in Paris (1919), London and Brussels (1921), London and Lisbon (1923), and New York City (1927) were organized by W. E. B. DuBois, who is often regarded as the father of Pan-Africanism. The movement gained momentum in the 1930s as a consequence of the Italian invasion of Abyssinia (Ethiopia), which came to be seen as a black homeland from around this time, the period in which Rastafarianism has its beginnings.

After World War II, Pan-Africanism was increasingly associated with the independence struggle of Sub-Saharan African nations and the Sixth Pan-African Congress convened by George Padmore and Kwame Nkrumah in Manchester in 1945 was attended by several future African leaders, among them Jomo Kenyatta from Kenya, Nkrumah, S. L. Akintola from Nigeria and Wallace Johnson from Sierra Leone. At this Congress the mercurial and controversial Nkrumah, who would later become the first post-independence Prime Minister of an Anglophone Sub-Saharan nation when Ghana attained independence in 1957, founded the West African National Secretariat to promote a so-called United States of Africa. Pan-Africanism entered a new phase with the foundation of the OAU (Organisation of African Unity) in 1963. In the post-independence era the movement has sought to promote co-operation among African nations, to end white minority rule in countries such as South Africa and to combat the NEO-COLONIAL economic exploitation of 'DEVELOPING COUNTRIES'.

Parsi, Parsee   Adherent of a contemporary form of Zoroastrianism, an ancient religion of Persia (Iran) that has origins dating back to the sixth century BC Zoroastrianism involved the monotheistic worship of a single deity, Ahura Masda, along with a belief in an ethical dualism, in which truth and falsehood were opposed, cp. Christianity. In the seventh and eighth centuries AD, Parsis fled from Persia to avoid Muslim persecution. Today India has the largest population of Parsis: about 120,000, approximately two-thirds of whom live in Mumbai (Bombay). Their significance in Indian society has far exceeded their small numbers, since they have occupied important positions in business, especially banking, and other spheres of Indian public life. Parsis are among the most Westernized of Indian communities. Pakistan has a small population of Parsis, estimated at 5,200 and mainly settled in Karachi. There are also Parsi communities in London and elsewhere, while in Iran, a sect called the Gabars continues Zoroastrian customs. The holy book of the Parsis is the Avesta. Parsis revere fire as a purifying element and traditionally left their dead on towers to be consumed by vultures to avoid contamination, a practice that has declined today. Notable Parsi novelists include Rohinton MISTRY and Bapsi SIDHWA.

Partition, partition   In its most obvious political usage, 'partition' (lower case) refers to the division of a country or region as a consequence of the drawing of new frontiers or the establishment of new nation–states. It is, however, a term with numerous other resonances, many of which have implications for post-colonial studies.

The main period of colonial partition in Africa took place in the late nineteenth century, at the time of the 'SCRAMBLE FOR AFRICA', when European nations divided much of the continent's territory among themselves. See also the BERLIN CONFERENCE. This division of the continent resulted in the creation of nation–states which ignored existing geopolitical realities and particularly led to tensions between rival tribal and other groupings at the time when political independences were being achieved and in the post-independence era, generating such conflict as the NIGERIAN CIVIL WAR and the more recent Tutsi–Hutu fighting in Rwanda. At an opposite extreme, artificially constructed FEDERATIONS such as that in former Yugoslavia and the USSR have generated a separate set of divisions, at the point when the federation has collapsed.

India was partitioned at the time of independence, resulting in the formation of the new nation–state of Pakistan, which itself split into two countries after a civil war between its eastern and western wings led to the formation of Bangladesh in 1971. Indian novels in English about Partition (capitalized), written in the years following the event include Khushwant Singh's *Train to Pakistan / Mano Majra* (1956) and Manohar Malgonkar's *A Bend in the Ganges* (1964). A slightly later phase of writing about Partition includes such novels as Nayantara Sahgal's *Storm in Chandigarh* (1969) and Chaman Nahal's *Azadi* (1975). Salman Rushdie's *Midnight's Children* (1981) and Amitav Ghosh's *The Shadow Lines* (1988) both foreground the consequences that Partition has on the lives of a particular family, while also suggesting its broader implications as a signifying practice that divides people in other ways. Set in Lahore in the years leading up to Independence – and Partition – Bapsi Sidhwa's *Ice-Candy-Man* (1988) also shows the impact of Partition on particular lives, with the young Parsi narrator ingenuously asking the question 'Can one break a country?' and the novel's representation of the increasing proliferation of communal divisions, suggesting an answer in the affirmative. Much of the Urdu writer Saadat Hasan Manto's fiction concerns itself with the consequences of Partition and his short story 'Toba Tek Singh', in which the Sikh and Hindu inmates of a Lahore mental asylum display various responses to the prospect of being transferred to India, is perhaps the most compressed masterpiece illustrating the absurdism of Partition. Nothing in the inmates' lunatic behaviour, the story suggests, is quite as insane as the political situation they are forced to confront. More generally, the implications of Partition in the sub-continent extend far beyond the geographical, and different communities have attached very different spiritual associations to it. Thus for Hindus it has been particularly associated with dismemberment, since Hindu myths relate the body politic to the human body, while Muslim responses have frequently seen parallels with Muhammad's departure from Mecca to Medina in AD 622, the year that was subsequently established as the beginning of the Muslim era.

Apart from the Indian sub-continent, several other Asian countries saw partition in the twentieth century. These include Korea (divided into North and South) and Vietnam. Numerous European countries, including Poland, Germany, Ireland and Cyprus have also been partitioned in modern times, as a consequence of various forms of colonialism and external intervention. In the case of Ireland, where partition occurred when Northern Ireland was established as a self-governing province in 1920 in an attempt to recognize the needs of the Protestant majority in this part of the country, but with less attentiveness to those of the province's Catholic minority, it has generated tensions similar to those in Kashmir (divided between India and Pakistan). Cyprus was partitioned in 1974, when the Attila (or Sahin) line was introduced as a frontier dividing Greek and Turkish communities. However, the most extensive partition in modern Europe came into force when the Iron Curtain (Winston Churchill's 1946 phrase) was introduced after World War II, splitting Germany into two halves and dividing the Warsaw Pact countries of Eastern Europe from Western Europe. The Berlin Wall (built in 1961 and dismantled in 1989) became the central physical symbol of the bifurcation of Western and Eastern Europe.

The implications of partition for post-colonial studies are various. While the borders they introduce can be seen as CONTACT ZONES, the imposition of artificial boundaries restricting freedom of movement tends to work against contact and the kind of interstitial encounters privileged in much recent post-colonial theory. FEDERATION ostensibly operates in a converse manner, but frequently imposes equally artificial political CARTOGRAPHIES, suggesting that the achievement of a positive transnational awareness needs to move beyond the notion of the nation–state itself.

Patchwork, patchwork quilting Elaine Showalter has argued that the patchwork quilt has replaced the MELTING POT as the central metaphor of American cultural identity (quoted in Rogerson 1998: 5). She sees it as representing the emergence of a traditionally female paradigm of identity (Showalter 1991: 146ff.), made up of a collage of fragments involving the need to adapt, make do, conserve and bond with other women (Showalter 1991: 148–50; Rogerson 1998: 5), as an alternative model for national identity, which disputes the homogenizing notion of ASSIMILATION engrained in the melting pot model. Another aspect of contemporary patchwork has been the phenomenon of the AIDS quilt, which could also be seen to admit a marginalized group into the national discourse (Rogerson 1998: 5).

From the point of view of literature, patchwork has provided the central organizing figure for a number of notable novels by women, among them Whitney Otto's *How to Make an American Quilt* (1991) and Margaret Atwood's *Alias Grace* (1996). In Atwood's novel, each of the sections is headed by a particular quilt design and patchwork becomes a trope for both identity – especially, but not exclusively, women's identity – and the composition of the novel itself, which on one level can be viewed as an album of different quilt designs. The novel's central revelation, that the key to the mystery of whether its protagonist, the supposed murderess Grace Marks, sometimes viewed as Canada's Lizzie Borden, is actually guilty lies in schizophrenia, since she temporarily assumed another identity at the time of her alleged crime, provides further striking evidence of the patchwork nature of identity that challenges the world-views of the various males who brand her a hysteric.

The use of the trope of the patchwork quilt is not, however, confined to North America. It is also prominent in other literatures where the piecemeal, fragmentary composition of identity is foregrounded and consequently has particular significance for post-colonial cultural models. Thus in Indian texts in English that embody a non-ESSENTIALIST view of both personal and national identity, complementing this with textual structures that offer a formal correlative, the patchwork is once again a central metaphor. Githa HARIHARAN describes her novels as patchwork quilts and in Rohinton MISTRY's *A Fine Balance* (1995), where one of the characters imagines God as a giant quilt maker, the various stories told by the four main characters are 'stitched into a quilt' (Morey 2000: 177). Mistry's novel lends itself to interpretation as NATIONAL ALLEGORY, as does Salman RUSHDIE's *Midnight's Children* (1981), where the central organizing figure of the perforated sheet, comes to stand not only for the fragmentation of personal and social identity, but also for India and for the novel's technique, which Rushdie has referred to as 'the world viewed in fragments' (Rushdie 1982a). Amitav

Gʜᴏsʜ's use of weaving as a defining trope for cultural interaction in texts such as *The Circle of Reason* (1986) and *In an Antique Land* (1992) offers an analogous model, in this case for cross-cultural contacts, while his later novel *The Calcutta Chromosome* (1996) displaces this trope onto a more recent network of supranational cultural interaction, the world-wide web.

Dorothy Jones (1994) offers an account of the importance of fabric in colonial and post-colonial texts, which includes discussion of the patchwork trope and insights into such subjects as Gᴀɴᴅʜɪ's refabrication of Indian national identity through his emphasis on *khaddar* (homespun) as feminine and implicit representation of himself as female through such activities as spinning.

Further reading

Weiner and Schneider (eds) (1989); Showalter (1991); Jones (1994); Rogerson (1998); Morey (2000).

Penal colonies Problems that Britain had been experiencing with its surplus prison population for some two hundred years came to a head in the late eighteenth century, when the loss of its American colonies after the War of Independence resulted in the ending of the transportation of convicts to North America. Australia was established as a penal colony, with the first prisoners arriving in New South Wales in 1788. While only a minority of Australia's Aɴɢʟᴏ-Cᴇʟᴛɪᴄ settlers originate from convict backgrounds, this aspect of the modern nation's provenance has *sometimes* been seen as having played a significant role in shaping notions of Australian national identity, particularly in relation to Australia's ᴀᴍʙɪᴠᴀʟᴇɴᴛ relationship with England. Robert Hughes's *The Fatal Shore* (1987) is a highly readable account of the history of Australian convictism.

Marcus Clarke's classic nineteenth-century Australian novel, *His Natural Life* (1870) achieved fame as an indictment of the convict system, but is concerned with a broader complex of issues including the psychology of colonial 'exile'. Notable recent novels that engage with aspects of the convict experience include Thomas Keneally's *The Playmaker* (1987) and Peter Carey's *Jack Maggs* (1997). *The Playmaker* is a fictional treatment of the first 'white' Australian theatrical performance, a staging of George Farquhar's *The Recruiting Officer* by the convicts of the First Fleet in 1789. *Jack Maggs* tells the story of a figure, loosely based on Magwitch, the convict in Dickens's *Great Expectations*, and in a complex, multi-faceted novel, which subverts colonial notions of ꜰɪʟɪᴀᴛɪᴏɴ, inverts the relationship between 'Mother Country' and antipodean colony, concluding by suggesting the superiority of the latter. Laurie Hergenhan's *Unnatural Lives* (1983) is a study of convict fiction.

Further reading

White, R. (1981); Hergenhan (1983); Hughes (1987).

Periphery   See CENTRE AND PERIPHERY, CENTRE AND MARGINS.

Phillips, Caryl   Born 1958. Caribbean-British novelist, travel-writer and film-maker. Born in St Kitts, Phillips was brought up in Leeds and Birmingham and has a degree in English from Oxford University. After being involved in student theatre and writing a number of plays, including *Strange Fruit* (1980), a naturalistic drama about family conflicts, he turned to fiction. He has held professorial appointments at the University of the West Indies, Barbados and Amherst College and Barnard College in the USA, where he currently lives.

Phillips's first novel, *The Final Passage* (1985) follows the fortunes of a Caribbean woman who migrates to England. *A State of Independence* (1986) describes a West Indian's return to his native island at the time of its independence celebrations and illustrates some of the difficulties surrounding this kind of homecoming and the failure of the islanders to achieve real freedom – as in V. S. NAIPAUL's *In a Free State* (1971), the title of the novel suggests the ironies of 'independence'. It was followed by a number of novels dealing with various aspects of the African DIASPORA and the experience of minorities in Europe, which employ multiple narrators and a POLYPHONIC technique.

Phillips's first major novel, *Cambridge* (1991), is set on a nineteenth-century Caribbean plantation. It is mainly concerned with the murder of an overseer by the eponymous hero, but tells its story from multiple viewpoints, which in turn draw on intertexts ranging from plantation owners' journals to Olaudah EQUIANO's *Narrative* (O'Callaghan 1993), thereby presenting competing versions of events that deny ultimate authority to any one character or set of interests. *Crossing the River* (1993) is similarly multi-optic, in this case interweaving stories which span a CONTINUUM of experience that includes excerpts from the journal of an eighteenth-century MIDDLE PASSAGE captain on the West Coast of Africa and a narrative of a World War II interracial romance and its legacy. The various component parts are linked by a common focus on the enduring consequences of the Atlantic Slave Trade and come together in the epilogue in a 'many-tongued chorus of the common memory', which though mainly comprised of African diaspora voices expands outwards to incorporate 'other children'. *Higher Ground* (1989) and *The Nature of Blood* (1997), which employs protagonists based on OTHELLO and Anne Frank, broaden Phillips's depiction of interracial issues by drawing analogies between black and Jewish experiences of racial discrimination. He has also written about Othello in his travel-book *The European Tribe* (1987), in which he journeys to a number of European countries, ironically subverting the method of many European travel-writers by turning a quasi-ETHNOGRAPHIC eye on Europe itself. In his second travel-book, *The Atlantic Sound* (2000), he journeys to the three corners of the TRIANGULAR TRADE.

Phillips's other works include the screenplay for his film, *Playing Away* (1987), in which a cricket match between a team from Brixton and a team from an English village provides a focus for an ironic cross-cultural comedy of manners that discovers both similarities and dissimilarities between visitors and hosts. His anthology *Extravagant Strangers: A Literature of Belonging* (1997) brings together a wide range of writing by British writers born outside the country and in so doing questions Britain's 'vision of herself as a nation that is both culturally and ethnically homogeneous', arguing instead that the country has been 'forged in the crucible of fusion – of hybridity' (ibid.: x). Phillips is General Editor of the Faber Caribbean Writers Series and has also edited an anthology of tennis writing, *The Right Set: The Faber Book of Tennis* (1999). *A New World Order* (2001) is a collection of his essays. His other film scripts include the screenplay for Ismail MERCHANT's film of Naipaul's *The Mystic Masseur* (2001).

Further reading

O'Callaghan (1993); Ledent (2002).

Pidgin   Believed to derive from a Chinese corruption of English 'business', a pidgin is a grammatically and lexically simplified form of an established language, used as a means of communication between groups that otherwise have no common language. Prominent pidgins have developed from English, French and Portuguese. Pidgins exist in all parts of the world, with particular prominence in the western Pacific Rim and Atlantic coastal regions and more generally in regions that have been colonized. They differ from CREOLES, which are generally distinguished from pidgins as the mother tongues of speakers and as lexically more complicated and capable of expressing *all* the linguistic needs of a speech community. The distinction is, however, less clear-cut than this suggests, since pidgins and Creoles characteristically operate on a 'post-Creole continuum', which itself may be seen as a linguistic expression of the flux of HYBRID CONTACTS. See also DIALECT, NATION LANGUAGE.

Further reading

Todd (1990); Holm (2000).

Plantocracy   The ruling planter class. Also the system of government that operated in many plantation-based colonial economies, through which this class ruled.

Plural, pluralism   'Pluralism' is loosely analogous with MULTICULTURALISM and is a term employed to describe societies, in which no single system, based on religion, class or creed, predominates. The term came into common usage in the late 1960s and 1970s and is generally used positively to connote tolerance and cultural diversity. As a signifier that is antithetical to monoculturalism, it usually has positive connotations in post-colonial contexts, though sometimes, like cultural diversity and multiculturalism, it is seen as part of a liberal discourse that fails to provide an adequate articulation of cultural difference. POLYPHONY is one of the characteristic formal modes of plural texts.

Polyphony, polyphonic   Multi-voicedness. Originally a term used to refer to music in which several parts are combined simultaneously, particularly compositions in which various voices are interwoven in counterpoint. The Russian formalist critic Mikhail Bakhtin's work on the 'dialogic' novel was influential in disseminating its application in literary contexts. Bakhtin used it to refer to texts in which several authorial voices are employed, without any one being privileged over the others. This differs from 'polysemy', which is used to indicate a multiplicity of meanings and hence the indeterminacy of the sign more generally.

Bakhtin's view of narrative polyphony sees it as enacting a democratic politics, in which mutually exclusive positions can co-exist without any one voice being allowed definitive authority, as tends to happen in narratives employing a unitary mode, especially those where a controlling authorial voice does have primacy. Bakhtin's usage of the term, to refer to the narrative practice of authors such as Dostoevsky, makes no direct reference to post-colonial discourse, but polyphony is widely used in post-colonial writing, where the opportunities it offers for the representation of alternative viewpoints that are given equal authority makes for a relativistic vision that disturbs the monocultural modes of perception, commonly associated with colonial discourse. More radically, it challenges assumptions about HEGEMONIC power, by destabilizing the binary classification systems of MANICHEAN ALLEGORY, in which the authorial voice separates itself from 'alterity' (see 'OTHERNESS'). Needless to say numerous canonical Western texts are dialogic in structure and similarly many post-colonial texts employ unitary narrative voices. Nevertheless it remains reasonable to associate polyphonic modes with an idealized post-colonial practice and unitary narrative modes with authoritarian forms of colonial discourse.

Examples of post-colonial texts that employ a polyphonic method include the short stories of Ama Ata AIDOO's *No Sweetness Here* (1970), Erna BRODBER's *Jane and Louisa Will Soon Come Home* (1980) and Caryl PHILLIPS's *Crossing the River* (1993). The use of multiple focalizers (or points of view) within the framework of a single, controlling narrative voice can have a similar effect, as in NGUGI wa Thiong'o's *A Grain of Wheat* (1967) and Anita DESAI's *Clear Light of Day* (1980), though it is usually more diluted in such instances.

Further reading

Bakhtin (1994).

Postcolonial, post-colonial   See the HYPHEN IN 'POST(-)COLONIAL' and the Preface.

Postcolonial Forum   A newsletter published three times a year by the Centre for Colonial and Postcolonial Studies at the University of Kent. The hard-copy newsletter contains listings of forthcoming conferences and events, calls for contributions, reviews of books and academic journal and details of other recent publications.

Postcolonial Forum also exists in an on-line version, which does not replicate the material published in the hard copy. Website: www.ukc.ac.uk/english/postcolonial/postcolonialforum.

Postcolonial Studies   Journal founded in 1998 and published by Routledge. It is mainly edited from Melbourne by Michael Dutton, Leela Gandhi and Sanjay Seth. Its fourth editor is Dipesh Chakrabarty (Chicago). The journal covers the fields of culture, politics and economics.

Prawer, Ruth   See Jhabvala, Ruth Prawer.

Présence Africaine   Journal founded in Paris in 1947 by a group of African intellectuals and students. Its first number was published simultaneously in Paris and Dakar and its founding editor, the Senegalese writer, Alioune Diop, outlined its purpose as 'to define African originality and hasten its insertion in the modern world'. This project inevitably involved it with Negritudinist thinking and also had the effect of associating it with the nationalist political causes predominant in Pan-African politics in the 1950s, although it had been established as a purely cultural journal.

Prospero and Caliban   Characters from Shakespeare's final play, *The Tempest*, who, like Defoe's Man Friday and Robinson Crusoe, have been widely used by post-colonial and other writers and theorists as archetypes of the colonizer and colonized.

The Quit India Resolution   A resolution to bring about the end of British rule in India passed by the Congress Party in 1942, after the rejection of its offer to co-operate with Britain in World War II, if India was granted immediate independence. Independence was attained in 1947 and the Quit India Resolution is generally thought to have been a decisive factor in bringing the Raj to an end, though some commentators point to a broader complex of causes, including the activities of the pro-Japanese 'Indian National Army' in Burma (Myanmar) and economic considerations that arose during and immediately after the war.

The Qur'an, The Koran, The Quran   The holy book of Islam, consisting of revelations uttered by the Prophet Muhammad at Mecca and Medina and believed to have been transmitted to him by the archangel Gabriel. The *Qur'an*'s revelations were transcribed into written Arabic in the seventh century AD and traditional believers consider them untranslatable into other languages, since they are the literal word of God. This belief also underlies the view that ascribing the apocryphal 'satanic verses' (see Salman RUSHDIE) to Muhammad is heretical. The authorized version of the *Qur'an* was established during the caliphate of Othman (AD 644–56) and consists of 114 *suras*, or chapters, of varying length. The revelations of the *Qur'an* relate to many areas of human experience, spiritual and secular, and provide the basis of SHARIA LAW.

The form *Qur'an* is often preferred to the alternative forms of *Koran* and *Quran* as a closer transliteration of the original Arabic form of the word.

R

'Race', racism   Classic anthropology endeavoured to classify the world's peoples as a number of physically distinct genetic types, using categories such as skin colour, hair type, physiognomy and other physical characteristics to do so. Such anthropological activity was at its height in the post-Darwinian late nineteenth century, when, for example, ABORIGINES' skulls were brought from Australia to England so that they could be measured and provided a pseudo-scientific underpinning for the colonial subjugation of supposedly less developed forms of humanity. The three main groups identified by such anthropology were Caucasian, Mongoloid and Negroid. Today the concept of 'race' is widely viewed as a discursive construction, which continues to be used to assert the superiority of particular groups of people over others or to legitimize stereotypical representations of 'alterity' (see 'OTHERNESS').

Nevertheless 'race' remains a potent force in popular belief and is frequently invoked to sanction the practice of various forms of ra*cism*, which base discrimination on the ascription of stereotypical qualities to particular ethnic groups. Debates about the extent to which human characteristics are the product of biological determinism rather than socialization continue to rage in various forms. Those who contend that specific abilities are the product of nurture rather than nature suggest, for example, that the success of black athletes in 'explosive' events such as sprinting, as opposed to events that require stamina, may have more to do with social expectations and conditioning than innate physical prowess, a view that is supported by the successes of Kenyan and Ethiopian athletes in long-distance running rather than sprinting.

While racism has long historical origins, the term dates from the 1930s, when Fascist attempts to assert the superiority of an Aryan master race led to the development of a complex hierarchical classification of ethnic groups. Ashcroft *et al.* (1998: 198–206) provide a valuable summary of the evolution of thinking about 'race' from the Renaissance period onwards, particularly focusing on its use in colonial contexts to enforce asymmetrical binary divisions that justify imperialism. These include the privileging of 'civilized' European values over those of 'primitive' peoples and of 'pure' blood over 'mixed' ancestry, a perspective that has been radically challenged by more recent post-colonial approaches that stress the positive aspects of HYBRIDITY. Ashcroft *et al.* conclude that the term 'ETHNICITY' is preferable to 'race', on the grounds that it places less emphasis on biological determinism and allows for more fluidity.

Further reading

Bolt (1971); Gates (1986); Malik (1996); Ashcroft *et al.* (1998).

Ramanujan, A. K. (1929–93). Indian poet and translator. After his early education in India, Ramanujan attended Indiana University as a Fulbright Scholar and subsequently worked for many years as a Professor of Linguistics and South Asian Civilization at the University of Chicago. One of India's most important twentieth-century poets, his own work has been composed in English and Tamil; and his translations from Kannada and Tamil have also been highly praised as major creative works. His volumes of verse in English include *The Striders* (1966), *Relations* (1971), *Selected Poems* (1976) and *Second Sight* (1986). *Speaking of Siva* (1976) brings together his acclaimed translations of Kannada devotional lyrics.

Ramanujan's poems frequently return to his South Asian BRAHMIN origins, reconstructing this past in memory and demonstrating a complex and AMBIVALENT response to his ancestral background. Thus in one of his best-known poems, 'Small-Scale Reflections on a Great House', the trope of the house seems to signify Hindu India, with the persona saying 'Sometimes I think that nothing/ that ever comes into this house/ goes out'. If initially this suggests an enclosed and suffocating world, the use of the trope also points, albeit not without irony, towards the inclusiveness of Hinduism and its capacity to accommodate and neutralize outside influences.

The *Ramayana* One of the two great epics of SANSKRIT literature, taking its title from its hero, Rama, the seventh avatar of the god Vishnu, often seen in Hinduism as the ideal man, embodying the virtues of courage, reason and virtue. The epic has some 24,000 lines in seven books and dates from around 300 BC. Its main episode concerns the abduction of Rama's beloved, Sita, sometimes equated with Mother India, by Ravana, the many-headed demon king of Lanka (modern Sri Lanka) and Rama's expedition to rescue her, in which he is assisted by the monkey god, Hanuman. Rama subsequently has doubts about Sita's chastity and tests her by subjecting her to an ordeal by fire, which proves her virtue. However, Rama later abandons her and banishes her to the forest, an act which undermines the romantic pattern of the earlier heroic journey and which has led some contemporary feminist commentators to question Rama's heroic status and to demand a re-interpretation of Sita's role.

Although it is only a fraction of the length of the other great Sanskrit epic, the MAHABHARATA, the *Ramayana* contains an abundance of other narrative strands and is believed, like Homer, to be an accretion of oral stories that were circulating during the period of its 'composition'. Its best-known version has been attributed to the scribe, Valmiki, but there are numerous other later versions in several of India's regional languages, such as the eleventh-century Tamil poet Kamban's, which R. K. NARAYAN used for his retelling (1972). Unlike the epics of Homer and Virgil, it remains part of everyday Hindu life, with dramatic performances being staged up and down the length of the sub-continent Its influence has also extended eastwards and performance forms based on its legends occupy an important place in various South-East Asian cultures.

Rao, Raja Born 1908. South Indian novelist born in Hassan, Mysore (now Karnataka), from a distinguished South Indian BRAHMIN family. Rao studied literature and history at the universities of Montpellier and Paris. Along with Mulk Raj ANAND and R. K. NARAYAN, he came to the fore as a novelist in the 1930s, as one of the 'BIG THREE' of Indian fiction in English. Most of his work has a strong metaphysical bent and is steeped in Vedantic Hinduism. His first novel, *Kanthapura* (1938), is his most accessible; it is also more obviously concerned with social issues than his subsequent writing. It deals with the Indian independence movement, as seen from the point of view of a South Indian grandmother, whose narrative draws extensively on oral myth and folklore. She gives an account of how her village's struggle against the Raj comes to be informed by AHIMSA, the GANDHIAN belief in non-violent resistance. The novel's Foreword stresses the degree to which Indian village society is permeated by legend and is also notable for its comment on the problem of conveying 'in a language that is not one's own the spirit that is one's own', which anticipates later comments on the process of adapting English for use in India, albeit without recognizing the inevitable Indianization that Standard English undergoes. After World War II, Rao lived in India and France before moving, in 1965, to the University of Texas in Austin, where he taught until 1983.

France provides the setting for most of his semi-autobiographical second novel, *The Serpent and the Rope* (1960), though geographical locale is secondary to the exploration of inner spiritual states. The novel is about the breakdown of the marriage of a young brahmin, who is researching the history of the Cathars (a MANICHEAN sect) and seeking spiritual truth through Vedantic philosophy in India and England, as well as France. Based on a story from the MAHABHARATA, it uses the marriage theme as a means for exploring relationships between India and Europe. The serpent of the title is *maya* (worldly illusion); the rope signifies reality. Considered by some to be not only Rao's masterpiece, but also the finest Indian-English novel of its period, *The Serpent and the Rope* has been criticized by others for Hindu ESSENTIALISM and androcentrism.

Rao's other novels are *The Cat and Shakespeare* (1965), *Comrade Kirillov* (1976) and *The Chessmaster and His Moves* (1988). He has also published the short story collections, *The Cow of the Barricades* (1947), *The Policeman and The Rose* (1978) and *On the Ganga Ghat* (1993), and a biography of GANDHI, *Great Indian Way* (1998). *The Meaning of India* (2000) is a collection of his essays.

Rastafari, Rastafarianism   A religious movement, which has its origins in a small sect that came into being in Kingston, Jamaica in the 1930s. Inspired by the PAN-AFRICANIST Marcus GARVEY, who is alleged to have told his followers to 'Look to Africa, where a black king shall be crowned', dispossessed urban Jamaicans found a spiritual leader in the figure of Ras Tafari, Haile Selassie (Tafari Makonnen, 1892–1975), the last Ethiopian Emperor. When Selassie returned to Ethiopia from a period of exile in Britain in 1941, Rastafarians viewed this as the fulfilment of Garvey's words and of a prophecy in *Revelations* and hailed him as the Messiah, although he resisted the categorization himself. They saw themselves as reincarnations of the exiled Israelites of the Bible, adopted aspects of the worship and beliefs of the Ethiopian Orthodox Church and advocated repatriation to 'Zion' (Africa) to escape oppression in 'Babylon' (Jamaica and the white Establishment more generally). While some of the movement's members have made this journey, the call to return is often interpreted symbolically, as an injunction to recognize the African aspects of Jamaican and other African DIASPORA communities and to live according to an African-derived set of values. These include anti-materialism, pacifism, eating *I-tal* (natural) food, the subordination of women, racial equality, the smoking of ganja (marijuana) to reach a heightened state of spiritual consciousness and the wearing of dreadlocks. Belief in Rastafarian values is seen as initiating a process of self-discovery, which involves recognition of one's inner identity. Rastafari has no churches or formal leaders.

In its early days the movement was vilified in Jamaica, but the University of the West Indies' influential *Report on the Rastafari Movement in Kingston Jamaica* (1960), co-authored by M. G. Smith, Roy Augier and Rex NETTLEFORD, served as a corrective to public misconceptions about its nature and beliefs. Over a period of decades, Rastafari spread throughout the Caribbean and then to Europe and North America, a phenomenon which lends support to Paul Gilroy's contention that the BLACK ATLANTIC is a single, transnational geopolitical area. Along with REGGAE, it became an important force in black identity politics, helping to create an international sub-culture, which, while sometimes more secular than spiritual in outlook, offered a framework for self-identification and cultural resistance that attracted many Afro-Caribbean youths, who espoused its dress codes and various other aspects of its life-style. Rastafarianism has influenced various reggae performers, most notably Bob MARLEY, whose international popularity played a major role in disseminating awareness of its beliefs, and DUB POETS such as Linton Kwesi JOHNSON, 'Mikey' SMITH and Jean 'Binta' Breeze, who draw on the distinctive speech of Rasta communities as well as NATION LANGUAGE more generally.

(Edward) Kamau Brathwaite's poem 'Wings of a Dove' (in *Islands*, 1969) is a complex early treatment of the figure of a Rastafarian. Fictional representations include Roger Mais's novel, *Brother Man* (1953), Orlando Patterson's *Children of Sisyphus* (1964) and N. D. Williams's *Ikael Torass* (1976).

Further reading

Campbell (1987); Barrett (1988); Alleyne (1988); Dawes (1999).

Ray, Satyajit (1921–92). Bengali film director and writer. Born in Calcutta, Ray was strongly influenced by the work of Rabindranath Tagore, whom he met as a young boy and whose university, Shantineketan in West Bengal, he attended. He later made a 1961 documentary about the Nobel Prize winner. Ray studied fine arts and subsequently worked as a commercial artist. He was fascinated with Hollywood cinema from an early age and during the 1940s found a departure point for the formation of his own distinctive style in the work of the European directors, Jean Renoir, René Clair and Vittorio De Sica. De Sica's *Bicycle Thieves* provided the inspiration for the neorealism of his first film, *Pather Pachali* (*The Song of the Road*, 1955). This marked the beginning of his long collaboration with the cinematographer, Subrata Mitra, who later became the cameraman for the early films of Merchant Ivory. The filming of *Pather Pachali*, which was mainly shot in southern India, began in 1952, but was interrupted midway, when funding ran out, and was not completed until three years later. Adapted from a novel by his fellow Bengali, Bibhutibhushan Bandyopadhyay, the film tells the story of a young boy called Apu born into a Brahmin family in rural Bengal. It immediately established Ray's characteristically reticent humanist style, which shows the influence of Tagore, and he has written of his admiration for 'far-eastern calligraphy, which goes to the heart of perceived reality and expresses it by means of minimal brush strokes applied with maximum discipline' (Ray 1976: 11). Despite its immersion in a local rural landscape, *Pather Pachali* immediately established Ray's international reputation and was followed by the two subsequent parts of his 'Apu trilogy', *Aparatijo* (*The Unvanquished*, 1956) and *Apu Sansar* (*The World of Apu*, 1958).

Subsequent major Ray films include *Charulata* (*The Lonely Wife*, 1964), a delicate study of a neglected wife who takes a lover, *Aranyer Din Ratri* (*Days and Nights in the Forest*, 1970) and *Jalsaghar* (*The Music Room*, 1958), the story of an elderly *zamindar* (landlord), a relic of an older generation who is both ridiculed and observed with affectionate nostalgia as he holds a final party in defiance of the new social order that has replaced the world he represents. The role of music in *Jalsaghar* is paralleled by that of chess in Ray's first Urdu (not, as is commonly thought, Hindi) film, *Shantranj Ke Kilari* (*The Chess Players*, 1977), which was adapted from a short story by Premchand, one of India's finest Hindi writers. Again the story depicts an elitist India which ignores the impact of external forces that are threatening its very existence: in this case two *zamindars* immerse themselves in playing chess during the period of the nineteenth-century British annexation of the kingdom of Oudh. Meanwhile the king devotes himself to artistic pleasures and eventually allows the British to dethrone him without any resistance.

Ray was an auteur who ensured he was involved in virtually every aspect of the production of his films, often writing his own screenplays and composing their musical scores. From *Charulata* onwards, he acted as his own cameraman. During the radical 1960s, his pre-eminence in Bengali cinema was challenged by the emergence of a younger generation of directors, including such film-makers as Mrinal Sᴇɴ, who felt his films lacked sufficient political commitment. However, with the exception of occasional forays into mythological subjects such as *Devi* (*The Goddess*, 1960), he continued to work in his characteristic mode of quietly understated realism and also made a number of documentaries. During the latter part of his career, a heart condition prevented him from shooting on location and, although his low-key technique had never placed much emphasis on external action, some commentators feel there was a slight falling off in the quality of his work.

Ray's other films include *Kanchenjunga* (1962), *Mahanagar* (*The Big City*, 1963), *Nayak* (*The Hero*, 1966), *Seemabaddha* (*Company Limited*, 1972) and *Ashani Sanket* (*Distant Thunder*, 1974), *Ghare-Baire* (*The Home and the World*, 1984), and *Agantuk* (*The Stranger*, 1991). *Pather Pachali* won the special jury prize for the 'Best Human Document' at the 1956 Cannes Film Festival and Ray's numerous other awards included a Hollywood Oscar for lifetime achievement (1992). *Our Films, Their Films* (1976) is a collection of his talks and articles on cinema. He also wrote numerous short stories in Bengali and is particularly known for his fiction for teenagers, which include detective stories and work in various fantasy genres.

Further reading

Ray (1976); Robinson (1989).

Reggae   The most widely known form of Jamaican popular music, which evolved from earlier Jamaican musical forms such as rock steady and sᴋᴀ in the 1960s. Its most distinctive feature is a strong accent on the upbeat in each bar. The international popularity of Bob Mᴀʀʟᴇʏ spread its influence internationally and its incantatory beat has pervaded the idioms of Western pop music, influencing such forms as rap, gansta rap and hip-hop. Other acclaimed reggae performers have included Jimmy Cliff, who starred in the first feature film to make extensive use of the music, Perry Henzell's *The Harder They Come* (1973) and Peter Tosh.

The music has been associated with the spread of Rᴀsᴛᴀꜰᴀʀɪᴀɴ beliefs and codes and, although often appropriated by the Westernized global music industry, has generally been seen as an importance force in the anti-colonial political struggle. It is perhaps best seen as an aesthetic practice, which encapsulates a whole way of perceiving the world and which, in Kwame Dawes's words, 'provided Jamaica (and the Caribbean region) with an artistic form that has a distinctively postcolonial aesthetic' (1999: 17). Steve Barrow and Peter Dalton's *Rough Guide to Reggae* (1997) is an immensely informative account of the music, with chapters on the earlier musical forms from which it developed. The expanded second edition of the *Guide* (2001) extends coverage into more contemporary offshoots such as ragga.

Further reading

Clarke (1980); Dawes (1999); Barrow and Dalton (2001).

Regionalism 'Regionalism' is a term that has been employed in two more or less diametrically opposed ways: sometimes to suggest the distinctiveness of particular geopolitical areas, e.g. the Prairie regions of the USA and particularly Canada, often asserting their differences from the centralist discourses of a particular nation–state, sometimes to suggest the overall coherence of an area comprising several countries, e.g. the Caribbean region. The former usage has the more interesting implications for post-colonial studies, since it expresses the felt need of what has traditionally been regarded as the periphery to separate itself from the HEGEMONIC authority of the supposed CENTRE, i.e. it is a project that involves emancipation from *internal* political and cultural colonization. Historically, marginalized regions were frequently expected to subordinate any sense of difference to the national discourse, e.g. as in Western Canada or the Basque region of Spain. Their increasing assertions of distinctiveness have found expression in political contexts, varying from separatist movements to campaigns for limited forms of devolved authority, and these have their cultural correlatives in art forms that suggest that the dominant discourse occludes expression of the concerns of the particular region.

Regional writing has passed through various phases. Early forms tend to be associated with 'local colour', usually represented in realist modes of writing. More recent forms have often extended the imaginative possibilities of 'region' by turning to fabulist modes such as MAGIC REALISM.

Further reading

Alonso (1990); Jordan (1994).

Reid, V(ictor) S(tafford) (1913–87) Jamaican novelist. V. S. Reid was involved with the FOCUS GROUP in the pre-independence NATIONALIST phase of Jamaican writing and worked as a journalist and editor of various publications. His most significant achievement, *New Day* (1949), has been seen as a novel that prefigures many of the concerns of the major generation of ANGLOPHONE Caribbean novelists that emerged in the 1950s. *New Day* is an historical novel, dealing with events in Jamaican history between 1865, the year of the MORANT BAY REBELLION, and 1944, the year when a new constitution which extended the franchise was introduced. Its gradualist approach to political change is said to reflect the policies of Norman Manley, on whom the hero of the later sections is based. It is notable for its use of a modified form of Jamaican Creole as the narrative medium of the novel, a technique that was unprecedented in a work of this length at the time when it appeared. Its narrator is an 87-year-old man, who in the first half of the novel remembers seeing the events of the rebellion as a young boy, an angle of vision which provides the novelist with an ideal perspective for discovering and documenting hitherto unrecorded aspects of the Jamaican landscape and folk experience. Drawing on personal testimony, the novel's oral method challenges the official HISTORIOGRAPHICAL account of the colonial society.

Reid also treated the events of the rebellion in his children's book, *Sixty-Five* (1960). His second novel *The Leopard* (1958), set in Kenya at the time of the Mau Mau insurgency, attempted to counter the negative representation of the movement in the Western media. Like Denis Williams's *Other Leopards* (1963), it employs a protagonist torn between different ancestral strands (in this case 'half Kikuyu, half Masai') in a manner which reflects the ambivalence of the Caribbean relationship to Africa. Reid published two further historical novels, dealing with resistance to colonial authority: *The Jamaicans* (1976), set in the seventeenth century; and *Nanny-Town* (1983), which tells the story of the Maroon woman warrior who led her people in the struggle against English rule. *The Horses of the Morning* (1985) is a biography of Norman Manley.

Further reading

Cooke (1993).

Research in African Literatures   One of the leading journals in its field, *Research in African Literatures* is published four times a year by Indiana University Press. Its founding editor was Bernth Lindfors and it was published by the University of Texas Press for more than 20 years. *RAL* prints work on both the oral and written literatures of Africa and includes reviews, information on African publishing and notes and queries. The journal also publishes special issues and symposia on particular topics. The current editor is Abiola Irele.

Rhizome   Like many post-colonial terms, including cross-pollination, HYBRIDITY and transplantation, the trope of the rhizome is taken from botany. Unlike roots, which grow downwards from the plant – just as a family tree centred on an individual traces ancestry, downwards or upwards, through multiple generations following a linear pattern – the rhizome grows haphazardly and is suggestive of the complex entanglement of factors that shape identity. It forms a central aspect of the Martinican writer and theorist, Édouard Glissant's work on Caribbean identity, which challenges originary and ESSENTIALIST conceptions of subjectivity. Glissant's use of the term derives from the French theorists, Gilles Deleuze and Félix Guattari.

Further reading

Deleuze and Guattari (1987); Glissant (1989).

Rhys, Jean (Ella Gwendolen Rees Williams) (1890–1979). Dominican-born novelist and short story writer of mixed Welsh and white CREOLE parentage who, after moving to England in 1907, lived in Europe for the remainder of her life, only returning to Dominica once. Rhys's autobiographically based early novels, published between 1928 and 1939, deal with female protagonists living on the margins of society in London or Paris. They attracted comparatively little attention when first published, but since the success of her masterpiece, *Wide Sargasso Sea* (1966), have come to be regarded as feminist classics, though some commentators have expressed reservations about the extent to which the typical Rhys heroine defines herself through relationships with and dependence on men. Three times married, Rhys lived in Paris during the 1920s, at one point in a *ménage à trois* with the writer Ford Madox Ford, who became her literary mentor, and his wife. The influence of Modernism manifests itself in *Wide Sargasso Sea* in the use of interior monologue and an emphasis on the subjectivity of perceptions. However, as Helen Carr (1996) points out, her version of Modernism is distinctively different from that of the major male Modernists.

Rhys disappeared from public attention for two decades, but was rediscovered when the BBC broadcast a dramatization of her novel, *Good Morning, Midnight* (1939) in 1957 and was encouraged to develop a novel that would reclaim 'the first Mrs Rochester' (her original working title for the book), the 'madwoman in the attic' of Charlotte Brontë's *Jane Eyre*, from the Gothic margins. While there are some similarities between her earlier fiction and *Wide Sargasso Sea*, in that the protagonist Antoinette (significantly renamed from the 'Bertha' of *Jane Eyre*) is another isolated victim of a patriarchal society, the novel's canvas is much larger and its fictional technique more complex. In telling the story of the Creole heiress, Antoinette's early life in the Caribbean, Rhys provides a compelling explanation of the factors that contribute to her alleged 'madness', while also dramatizing her husband's (he is never called 'Rochester') sense of alienation in the tropics. The long central section of the novel is located in her home island of Dominica and draws both on her own early life and a novel by another white Dominican writer, Phyllis Shand Allfrey's *The Orchid House* (1953). Although its action is circumscribed by events in *Jane Eyre*, *Wide Sargasso Sea* ends with Antoinette dreaming of leaping back to the Caribbean and her childhood, an act that suggests resurrection as opposed to the destructiveness of the suicidal act of arson that ends Bertha's life in *Jane Eyre*. It also involves a conscious choice of the other side of the 'wide Sargasso Sea', a region that has been represented as hellish in the earlier novel. Rhys's other fiction includes the novels *Quartet* (original title: *Postures*, 1928), *After Leaving Mr Mackenzie* (1930), *Voyage in the Dark* (1934) and her *Collected Short Stories* (1987).

Her 'unfinished autobiography', *Smile Please* (1979) was published posthumously. Carole Angier's *Jean Rhys* (1990) is the definitive biography.

Further reading

Carr (1996); Angier (1990); Howells (1991); Thomas (1999).

***Robinson Crusoe*, post-colonial responses to** Along with *The* TEMPEST and CONRAD's *Heart of Darkness*, Daniel Defoe's *Robinson Crusoe* (1719) is one of three canonical English texts that overtly engage with particular phases of English colonialism and, like Caliban and Prospero in *The Tempest*, Defoe's Friday and Crusoe have frequently been seen by post-colonial commentators as archetypes of the colonizer and colonized. *Robinson Crusoe* is specifically concerned with the expansionist mercantilist culture of the late seventeenth and early eighteenth centuries and political economists such as Karl Marx have seen Crusoe as a type of *homo economicus* (economic man), a figure for whom everything can be rendered in terms of double-entry book-keeping. Edward SAID comments on the colonial dimension of this in *Culture and Imperialism*: 'Robinson Crusoe is virtually unthinkable without the colonizing mission that permits him to create a new world of his own in the distant reaches of the African, Pacific, and Atlantic wilderness' (1994: 75). Defoe's novel not only thematizes the capitalist ethic in a Caribbean context, which allows his castaway to construct an island kingdom that has virtually all the aspects of a plantation economy, including a one-man labour force in the figure of Friday and only lacks a market-place in which Crusoe can trade, it also embodies it within the verisimilitude of its Puritan fictional practice, which has led to its being seen as the founding text of English fictional realism. As such, 'it is a materialist text in two senses: a work in which the profit motive is the driving force of the hero *and* a text in which everything can be assigned a material value, in terms of its weight, worth or magnitude' (Thieme 2001: 54–5). Consequently, it has become a doubly significant text for post-colonial COUNTER-DISCOURSE that 'writes back' to the canon.

Caribbean responses to *Robinson Crusoe* include revisionist comic treatments of the Friday–Crusoe relationship in Sam SELVON's *Moses Ascending* (1975), the second novel of his trilogy about Caribbean-British migrants, and Derek WALCOTT's play, *Pantomime* (1980), a two-hander set in a Tobago hotel. Both work playful variations on the roles of Friday and Crusoe, appropriate to the renegotiations of the colonized/colonizer relationship taking place in the post-colonial period, but ultimately, like most counter-discourse, are more notable for destabilizing the very basis of the hierarchical binary relationships constructed by colonialism rather than for inverting them.

Several of J. M. COETZEE's novels respond to aspects of Defoe's work, particularly *Robinson Crusoe*. The Coetzee novel which does this most obviously is *Foe* (1986), in which Cruso (Coetzee changes the name by omitting the final 'e') dies in the opening section and a tongueless Friday comes to London, where most of the action is set, with a woman castaway, Susan Barton, who has been on the island with the two men. Race and gender norms are destabilized, but the novel's most radical interrogation of canonical conventions comes in its postmodernist fictional practice: Susan searches for the elusive male author, Daniel Foe, whom she hopes will tell her story, and the text's dislocations increasingly unsettle the very basis of fictional authority. Other post-colonial responses to *Robinson Crusoe* include poems by Derek Walcott in his early collection, *The Castaway* (1965), in which the main emphasis is on the Crusoe figure as a Caribbean archetype, a shape-changing Adamic figure hewing a culture from scant raw materials and hence, in Walcott's view, having affinities with the Caribbean artist, Walcott's essay 'The Figure of Crusoe' (Hamner (ed.) 1993: 33–40), a companion piece to the Crusoe poems in *The Castaway*, and V. S. Naipaul's essay, 'Columbus and Crusoe' (Naipaul 1972: 203–7), in which the emphasis is also on the Crusoe figure.

Further reading

Said (1994); Spass and Stimpson (eds) (1996); Thieme (2001).

Rodney, Walter   (1942–80). Guyanese historian and political leader, educated in Jamaica at the University of the West Indies and at the University of London, where he obtained his doctorate. His radical beliefs led to his being expelled from a lecturing post at the Jamaican campus of the University of the West Indies and he subsequently worked as a Professor of African History at the University of Dar es Salaam. In 1974, Rodney returned to his homeland to take up an appointment as Professor of History at the University of Guyana, but was prevented from doing so by the intervention of the Guyanese government. He formed the Working People's Alliance (WPA), a political party that attempted to cut across the racial binarism (between the predominantly Afro-Guyanese People's National Movement and the predominantly Indo-Guyanese People's Progressive Party) that had characterized Guyanese political life in the post-independence era. He was killed in mysterious circumstances in 1980, allegedly the victim of an assassination carried out by forces working on behalf of the Guyanese government and, as well as being revered for his work as a historian, has been seen as a martyr to the cause of political freedom within the nation. He is best known for *How Europe Underdeveloped Africa* (1972), an analysis of the means through which Europe systematically destroyed African political economies, and also published *The Groundings with My Brothers* (1969), a plea for Black Power solidarity, and *A History of the Guyanese Working People, 1881–1905* (1981).

Further reading

Rodney (1972); Campbell (1987).

Roumain, Jacques (1907–44). Haitian novelist and political activist. Educated in Europe, Roumain played a significant part in the Haitian resistance movement against the American occupation of the country which had begun in 1915, founding the Haitian Communist Party in 1934. He spent three years in prison in the 1930s and subsequently travelled in Europe and the United States. On his return to Haiti he was active in attacking the ASSIMILATIVE values of the local middle classes and in promoting the study of Haitian peasant culture, particularly championing the role of VODUN and CREOLE, both in his fiction and in his journal, *La Revue indigène*. In his best-known work, the novel, *Gouverneurs de la rosée* (1944; *Masters of the Dew*, 1947), a notable contribution to the genre of the peasant novel, a returnee from Cuba tries to raise political awareness among the inhabitants of a drought-stricken village, *Bois d'ébène* (1945; *Ebony Wood*) is a collection of his poetry

Further reading

Ormerod (1985).

Roy, Arundhati Born 1965. Indian novelist and activist. Born in Bengal and brought up in Kerala in a Syrian Christian community, Roy trained as an architect, before turning to film-writing and producing a number of acclaimed scripts. Her only novel to date, *The God of Small Things* (1997), won the 1997 BOOKER PRIZE. Set in Kerala, it focuses on the intense relationship between two twins, whose lives are traumatized by the drowning of their nine-year-old half-English cousin, and on an adult relationship between the twins' divorced mother and an UNTOUCHABLE. The novel employs a complex time-structure, which cross-cuts between the late 1960s and the 1990s, suggesting the interpenetration of past and present events, and is notable for a lyrical style whose verbal inventiveness reflects its characters' HYBRID identities. Its international success has been variously attributed to its stylistic distinctiveness, the sensationalism of its themes, shrewd marketing and its appeal to global notions of Indianness. Such explanations pay comparatively little attention to the specifics of the novel, which suggest a highly individual vision, coupled with a self-conscious response to the globalization of India over the decades. The more local dimension of *The God of Small Things* was highlighted when the Keralan Communist E. M. Namboodiripad claimed that he had been grossly caricatured in the novel and that this was an affront to Communism more generally. Roy also had to contend with another objection, when a court case was brought against her by a lawyer who complained that the novel's representation of lovemaking that infringed CASTE taboos was obscene.

Roy has subsequently involved herself in various ecological campaigns, most notably the movement for nuclear disarmament in the sub-continent and the campaign against the American bombing of Afghanistan. She also took a leading role in a campaign to prevent the building of a dam on the Narmada River that would submerge local villages. Her other publications include *The Cost of Living* (1999), which brings together essays on the Narmada Dam project and the Indian atomic bomb, and *Power Politics* (2001), an essay collection, which again expresses her ecological concerns and hostility to American policy in Afghanistan.

Further reading

Mullaney (2002).

Rushdie, Salman   Born 1947. Indian novelist and short story writer. Born into a Muslim family in Bombay, Rushdie moved to England, where he was educated at Rugby School and King's College, Cambridge. Prior to the success of his second novel, *Midnight's Children* (1981), which won the Booker Prize, he worked as an advertising copy-writer. *Midnight's Children* took Indian fiction in English in new directions by employing a distinctive fusion of Eastern and Western fabulist modes and its popularity has been seen as a major factor in the renaissance of Anglophone Indian fiction that has occurred during the last two decades. The novel stresses the diversity of contemporary Indian society and brings together a number of non-realist narrative modes, among them traditional Hindu and Islamic storytelling, Latin American magic realism and the hybrid cinematic style of the Bombay Talkie. Its narrator Saleem Sinai feels that he is 'handcuffed to history', because he is born at the exact moment of Indian independence (Rushdie was born in the same year) and Rushdie uses this analogy to trace an intricate network of comic parallels between personal and national historiography, with Saleem increasingly viewing himself as a rival to India's Prime Minister, Indira Gandhi, as a protagonist who represents India. As the novel moves from the optimism of the Independence era to events connected with the 'Emergency' declared by Mrs Gandhi in the mid-1970s, its mood becomes increasingly sombre and the comedy is supplanted by a more pessimistic political vision. *Shame* (1983) blends fairy tale and social realism in an allegory about contemporary Pakistan. Although it draws on the fabulist storytelling traditions of *The Thousand and One Nights* and has a hero, Omar Khayyam Shakil, whose name evokes the supposed author of the *Rubaiyat*, it is again a highly political novel, whose characters have been identified with the major power-players in the national struggles of the period, General Zia Ul-Haq, Zulfikar Ali Bhutto, and Bhutto's daughter, Benazir.

Rushdie became a household name around the world in February 1989, when Iran's Ayatollah Khomeini pronounced a fatwa on his life because of the alleged blasphemy of his treatment of aspects of the life of the Prophet Muhammad in his novel *The Satanic Verses* (1988). He subsequently spent many years in hiding under police protection, until the Iranian leadership rescinded the *fatwa* in September 1998. The controversy surrounding *The Satanic Verses* has tended to obscure the book's central concerns, which have more to do with migration and hybridized identities than Islamic doctrine, though arguably these two areas intersect in the novel's interrogation of the notion of 'pure' or authentic cultures. Its two migrant protagonists, Saladin

Chamcha and Gibreel Farishta, who begin the novel in a kind of limbo as they fall to earth in Vilayet (England) from a bombed aircraft, represent opposed responses to the predicament of being 'TRANSLATED' men: Saladin is motivated by a desire to be assimilated into England; Gibreel, who loses his ability to distinguish between dream and reality, is a vivid study in CULTURAL SCHIZOPHRENIA. *The Moor's Last Sigh* (1995) focuses on a hybridized Indian hero, an amalgam of Catholic, Jewish and Moorish cultural strains, for another investigation of cross-cultural identity and the problems of communal and sectarian divisions. *The Ground Beneath Her Feet* (1999) is a modern-day reworking of the Orpheus myth, set in the world of pop music, which once again explores transformations in the cultural traffic between East and West.

Rushdie's other works include: the science-fiction novel *Grimus* (1975); *The Jaguar's Smile* (1987), a Nicaraguan travel journal; *Haroun and the Sea of Stories* (1990), a children's book that lends itself to a range of allegorical interpretations; *East West* (1994), a collection of short stories; and the novel *Fury* (2001). *Imaginary Homelands* (1991) is a collection of his essays, which have affinities with the work of Homi K. BHABHA in their resistance to ESSENTIALIST definitions of cultures and emphasis on the 'translated' situation of the migrant. *Step Across This Line: Collected Non-Fiction 1992–2002* (2002) includes essays on the *fatwa*, rock music literature, politics and soccer. With Elizabeth West, Rushdie co-edited *The Vintage Book of Indian Writing 1947–1997* (1997), an anthology that aroused controversy on the sub-continent, because of its exclusion of Indian writing in languages other than English, with the single exception of Saadat Hasan Manto's short story 'Toba Tek Singh' (see PARTITION). Reder (ed., 2000) and Chauhan (ed., 2001), taken together, provide a fairly comprehensive selection of the many interviews that Rushdie gave over a period of two decades.

Further reading

Ruthven (1990); Fletcher (ed.) (1994); Cundy (1996); Kuortti (comp.) (1997); Mukherjee, M. (ed.) (1999); Reder (ed.) (2000); Chauhan (ed.) (2001).

S

Saadawi, Nawal El Born 1931. Egyptian writer and feminist activist. El Saadawi is a medical doctor, with a degree in psychiatry from Cairo University. She practised psychiatry and rose to become Egypt's Director of Public Health, but was dismissed from this position after the publication of her controversial book *Women and Sex* (1972), which challenged conventional perceptions of Arab women's roles. She subsequently became the United Nations Adviser for the Women's Programme in Africa and the

Middle East. Her work on women's neuroses and sexuality has brought her into conflict with both political and religious authorities in Egypt on various occasions and she was arrested in 1981. After her release in the following year, she founded the Arab Women's Solidarity Association (AWSA), an organization committed to liberating Arab women from the constraints placed upon them.

El Saadawi has published more than 30 books in Arabic. English translations, which have helped to secure an international readership for her work, include those of her best-known book, *The Hidden Face of Eve: Women in the Arab World* (1980), *Memoirs of a Woman Doctor* (1980), the novel *Woman at Point Zero* (1983), *God Dies by the Nile* (1985), *The Fall of the Imam* (1988), *The Innocence of the Devil* (1994) and *Daughter of Isis* (1999). *The Hidden Face of Eve* treats a range of topics that are traditionally taboo in Arab society, including female 'circumcision', divorce and prostitution. *North/South* (1997) is a reader in her work containing essays, articles and excerpts from her other books. El Saadawi has held teaching positions at American universities and her work has been widely translated into languages other than English. She shares a website with her husband, the doctor and novelist, Sherif Hetata.

Further reading

www.nawalsaadawi.net

Sahgal, Nayantara Born 1927. Indian novelist and political commentator. A member of post-independence India's most prominent family, Sahgal is a niece of Jawaharlal NEHRU, a first cousin of Indira Gandhi, during whose 'EMERGENCY' she was imprisoned, and the daughter of India's first ambassador to the United Nations. Prior to becoming known as a novelist, she was a prominent political journalist and her non-fiction work includes *Prison and Chocolate Cake* (1954), *From Fear Set Free* (1962), and *Indira Gandhi: Her Road to Power* (1982). *A Voice for Freedom* (1977) is a collection of her speeches and writings, protesting against the plight of 'imprisoned India' under the 'Emergency'. She has also published a more recent essay collection, *Point of View: A Personal Response to Life, Literature and Politics* (1997).

Beginning with *A Time to Be Happy* (1958) and *This Time of Morning* (1965), Sahgal's novels characteristically use personal situations to represent larger political themes, offering critiques of both contemporary and past political corruption and patriarchal oppression. Their foregrounding of the public dimension of personal situations is in marked contrast to the understated fictional technique of Sahgal's contemporary, Anita DESAI. *Storm in Chandigarh* (1969) deals with the PARTITION of Punjab into two states. *Rich Like Us* (1983) is a complex novel, which moves between the contemporary India of the 'Emergency' and a historical account of the practice of *sati*, while also dramatizing relationships between India and England. Set in a Himalayan hill station in the summer of 1914, *Plans for Departure* (1986) takes a progressive Danish protagonist as its vantage point for observing a social group that serves as a microcosm for the twentieth-century Raj and its impending retreat from India. Sahgal has also published the novels *The Day in Shadow* (1975), *A Situation in New Delhi* (1977) and *Mistaken Identity* (1988).

Further reading

Crane (1998).

The Sahitya Akademi India's national academy of letters, founded by the Government of India in 1954. The Akademi's headquarters are located in New Delhi, but it is a pan-Indian organization, involved in mounting seminars, readings, colloquia and other activities throughout the country. Arguably its most significant single achievement has been its extensive TRANSLATION programme, which has published translations of 2,000 works into twenty-four Indian languages. The extent of iits 'inter-language' translations, which bypass the nation's official languages of English and Hindi, is not matched in the translation programmes of India's commercial publishers. It has played an important role in widening awareness of work in the country's regional literatures and broadening a pan-Indian consciousness of difference and diversity within the context of a secular discourse of national unity. The Akademi makes annual awards which honour work in the 22 Indian languages it formally recognizes and also makes special awards (known as Bhasha Samman Awards) to work in other languages. Its major publications include the *Encyclopedia of Indian Literature*, the *Who's Who in Indian Literature* and the ongoing 10-volume *History of Indian Literature*. Its other work includes cultural exchange programmes, a Tribal Oral Literature Project and histories of particular Indian literatures. Its useful website contains a select glossary of Indian literature, as well as full details of recipients of its awards and its activities more generally.

Further reading

Official website: www.sahitya-akademi.org/sahitya-akademi

Said, Edward W. Born 1935. One of the most influential of post-colonial theorists, Said was born in Jerusalem and attended school in Cairo between 1948 and 1951 before migrating to the United States. He attended Princeton and Harvard, writing his doctoral thesis on Joseph CONRAD, and was subsequently appointed as a Professor in Comparative Literature at Columbia University, New York, where he has worked ever since. The Arab-Israeli war of 1967 marked a turning-point in his life. Living in the USA in a climate partial to the Israeli viewpoint, he aligned himself with the Arab cause and, although he is sometimes seen as the epitome of a DIASPORA intellectual, AFFILIATED himself with the Palestinian side of his ancestry. He was a member of the PNC (Palestine National Council) from 1977 to 1991 and his books on Palestinian issues include *The Question of Palestine* (1979) and *The Politics of Dispossession* (1994).

In 1998 he was elected President of the MLA (Modern Language Association of America), an appointment which caused controversy in some quarters, because of his links with the Palestinian cause.

While Said's work is wide-ranging, both in terms of its historical and geographical sweep and its disciplinary coverage, it is rooted in literature and cultural theory and is invariably informed by his concern with IMAGINATIVE GEOGRAPHY and the extent to which the cultures of apparently discrete areas are intertwined. He emphasizes the way geopolitical categorizations and power formations are distributed into aesthetic contexts. His analysis of the discursive constitution of power HEGEMONIES draws on the work of Antonio Gramsci and Michel Foucault. Said's most famous work *Orientalism: Western Conceptions of the Orient* (1978) (see ORIENTALISM), which deals with the West's discursive construction of 'the East', was a landmark text not only for post-colonial studies, but also for twentieth-century cultural theory more generally. Despite various attacks, it remains a definitive work on European constructions of 'alterity' (see 'OTHERNESS'), on the stereotyping of Asian and North African cultures and on the formation of notions of cultural identity more generally. Its second edition (1995) responds to some of the criticisms levelled against the work in the intervening years.

Other important works by Said include *Beginnings* (1975), which interrogates notions of origins and lineages and demarcates the conceptual terrain that he revisits in all his subsequent work, and *The World, the Text and the Critic* (1983), which is centred on a discussion of the tension between FILIATION AND AFFILIATION. *Culture and Imperialism* (1993) ranges across various forms of European cultural production, including literature, opera and contemporary media representations, with a particular emphasis on English and French novels that have engaged with colonialism, among them Jane Austen's *Mansfield Park*, Conrad's *Heart of Darkness* and Albert Camus' *L'Etranger*. It examines the relationship between culture and imperial attitudes, arguing that the former cannot be divorced from mercantile realities and promulgating a position which challenges separatist and chauvinistic discourses. *Out of Place* (1999) is a memoir of his early years in Palestine, Egypt and Lebanon, which also provides a powerful account of the changes in the Arab world in the years after World War II. The displacement referred to in its title is both personal and cultural and also relates to Said's sense of linguistic AMBIVALENCE.

Further reading

Sprinker (ed.) (1992); Ashcroft and Ahluwalia (2001).

Salih, Tayeb   Born 1929. Sudanese-born novelist educated in Khartoum and London, who has spent much of his life abroad and took up writing in mid-career. He has worked as Head of Drama for the Arabic section of the BBC World Service, Director of Sudanese national radio, Director General of Information in Qatar and for UNESCO in Paris and Qatar. Written in Arabic, his fiction draws on classical Arabic texts and a range of other Islamic sources. His masterpiece, *Mawsin al-Hijra ila al-Shamal* (*Season of Migration to the North,* 1969) has been viewed as a *Thousand and One Nights* in reverse. It is a powerful study of split consciousness, centred on a mysterious protagonist who has travelled 'north' to Europe and returns to the Sudan, where he attempts to revenge the exploitation of Africa by preying on white women, acting out the role of an OTHELLO-like 'Arab-African'. His story is told by an unnamed narrator who shares certain affinities with him and the novel has been seen as a post-colonial response to Conrad's *Heart of Darkness* (1902). Although it moves in an opposite direction, it resembles Conrad's novella in its probing of larger socio-economic issues through its psychoanalytic approach and the doubling of its two main characters. It also draws on Conrad's *Nostromo* (1904), Shakespearean tragedies and the writings of Sir Richard Burton. Its representation of divisions in Sudanic society, which relate to those in the characters' psyches, parallels DENIS WILLIAMS's *Other Leopards* (1963).

Salih's other fiction also probes the tensions between North African village life and Western cultural values. *Bandarshah* (1996) is a similarly enigmatic novel about a stranger with no discernible markers of identity, who transforms the lives of a group of villagers. It initiates its readers into a fabulist world of Arab village customs, while always foregrounding the social dimensions of its action. Salih's other works include *Urs al Zayn* (*The Wedding of Zein and Other Stories,* 1969) and *Al-Rajul al Qubroshi* (*The Cypriot Man,* 1978).

The Salt March   A central event in Mahatma GANDHI's SATYAGRAHA campaign. In 1930 Gandhi chose to protest against the British Raj's monopoly of the manufacture and taxing of salt, a necessity that was readily available without cost in India, as the focal point for his struggle against colonial misrule. Along with 78 followers, he embarked on a march from Sabarmati to the coastal town of Dandi some 240 miles away. The number of marchers grew daily and estimates of the column's length at the end of the journey, 23 days later, have put it at two miles. The episode shows Gandhi's flair for symbolic gesture that could initiate political change at its best: on the seashore he picked up a lump containing salt, boiled it in saltwater and instructed others to follow him in breaking the law. Thousands did so and Gandhi was arrested in the following month (May 1930), while still at Dandi.

As with the American revolutionaries' choice of tea as a target for protesting against British economic exploitation (at the Boston Tea Party), Gandhi's decision to make salt the central focus of his campaign for home rule was an inspired choice that captured the Indian public's imagination, uniting people of different backgrounds and political persuasions. The Salt March was followed by Gandhi's advocacy of the use of *khaddar* (homespun cloth) and a boycott on imported Lancashire cotton. See PATCHWORK.

Further reading

Jones (1994).

Sancho, Ignatius (1729–80). Afro-British letter-writer. Allegedly born on a Middle Passage ship *en route* to South America, he was subsequently sold into slavery in England. Employed as a butler in the service of the Duchess of Montagu, he later became a grocer in Westminster and with a clientele that included many fashionable artists, he found a niche for himself in English polite society. Thomas Gainsborough painted his portrait and he was befriended by the novelist Laurence Sterne and the actor David Garrick. Sancho is known to posterity as the author of the posthumously published *Letters of the Late Ignatius Sancho: An African* (1782). The letters mainly deal with domestic subjects and differ in tone from the work of Britain's other major eighteenth-century 'African' writer, Olaudah Equiano in that Sancho seems to have been comfortably assimilated into English society and only rarely comments on 'race', usually in an ironic manner which is ambivalent rather than adversarial. Sancho's most famous letter, written to Sterne in 1776, draws on the contemporary vogue for sentimentality, for which Sterne himself was famous. The *Letters* were republished in a scholarly edition in 1994.

Further reading

Edwards and Rewt (eds) (1994).

The San Domingo Revolution See the Haitian Revolution.

Sanskrit The language of ancient India, in which most of the classic North Indian Hindu texts were written. Classical Sanskrit derives from the earlier Vedic form of the language, which flourished from around 1500 BC to 200 BC. 'Sanskrit' means 'perfected', referring to the view that the classical form of the language represented an improvement on its Vedic precursor, though the two co-existed for a period.

Traditionally Sanskrit was the prerogative of the Brahmin caste of priests and scribes, who controlled its traditions and transmission. As the writer-protagonist of Shashi Deshpande's *That Long Silence* (1988) points out, Sanskrit drama did not allow women to speak the language; instead they were required to speak the less prestigious language of Prakit.

Sanskrit remained an important link-language in India until the passing of Macaulay's Minute in 1835 established the primacy of English as a pan-Indian medium of communication. Although it is in *one* sense a 'dead' language, an Indian equivalent of Latin, it was reinstated, along with 14 modern languages as one of the 'major' languages of post-independence India, at the time when the post-Independence Constitution established Hindi and English as the nation's two 'official' languages; and, just as texts such as the *Ramayana* and the *Mahabharata* (which also exist in non-Sanskrit versions) continue to occupy an important place in contemporary Indian discourse, it retains a significance no longer enjoyed by Europe's classical languages. See also Hindu texts.

Saro-Wiwa, Ken   (1941–95). Nigerian writer, television producer and political activist. His execution by the Nigerian military government on charges of incitement to murder, after a campaign to secure his release, in which Nelson MANDELA played a leading role, provoked international condemnation. In his best-known novel *Sozaboy: A Novel in Rotten English* (1985), Saro-Wiwa brought together a range of language registers including PIDGIN and Standard English to tell the story of its 'sozaboy' (soldier) hero, whose disillusioning experience of the NIGERIAN CIVIL WAR, during which Saro-Wiwa himself had served as an administrator, provides an apt vehicle for an attack on the exploitation of minorities in Nigeria. His writing has been divided into two main categories: early works for a youthful audience and later works concerned with the plight of the Ogoni people. However, his concern with political corruption and the exploitation of minorities is already manifest in *Sozaboy*, which is also his most significant literary achievement. His other novels include *Prisoner of Jebs* (1988) and *Pita Dumbrok's Prison* (1991). He also published the short story collections, *Forest of Flowers* (1987) and *Adaku* (1989). Work in other genres includes *Basi and Company: A Modern African Folktale* (1987) and *Four Farcical Plays* (1989), which were adapted from his popular television series *Basi and Company*; *On a Darkling Plain* (1989), an autobiographical account of the Nigerian Civil War; and *The Singing Anthills* (1991), a collection of Ogoni folktales.

The circumstances that initiated the events that led to his arrest and hanging are detailed in *Genocide in Nigeria: The Ogoni Tragedy* (1992), in which he attacks the Shell Oil Company's pollution of Ogoniland in the Southern Niger Delta, a protest significant for its specific advocacy of the rights of the Ogoni people and more generally for its support for minority interests that are subordinated to those of global multinational corporations. *A Month and a Day* (1995) is an account of his imprisonment for alleged treason in 1993.

Sati, suttee   The former Hindu practice of a woman's committing suicide after the death of her husband, by burning herself on the husband's cremation pyre. The term was also applied to the widow who immolated herself in this fashion. It derives from the SANSKRIT for 'true wife' and the practice is mentioned in texts dating back to the fourth century BC. Muslim attempts to suppress *sati* during the period of the Mughal Empire stopped short of a complete prohibition and when the British did ban it in 1829, their action aroused the opposition of some Hindu traditionalists, who defended the widow's right to die as one of Hinduism's traditional customs. *Sati* has continued to attract attention in the work of post-colonial theorists such as Gayatri Chakravorty SPIVAK, who discusses it in her essay 'Can the Subaltern Speak?' (1988b), and writers such as Nayantara SAHGAL, who traces analogies between contemporary and older forms of patriarchal repression with reference to *sati* in her novel *Rich Like Us* (1983).

Further reading

Spivak (1988b).

Satyagraha   Non-violent resistance, as advocated by GANDHI, first in South Africa and then in his campaign of civil disobedience against British rule in India. It derives from the SANSKRIT words for 'truth' and 'obstinacy' and the belief in AHIMSA and affords an excellent example of Gandhi's transformation of older religious concepts into a contemporary political philosophy that would mobilize the Indian populace. See also the SALT MARCH.

Schwarz-Bart, Simone   Born 1938. French-born writer of Guadeloupean parentage who returned to Guadeloupe at the age of three and spent her early life there. As an adult she studied in France and lived in Senegal and Switzerland, before once again settling in Guadeloupe. She is best known for *Pluie et vent sur Telumée Miracle* (1972; *The Bridge of Beyond*, 1974), a novel about women's survival in adversity, which looks back to the period of SLAVERY, spans five generations of a family and emphasizes continuity and the spiritual resilience that is conveyed by its English title. Schwarz-Bart's other novels include *Ti-Jean L'Horizon* (1979; *Between Two Worlds*, 1981), based on a popular hero of FRANCOPHONE Creole tales, who also provides the focal point for Derek WALCOTT's play, *Ti Jean and His Brothers*. With her husband André Schwarz-Bart, she co-wrote the novel, *Un Plat de porc aux bananes verts* (1967), in which an elderly Martinican woman, immured in an old people's home in Paris, looks back over her earlier Caribbean life. Schwarz-Bart has also published the play *Ton beau capitaine* (1987) and the six-volume *Homage à la Femme Noire* (1989; publication in English as *In Praise of Black Women* ongoing at the time of the Glossary's compilation).

The 'Scramble for Africa'   Although the colonization of Africa began centuries earlier, it was in the last quarter of the nineteenth century that European economic and political rivalries resulted in the wholesale appropriation of African territory that became known as the Scramble for Africa. The BERLIN CONFERENCE of 1884–5 established 'spheres of influence' that legitimized the control of large sections of the continent by European powers and provided a framework for further colonial expansion. The Scramble resulted in a redrawing of the map of Africa, which has continued to have repercussions in the post-independence period, since its new arbitrarily imposed borders cut across traditional tribal and other boundaries; and traumatic experiences in more recent African history such as the NIGERIAN CIVIL WAR can be attributed to such political CARTOGRAPHY.

The Berlin Conference was convened after Belgium's King Léopold II had laid claim to a large section of central Africa in the region of the Congo River and Germany had assumed control of South West Africa (later Namibia), the Cameroons and parts of

East Africa in the early 1880s. France and Britain sought recognition of their interests in Africa. France obtained extensive rights in Saharan Africa and parts of West Africa, including Dahomey, the Ivory Coast and Senegal. British HEGEMONY in several parts of West Africa, including Nigeria and Ghana, was confirmed, while in East Africa Britain was granted British East Africa (later Kenya and Uganda) and, further south, Southern and Northern Rhodesia (later Zimbabwe and Zambia), Bechuanaland (Botswana) and Nyasaland (Malawi). Portugal obtained Angola and Mozambique.

Further reading

Pakenham (1991).

Seacole, Mary (1805–81). Jamaican nurse, famed for her activities during the Crimean War. Recent scholarship has suggested that she was a figure of equivalent importance to Florence Nightingale. Seacole was born of mixed parentage in Kingston and spent her early adult life running a boarding house established by her mother. She married Viscount Nelson's godson on a visit to England, but returned to Jamaica after his death in 1836. She subsequently spent time in Colombia and Panama, nursing, prospecting for gold and keeping hotels. When the Crimean War broke out, she went to England and volunteered her services as a nurse, having acquired considerable experience of the profession during cholera and yellow fever outbreaks in Jamaica and her time in Colombia and Panama. She was refused, allegedly on racist grounds, but nevertheless travelled to the war zone, where she became a trader and hotel-keeper, nursing the wounded at her hotel in Balaclava. Revisionist historical accounts of the period have suggested that her actual contribution to the nursing of the wounded was greater than that of the better-known Florence Nightingale, who became an imperial icon of femininity, while Mary Seacole remained comparatively ignored because of her race. She worked nearer the front, relieving ailments such as jaundice, dysentery and frostbite and reputedly saving many lives through her insistence on a regime of strict hygiene. Her activities were reported in such imperial organs as *The Illustrated London News* and when her autobiography, *Wonderful Adventures of Mrs Seacole in Many Lands*, was published in 1857, her reputation increased. Ziggi Alexander and Audrey Dewjee's Introduction to a 1984 reprint of the second edition of the *Wonderful Adventures* provides details of her later life.

Further reading

Seacole (1984).

Selvon, Sam (1923–94). Trinidadian-born novelist, short story writer and dramatist, who lived much of his life in Britain and Canada. Selvon worked as a journalist and wireless operator before emigrating to Britain in 1950, travelling to England on the same boat as George LAMMING in 1950, an experience which Lamming recalls in *The*

Pleasures of Exile (1960). He became a regular contributor to the BBC's Caribbean Voices programme and also published stories in London's *Evening Standard*.

Selvon's work falls into two main categories: books about Indo-Caribbean life in Trinidad and books about Caribbean migrants of the Windrush Generation in London. The former are mainly written in Standard English; the latter in stylized forms of Caribbean Creole, which exhibit shifts in register with the passing of the years – an index of the changes affecting the community he depicts. The Trinidadian novels are *A Brighter Sun* (1952), a coming-of-age novel about a young Indo-Caribbean man, *An Island is a World* (1955), *Turn Again Tiger* (1958), a sequel to *A Brighter Sun*, *I Hear Thunder* (1963), *The Plains of Caroni* (1970) and *Those Who Eat the Cascadura* (1972). The London novels describe the lives of the post-World War II generation of Caribbean migrants into Britain, centring on the figure of Moses Aloetta, the protagonist of Selvon's 'Moses' trilogy, *The Lonely Londoners* (1956), *Moses Ascending* (1975) and *Moses Migrating* (1983). *The Lonely Londoners* is Selvon's finest achievement. Written in an anecdotal style that moves between humour and pathos, it is an episodic novel about the picaresque adventures of a group of mainly male migrants, which depicts both the comic vibrancy and the underlying aimlessness of their lives in the metropolis. In *Moses Ascending*, the protagonist has joined the landlord class and his narrative voice mixes Creole with some oddly archaic English. In *Moses Migrating*, he returns to Trinidad at Carnival time and becomes involved in some oddly anachronistic role-playing. The end of the novel finds him ambivalently poised between England and Trinidad. London also provides the setting for Selvon's comic stories of Caribbean migrants' lives in the second half of his short story collection, *Ways of Sunlight* (1957) and his novel, *The Housing Lark* (1965), where he particularly focuses on discrimination in housing, again in his characteristically comic vein.

Other books by Selvon include *Eldorado West One* (1988), seven one-act plays about the characters of *The Lonely Londoners*, *Highway in the Sun and Other Plays* (1991) and *Foreday Morning: Selected Prose, 1946–1986* (1989). He wrote the screenplay for Horace Ové's film, *Pressure* (1976).

Further reading

Nasta (ed.) (1988); Zehnder (ed.) (2003).

Sembène, Ousmane   Born 1923. Senegalese film director and novelist, generally regarded as the founder of Sub-Saharan cinema. Sembène worked as a fisherman before being conscripted to serve in the French army in World War II. After the war, he was a longshoreman in Marseilles, an experience which provided the material for his first novel, *Le Docker noir* (1956; *The Black Docker*, 1981). *Les Bouts de bois de Dieu* (1960; *God's Bits of Wood*, 1962) deals with a strike on the Dakar–Niger railroad in the late 1940s. Like all of his subsequent work, it protests against economic exploitation, whether it be colonial or neo-colonial. A committed trade union activist for many years, Sembène prefers to see himself as an artist who dramatizes social injustice in an interrogative manner rather than as someone who offers a prescriptive recipe for change. His commitment to pragmatic social realism and distrust of abstractions brought him into conflict with Senegal's President Léopold SENGHOR, whose doctrine of NEGRITUDE has been seen by Sembène as having little relevance to lived West African experience.

In the early 1960s Sembène studied film production in Moscow. After returning to Senegal in 1963, he made the first African feature film, *La noire de . . .* (*The Black Girl*, 1966), which deals with the mistreatment and suicide of a black domestic in the south of France. With *Mandabi* (*The Money Order*, 1968), adapted from his novel *Le mandat* (1964), he began producing films in the Wolof language, thus making them available to the local populace, in much the same way as NGUGI wa Thiong'o's use of Gikuyu has enabled him to reach a larger Kenyan audience. Like his writing, Sembène's cinema communicates in a direct and accessible manner, exhibiting similar narrative skills to those of the traditional GRIOT. *Le mandat/Mandabi* follows the struggles of an unemployed and illiterate Senegalese man as he tries to get a money order cashed and in so doing provides a vivid satirical portrait of conflicts occasioned by modernization. It was followed by *Emitai* (1971), *Xala* (1975), adapted from Sembène's novel of the same title (1971), and his masterpiece *Ceddo* (*Outsiders*, 1977), a powerful historical drama which offended sensibilities in Senegal by portraying African complicity in the Slave Trade, and was consequently banned. Sembène's later films have continued to explore social and political issues, often focusing on the predicament of African women. They include *Le Camp de Thiaroye* (1987), *Guelwaar* (1993) and *Faat-Kine* (2000). *The Money Order* (with *White Genesis*, 1972) and *Xala* (1976) have also been published in English translations. His other fiction includes *Voltaïque* (1962; *Tribal Scars and Other Stories* 1974), *L'Harmattan* (1963), *Le Dernier de l'empire* (1981; *The Last of the Empire* 1983), and *Niiwam suivi de Taaw* (1987; *Niiwam and Taaw* 1991).

Further reading

Pfaff (1984); Petty (ed.) (1996).

Sen, Mrinal   Born 1923. Indian film director, often compared with his famous Bengali contemporary Satyajit RAY, generally in the context of their different political stances and Sen's greater commitment to socialist cinema. Sen joined the Communist Party of India at an early age and from the beginning of his career encountered hostility to his Marxist politics, which led to the temporary banning of *Neel Akasher Neechaley* (*Under the Blue Sky*, 1958). Challenges to bourgeois Calcutta society form the subject of several of his finest films, including *Baishey Shravana* (*A Wedding* Day, 1960) and *Punascha* (*Over Again*, 1962), which deal with middle-class marriages, *Ek Din Pratidin* (*And Quiet Rolls the Day*, 1979) and *Kharij* (*The Case is Shut*, 1982). His 'Calcutta Trilogy' – *Interview* (1970), *Calcutta 71* (1972) and *Patalik* (1973) – focuses on the

Marxist-Leninist Naxalite Movement. His later films are often more self-referential, examining the mechanics of film-making and foregrounding issues of agency. *Akaler Sandhaney* (*In Search of Famine*, 1980), which deals with a film crew's attempt to recreate famine conditions in a Bengali village, suggests the extent to which the crew becomes implicated in the very practices it is supposedly attacking.

Sen's desire to reach a wider Indian audience led him to make films in Hindi, Telugu and Oriya, as well as Bengali. While his international reputation has remained second to Satyajit Ray's, his unwavering commitment to attacking social injustice and the integrity of his austere style have made him more popular with many Indian intellectuals. His other films include *Akash Kusum* (*The Daydream*, 1965) and *Khandhar* (*The Ruins*, 1983). *Ten Days in Calcutta* (1984) is a 'portrait' of Sen by the German director, Reinhard Hauff.

Sen, Sudeep   Born 1964. Indian poet born in New Delhi, who has lived in the USA, Britain and Bangladesh, as well as India. Sen is arguably the most cosmopolitan of the contemporary generation of Indian poets writing in English, a writer whose minimalist, carefully crafted work avoids both obvious 'Indian' themes and the more fashionable fusions generated by the Western vogue for things Indian. It remains distinctly eclectic and technically assured volumes such as *Kali in Ottava Rima* (1992) bring Western and Eastern discourses together in a manner that resists easy pigeon-holing. Sen's collections of poetry include *The Lunar Visitations* (1990), *New York Times* (1993) and a later 'American' volume *Retracing American Contours* (1999), *Mount Vesuvius in Eight Frames* (1994), *South African Woodcut* (1994), *Dali's Twisted Hands* (1995), *Lines of Desire* (2000) and *Almanac* (2000). *Postmarked India: New and Selected Poems* (1997), a collection of much of his best verse, provides the best introduction to his work. He has also published *Bodytext: Dramatic Monologues in Motion* (1999), a series of monologues in poetic prose and *Monsoon* (2002), a reflection on the 'passion and politics' of rain, in which his limpid prose is accompanied by photographs by the Dhaka-based photographer, Mahmud. Sen has edited and translated various collections of poetry and is also a film-maker. Kwame Dawes's useful introduction to *Postmarked India* provides biographical information and an overview of Sen's work and its critical reception.

Further reading

www.sudeepsen.org.

Senghor, Léopold Sédar   (1906–2001). Senegelese writer and politician, one of the main architects of the Negritude movement. Born into a peasant family, Senghor was educated at Catholic mission schools and in France. He met Aimé Césaire and Léon-Gontran Damas during his studies in Paris. After World War II, Senghor entered politics, first serving as a deputy from Senegal to the French National Assembly and later founding the Union Progressive Sénégalaise (UPS) at home. The party emerged as the major force in Senegalese politics and Senghor became President of post-independence Senegal in 1960, an office that he held until 1980. Both a nationalist and a believer in FRANCOPHONE West African unity, Senghor established the short-lived Mali FEDERATION in the late 1950s, but this collapsed in 1960.

Beginning with *Chants d'ombre* (1945) and *Hosties noires* (1948), his poetry received considerable critical acclaim and played a leading role in the formation of the ideology of Negritude. His verse attempted to assert the simple dignity of African experience as a corrective to negative Western stereotyping. Subsequent volumes included *Ethiopiques* (1956) and *Poèmes* (1984). A bilingual (French with English translations) collection of his *Selected Poems* appeared in 1976 and an English edition of his *Collected Poetry* was published in 1998.

Senior, Olive   Born 1941. Jamaican short story writer and poet. Senior was born and raised in rural Jamaica. She studied journalism in Canada and Britain and subsequently played an important part in Jamaican cultural life, as Managing Editor of *JAMAICA JOURNAL* and as head of the publications division of the Institute of Jamaica. She now lives in Canada. Her first collection of short stories, *Summer Lightning* (1986), won the inaugural COMMONWEALTH WRITERS PRIZE (1987). Most of its stories are set in the late colonial period and focus on child protagonists, several of whom find themselves transplanted into another household, an experience that replicates that of Senior's own childhood which involved a similar movement between houses and, she says, made her a child of two worlds. In the stories this movement between different social worlds enables her to dramatize the competing claims of Jamaica's middle-class and folk cultures and to explore the major forces in her protagonists' socialization, including religion, education, race, colour and class. The title-story, 'Bright Thursdays' and the longer final story, 'Ballad', a comic *tour de force*, which like several others in the collection is written in CREOLE, are particularly outstanding. Senior has also published the short story collections, *Arrival of the Snake Woman* (1989) and *The Discerner of Hearts* (1995). Like the work of her Jamaican contemporary, Erna BRODBER, her fiction provides a vivid portrayal of the double socialization of Jamaicans of her generation, caught in the AMBIVALENT interstices between colonial and local folk cultures. It does so in a style that is ostensibly less exploratory than Brodber's, but equally successful in offering a metonymic representation of the CULTURAL SCHIZOPHRENIA engendered by colonialism. Her other books include two poetry collections, *Talking of Trees* (1985) and *Gardening in the Tropics* (1995), a one-woman encyclopaedia of Jamaican life and customs, *A-Z of Jamaican Heritage* (1983) and *Working Miracles: Women's Lives in the English-Speaking Caribbean* (1991).

Further reading

Patteson (1998).

The Sepoy Mutiny, The Indian Mutiny, The Great Indian Uprising   An Indian rebellion against colonial rule which, in Denis Judd's words, 'inflicted a deep wound upon the Victorian psyche' (1996: 66). The English public was particularly scandalized by attacks on British civilians, including women and children, and the word 'mutiny' was widely used as part of a discourse that located the rebellion in a purely military context, although it was more general, and suggested the disloyalty of Britain's colonial subjects. It did, however, begin among the sepoys (soldiers) of the Indian army who were outraged by the introduction of a new type of greased cartridge (offensive to both Hindus and Muslims, in different ways), an act that demonstrated insensitivity to local customs and beliefs and appeared to confirm local suspicions that the colonial authorities were bent on undermining basic tenets of Hinduism. There were numerous uprisings in garrison towns, in which white soldiers and other residents were killed. After various encounters, most notably the Siege of Lucknow, which received extensive coverage in the Victorian press, the rebellion was put down, but the events that had occurred had shattered the illusion of the FILIAL relationship between the Raj and the subjects of Britain's most prized colony. The rebellion resulted in direct Crown rule being introduced in place of the administration of the East India Company.

Further reading

Judd (1996).

Seth, Vikram   Born 1952. Indian writer. Seth's work has generally been seen as more 'realistic' in orientation than that of contemporaries such as Salman RUSHDIE and Arundhati ROY. However, although his individual books lack their generic HYBRIDITY, he has shown a similar interest in formal plurality, by producing work in numerous genres: 'classic realist' novel; travel-book; animal fable; verse; translation; libretto; and verse-novel.

Born in Calcutta, he attended one of India's leading boarding schools, the Doon School in Dehra Dun and subsequently studied politics, philosophy and economics at Oxford and economics at Stanford University in California, an area he used as the setting for his verse-novel *The Golden Gate* (1986). He subsequently spent two years in China, doing research for an uncompleted doctorate on the economic demography of village life. His travel-book, *From Heaven Lake: Travels through Sinkiang and Tibet* (1983), describes a journey he made in 1981, hitch-hiking from Beijing to Delhi along routes that took him off the beaten track. *The Golden Gate*, a sequence of some six hundred sonnets about the lives of young professionals in California's Silicon Valley, won the Commonwealth Poetry Prize.

Seth is best known for his family saga, *A Suitable Boy* (1993), a vast novel set in the period just after Indian independence, which won the Best Book award of the COMMONWEALTH WRITERS PRIZE. Its epic sweep has attracted comparisons with such nineteenth-century masterpieces as George Eliot's *Middlemarch*. Focusing on the fortunes of four families and, like Jane Austen, using marriage as a central trope for social organization, *A Suitable Boy* examines the emergence of a new Indian middle class during this period of nationalist assertion. In *An Equal Music* (1999), Seth once again shifted direction, this time producing a novel centred on the emotional life of an English musician and the lost love he rediscovers, only to lose again. His other volumes of verse are *Mappings* (1980), *The Humble Administrator's Garden* (1985) and *All You Who Sleep Tonight* (1990). *Three Chinese Poets* (1992) is his translation of three Tang dynasty poets from the eighth century: Wang Wei, Li Bai and Du Fu. *Beastly Tales from Here and There* (1993) brings together animal fables from India, China, Greece, the Ukraine and 'the Land of Gup'. *Arion and the Dolphin* (1994) is a children's book based on a libretto he wrote for an English National Opera production.

Settler colonies   Term used to describe countries such as Canada, Australia and New Zealand that were colonized by European migrants, who usually dispossessed the pre-existing NATIVE populations of their ancestral lands. Changes in the demographic composition of such nations, as a consequence of different patterns of migration in the post-World War II period, and parallel changes in public policy have rendered the term increasingly problematic in contemporary usage. Revisionist HISTORIOGRAPHY has also questioned the appropriateness of using it to describe the nation's identities in *earlier* periods. Today MULTICULTURAL policies, which recognize the PLURAL nature of Australian, Canadian and New Zealand, have dismantled such ANGLO-CELTIC constructions of the nations' cultural identity. See also the LEGEND OF THE NINETIES.

Shaka, Chaka   (*c.*1787–1828). Zulu chieftain, who is generally regarded as the founder of his nation. Historical information about Shaka is comparatively scarce and most representations of him are founded on white mythologizing practices that have demonized him as a metonym for the 'savage' Zulu. Dan Wylie's *Savage Delight: White Myths of Shaka* (2000) traces the evolution of the literary mythology of Shaka, offering four case-studies of influential white writing on Shaka and demonstrating how they reveal more about their authors' need to define themselves in contradistinction from 'alterity' (see 'OTHERNESS') than the historical Shaka or the Zulu. Wylie's study illustrates how popular conceptions of 'Shaka' were shaped by notions of the 'NOBLE SAVAGE', compounded with a representation of the Zulu as a people who needed to be tamed by the intervention of white 'civilization'. As such, the mythography of Shaka offers a particularly stark example of a colonial discourse that enforced a white supremacist ethic. It continued to have currency during the APARTHEID era. Cy Enfield's film *Zulu* (1964), which depicts the 1879 battle of Rorke's Drift in the Anglo-Zulu War as an instance of heroic British resistance against insuperable odds, is perhaps the most widely disseminated example of the stereotype of the 'savage' and warlike Zulus.

The historical Shaka became chief of the Zulus around 1816, unified the nation and initiated the period of warfare known as the *Mfecane*. According to legend, he was murdered by his half-brothers. Thomas Mofolo's *Chaka* (1931) provides a partial antidote to the white stereotyping of Shaka.

Further reading

Wylie (2000).

Shakespeare, post-colonial responses to   See particularly the more·detailed entries on post-colonial responses to *The TEMPEST* and *OTHELLO*.
   Revisionist perspectives on Shakespeare in the last two decades have occasioned a proliferation of readings of his work from post-colonial perspectives. Such attention has engaged with a wide range of his drama and poetry, expanding outwards from plays such as *The Tempest* and *Othello* which are directly concerned with colonialism and 'race' to discussions that examine the representation of 'alterity' ('OTHERNESS'), LOCATION and cultural difference more generally.

Further reading

Loomba and Orkin (eds) (1998); Cartelli (1999).

Shamanism   Shamanism is a set of religious practices, in which individuals believed to possess heightened spiritual awareness function as intermediaries between the members of their tribal grouping and the spirit world. Shamans are generally believed to possess healing and other magical powers. The term derives from a Siberian word, but shamanistic beliefs are also practised in other parts of Asia and inform the cultures of many NATIVE American peoples. Shamanistic communion with the spirit world is sometimes achieved through a trance-like state. Jungian anthropologists, such as Paul Radin, have seen the shaman as a creative trickster figure who is able to assist others in achieving psychic integration. Michael Taussig's *Shamanism, Colonialism, and the Wild Man* (1987), which is more alert to contemporary anthropological dilemmas such as the question of agency, locates shamanism in relation to the interventions of colonialism. Post-colonial writers such as Wilson HARRIS have used shamanism as a trope for the process of transforming consciousness more generally.

Further reading

Radin (1956); Jung *et al.* (1964); Taussig (1987).

Shankar, Ravi   (Robindro Shaunkor Chowdhury) Born 1920. Indian musician, renowned as the world's foremost sitar-player, especially after his association with the Beatles in the 1960s propelled him to the forefront of international attention. He performed at the Monterey Pop Festival and Woodstock and also worked with more classical Western musicians, such as the violinist Yehudi Menuhin. His numerous pupils included George Harrison and his daughter, Anoushka Shankar, who now also has an international reputation as a sitarist. Ravi Shankar's achievements include the composition of the music for Satyajit RAY's 'Apu trilogy' and various other film scores, two concertos for sitar and orchestra, numerous *ragas* and several ballets. He has been involved in various forms of fusion music, including work that combines Indian classical instruments with electronic technology. He published his autobiography in 1997. His website includes an 'Appreciation of Indian Classical Music', which provides a succinct introduction to the *raga*.

Further reading

Shankar (1997); official website: www.ravishankar.org.

Sharia law   The traditional law of Islam, based on the QUR'AN and other utterances by the Prophet Muhammad. It lays down the ethical codes according to which Muslims are supposed to lead their lives and in some cases is reinforced by a strict penal system. In modern times, many Muslim countries have synthesized Sharia law with westernized legal practices, while others such as Saudi Arabia have maintained it as the country's legal system, usually in forms that have seen recent accretions. In countries such as Nigeria, Islamic revivalist attempts to enforce strict Sharia law have generated conflicts between Muslim and Christian communities.

Sharpeville   Like the AMRITSAR MASSACRE in India, 'Sharpeville' was a defining moment in South African history. On 21 March 1960, South African security forces fired on an anti-APARTHEID protest in the black township of Sharpeville, south of Johannesburg, killing 69 demonstrators and wounding a further 180. Sharpeville was followed by an extension of the apartheid regime's repressive policies, which included the banning of the AFRICAN NATIONAL CONGRESS and the Pan-Africanist Congress. The massacre was widely condemned internationally and with pressure on his government mounting, South African Premier, Hendrik Frensh Verwoerd (1901–66) declared the country a republic and in the following year withdrew South Africa from the COMMONWEALTH. The name 'Sharpeville' became synonymous with the brutality of the regime and anniversaries of the massacre provoked similar further demonstrations. In 1985, on the twenty-fifth anniversary, police opened fire on a funeral procession for black activists, killing some 20 people. This event, which led to widespread rioting in the townships, after the ANC had called on its supporters to make them 'ungovernable', and the imposition of trade sanctions on South Africa, were major factors in the demise of apartheid.

Shia, Shiite   Shia is one of the two main branches of Islam. Shiites differ from the more orthodox SUNNI Muslims in their interpretation of Islamic tradition and in their rejection of the first three Sunni caliphs. They regard the Prophet Muhammad's son-in-law, Ali, the fourth caliph, as his true successor. Sunnis did not recognize Shi'ism as a legitimate school of Islam until the second half of the twentieth century and conflicts between the two factions continue. While most Islamic nations are predominantly Sunni, Shiites form the vast majority of the population in Iran, and also outnumber Sunni in Iraq, Lebanon and Bahrain.

Sidhwa, Bapsi Born 1938. Pakistani novelist of Parsi descent, who was born in Karachi, grew up in Lahore and now lives in Houston, Texas. She has been active in campaigning for Asian women's rights. Sidhwa's fist novel, *The Crow Eaters* (1979), is a satirical portrait of Parsi life, centred on the fictional figure of Freddy Junglewalla, the head of the community in Lahore. One of the finest South Asian comic novels, its satire still demonstrates considerable affection and empathy for the idiosyncratic community it represents. *Ice-Candy-Man* (1988; republished as *Cracking India*, 1992) offers a vivid account of PARTITION, as seen through the eyes of Lenny, a young Parsi girl growing up in Lahore, who is afflicted with polio. As Independence and Partition approach, she ingenuously asks the question, 'Can one break a country?' and the events of the novel provide a microcosm that answers this in the affirmative. *Ice-Candy-Man* is also a compelling coming-of-age novel, which chronicles Lenny's gradual awakening into a sense of her sexuality and her personal identity more generally. Sidhwa's other novels are *The Bride* (1982) and *An American Brat* (1993). The four novels she has published to date have been published together in a Pakistani omnibus edition (2001). *Earth* (1999), directed by Deepa Mehta, is a film version of *Ice-Candy-Man*.

Further reading

Dhawan and Kapadia (eds) (1996).

Signifying, the signifying monkey 'Signifying' is an African American term for 'bragging' and the monkey of various animal fables is a trickster figure who lives by his wits, eluding definition through his capacity to talk. Henry Louis GATES, Jr sees signifying as representative of the double-voiced tradition of African American discourses such as slave narratives, contending that they make 'the white written text speak with a black voice' (1988: 131). The 'signifying monkey' is Gates's term for the interpretive practices of African American and other New World African DIASPORA discourse. In his now-classic 1988 study with this title, he identifies the signifying monkey as a central figure in the transmission of African forms in the Americas. He argues that a trickster of the kind to be found in the Esu-Elegbara figure of Yoruba culture is a recurrent topos in the myths of New World Africans and relates the double-voiced 'talking book' aspect of vernacular retellings of trickster tales, whether in early slave narratives or more contemporary urban 'toasts' to the practices of African American writers, such as Zora Neale Hurston and Ralph Ellison. In so doing, he draws on some of the more accessible aspects of European poststructuralist theory to identify what he sees as the distinctive features of a black rhetorical tradition in the New World.

His stress on the trickster invokes parallels with the most popular Caribbean incarnation of the figure, the spiderman ANANCY, who, like the Esu archetype, serves as a bridge between oral tales and the work of writers such as (Edward) Kamau BRATHWAITE and Wilson HARRIS who have employed Anancy as a trope for the possibility of psychic and other forms of transformation. While Gates's concern is with the African DIASPORA experience, his approach has implications for marginalized cultures more generally and in New World contexts bears an interesting relationship to the importance accorded to the SHAMAN/trickster figure in NATIVE American and other AMERINDIAN mythologies.

Further reading

Gates (1988).

Singlish   Singaporean English, particularly in its colloquial forms, as opposed to the international Standard English used in official contexts, business and the media. 'Basilect' forms of Singlish (see CREOLE) are influenced by Chinese and Malay.

Sistren   Jamaican women's theatre collective. Sistren ('Sisterhood') was formed in Kingston in 1977, when Honor Ford-Smith of the Jamaican School of Drama staged a sketch about the lives of women working in a garment factory. Numerous later plays, generally employing improvisational methods, have explored the exploitation of women in Jamaican society. The collective's plays draw on local folk traditions and most of their dialogue is in Jamaican CREOLE. Sistren's success led to tours in the Caribbean, North America and Europe. Its best-known plays include *Bellywoman, Bangarang* (1978), *QPH* (1981; published in Gilbert (ed.) 2001: 157–78) and *Muffet Inna All A We* (1985). Sistren's activities have developed to include participatory educational projects, which also aim to analyse and increase awareness of gender discrimination. *Lionheart Gal* (1986) is a collection of 'life stories' of Sistren women, produced in collaboration with Honor Ford-Smith.

Further reading

Sistren with Ford-Smith (1986); Gilbert (ed.) (2001).

Ska   A form of Jamaican music, generally played at a fast tempo and with the emphasis on the offbeat. The music was also known as 'blue beat', the name of the record label on which it mainly appeared, and played an important part in the evolution of REGGAE in the 1960s. Leading performers included the so-called 'King of Ska', Prince Buster (Cecil Bustamante Campbell, born 1938), whose most famous recordings include 'Al Capone' and the half-spoken compositions 'Madness' and 'Judge Dread', both of which gave their names to British performers who came to the fore in the 1970s.

Further reading

Barrow and Dalton (2001).

Slavery   The situation in which human beings are treated as chattels, who have become the property of another person, group or institution either as a consequence of capture and/or trade or by virtue of being born into such a situation. Slavery has existed in most periods of human history, e.g. ancient Egypt and classical Greece, though in the feudal system of medieval Europe it was supplanted by the more modified form of bondage of serfdom.

In imperialist contexts, slavery is particularly but not exclusively associated with the Atlantic Slave Trade that took some nine million Africans to the New World, during a period beginning in the sixteenth and ending in the nineteenth century. Slaves were brought to provide a labour force for the plantation economies of the southern USA, the Caribbean and parts of Central and South America. On arrival in the New World, the conditions experienced by slaves varied, but they suffered from widespread brutalization and attempts to eradicate African cultural retentions. Newly arrived slaves were sold at market, having been advertised in bills of fare that used language humane society would normally reserve for animals, with families, kinship groups and people that shared a common language often being deliberately separated. As plantation field workers, slaves usually worked from sunrise to sunset, only being allowed to rest on Sundays and with no right to own property or lead family lives. See the TRIANGULAR TRADE, ABOLITIONISM and William WILBERFORCE for details of the end of the Slave Trade and slavery itself.

The League of Nations passed a Slavery Convention in 1926, which was adopted by the United Nations in 1953. Slavery remained legal in certain countries at that time, only being abolished in Saudi Arabia in 1963 and it continues in many parts of the world today. A recent United Nations estimate put the number of people working as slaves (i.e. in situations of enforced labour) in Africa, Asia and South America at 200 million.

Smith, Michael ('Mikey')   (1954–83). Leading exponent of Jamaican NATION LANGUAGE poetry, best known for the title-track of his classic album, *Mi Cyaan Believe It* (1982), which expresses his incredulity at poverty and social injustice in Jamaican society. Like many Caribbean oral poets, Smith's work found its most powerful expression in performance, though recordings capture some of its force. It is collected in the posthumous volume, *It a Come* (1986). Smith died tragically young, stoned to death the day after he had heckled Jamaica's Minister of Education at a political meeting.

Soca   See CALYPSO.

Social Text   A leftist quarterly journal of cultural and political analysis founded in the late 1970s – around the same times as companion publications such as *Diacritics*, *Critical Inquiry* and *Signs* – with the broadly Marxist sub-title 'Theory, Culture, Ideology'. Although its concerns are not specifically post-colonial, *Social Text* has published a number of important interventions in the field. The original editors were Stanley Aronowitz, John Brenkman and Fredric Jameson. Today *Social Text* is produced by an editorial collective made up of scholars, critics, artists and writers based in New York. A 2002 editorial suggested that much of the journal's original purpose had been achieved and in the changed cultural climate of the early twenty-first century restated its mission as 'the elaboration of cultural politics after cultural studies'.

South   Term sometimes used in preference to 'THIRD WORLD' and 'DEVELOPING COUNTRIES' to identify the world's poorer regions, in contradistinction to the affluent regions of the North. It is used to refer to Africa, Latin America and the southern parts of Asia, but not the more 'Westernized' southern hemisphere nations of Australia and New Zealand.

Soweto   The best known of South Africa's black townships, Soweto is in fact an area south-west of Johannesburg made up of several different townships. In 1976 it was the scene of demonstrations against the imposition of Afrikaans as the compulsory language of education. This was successfully resisted, but the demonstrations resulted in the killing of some five hundred black and coloured South Africans and the anniversary of this event continued to be marked until the multi-racial elections of 1994 ended minority rule. 'Soweto' is an acronym for the South West Township of Johannesburg.

Soyinka, Wole   Born 1934. Nigerian dramatist, novelist, poet and autobiographer, who was awarded the 1986 NOBEL PRIZE FOR LITERATURE. Soyinka was born near Abeokuta in the western part of Nigeria. His autobiographical volumes, *Aké: The Years of Childhood* (1981), *Isara: A Voyage around Essay* (1989) and *Ibadan: The Penkelemes Years: A Memoir 1946–1965* (1994) provide a compelling account of his early years, though their emphasis is as much on the community and the particular individuals who shaped his sensibility as on himself. He was educated at the Universities of Ibadan and Leeds and worked as the Royal Court Theatre in London before returning to Nigeria in 1960. Back in Nigeria, he founded the Masks and the Orisun theatre companies and worked at the universities of Ibadan, Ife and Lagos. He spent 27 months in jail during the NIGERIAN CIVIL WAR.

His earliest plays, *The Swamp-Dwellers* (1958) and *The Lion and the Jewel* (1959), were followed by one of his most demanding and theatrically ambitious works, *A Dance of the Forests* (1960). Staged as part of Nigeria's independence celebrations, the play is a complex allegory which makes extensive use of Yoruba myth, ritual and theatrical practices and has been interpreted as an enigmatic comment on the promise of Nigerian independence. In *The Trials of Brother Jero* (1960) and *Jero's Metamorphosis* (1973), Soyinka took a trickster as his protagonist and it is perhaps a measure of his growing disillusionment with post-independence Nigerian society that the essentially comic creation of the first play becomes a more ominous figure in the second. The provocatively titled *The Bacchae of Euripides* (1973), which finds Yoruba equivalents for the Apollonian–Dionysian conflict of the Greek tragedy, also makes extensive use of Yoruba customs, so that it is as much a *Nigerian Bacchae* as Derek WALCOTT's *Omeros* (1990) is a Caribbean *Iliad*. Soyinka also turned to a European 'original' for his *Opera Wonyosi* (1977), which took its departure point from Brecht's *Threepenny Opera*. Such cross-cultural work, which suggests the universality of African experience – in a neat reversal of the Western appropriation of UNIVERSALISM for its own ideologies and representational practices – has, however, led to Nigerian writers such as Chinweizu *et al.* (1980) criticizing Soyinka for being excessively EUROCENTRIC in outlook. Other notable plays from the first part of his career include *Kongi's Harvest* (1965), *The Road* (1965), *Madmen and Specialists* (1970) and *Death and the King's Horseman* (1975), a tragedy which again draws on Greek and Yoruba elements to stage a complex debate about the ethics of a ritual suicide, which serves as a metonym for the conflict of Yoruba and Western cultural codes. His later plays include *A Play of Giants* (1984), an attack on African dictatorships, *From Zia with Love* and *A Scourge of Hyacinths* (1992) and *The Beatification of Area Boy* (1995).

Although Soyinka is best known as a dramatist, his prolific output also includes major work in a number of other genres. He is the author of the novels *The Interpreters* (1965) and *Season of Anomy* (1973) and the poetry collections *Idanre and Other Poems* (1967), *Poems from Prison* (1969), *A Shuttle in the Crypt* (1972), *Ogun Abibiman* (1976) and *Mandela's Earth* (1989). *The Man Died: Prison Notes* (1972) is an account of his experience of imprisonment during the Nigerian Civil War and, beginning with *Aké*, he has proved himself to be an outstanding and innovative autobiographer. *Myth, Literature and the African World* (1976) is a collection of his challenging critical writing, which again takes much of its inspiration from Yoruba mythology and cosmogony, seeing the artist's role in society as equivalent to that of Ogun, the Yoruba god of creativity. *Art, Dialogue and Outrage* (1988) is a second collection of essays.

His plays are available in several collected editions, including *Collected Plays*, Vol. 1 (1973), Vol. 2 (1974) and *Six Plays* (1984).

Further reading

Soyinka (1976); Chinweizu *et al.* (1980); Wright (1993): Maja-Pearce (ed.) (1994).

SPAN The twice-yearly journal of the South Pacific Association for Commonwealth Literature and Language Studies (a chapter of ACLALS), currently published from the University of the South Pacific, Suva, Fiji.

Sparrow, The Mighty (Slinger Francisco.) Born 1935. The most famous of Trinidadian calypsonians. Born in Grenada, Sparrow shot to public fame in Trinidad, when he became CALYPSO King in 1956 with his composition 'Jean and Dinah', a satirical comment on the post-war fate of the good-time 'girls', who had benefited from the American military presence in Trinidad in World War II. He subsequently won the title of Calypso King (later Monarch) on ten further occasions, despite boycotting Carnival for several years when he was at the height of his powers. 'Jean and Dinah' also brought him the first of eight Road March titles. Its playful treatment of the man–woman relationship is typical of many later Sparrow calypsoes, such as 'The Village Ram' (1964), in which he characteristically cultivates a macho persona. Throughout his career Sparrow has also been a commentator on various aspects of Trinidadian social and political life. Initially a supporter of ERIC WILLIAMS's PNM (People's National Movement), he turned to criticizing its policies in the post-independence period, in such compositions as 'Get to Hell Outa Here' (1965). Other political calypsoes include 'FEDERATION' (1962), 'Kennedy and Khruschev' (1963) and 'Wanted Dead or Alive' (1980). 'Dan is the Man in the Van' (1963) is an inspired CARNIVALESQUE satire on the injurious effects of the English-oriented Caribbean educational curriculum of his youth (see also ORALITY). Other famous Sparrow calypsoes include 'Ten to One is Murder' (1960), 'The Congo Man' (1965), an AMBIVALENT response to Africa which plays on stereotypes of CANNIBALISM, 'Obeah Wedding' (1966) and 'Drunk and Disorderly' (1972).

Sparrow's only major rival during his prime was Lord Kitchener (Aldwin Roberts) (1922–2000), who won ten Road March titles. His capacity for self-reinvention repeatedly enabled him to win over audiences, when he returned to Trinidad from extensive tours abroad, but his blend of entertainment and social commentary became less popular in the politically charged years of the 1970s, when calypsonians such as The Mighty Chalkdust (Hollis Liverpool, born 1941) and Black Stalin (Leroy Calliste, born 1941) found more favour with the public. Sparrow has received numerous honours, including a doctorate from the University of the West Indies, a Yoruba chieftainship and the Order of the Caribbean Community.

Spivak, Gayatri Chakravorty Born 1942. Indian cultural theorist and translator. Born into a Bengali BRAHMIN family, Spivak studied at the University of Calcutta and Cornell University, where she was heavily influenced by the work of Jacques Derrida, whose *De la Grammatologie* (1967; *Of Grammatology*, 1976) she later translated into English. Like the style of several of the French deconstructionists, the complexity of her writing frequently presents her readers with a considerable challenge, on the most basic level of comprehension. However, as with the work of Homi K. BHABHA, its apparent hermeticism works to destabilize habitual ways of thinking and can be seen as a necessary corollary of her project of articulating innovative theoretical ideas outside the framework of conventional academic discourse. She has disseminated her ideas through a range of modes, including interviews – in *The Post-Colonial Critic: Interviews, Strategies, Dialogues* (1990) – and TRANSLATIONS, most notably of the work of her Bengali compatriot, MAHASWETA Devi.

Spivak's range of interests is more eclectic than that of either Bhabha or Edward SAID and it is difficult to summarize the main principles of her theory, both because of its breadth and because of the tensions generated by its Derridean emphasis on the deferral of signification on the one hand and its commitment to the lived experience of real people on the other. Her work moves between a poststructuralist account of the difficulties of representing subjectivity and a Marxist concern with recuperating occluded subaltern experience. This particularly informs her engagement with the SUBALTERN STUDIES project. She views the attempt to articulate subaltern experience as especially problematic because of her resistance to the concept of unified subjectivity, but nevertheless supports the use of STRATEGIC ESSENTIALISM in particular situations. Her approach to subjectivity emphasizes its staged nature, a perspective which again frustrates attempts at definition through notions of originary or AUTHENTIC identity.

Other central aspects of Spivak's theory include her stress on the heterogeneity of post-colonial experience and the extent to which gendered readings of the subaltern, which privilege feminist over post-colonial elements, distort. This view informs her attempt, in 'Three Women's Texts and a Critique of Imperialism' (Spivak 1985), to reclaim Charlotte Brontë's Bertha from what she sees as the appropriation of Western feminist critics, whose claims for the feminism of *Jane Eyre* have overlooked the extent to which Jane's iconic status is achieved through the dispossession of her colonial double. Equally, it could be argued that Spivak's complex discussion of this issue adds comparatively little to the position dramatized by several earlier commentators and explored at length in Jean RHYS's novel *Wide Sargasso Sea* (1966), which is one of the other two texts discussed in Spivak's essay.

Spivak is painstakingly discriminating in her accounts of Western critics' analyses of post-colonial subjects. She resists the suggestion that such commentators lack the authority to comment on post-colonial topics as a form of 'reverse ethnocentrism' (see Moore-Gilbert 1997: 108ff.), a position that *could* be seen as a partial justification of her own situation within the Western academy. However, she frequently foregrounds her privileged subject-position in a manner that is in marked contrast to several of her peers. At the same time, in her essay 'French Feminism in an International Frame' (Spivak 1988a: 134–53), she attacks discussions such as Julia Kristeva's *Des Chinoises* (1974; *About Chinese Women*, 1977) for being insufficiently sensitive to the specifics of its subjects' situations, so that the approach becomes a form of latter-day ORIENTALISM, in which the exploration of 'alterity' (see 'OTHERNESS') says more about the identity of the author and her reading community than that of her subjects.

Spivak's other works include *Outside in the Teaching Machine* (1993) and *A Critique of Postcolonial Reason: Toward a History of the Vanishing Present* (1999). With Ranajit Guha, she edited *Selected Subaltern Studies* (1988). *The Spivak Reader* (1996), edited by Donna Landry and Gerald MacLean, is a selection of her work, which includes a checklist of her writings. See also GENDER AND POST-COLONIALISM and WORLDING.

Further reading

Spivak (1985, 1988a, 1988b, 1990 and 1999); Landry and MacLean (eds) (1996); Moore-Gilbert (1997).

Staffrider   South African literary and cultural magazine, first published in 1978. It initially operated with a self-editing policy that attempted to release and nurture voices previously repressed in the struggle against racial oppression. This policy was later reversed Its contributors have included Miriam TLALI, Chris van Wyk (who later became its editor), Njabulo Ndebele, Mongane Wally Serote, Ahmed Essop and Kelwyn Sole. *Staffrider* has attempted to break down traditional notions of genre classification and includes photographs, graphics and revisionist histories, along with fiction and poetry. It has been published by Ravan Press, and more recently by COSAW (the Congress of South African Writers).

Steelband   Popular musical form, which evolved in Trinidad in the 1930s, when 'pans' were fashioned from various metal objects as an alternative to the 'African' drums that had been banned from Port of Spain's annual CARNIVAL celebrations. So steelband has its origins in a strategy that slyly subverted a colonial prohibition on an Afro-Caribbean form of expression. In the 1940s, the exponents of this art of *bricolage* (the term, adapted from do-it-yourself vocabulary, by the French anthropologist Claude Lévi-Strauss to describe cultural formations fashioned from materials that are readily to hand, as an index of a world-view predicated upon pragmatic utilitarianism, often as a consequence of necessity) found the perfect material for their music in the discarded drums used in the island's oil industry. Players developed their instruments to sound a range of pitches that covered full chromatic octaves and the music became a central part of Carnival celebrations. Bands competed with one another in warrior-like competition and developed repertories that extended from CALYPSO to European symphonies. They boasted names such as Renegades and Desperadoes and their members traditionally rehearsed in yards, forming closed gang-like communities, an aspect of Trinidad urban culture vividly portrayed in Earl LOVELACE's novel *The Dragon Can't Dance* (1979), which celebrates the warriorhood aspects of the music, while lamenting its commercialization and the middle-class appropriation that betrays its original driving force. In recent decades steelband music has spread through the Caribbean and become popular in North America and Europe.

Strategic essentialism   Term coined by Gayatri Chakravorty SPIVAK to refer to the need to employ ESSENTIALISM in order to understand how such thinking operates. Her advocacy of such usage remains deconstructivist and she likens it to the process of trying to enter the criminal mind in order to understand its operation better. Writing on the work of the SUBALTERN STUDIES scholars 'from within but against the grain', she suggests that 'elements in their text would warrant a reading of the project to retrieve the subaltern consciousness as the attempt to undo a massive historiographic metalepsis and "situate" the effect of the subject as subaltern' and says that reading their work as a '*strategic* use of positivist essentialism' (Spivak 1988a: 205; italics in original) would locate them in a Marxist tradition of analysis that includes aspects of the writing of Marx himself, Nietzsche, Foucault, Barthes and Derrida. Despite this top-heavy listing of European theorists to legitimate a non-European practice and the use of poststructuralist terminology that many would see as operating against the retrieval of subaltern discourse, Spivak's use of 'the concept of an essential subject' can be justified 'as part of a wider political project' (McLeod, J. 2000: 194). John McLeod, who makes this point, cites NEGRITUDE as an example of strategic essentialism.

Further reading

Spivak (1988a); McLeod, J. (2000).

Subaltern Studies   A project led by historians, which attempted to promote discussion and awareness of 'subaltern' themes in South Asian studies. Ten volumes of essays, on history, politics economics, sociology and law, entitled *Subaltern Studies: Writings on South Asian History and Society*, were published by Oxford University Press India between 1982 and 1999. The first six volumes were edited by Ranajit Guha, who founded the series; and each of the four subsequent volumes was edited by two or more of the Subaltern Studies collective, whose members have included Partha Chatterjee, Gyanendra Pandy, Shahid Amin and Dipesh Chakrabarty. An eleventh volume, edited by Partha Chatterjee and Pradeep Jeganathan was published by Columbia University Press and Permanent Black, New Delhi, in 2000. A volume of *Selected Subaltern Studies*, edited by Guha and Gayatri Chakravorty SPIVAK was published in 1988; and the work of the group has yielded numerous other monographs and journal articles.

In his Preface to the first volume, Guha cites the *Concise Oxford* definition of a subaltern as someone 'of inferior rank' and links the group's projected work with that of the Italian political theorist, Antonio Gramsci (*Subaltern Studies* 1 [1982]: vii). In the inaugural essay of the first volume, 'On Some Aspects of the Historiography of Colonial India', Guha effectively outlines its aims, pointing out that

> Parallel to the domain of elite politics there existed throughout the colonial
> period another domain of Indian politics in which the principal actors were
> not the dominant groups of the indigenous society or the colonial authorities
> but the subaltern classes

and arguing that 'This was an autonomous domain . . . . Far from being destroyed or rendered virtually ineffective . . . it continued to operate vigorously . . . adjusting itself to the conditions prevailing under the Raj' (*Subaltern Studies* 1 [1982]: 4). Notable later essays include Guha's 'The Prose of Counter-Insurgency'(2 [1983]: 1–42), Spivak's 'Subaltern Studies: Deconstructing Historiography' (4 [1985]: 330–65; repr. in Spivak 1988a), Amitav GHOSH's 'The Slave of MS. H. 6' (7 [1992]: 151–220) and Upendra Baxi's '"The State's Emissary": The Place of Law in Subaltern Studies' (7 [1982]: 247–64).

The phrase 'subaltern' is best known in post-colonial contexts through Spivak's influential essay 'Can the Subaltern Speak?' (Spivak 1988b). This is often assumed to deal with the problems of giving voice to subaltern discourse, but is predicated on an attack on the Western notion of unified subjectivity, endemic in the approach taken by Guha and the Subaltern Studies scholars. In Spivak's view the subject is a discursive construct rather than a sovereign whole. While such an approach resists Western ESSENTIALISM, it has laid her open to the charge of being indebted to a later mode of Western thinking, French poststructuralist theorizing, and consequently failing to engage with social 'realities'. Such a view is, however, simplistic, given Spivak's self-conscious foregrounding of her position and her advocacy of the need for STRATEGIC ESSENTIALISM. Ostensibly Amitav Ghosh's essay 'The Slave of MS. H. 6', which was subsequently incorporated into *In an Antique Land* (1992), moves in an opposite, less theoretical direction. It describes its narrator's attempts to discover the fugitive material traces of a medieval subaltern, who was the slave of a Jewish merchant and, in *In an Antique Land*, it is juxtaposed with a parallel contemporary narrative of a Ghosh persona's life among *fellaheen* subalterns in Egypt, where he is engaging in anthropological research. Equally one might take the view that Ghosh's 'slave' is a paradigm of the discursively constructed subaltern, since his only existence is in the margins of the HISTORIOGRAPHICAL records, through which the Ghosh persona pursues him.

Further reading

Guha *et al.* (eds) (1982–99); Spivak (1988a and 1988b); Ghosh (1994); Chakrabarty (2002).

The Suez Crisis   A defining moment in the latter days of Britain and France's roles as imperial powers, the Suez Crisis has been seen as signalling the end of the two nations' HEGEMONIC influence in the Middle East. In 1956, Egypt's President, Gamal Abdel NASSER, nationalized the Suez Canal, a waterway owned by a British and French consortium. Israeli interests were also threatened and Israel invaded the Sinai, while British and French forces launched attacks on Egyptian bases. They were forced to withdraw under pressure from the USA and USSR and the British Prime Minister Anthony Eden's resignation in early 1957 has been attributed to the Suez débâcle.

Further reading

Judd (1996).

Suleri Goodyear, Sara   Pakistani-born American-based writer and critic. Born to a Pakistani father, who was a leading political journalist, and a Welsh mother, Suleri has degrees from Punjab University, Lahore and Indiana University and has taught at Yale since 1983. Although her work is centrally concerned with identity politics, she characterisitically employs strategies that frustrate simplistic categorization. *Meatless Days* (1989) is an autobiographical memoir of her early years in Pakistan, which juxtaposes personal and public history and has been highly praised for its lyrical prose. *The Rhetoric of English India* (1992) develops a view of Anglo-India literary transactions, which emphasizes the interdependence of supposedly opposi-tional British and Indian elements. Covering a broad sweep of material, including the writing of Edmund Burke and travel journals by nineteenth-century British women, along with work by Rudyard Kipling and E. M. Forster and contemporary authors such as V. S. NAIPAUL and Salman RUSHDIE, Suleri's demonstration of the degree of cultural interchange that took place challenges approaches that insist on the separateness of English and Indian traditions and in so doing problematizes the issue of post-colonial literary genealogies more generally. Suleri was a founding editor of *The Yale Journal of Criticism*.

Sunni, Sunnite   One of the two main branches of Islam and the form followed by the majority of the religion's adherents. Sunni is derived from '*Sunna*', the Arabic word for tradition. It bases its practices on the teachings of the Prophet Muhammad and the *Sunna* represents the ideal way of life, as followed by Muhammad and as expressed in the QUR'AN and his variôus other teachings. See also SHIA.

Survival   Title of Margaret Atwood's classic 1972 'thematic guide to Canadian litera-ture'. Atwood sees survival as the dominant symbol of Canadian writing and con-trasts this with the expansionist confidence embodied in the American Frontier ethic. She contends that, unlike American writing, Canadian literature represents the nation's people as suffering from a victim syndrome and identifies four charac-teristic victim positions, culminating in that of 'creative non-victim'. Atwood's novel *Surfacing* (1972), in which an unnamed narrator-protagonist progresses from a state of mind in which she represses the truth about her past to a resolution that she will 'refuse to be a victim', has been seen as a fictional dramatization of positions expressed in *Survival*. It has been read as both a feminist and as a Canadian nation-alist text. The two strands are interlinked and the novel contains numerous refer-ences that support a reading of it as a NATIONAL ALLEGORY, in which Canada is engendered as feminine and American NEO-COLONIALISM as masculine. *Survival* was a best-seller, but attracted criticism in the 1970s from those who took issue with its view of Canadian identity. Three decades later, it can be seen as a witty and illumi-nating, albeit polemical, analysis of Canadian literature published prior to its appearance and as a nationalist text asserting Canadian distinctiveness. It was a major Canadian contribution to the then-popular school of myth criticism, in the tradition of the work of Atwood's fellow-Canadian Northrop Frye and its analysis of archetypal patterns in Canadian literature demonstrates a debt to Frye's *The Bush Garden* (1971).

Further reading

Atwood (1972).

Suttee   See SATI.

Syncretism   In general usage, 'syncretism' is a term mainly deployed in philosophical and theological contexts to refer to the actual or attempted merging of two diverse practices or sets of beliefs, e.g. as in Neo-Platonism, which combined elements from Greek philosophy and Eastern religions and which in turn influenced the early development of Christianity. 'Syncretism' has a more specific meaning in linguistic contexts, where it indicates words that are identical in form, but belong to different linguistic categories (e.g. different noun cases or tenses of the verb).

   In post-colonial contexts, syncretism has particularly been used to refer to the various kinds of cultural – and theological – fusions that occur in post-CONTACT situations. Post-colonial forms of syncretism range between the processes by which SUBALTERN groups adopt and adapt forms of a dominant culture through CREOLIZATION, e.g. the incorporation of Christian elements into African-based Caribbean rites such as MYAL and VODUN, and converse processes of colonial ASSIMILATION. Consequently syncretism is best seen as operating on a social – and linguistic – CONTINUUM, in which disparate strands come together in variable and unstable relationships and the interaction produces distinctly new formations. In the case of Caribbean cultures this supports a view that acknowledges the residual and transformed presence of both African and European 'retentions', along with other ancestral elements, rather than the predication of an ETHNOCENTRIC model that privileges a single originary culture.

Taban Lo Liyong   Born 1939. Sudanese-born writer and critic of Uganda parentage, who has taught in universities in Papua New Guinea, Nairobi and Khartoum and most recently at the University of Venda in South Africa. Taban's work defies conventions and easy literary categorizations. It draws on Luo folktales and other oral forms, English literature and a range of African writing. It includes *Fixions and Other Stories* (1969), *Meditations in Limbo* (1970), a more extended prose work, and the poetry collections, *Another Nigger Dead* (1972) and *Ballads of Underdevelopment* (1976). His criticism particularly focuses on Luo aesthetics and traditional African values. It includes *The Last Word* (1969) and *Culture is Rustan* (1991).

Tagore, Rabindranath   (1861–1941). Bengali writer and philosopher. The first and to date the only Indian winner of the NOBEL PRIZE FOR LITERATURE, Tagore was born in Calcutta, studied law in England (1878–80) and then, for nearly two decades, managed his distinguished BRAHMIN family's estates in East Bengal. His short stories combine realistic depictions of rural life with protests against social injustice and were mostly written during the early 1890s for the magazine *Sadhana*, of which he became editor in 1894. His early collections of poetry, which include *Manasi* (1890) and *Sonar Tari* (1895), employ a colloquial register that represented a significant departure from the formal language of the Bengali verse of the period.

A believer in dialogue between cultures, Tagore founded the Santiniketan communal school, which sought to integrate Eastern and Western educational thinking and methods, at Bolpur, approximately a hundred miles from Calcutta. Unlike Mahatma GANDHI's *ashram* at Ahmedabad, its programme for cultural and spiritual regeneration only occasionally engaged with *swaraj*, the campaign for home rule, instead promoting a more individual humanitarian, approach to self-fulfilment. The English publication of *Gitanjali* (1912), his most famous collection of lyrics, with an introduction by W. B. Yeats, was influential in his being awarded his Nobel Prize in 1913. After its award, Tagore added an agricultural school to Santiniketan in 1914 and an international university in 1921. He was knighted in 1915, but returned this honour in 1919 as a protest against the AMRITSAR MASSACRE.

Among the best-known works from his prolific output are: the novels, *Gora* (1908) and *Ghare Bhaire* (1918; *The Home and the World*); and *The Gardener* (1913), which, like *Gitanjali*, is a collection of spiritual lyrics with an introduction by Yeats. His plays include *Chitra* (1895), taken from an episode in the MAHABHARATA, *Raja* (1910; *The King of the Dark Chamber*), *Dakghar* (1910; *The Post Office*) and *Rakta Karabi* (1924; *Red Oleanders*). Tagore was also a prominent force in Bengali music, writing over 2,000 songs, including compositions that later became the national anthems of India (1947) and Bangladesh (1971), and in his later years turned his eclectic artistic talents to painting. His own translation of his *Collected Poems and Plays* (1936) includes *Gitanjali, The Crescent Moon, The Gardener, Chitra, Fruit-Gathering, The Post Office, Lover's Gift, Crossing, Stray Birds, The Cycle of Spring, The Fugitive and Other Poems* and five further short plays. William Radice's translations of his *Selected Poems* (1985; revised 1987) and his *Selected Short Stories* (1991) are widely regarded as the finest recent versions of his work in their respective genres. Tagore's philosophical works include *Sadhana* (1913) and *Manab Dharma* (1930; *The Religion of Man*). *My Reminiscences* (1917) and *Chhelebela* (1940; *My Boyhood Days*) are autobiographical works.

After the award of the Nobel Prize, Tagore made numerous lecture tours to the West and some of his international fame can be attributed to his role as a cultural broker, who interpreted Hindu spiritual thinking for other cultures at a time when belief in scientific and technological progress had been undermined by the horrors of World War I. However, the uniqueness of his stylistic achievement and his role in forging a new outlook at home were very considerable and his later work in particular frequently departs from the mystical image, with which his reputation has been associated (Chaudhuri 1987; Desai 1994). He occupies a particular place in the development of Bengali humanism, a discourse which he helped shape from the various cross-currents that were influential in the region in the late nineteenth and early twentieth centuries. Insofar as he was a universalist, his supra-national vision remains a product of his particular Indian milieu and he contributed very significantly to its evolution. His influence can be seen in the work of major later Bengali artists, such as the film-maker Satyajit Ray and the novelist, Amitav Ghosh, both of whom have acknowledged their debt to him.

Further reading

Chaudhuri (1987); Desai (1994).

The Tempest, post-colonial responses to   Of all Shakespeare's plays, his last major work, *The Tempest*, has most readily lent itself to staging as an allegory about colonialism. The play suggests Shakespeare's own interest in early debates about colonialism. He appears to have read the contemporary 'Bermudas Pamphlets', which gave an account of the wreck of a ship bound for the newly founded colony of Virginia, and to have been familiar with various other narratives about the imaginative possibilities of 'America' and encounters with 'alterity' (see 'OTHERNESS'), including Montaigne's essay 'Of Cannibals' (1580). The shipwrecked sailors were stranded in a 'natural' state for nearly a year (1609–10) and their extra-social situation stimulated debates about the competing claims of nature and nurture in the process of shaping identity, as well as being seen as a microcosm for colonialism. *The Tempest* itself resists the temptation to sentimentalize its most obvious 'natural man', the 'salvage and deformed slave' Caliban (*Tempest*, 'Names of the Actors'), while also introducing a number of other figures whose characters lend themselves to colonial interpretation. Although Caliban and his master, the magician/colonizer figure of Prospero, have attracted the most attention in post-colonial re-readings of *The Tempest*, other characters in the play, particularly Prospero's daughter, Miranda and the spirit, Ariel, have also figured prominently in such revisionist readings and performances.

In the NATIONALIST period, before and after various territories colonized by European powers attained their independences, several FRANCOPHONE writers employed Prospero and Caliban as archetypes of the colonizer and colonized, placing particular emphasis on two related areas: the psychology of colonialism, as it affects both figures; and

Caliban's response to the imposition of Prospero's language, a reading supported by his complaint 'You taught me language; and my profit on't/ Is, I know how to curse' (*Tempest* 1.2.364–5). Octave MANNONI's classic study *Psychologie de la colonisation* (1950; *Prospero and Caliban*, 1956) particularly focuses on Caliban's dependence complex, while Frantz FANON's *Peau noire, masques blancs* (1952; *Black Skin, White Masks*, 1967) suggests the extent to which the colonizer/colonized relationship involves the suppression of integral aspects of Caliban's personality. Later Francophone responses include Aimé CÉSAIRE's play, *Tempête* (1969; *A Tempest*, 1986) and Max Dorsinville's *Caliban without Prospero* (1974), which mainly discusses Québecois and African American writing.

George LAMMING's non-fictional work *The Pleasures of Exile* (1960) and his novel *Water with Berries* (1971) include some of the most probing post-colonial analysis of *The Tempest*'s archetypes to have appeared to date. *The Pleasures of Exile* begins from the premise that 'Caliban is [the] convert, colonized by language and excluded by language' (Lamming 1960: 15) and, with a particular focus on the 'exile' experienced by the Caribbean artist, both diagnoses and seeks emancipation from this predicament, demonstrating the multiple transformations that the character of Caliban has undergone and his capacity to mimic all the parts in the colonial repertory. Such MIMICRY, which unsettles the asymmetrical binary power structures engrained in the colonial relationship, also informs the treatment of Caliban in *Water with Berries*, but despite Lamming's demonstration that Shakespeare's 'slave' is well able to play *all* the roles in *The Tempest*, including that of the artist-magician, Prospero, the novel ends in a holocaust of violence that appears to express some of the pessimistic aspects of the thinking of the Black Power movement of the late 1960s and early 1970s. (Edward) Kamau BRATHWAITE's 'Caliban' (in *Islands*, 1969) also offers a number of versions of its eponym, variously representing him as a victim of American NEO-COLONIALISM, as a CARNIVAL masquerader and as a LIMBO dancer. However, Brathwaite arrives at a rather more optimistic assessment of Caliban's potential for creative transformation.

From around the middle of the twentieth century, critical analyses of *The Tempest* also began to devote particular attention to its colonial and post-colonial implications. Significant contributions to this body of writing include Frank Kermode's Introduction to the second Arden edition of the play (1954), Trevor R. Griffiths's '"This Island's Mine": Caliban and Colonialism' (1983) and Jerry Brotton's '"This Tunis, sir, was Carthage": Contesting Colonialism in *The Tempest*' (1998). Alden T. and Virginia Mason Vaughan (1991) examine the various incarnations of Caliban across the years. Peter Hulme and William H. Sherman (2000) offer a broader overview of interpretations that have seen *The Tempest* as an allegory of colonialism. Christine Dymkowski (ed.) (2000) provides a more general account of the play's performance history. John Thieme (2001) compares and contrasts Caribbean and Canadian creative writers' responses to the colonial aspects of the play.

See also *ROBINSON CRUSOE*, POST-COLONIAL RESPONSES TO.

Further reading

Kermode (1954); Lamming (1960); Griffiths (1983); Vaughan and Vaughan (1991); Loomba and Orkin (eds) (1998); Cartelli (1999); Hulme and Sherman (eds) (2000); Dymkowski (ed.) (2000); Thieme (2001).

Terra nullius   A doctrine introduced by the British colonizers of Australia, which dispossessed the Aboriginal peoples of the continent by decreeing that it had hitherto belonged to no-one, since its inhabitants lacked social organization and other trappings of 'civilization'. It remained in force until the Mabo Case successfully established Aboriginal rights to land ownership in the 1980s.

Te Tiriti O Waitangi   See the Treaty of Waitangi.

Theravada   One of the two main forms of Buddhism, widely practised in Sri Lanka, Myanmar (Burma), Thailand, Cambodia and Laos. The older, more conservative tradition of Buddhism, it emphasizes personal enlightenment.

Third Space   Homi K. Bhabha's term for the enunciative 'passage', in which meaning is produced. Drawing on the poststructuralist theorist, Jacques Derrida's theory of *différance*, Bhabha writes:

> The pact of interpretation is never simply an act of communication between the I and the You designated in the statement. The production of meaning requires that these two places be mobilized in the passage through a Third Space, which represents both the general conditions of language and the specific implication of the utterance in a performative and institutional strategy of which it cannot 'in itself' be conscious. (1994: 36)

While this may seem to represent a general statement about the enunciative process, Bhabha points out that it has particular implications for cultural analysis, because it disrupts the temporal logic on which most Western models of cultural authority are based, replacing the teleological 'narrative of traditionalism' with an ambivalent 'time of cultural uncertainty' (ibid.: 35). He cites a comment by Wilson Harris on '"the void or [Bhabha subsequently renders this as "of"] misgiving attending every assimilation of contraries"' (Bhabha 1994: 38; Harris 1967: 62) in colonial discourse as a precondition for the articulation of cultural difference. In short, although the concept of Third Space has broad, transcultural applicability, it has a particular 'colonial or postcolonial provenance' that makes it possible to conceptualize 'an *inter*national culture, based not on the exoticism of multiculturalism or the *diversity* of cultures, but on the inscription and articulation of culture's *hybridity*' (ibid.: 38; italics in original). Whether Bhabha's reading of Harris is definitive is questionable, since the Guyanese writer's aesthetics demonstrate a commitment to signifying practices that resist deferral. Moreover, Bhabha's use of poststructuralist theory as an alternative to nationalism has been attacked by Marxist commentators such as Aijaz AHMAD, who question the relevance of his stress on postmodernity to those who live 'in places where a majority of the population has been denied access to such benefits of "modernity" as hospitals or better health insurance or even basic literacy' (Ahmad 1992: 68–9). Nevertheless the notion of Third Space is crucial to Bhabha's conception of HYBRIDITY as a condition which maintains the ontological undecidability of cultural difference, as opposed to the epistemological certainty of cultural diversity, and destabilizes traditional models of HISTORIOGRAPHY and authority in favour of 'the articulation of a historical politics of negotiation' (Bhabha 1994: 35).

Further reading

Harris (1967); Ahmad (1992); Bhabha (1994).

Third Text   A quarterly journal offering 'critical perspectives on contemporary art and culture'. It is published by Routledge and first appeared in 1987. Its editors are Rasheed Araeen and Ziauddin Sardar. *Third Text* aims to provide 'a forum for the discussion and (re)appraisal of theory and practice of art, art history and criticism, and the work of artists hitherto marginalised through racial, gender, religious and cultural differences'. As such, it sees itself as posing a challenge 'to Eurocentrism and ethnocentric aesthetic criteria'. It encourages the development of new interdisciplinary approaches to art and culture.

Third World   A term, taken from the French *tiers monde*, widely used to refer to countries in Africa, Asia and Latin America, in contradistinction to the capitalist (First World) and Communist (Second World) countries. The term originated in the 1950s and is said to have first been used by Alfred Sauvy, in his article, *Trois mondes, Une planète*, published in *L'Observateur* in 1952, to promote a socialist alternative to the two dominant world orders of the period. Despite vagueness in its usage, it remained popular in some circles for over two decades, but lost much of its residual appeal with the collapse of the Soviet bloc in the late 1980s. It is now often considered to have pejorative connotations, since it implies that First and former Second World societies have primacy. Alternatives used to describe the same geopolitical areas include 'DEVELOPING' and 'SOUTH', when used in opposition to 'North'.

Thumboo, Edwin   Born 1933. Singaporean poet and academic. Born into a mixed-race background, Thumboo pursued a distinguished academic career as Professor of English at the National University of Singapore and played an important role in promoting Commonwealth literary studies in Singapore and internationally. His early collection of verse *Rib of Earth* (1956) represents a movement beyond the derivative verse that characterized much Singaporean poetry of the period, but his main achievement lies in his two later volumes, *Gods Can Die* (1977) and *Ulysses by the*

Merlion (1979). Tong Chee Kiong *et al.* (eds, 2001) contains a fairly full select bibliography of Thumboo's work.

Further reading

Ee Tiang Hong (1997); Tong Chee Kiong *et al.* (eds) (2001); Quayum and Wicks (eds) (2002).

Tlali, Miriam Born 1933. South African novelist, born in Johannesburg. Her popular novel *Muriel at Metropolitan* (1975) was the first to be published by a black woman in South Africa. Based on her own experiences as an office worker in a Johannesburg furniture store, it depicts the problems of a protagonist who struggles to reconcile her own sense of racial loyalty with the demands of the white company for which she works, as she finds herself forced to act as 'part of a conspiracy, a machinery deliberately designed to crush the soul of people'. The novel's dramatization of the everyday discrimination experienced by black South Africans under the APARTHEID regime resulted in a complicated publishing history. Completed in 1969, it was only published, in a censored version, in 1975 and, when an international edition subsequently appeared in 1979, both versions were banned within South Africa. Tlali's second novel, *Amandla* (1981), which deals with events arising from the 1976 SOWETO uprising, was also banned by the South African authorities shortly after its publication. She has been a regular contributor to STAFFRIDER, from its inaugural issue in 1978 onwards, writing a column entitled 'Soweto Speaking' that has particularly addressed the concerns of black South African women, and has also published the short story collection, *Footprints in the Quag: Stories and Dialogues from Soweto* (1989; a.k.a. *Soweto Stories*).

Toussaint L'Ouverture (François Dominique) (*c*.1743–1803). Haitian revolutionary leader, who played a key role in the country's emergence as the first black-governed republic in the Americas. Toussaint was a self-educated slave, who was freed shortly before the San Domingo Revolution of 1791 and became the military genius behind its first phase, which secured the EMANCIPATION of the island's slaves by 1793. He adopted the name 'L'Ouverture' ('the opening') around this time. In 1797 he was appointed Governor-General by the revolutionary government in France and fought to expel the British and Spanish from the western half of the island of Hispaniola, a goal he achieved in 1801, having previously succeeded in putting down a MULATTO rebellion. When Napoleon proclaimed the reintroduction of slavery, Toussaint resisted. He was defeated in 1801, taken prisoner and died in exile in France two years later.

Toussaint has been seen as one of the pioneer figures of New World African liberation and his fame has outstripped that of his fellow-leaders in the various phases of the bitter and divisive revolutionary struggle. Among the numerous Caribbean literary works that discuss and celebrate his achievements are C. L. R. JAMES's classic study of the HAITIAN REVOLUTION, *The Black Jacobins* (1938), and Derek WALCOTT's *Haitian*

Trilogy (2001). Toussaint's struggle for liberty is also celebrated in William Wordsworth's famous sonnet, 'To Toussaint L'Ouverture' (1802), written shortly before Toussaint's death.

Further reading

James, C. L. R. (1938).

Translation studies and theory   While translation is often seen simply as the rendering of words from one language into another, such transmission is invariably culturally encoded. Traditional accounts of translation make a distinction between literal and free translation, which operates on a CONTINUUM that has transliteration (when the two languages involved have different scripts) and verbatim rendering at one end of its spectrum and creative reworking, to provide a version that has more idiomatic fluency in the 'new' language, at the other. Such a distinction can, however, be seen as reductive, given that the signifier-signified relationship involves indeterminacy and signifiers carry contextual associations that subvert the possibility of straightforward literal translation. So meaning invariably gets transformed in the process of brokering words from one language to another; and in certain contexts has been considered an impossibility. Thus many Muslims contend that the QUR'AN is untranslatable, since its text is the literal word of God, as revealed to the Prophet Muhammad. Hence, although the *Qur'an* has been translated into numerous other languages, they take the view that it only exists in its pure, unmediated Arabic form.

Translation's central role in the forms and processes of cultural exchange have made it a crucial area of investigation for post-colonial studies. Stressing the broader cultural aspects of the continuum along which translation operates, Susan Bassnett and Harish Trivedi point out:

> translation does not happen in a vacuum, but in a continuum; it is not an isolated act, it is part of an ongoing process of intercultural transfer. Moreover, translation is a highly manipulative activity that involves all kinds of stages in that process of transfer across linguistic and cultural boundaries. Translation is not an innocent, transparent activity but is highly charged with significance at every stage; it rarely, if ever, involves a relationship of equality between texts, authors and systems. (1999: 2)

Bassnett and Trivedi question the widely held belief that translations are inferior to their originals, and in so doing also implicitly interrogate the notion of originary purity more generally. Two notable Indian bodies of translation provide instances of translation as *discovery* (the phrase is Sujit Mukherjee's – see Mukherjee 1994): A. K. RAMANUJAN's translations of Kannada devotional lyrics re-invent their 'originals' to a point where they have been acclaimed as major creative works in their own right, while Gayatri Chakravorty SPIVAK's translations of the work of MAHASWETA Devi are

261

self-consciously theorized responses to the Bengali writer's work that come to form part of *Spivak's* project of retrieving the voices of India's Subaltern groups.

Translation also has numerous resonances that extend beyond the area of language itself. In a parenthetical comment in the title-essay of his collection *Imaginary Homelands* (1991), Salman Rushdie stresses the positive value of 'translation', tracing the derivation of the word in a discussion that relates it to the situation of the Indian writer in England and argues for its positive benefits on migrant subjectivity:

> The word 'translation' comes, etymologically, from the Latin for 'bearing across'. Having been borne across the world, we are translated men. It is normally supposed that something always gets lost in translation; I cling, obstinately, to the notion that something can also be gained. (Rushdie 1991: 17)

So, although DIASPORA Indians may sometimes see themselves as 'post-lapsarian men and women ... Hindus who have crossed the black water [and therefore lost their CASTE identity]; ... Muslims who eat pork' (ibid.: 15), Rushdie sees such translation as opening up possibilities for a creative reinvention of identity. Such a view accords with that of writers such as Derek WALCOTT and Nayantara SAHGAL, who have also emphasized the positive benefits of CULTURAL SCHIZOPHRENIA, suggesting that the interchange that occurs at the interface of different, often competing, cultural discourses, is as important an issue for those post-colonial subjects who stay at home as those who migrate. Despite its having attracted attention for other reasons, Rushdie's novel, *The Satanic Verses* (1988) turns on a pivotal contrast between two complementary 'translated' men, Saladin Chamcha and Gibreel Farishta, who respectively represent a migrant who tries to reinvent himself through his adopted conception of Englishness and an Indian who 'stays home', but performs constants restagings of self in his profession as a BOMBAY TALKIE film-star.

Homi K. BHABHA extends such thinking by foregrounding the importance of translation in relation to the central tenets of his theoretical approach, i.e. as an activity that occurs in the interstitial borderlands of culture which resist ESSENTIALIST appropriation, acting as crucibles in which transformative meanings can be produced:

> we should remember that it is the 'inter' – the cutting edge of translation and negotiation, the *in-between* space – that carries the burden of the meaning of culture. It makes it possible to begin envisaging national, anti-nationalist histories of the 'people'. And by exploring this Third Space, we may elude the politics of polarity and emerge as the others of our selves. (Bhabha 1994: 38–9; italics in original)

Translation is also important to post-colonial studies in various other ways, and today perhaps most importantly as an activity that offers alternatives to the HEGEMONIC dominance of European languages and particularly to the spread of GLOBAL ENGLISH. Although an increasing number of post-colonial writers have turned to English in order to reach an international audience and in many cases this has led to an over-valuing of English-language writing at the expense of work produced in other languages, translation projects that attempt to resist, or at least to counterbalance, this tendency have been, and are, of major importance in establishing cultural dialogue. Such projects include the SAHITYA AKADEMI's extensive 'inter-language' programme of translations between the 22 Indian languages it recognizes (as well as work in some others) and NGUGI wa Thiong'o's commitment to publishing his work in Gikuyu, only subsequently, and secondarily, allowing it to be rendered into English. And the use and promotion of CREOLE and other non-'Standard' forms of English, such as Rasta talk (the language of RASTAFARI), are acts of political self-determination that also resist the homogenizing tendencies of global English.

Further reading

Rushdie (1991); Bhabha (1994); Mukherjee, S. (1994); Clifford (1997); Bassnett and Trivedi (eds) (1999).

Travel writing, travelling theory   Introducing a 1982 volume of essays on British travel writing, its editor claimed that it was the 'first collection' of its kind (Dodd 1982: vii). Just over two decades later, a proliferation of such collections reflects a massive expansion of interest in the genre, which has coincided with the development of post-colonial studies and which can be related to the recognition that BORDER spaces are the locations where new cultural formations come into being.

Most post-medieval European travel writing operated as a discourse that demarcated the boundaries between the 'civilized' world of its narrating agents and the 'savage', 'exotic' or 'strange' worlds, into which they were journeying, e.g. Sir Walter Raleigh's *Discoverie of the Large, Rich and Bewtiful Empyre of Guiana* (Whitehead (ed.) 1997) and William Dampier's *Voyages*. The writings of such European travellers often seek to render the unfamiliar familiar by processes of adaptation and reshaping within known frames of reference. The extent to which they attempt 'neutrality' in their depiction of observed experience varies considerably, but even those travel-writers who seem comparatively unencumbered with the cultural baggage they have brought with them resort to forms of analogy to make sense of the 'strange' and accommodate it within their own epistemologies.

At the same time, from the early Renaissance phase of European expansionist colonization through to the late nineteenth century, travel writing was a discourse that invariably manufactured a sense of self through the creation of binary oppositions that contrasted Europe with its 'OTHERS'. As Mary Louise Pratt puts it, it served to produce 'Europe's differentiated conception of itself in relation to something it became possible to call "the rest of the world"' (1992: 5; quoted by Loomba 1998a: 57). Ania Loomba develops this in relation to European travellers' reworking of the stereotypes (e.g. of CANNIBALISM) that they took with them on their journeys into 'unknown' or newly colonized territory and their return with exhibits, such as the 'Eskimo' that the

Elizabethan Arctic explorer Sir Martin Frobisher put on display in England (Loomba 1998a: 59). While it is possible to see the first phase of European colonial travel writing as informed by a fairly innocent, albeit ETHNOCENTRIC, curiosity about the 'unknown', by the late seventeenth century this was supplanted by a vision of world geography, which asserted the centrality of Europe, and particularly England, in a more overtly imperialistic manner. See CARTOGRAPHY and GREENWICH.

Post-colonial theory has generally viewed travel in a different light, seeing it as an activity which, since it occurs in the LIMINAL space between cultures, opens up possibilities for cultural interchange in an AMBIVALENT environment. One of Edward SAID's best-known essays, 'Traveling Theory', takes travel as a trope for the activity of theory itself, suggesting that it establishes connections that erode notions of fixed positionality and discrete subjectivity, i.e. it functions as a *discursive* CONTACT ZONE (Said 1984: 226–47). Along with that of Said and Pratt, the work of Anne McClintock, who particularly analyses the sexual aspects of travel imagery, and Robert Young, whose discussion of HYBRIDITY focuses on colonial desire and miscegenation, is also concerned with travel as a site of cultural exchange; and Homi K. BHABHA's ubiquitous focus on interstitial locations and migrant subjectivity is centrally relevant to the function of travel writing as a discourse that challenges monocultural versions of identity. The work of the social anthropologist, James Clifford, has also been a major intervention in the hermeneutics of travel. Like Said, Clifford links travel with theory itself, seeing both as challenging notions of 'home' and fixed positionality and hence as particularly relevant to the contemporary world situation in which 'borderland' places and transnational discourses have replaced older notions of stable, discrete locations (Clifford 1997).

Numerous contemporary writers of actual travel-narratives demonstrate a self-conscious awareness of issues of agency, which is in marked contrast to the positions adopted by the majority of their precursors in the genre. Michael ONDAATJE's *Running in the Family* (1982), Caryl PHILLIPS's *The European Tribe* (1987) and Amitav GHOSH's *In an Antique Land* (1992) are all examples of works that foreground the particular subject-position of the travelling narrator and in so doing undermine the illusion of definitive authority that characterizes the voice of much earlier travel writing. In contrast, the early travel books of V. S. NAIPAUL, such as *The Middle Passage* (1962) and *An Area of Darkness* (1964), which acknowledge an indebtedness to the Victorian travel-writers Charles Kingsley, Anthony Trollope and, most notoriously, James Anthony Froude (whose *The Bow of Ulysses, or The English in the West Indies* [1887] has been roundly condemned in the Caribbean for its 'negrophobia'), resist the positive possibilities of DIASPORA in favour of an exilic view that expresses nostalgia for the loss of 'pure' monocultures. As such, the Naipaul works in question become fascinating examples of post-colonial travel texts, which attempt to work within the conventions of their English intertexts and which, in so doing, generate a range of tensions that unwittingly bring new mixed-mode forms into being.

Further reading

Naipaul (1962 and 1964); Dodd (ed.) (1982); Ondaatje (1982); Said (1984); Pratt (1992); Phillips (1993); Ghosh (1994); Bhabha (1994); McClintock (1995); Young (1995); George (1996); Clifford (1997); Loomba (1998a); Gilbert and Johnston (eds) (2002).

The Treaty of Waitangi/Te Tiriti O Waitangi A controversial treaty signed between some 45 Maori chiefs and representatives of Queen Victoria's government, which was a defining moment in the post-settlement history of Aotearoa/New Zealand. Signed in February 1840, Te Tiriti/The Treaty effectively established colonial authority in New Zealand, while from the Maori point of view it secured land rights. It was followed by British annexation of New Zealand/Aotearoa in May of the same year. According to the British version, the Maori ceded sovereignty to the British Crown, while the chiefs were guaranteed protection and territorial rights from unregulated PAKEHA encroachments into their lands. However, the Maori subsequently disputed that they had ceded sovereignty and many tribes were not signatories to the compact in the first place. The Treaty/Te Tiriti has remained a source of grievance until the present day, with arguments about whether the Maori or English-language version has primacy being central to the debate.

The Triangular Trade The commerce of the three-legged Atlantic shipping routes that flourished during the period of the Slave Trade. The first leg carried items such as textiles, utensils, cowrie shells (used as money) and guns from Europe to West Africa, where they were exchanged for slaves. The slaves were then taken across the MIDDLE PASSAGE from West Africa to the Americas to provide a labour force for the plantation-based economies of areas such as the Caribbean and Virginia. The third leg carried crops such as sugar, coffee, cotton and tobacco from the Americas to Europe. During the early period of the trade, the main British terminus was Bristol; Liverpool subsequently succeeded it in this role. Caryl PHILLIPS's *The Atlantic Sound* (2000) is a travel journal, in which Phillips revisits three ports that formed points of the triangle: Liverpool, Accra and Charleston, South Carolina.

In colonial North America, the term was used to describe a similar rum- and slave-based trade that operated between New England, the West Indies and West Africa, and also a trading nexus that involved the movement of goods between New England, the Caribbean and Britain and did not involve the transportation of slaves. In the latter instance, provisions were shipped to the West Indies, where they were exchanged for sugar, which was taken to England to be exchanged for manufactured goods that were in short supply in North America.

The Trinidad Theatre Workshop Theatre company, founded by Derek WALCOTT in 1959, which played a pioneering role in establishing local theatre in the Caribbean as part of Walcott's attempt to develop a distinctive regional theatre aesthetics. The Workshop's productions challenged metropolitan theatre-going habits, e g. by staging Sunday morning theatre-in-the-round performances, and expanded the repertory of Caribbean theatre by including drama from an eclectic range of sources. Its productions included plays by SOYINKA, Genet, Beckett, Albee and Ionesco and the Caribbean dramatists E. M. Roach, Dennis Scott and Errol John. The company also premiered several of Walcott's own plays, including his two musical collaborations with Galt McDermot, *The Joker of Seville* (1974), a CREOLIZED reworking of the original Spanish Don Juan play which made extensive use of CARNIVAL forms, and *O Babylon!* (1976), and performed several of his plays that had been premiered elsewhere, including *Dream on Monkey Mountain* and *Ti-Jean and His Brothers*. Leading actors and actresses in the company included Errol Jones, Wilbert Holder, Norline Metivier and Albert Laveau. In 1976, Walcott parted company with the Workshop, and his play *A Branch of the Blue Nile* (1983), first performed in Barbados, is said to be loosely based on this event. The company continued to mount productions under the artistic directorship of Albert Laveau after Walcott's departure. He later rejoined it in 1993.

Further reading

King (1995a).

Tutuola, Amos (1920–97). Nigerian novelist. Tutuola was the first Nigerian writer to receive international critical acclaim, when *The Palm-Wine Drinkard*, an episodic quest novel, written in what was regarded as a highly individualistic and unconventional form of English, was published in 1952. Rooted in village storytelling traditions, it tells the tale of a drunkard who enters a magical world populated by devils and various other supernatural beings. It received a mixed critical reception and its linguistic distinctiveness proved less popular in Nigeria, where it was attacked for primitivism, than in the West. The novel is typical of Tutuola's narrative technique in that it makes extensive use of Yoruba oral narrative modes and customs, and in recent years this has been recognized as a distinctively West African form of fabulation that has affinities with MAGIC REALISM.

The Palm-Wine Drinkard was followed by *My Life in the Bush of Ghosts* (1954), in which a young boy who enters the bush finds he has embarked on an INTERIOR JOURNEY that involves his choosing between the various 'ghosts' he encounters. These represent both local and Western values, often embodying elements of both. Tutuola's subsequent novels, *Simbi and the Satyr of the Dark Jungle* (1955), *The Brave African Huntress* (1958), *Feather Woman of the Jungle* (1962), *Ajaiyi and His Inherited Poverty* (1967) and *The Witch-Herbalist of the Remote Town* (1981), were generally less successful. They are similarly fantastic in conception and execution and in their unselfconscious creation of fictional worlds in which ghosts and devils rub shoulders with Western consumer goods. As such, they represent a salutary corrective to conceptions of culture in which such elements are paired in binary oppositions. Tutuola also published *Yoruba Folktales* (1986) and *The Village Witch Doctor and Other Stories* (1990).

Further reading

Lindfors (ed.) (1975); Owomoyela (1999).

Universalism   The belief that there are aspects of behaviour and culture that transcend particular social situations and contexts and are shared by all humankind. Although it is generally considered to be a humanist creed, universalist beliefs have frequently been the products of Western thinking and their erosion of cultural differences played a significant part in the brainwashing of colonized subjects, e.g. in their Christianization. Thus Chinua ACHEBE says,

> I should like to see the word 'universal' banned altogether from discussions of African literature until such time as people cease to use it as a synonym for the narrow, self-serving parochialism of Europe, until their horizon extends to include all the world. (1988: 52)

As Ashcroft *et al.* point out (1998: 235–7), universalism was one of the lynchpins on which the study of English literature has been based. A definition of 'culture' such as Matthew Arnold's view of it (in his Preface to *Literature and Dogma*, 1873) as the process of 'acquainting ourselves with the best that has been known and said in the world, and thus with the history of the human spirit' (Arnold M. 1954: 536), which was to become a cornerstone of the discipline of literary studies and remain popular until the middle of the twentieth century, is innocent enough on the surface, but begs the question of what constitutes both 'the best' and 'the world' and, while its own project involved a revisionist re-reading of biblical authority, never considers the possibility that there is more in heaven and earth than Judaeo-Christian 'culture' and 'universal' European norms allow.

Based on such a view, many of the literary and cultural codes exported by Western nations to their colonies served to interpellate colonial subjects into sets of values presented as 'universalist', but actually expressive of very specifically encoded beliefs. Such interpellation involved the repression of central aspects of their subjectivity, such as their class, gender, sexual orientation, cultural identity and ethnicity. The educational implications for colonial students of literature and culture – and to a lesser extent those from 'minority' backgrounds at 'home' within Europe – was a felt need to con-form to such 'universalist' norms, a process of ASSIMILATION that partly co-opted them into the colonizer's value-systems, while also generating the AMBIVALENCE that Homi K. BHABHA sees as a prime characteristic of colonial MIMICRY.

The implications of universalism as a form of putative co-optation extend far beyond literature and education. Thus while a concept such as 'love' may seem to transcend particular social situations, West Africans from polygamous cultures are unlikely to conceptualize it in the same way as middle-class English readers. Moreover, even within cultures the appeal to universalism is invariably undermined by the slip-page involved in signifying processes. As the unnamed narrator of Margaret Atwood's novel *Surfacing* (1972) points out, if the Eskimos have fifty-two words for 'snow', per-haps Western society needs as many for 'love'.

While the West's appropriation of 'universal' human values has had the effect of discrediting such concepts in the eyes of many post-colonial readers and commen-tators, the appeal to belief-systems that cut across national, communal and other divisions is, of course, not confined to Western colonial societies and discourses as varied as the notion of international human rights and Hindu-derived belief systems such as Bengali humanism (see Rabindranath TAGORE, Satyajit RAY and Amitav GHOSH) also make an appeal to values that transcend human differences. So, just as it is reasonable to distinguish between forms of NATIONALISM that promote the interests of the disempowered and forms that serve the interests of a ruling elite or would-be master-race, universalism can be seen as operating on a CONTINUUM and, like STRATEGIC ESSENTIALISM, be used to resist rather than promote coercive, HEGEMONIC authority.

Further reading

Achebe (1988); Ashcroft *et al.* (1998).

Untouchables   Members of the pariah classes excluded from the four main CASTES of Hindu society and seen as a source of pollution by those within the system. 'Untouchables' were sentenced to perform menial occupations and denied basic human rights, until Mahatma GANDHI, who renamed them '*HARIJANS*', and others began to campaign against caste discrimination in the 1930s. More militant 'untouchables' prefer the term '*DALIT*'. *Untouchable* is also the title of Mulk Raj ANAND's first novel, published in 1935, which was influenced by Gandhian political thinking.

After Indian independence, in 1955, the Untouchability Act declared discrimina-tion against 'untouchables' illegal and various affirmative action policies were intro-duced to promote and secure rights for the 'scheduled classes'. In 1997, K. R. Narayanan, an avowed champion of the rights of ordinary Indians, became the first Indian President, born as an 'untouchable'. Today there are approximately sixty million 'untouchables' in India, i.e. they form about 15 per cent of the nation's population.

Further reading

Mendelsohn and Vicziany (1998).

Vassa, Gustavus   See EQUIANO, Olaudah.

Vassanji, M(oyez) G.   Born 1950. Kenyan-born novelist and short story writer from an Asian background. Vassanji grew up in Tanzania and subsequently moved to the USA. He studied at the Massachusetts Institute of Technology and the University of Pennsylvania, where he obtained his doctorate in nuclear physics. Since 1978 he has lived in Canada. His novels mainly deal with attempts to trace continuities between the past African experience of his community and their contemporary Canadian experience. They include *The Gunny Sack* (1989), *No New Land* (1991), which deals with the experience of an immigrant family in Toronto, suggesting, as the title implies, that they carry many aspects of their past with them, and *Amriika* (1999), which spans three generations of immigrant life in North America, moving between Massachusetts, Toronto and California. Vassanji's most impressive achievement to date, *The Book of Secrets* (1994), in which a retired schoolteacher reads the diary of a colonial administrator and gradually begins to unpick the threads of his own personal past, works as both a mystery story and as another novel that chronicles the complex interrelationships between individual and community and between personal and public history. *Uhuru Street* (1991) is a collection of linked short stories about the often-eccentric inhabitants of a street in Dar es Salaam. Its use of the street as a unifying device, its characterization and its blend of irony and pathos are reminiscent of V. S. NAIPAUL's *Miguel Street* (1959). Vassanji has edited *Meeting of Streams: South Asian Canadian Literature* (1985) and *The Journey Prize Anthology* (1995), a collection of short fiction. He was the founding editor of *The Toronto South Asian Review* (now *The Toronto Review of Contemporary Writing Abroad*).

Vera, Yvonne   Born 1964. Zimbabwean novelist and short story writer. Born in Matabeleland into a Shona family, Vera worked as a schoolteacher prior to receiving her tertiary education in Toronto, where she studied at York University and obtained her doctorate in 1995. In 1997 she was appointed as Director of the National Gallery of Zimbabwe, whose mission she has tried to localize and extend through outreach activities and workshops that attract marginalized sections of the community. One of the most technically accomplished stylists of contemporary African fiction, Vera characteristically employs a compelling poetic prose that lays more emphasis on the evocation of character and milieu – both landscape and socio-political setting – than narrative.

Her first novel, *Nehanda* (1993), takes a late nineteenth-century Zimbabwean woman who led an uprising against colonial rule as its heroine. *Without a Name* (1994) deals with a later phase of Zimbabwean resistance to white minority rule, as its protagonist experiences the dual, but very different, horrors of rural experience and life in Harare during the late colonial period. In *Under the Tongue* (1997), which won the African section of the COMMONWEALTH WRITERS' PRIZE, the narrative moves between third-person reportage and the interior monologue of its adolescent protagonist, who is raped by her father and retreats into a private world of silence, while describing her predicament in a densely imagistic prose style that makes the novel Vera's most demanding work to date. *Butterfly Burning* (1998) is a love story set in a Bulawayo township in the 1940s, which, like *Without a Name*, demonstrates the limitations placed on a woman's life by an unwanted pregnancy. *The Stone Virgins* (2002) comes closer to the present in examining the effects of Zimbabwe's liberation struggle on the lives of contemporary women. Like most of Vera's fiction to date, it remains tragically pessimistic about the possibilities for effecting social change, while representing the resilience of its disempowered women in the face of adversity. Vera has also published the short story collection, *Why Don't You Carve Other Animals? (1992)* and is the editor of *Opening Spaces: An Anthology of Contemporary African Women's Writing* (1999).

Further reading

Primorac (2001).

Vodun, vodou, voodoo   New World African religious practice, which particularly thrives in Haiti, where it evolved from Dahomean and other West African forms. Popularly known in the USA and Europe as 'voodoo' and as such equated with 'black magic' (hence the tendency to prefer the name 'vodun' as a means of escaping its stereotypical demonizing), vodun is a complex belief-system that has transformed various elements into a spirit-possession religion, based on the belief that sacrifices and offerings to the natural forces that control human life are necessary to secure good fortune and success for its devotees. Although Haitian vodun rites contain many SYNCRETIST elements, similar forms elsewhere in the Caribbean and other parts of the Americas are generally more CREOLIZED and Haitian cultural forms have frequently provided an inspiration for Caribbean artists and intellectuals seeking to discover 'pure' African retentions. The more 'African' fusion of elements in Haitian religious practices has generally been seen as a consquence of Haiti's having liberated itself from European colonialism at an earlier point in history than other American plantation societies.

Vodun's importance as a repository of African cultural traditions has been stressed by (Edward) Kamau Brathwaite, who, in *Islands* (1969), invokes several rites and gods from the Haitian pantheon and suggests that deities such as Legba, the god of gateways, who acts as an intermediary between humanity and the other gods, can perform a crucial role in the threshold encounter between New World Africans and their ancestral culture. Brathwaite plays on the word 'possession' to suggest that the trance-like state achieved by some of the religion's acolytes during its rites is a LIMINAL experience that opens the way towards repossessing their past. His fellow-Barbadian George Lamming takes a similar view in his novel, *Season of Adventure* (1960), in which the middle-class Fola is initiated into the African aspects of her personality through a 'Ceremony of Souls', a rite which Lamming also uses as a central trope for the Caribbean engagement with submerged African cultural and psychic elements in his non-fiction work *The Pleasures of Exile* (1960) and his novel *Natives of My Person* (1971). Haitian writers who have explored the artistic possibilities of vodun and defended it – and Haitian culture more generally – against charges of primitivism and savagery include Jean Price-Mars in *Ainsi parla l'oncle* (1928; *So Spoke the Uncle*, 1983). See also OBEAH.

Further reading

Leyburn (1941); Deren (1953); Lamming (1960); Rohlehr (1981); Cosentino (ed.) (1995); Torres-Saillant (1997).

Walcott, Derek   Born 1930. St. Lucian poet and dramatist. Walcott and his twin brother, Roderick, who is also a notable dramatist, were born into an English-speaking Methodist family in the primarily FRANCOPHONE island of St. Lucia. His first published poem was published in the island's newspaper, when he was only 14 and by the time he was 21 he had published three volumes of poetry, written several plays, including the first of three that deal with the HAITIAN REVOLUTION, *Henri Christophe* (1950), and co-founded the St Lucia Arts Guild. He attended St Mary's College, Castries and the Jamaica campus of the University of the West Indies and subsequently lived in Trinidad, where he was an arts correspondent for the *Trinidad*

Guardian and founding director of one of the region's most influential theatre companies, the TRINIDAD THEATRE WORKSHOP. Walcott was awarded the NOBEL PRIZE FOR LITERATURE in 1992, after the publication of what has become his best-known poem, the book-length *Omeros* (1990). In recent decades he has divided his time between St Lucia and the USA, where he has held positions in universities in Boston and where he developed friendships with fellow Nobel Laureates, Seamus Heaney and Joseph Brodsky.

Walcott's first collection of poetry published outside the Caribbean, *In a Green Night* (1962), immediately demonstrated his technical virtuosity, his gift for striking imagery rooted in the Caribbean landscape and his capacity for transforming a range of primarily European intertexts into work that is uniquely his own. It was followed by *The Castaway* (1965), notable for its poems on the figure of ROBINSON CRUSOE, whom Walcott presents as a type of the Caribbean artist, and *The Gulf* (1969). *Another Life* (1972) is a poetic autobiography of the same kind as Wordsworth's *Prelude* in that it traces 'the growth of a poet's mind' (the sub-title of Wordsworth's poem) and is centrally concerned with mapping the landscape it depicts. It expands outwards from autobiography to epic, as Walcott becomes increasingly concerned with representing the 'sociological contours' of St Lucia, and in so doing moves in an opposite direction from that which Walcott would later follow in *Omeros*. Towards the end of the poem, Walcott shares a vow not to leave his homeland until he has performed 'Adam's task of giving things their names' and the portrayal of the island's hitherto unchronicled landscape in verse has been part of his life-long endeavour.

Walcott has written more than 40 plays, less than half of which have been published and, although he is rightly regarded as the Caribbean's finest dramatist, his plays received less attention than his poetry until comparatively recently. His collection *Dream on Monkey Mountain and Other Plays* (1970), takes its title from his dramatic masterpiece, an expressionist play in which a St Lucian charcoal-burner, influenced by a white Muse, has a dream of African chieftainship. The collection also includes *Ti-Jean and His Brothers* and two other plays drawing on St Lucian folk experience. In *The Joker of Seville*, a CREOLIZED reworking of the original Spanish Don Juan play and *O Babylon!* (published together in 1978), Walcott collaborated with Galt MacDermot to produce musicals which respectively drew on Trinidadian and Jamaican musical forms. A later musical, *The Capeman*, in which he collaborated with Paul Simon, premiered on Broadway in 1998, but was less successful and closed after a very short run. *Pantomime*, published along with *Remembrance* in 1990, is a comic two-hander, which uses the Friday–Crusoe relationship to explore the renegotiations of roles taking place in the post-independence Caribbean. *Three Plays* (1986) includes *The Last Carnival, Beef, No Chicken* and *A Branch of the Blue Nile*. *The Odyssey: A Stage Version* (1993), a play commissioned and performed by the Royal Shakespeare Company, is a partly creolized adaptation of its Homeric 'original' that nevertheless stays closer to it than *Omeros*. *The Haitian Trilogy* (2001) includes *Henri Christophe, Drums and Colours*, a (historical pageant focused on seminal moments in Caribbean history, which Walcott had written to commemorate the inauguration of the West Indian FEDERATION in 1958), and *The Haitian Earth. Walker* and *The Ghost Dance* (2002) are plays which take American minorities as their subjects. Walcott's other plays include *The Wine of the Country* (1956), *Franklin* (1969) and *To Die for Grenada* (1986).

Walcott remains a prolific writer and, although his output as an essayist is more slender than his work in verse and drama, he is also one of the Caribbean's finest prose stylists. His essays are collected in *What the Twilight Says* (1998). *Tiepolo's Hound* (2000), a volume in which the primary focus is on the impressionist painter, Camille Pissarro, who was born in St Thomas in the Virgin Islands and with whom Walcott identifies, includes reproductions of twenty-six of Walcott's own paintings. It is his most sustained account of the difficulties of capturing visual experience in art. Walcott's other volumes of verse include *Sea Grapes* (1976), *The Fortunate Traveller* (1981), *The Arkansas Testament* (1987) and *The Bounty* (1997).

Further reading

Terada (1992); Hamner (ed.) (1993); King (1995a and 2000); Walcott (1998); Thieme (1999); Burnett (2001).

Wasafiri   Journal devoted to critical and creative writing, founded in 1984 under the editorship of Susheila Nasta. *Wasafiri* originated as the journal of ATCAL, the British Association for the Teaching of Caribbean and African Literature, which had been established in 1978. Its title is taken from the Kiswahili word for 'travellers', which the inaugural issue says

> was chosen because many of those who have created the literatures in which we are especially interested, whether of Caribbean, African or Asian origin, have all in some sort been travellers, either through migration, transportation, or else in the more symbolic sense of seeking for a cultural home. (*Wasafiri* 1,1 [1984]: 2)

Wasafiri includes material on Black British, African, Asian and Caribbean literatures and is currently published three times a year from Queen Mary and Westfield College, University of London.

Websites   Numerous websites provide valuable information on post-colonial issues, writers and topics, but inevitably their quality, longevity and contemporaneity are variable. At the time the Glossary was completed, the most useful included the 'post-colonial studies' website at Emory University and George Landow's website on 'contemporary postcolonial and postimperial literature in English', now located at the National University of Singapore. The Emory site, devised by Deepika Bahri, contains over a hundred entries on post-colonial authors, theorists, terms and issues and is particularly strong on South Asian authors. The Singapore site also offers a broad range of material, though in some cases its title is misleading, since it includes English writers such as A. S. Byatt and Graham Swift, who are not normally classified as 'post-colonial'. The University of Florida libraries' site includes useful information on several African writers.

More general Internet resources that are often at least as valuable as dedicated post-colonial sites include the rapidly expanding on-line Literary Encyclopedia, developed by Robert Clark of the University of East Anglia, which is including extensive coverage of post-colonial writers. Web reference-tools, such as xrefer and the Columbia Encyclopedia and searchable newspaper sites such as those of *The Guardian/Observer* (UK), *The New York Times* (USA) and *The Hindu* (India) can also be extremely useful. The *Black World* site provides essential information on African and African DIASPORA topics (through africana.com). These suggestions are, however, only indicative of the kinds of searches that individuals may wish to pursue, through such search engines as google. Additionally numerous writers now have their own sites or homepages, some of which are listed in the Glossary's particular 'further reading' suggestions.

Further reading

www.emory.edu/ENGLISH/Bahri; www.scholars.nus.edu.sg/landow/post/; www.uflib.ufl.edu/cm/africana; www.litencyc.com; www.xrefer.com; www.Bartleby.com (Columbia Encyclopedia); www.observer.co.uk; www.newyorktimes.com; www.hinduonline.com; www.africana.com; www.google.com

Wilberforce, William   (1759–1833). The leading figure in the campaign for the ABOLITION of the Slave Trade within the British Empire. Wilberforce's involvement in the campaign began in the 1780s when he was converted to Evangelical Christianity and became a member of the Clapham Set, a group centred on the Anglican rector, John Venn, whose members also numbered another noted abolitionist, Granville Sharp. (See also Olaudah EQUIANO.) His first motion to abolish the Slave Trade was defeated in the House of Commons in 1791, but a subsequent attempt was successful and the Trade was abolished from 1807. Despite Wilberforce's central role in the campaign to abolish the Slave Trade, he was less committed to the abolition of SLAVERY itself, believing that both the slaves and their masters would be harmed by hasty legislation to EMANCIPATE them. He was eventually persuaded to join the campaign for the abolition of slavery within the British Empire, but played a minor part in this struggle, which realized its goal when legislation was passed in 1833, a month after his death.

His contribution to the struggle against slavery is commemorated in a museum located in his seventeenth-century house in Hull, which is dedicated to depicting the harshness of the conditions of the MIDDLE PASSAGE and of plantation life and also to the work of the abolitionists.

Williams, Aubrey (1926–90). Guyanese artist. Williams worked in the colonial Civil Service, spending two years living with the Amerindian Warrau tribe and subsequently participated in a working people's art class in Georgetown. He moved to Europe in 1952, eventually settling in London, where he studied at the St Martin's School of Art, in 1954. The most acclaimed Guyanese painter of his generation, Williams held numerous one-man exhibitions and won several awards including the 1964 Commonwealth Prize for Painting. His artistic practice rejected narrative and representational modes in favour of an expressionist style that linked pre-Columbian pictorial forms with a post-colonial vision and attempted to recuperate aspects of the indigenous Caribbean folk imagination that had been occluded during the colonial era. His most important works include his Dalhousie Murals (completed in 1978 for the University of Dalhousie, Nova Scotia), which drew on totemic motifs from Guyana's Carib, Warrau and Arawak tribes, his Shostakovich series, exhibited at the Commonwealth Institute (1981) and the Royal Festival Hall, London (1984) and his Olmec-Maya paintings, originally exhibited at the Commonwealth Institute in 1985. Other important commissions included murals for Guyana's Timehri airport, the Guyana Museum and the Olympia Art Centre, Jamaica. Eighteen of his finest paintings are reproduced in *Guyana Dreaming: The Art of Aubrey Williams* (1990), a compilation which also includes examples of his comments on art and critical observations on his work.

Further reading

Walmsley (comp.) (1990).

Williams, Denis   (1923–98). Guyanese artist, novelist, art historian and archaeologist. Denis Williams won what was then British Guiana's first scholarship to study art in London, where his paintings were acclaimed by Wyndham Lewis and he held a number of one-man and group exhibitions of his paintings. He subsequently taught art history in the Sudan, where he studied the remains of ancient Napatan and Meroitic cultures, and Nigeria, where he did similar fieldwork on the various bronze and iron-working societies of the region. This research formed the basis of his most important work as an art historian, *Icon and Image: A Study of Sacred and Secular Forms of African Classical Art* (1974), a monumental investigation into the techniques and cults associated with bronze and iron metallurgy which attempted to develop an aesthetic relevant to the whole field of African art. Williams returned to Guyana in 1968, settling in the interior Mazaruni region and devoting himself to archaeological work on prehistoric AMERINDIAN cultures. In 1974 he was appointed Director of the Walter Roth Museum of Archaeology and Art History where he founded the journal, *Archaeology and Anthropology.*

His comparatively little-known novel *Other Leopards* (1963) is a classic account of the dilemmas of a Caribbean man, who 'returns' to Africa, vainly hoping to discover his 'origins'. Its protagonist Lionel/Lobo – he speaks at the outset of being 'plagued ... by two names' – is an archaeological draughtsman working in the Sudanic region, where Williams taught from 1957 to 1962. Surnamed Froad (suggestive of 'fraud' and also the British imperial historian, James Anthony Froude, notorious in the Caribbean for his contemptuous indictment of black West Indians in his travel-book, *The English in the West Indies*, 1887), he is an INAUTHENTIC protagonist who is very self-consciously aware of his split cultural allegiances. Left in limbo up a tree at the end of the novel, he decides that he now knows who he is: 'a man hunting and running, neither infra nor supra, not Equatorial black, not Mediterranean white. Mulatto, you could say, Sudanic mulatto, looking both ways. Ochre. Semi. Not desert, but not yet sown.' These words come close to echoing the summary of his Sudanic location that he has provided at the beginning of the novel; now they are revived in a context which foregrounds their relevance to his own LIMINAL situation. Cultural division also informs his relationships with two women protagonists of the novel, who reflect the African and European sides of his identity, the Sudan's split between Arab and black African identities, its 'dual rape' by Christianity and Islam and the ambivalence of the archaeological site that Froad and his colleagues excavate. Appearing at a time when the African DIASPORA quest for roots sought an AUTHENTIC Old World experience, *Other Leopards* received a certain amount of critical acclaim, but its 'MULATTO' positioning led to its failing to find the audience it deserves as a major imaginative exploration of Caribbean CULTURAL SCHIZOPHRENIA that merits comparison with the work of Wilson HARRIS, Derek WALCOTT and Erna BRODBER. Williams also wrote another novel, *The Third Temptation* (1968), a highly experimental but less successful work, set in Wales.

Williams, Eric (1915–81). Trinidadian historian and statesman, who was the country's first post-independence Prime Minister. Williams was educated at Trinidad's leading secondary school, Queen's Royal College, and Oxford, experiences he describes in *Inward Hunger: The Education of a Prime Minister* (1969). His first book, *Capitalism and Slavery* (1944), adapted from his doctoral thesis, was a major contribution to the literature of SLAVERY, which documented its economic basis. He taught history in the USA, at Howard University, from 1939 to 1948, leaving this position to head the research branch of the Caribbean Commission, a post-World War II organization set up by Britain and the USA to consider the future of the Caribbean region. Williams gradually became disillusioned with what he saw as its colonialist approach and returned to Trinidad, where he founded the PNM (People's National Movement) in 1956. The party won elections in that year and he became Chief Minister (1956–62) and subsequently Prime Minister, after Trinidad attained independence in 1962. His political style blended academic detachment and populist appeal and his public lectures at 'the University of Woodford Square', an outdoor Port of Spain venue that has become synonymous with freedom of speech, did much to secure his reputation as a people's leader. However, his populist appeal declined in later years, when he came to be seen as a rather aloof figure and CALYPSONIANS and other satirists quipped that he turned his hearing aid off when he attended parliamentary sessions (see, e.g., Derek

Walcott's poem 'The Spoiler's Return' in *The Fortunate Traveller*, 1981). Williams's other publications include *History of the People of Trinidad and Tobago* (1962), *Documents from West Indian History* (1963), *British Historians and the West Indies* (1966) and *From Columbus to Castro: The History of the West Indies, 1492–1969* (1970).

The Windrush Generation   Name given to the first generation of post-World War II Caribbean immigrants to settle in Britain. It was so called after the name of the ship, the *SS Empire Windrush*, that brought 495 mainly Jamaican passengers, who were to become a symbol of post-war Caribbean migration to Britain, to Tilbury in June 1948. The term 'Windrush Generation' has, however, been applied more generally to Caribbean migrants, who came to Britain in the years following the arrival of the *Windrush* itself. The fiftieth anniversary of its arrival in 1998 saw several commemorative publications and a BBC television series that celebrated the lives of Caribbean-British people, telling the story of the Windrush Generation and their descendants mainly through oral testimony and assessing their larger impact on British life. Mike and Trevor Phillips's *Windrush: The Irresistible Rise of Multi-Racial Britain* (1998) was published as a companion to this series. Onyekachi Wambu's *Empire Windrush* (1998) is an anthology of fifty years of Caribbean- and Asian-British writing that also includes work by white commentators.

Prominent writers from the Windrush Generation include the novelists George Lamming and Sam Selvon, who came to Britain on the same ship in 1950, the poet James Berry and the novelist Andrew Salkey. See also Caribbean Artists Movement.

Further reading

Phillips and Phillips (1998); Wambu (ed.) (1998). See also the BBC Windrush website: www.bbc.co.uk/history/society_culture/multicultural/windrush/

'The winds of change'   Classic phrase, referring to the process of DECOLONIZATION, coined by the British Prime Minister, Harold Macmillan, in a watershed 1960 speech in Cape Town. The speech signalled a significant shift in Britain's foreign policy in Africa, by indicating that it would henceforth support democratic majority rule. It had particular implications for white minority regimes in East Africa and southern Africa: Britain's West African colonies had achieved or were moving towards independence at this point in time. Macmillan located the 'awakening of national consciousness' in colonized peoples in the contexts of the creation of European nation–states after the break-up of the Roman Empire and similar movements that had surfaced in Asia some 15 years before [sic]. In the speech's most famous passage, he asserted,

The wind of change is blowing through this continent, and, whether we like it or not, this growth of national consciousness is a political fact. We must all accept it as a fact, and our national policies must take account of it.

Macmillan returned to the phase for the title of his 1966 book, *Winds of Change*.

WLWE See World Literature Written in English.

Worlding Gayatri Chakravorty Spivak's term for the process by which colonialism appropriates the right to define the other space of the colonial world it has constructed. Thus cartography which defines and names supposedly unnamed colonized territory is a central part of the project of worlding. Instances of this include the activities of European nations during the period of the 'Scramble for Africa' and the Anglo-Celtic construction of Australia made possible by the continent's being designated *terra nullius*. See also the 'Dark Continent' and Joseph Conrad's *Heart of Darkness* (1902), where the narrator Marlow remembers his boyhood fascination with maps in which an equatorial region (clearly representative of Africa, but significantly left unnamed throughout the text), was 'the biggest, the most blank' space on earth, going on to explain that by the time he was actually able to travel there as an adult it had become known as a place of darkness.

Spivak also relates worlding to the appropriation of individuals' identities through 'epistemic violence'. Thus, in her discussion of *Jane Eyre* in 'Three Women's Texts and a Critique of Imperialism' she argues that Brontë's novel secures Jane's feminist status through the worlding of her colonial double, Bertha, whose dispossession legitimates Jane's promotion in English society (Spivak 1985). Sue Thomas's *The Worlding of Jean Rhys* (1999) uses this as a departure-point for her extended study of the Dominican-born novelist, whose *Wide Sargasso Sea* (1966) 'writes back' to *Jane Eyre* by reinventing Bertha as Antoinette and telling her story from inside as a kind of prequel that contests her worlding by both Rochester and Charlotte Brontë's novel more generally.

Further reading

Spivak (1985); Thomas (1999).

World Literature Today Oklahoma-published journal, which developed from one of the oldest American journals of 'international' writing, *Books Abroad*, originally founded in 1927. *Books Abroad* became *World Literature Today* in 1977. The journal is eclectic in scope and publishes symposia on particular writers, e.g. on Raja Rao (1986), Édouard Glissant (1989), Maryse Condé (1993), (Edward) Kamau Brathwaite (1994) and Nuruddin Farah (1998). It expanded its activities, by adding a new publication, *World Literature Today: The Magazine*, aimed at a more general readership, in 2001. The more academic journal is now known as *World Literature Today: The Journal*.

World Literature Written in English (WLWE) Literary journal founded at the University of Texas at Austin in 1968 under the editorship of Joseph Jones. It developed from the earlier newsletter of the Conference on British Commonwealth

Literature, which Jones had edited from around 1962. From 1978 *WLWE* was published in Canada at the University of Guelph, under the editorship of G. D. Killam and later Diana Brydon. More recently it has been published from Nanyang Technological University in Singapore under the editorship of Kirpal Singh and University College, Northampton, UK, under the editorship of Janet Wilson.

Writing back   See COUNTER-DISCOURSE and *The Empire Writes Back*.

Yard novel   A naturalistic form of Caribbean novel which emerged in the 1930s in the fiction of the Beacon Group. Its most notable early exponents were Alfred Mendes, in *Black Fauns* (1935) and C. L. R. James, in *Minty Alley* (1936). In focusing on the lives of the inhabitants of urban yards, such novels endeavoured to provide a warts-and-all portrait of the everyday realities of working-class Port of Spain society, which had hitherto been neglected in the literature read by the island's middle-class public. Although the writers concerned were themselves middle class, they acted as intermediaries between their subjects and their readers. Mendes researched his novel by living in a yard, while James used the point of view of a middle-class outsider, who has fallen on hard times financially and has to move into a poorer social milieu, as a way of providing a window on 'ordinary' Trinidadian urban life. The form has also been used in several later Trinidadian and Jamaican novels, including Roger Mais's *The Hills Were Joyful Together* (1953) and *Brother Man* (1954), in which the picture of ghetto life is bleaker, but the emphasis on community stronger.

Further reading

Sander (1995).

Z

Zion   See Rastafari.

Zobel, Joseph   Born 1915. Martinican novelist. He worked in the south of France and Senegal for nearly two decades and has resisted attempted to classify him as a Negritudinist, preferring to be seen simply in terms of his individuality, as a writer, *tout court*. His semi-autobiographical novel *La Rue Cases Nègres* (1950; *Black Shack Alley*, 1980) is a realistic work that makes highly effective use of a young boy's perspective to expose the hardships of life on a Martinican plantation. Its first part is notable for its rendition of older Caribbean oral storytelling traditions. Its social criticism of the conditions of plantation workers caused controversy. *La Rue Cases Nègres* was made into a critically acclaimed film by Euzhan Palcy. He has also published *Diab'là* (1942), *La Fête à Paris* (1953), a sequel to *La Rue Cases Nègres* and *Et si la mer n'était pas bleue* (1982).

Further reading

Knight (ed.) (1975).

Bibliography

Achebe, Chinua (1988) *Hopes and Impediments: Selected Essays, 1965–87*, Oxford: Heinemann.

Adam, Ian and Tiffin, Helen (eds) (1991) *Past the Last Post: Theorizing Post-Colonialism and Postmodernism*, Hemel Hempstead: Harvester Wheatsheaf.

Ahmad, Aijaz (1992) *In Theory: Classes, Nations, Literatures*, London and New York: Verso.

Alam, Fakrul (1996) *Bharati Mukherjee*, New York: Twayne.

Alden, Patricia and Tremaine, Louis (1999) *Nuruddin Farah*, New York: Twayne.

Ali, Tariq (1985) *The Nehrus and the Gandhis: An Indian Dynasty*, London: Pan.

Alleyne, Mervyn (1988) *Roots of Jamaican Culture*, London: Pluto Press.

Allis, Jeannette B. (comp.) (1981) *West Indian Literature: An Index to Criticism*, Boston: G. K. Hall.

Alonso, Carlos J. (1990) *The Spanish American Regional Novel: Modernity and Autochthony*, Cambridge: Cambridge University Press.

Anderson, Benedict (1983) *Imagined Communities: Reflections on the Origin and Spread of Nationalism*, London: Verso.

Angier, Carole (1990) *Jean Rhys*, London: André Deutsch.

Appiah, Kwame (1992) *In My Father's House: Africa in the Philosophy of Culture*, London: Methuen.

Arnold, A. James (1981) *Modernism and Negritude: The Poetry and Poetics of Aimé Césaire*, Cambridge, MA: Harvard University Press.

Arnold, Matthew (1954) *Matthew Arnold: Poetry and Prose*, ed. John Bryson, London: Rupert Hart-Davis.

Ashcroft, Bill (1996) 'On the Hyphen in "Post-Colonial"', *New Literatures Review* 32: 23–31.

Ashcroft, Bill and Ahluwalia, Pal (2001) *Edward Said*, London and New York: Routledge.

Ashcroft, Bill, Griffiths, Gareth and Tiffin, Helen (1989) *The Empire Writes Back: Theory and Practice in Post-Colonial Literatures*, London and New York: Routledge.

Ashcroft, Bill, Griffiths, Gareth and Tiffin, Helen (eds) (1995) *The Post-Colonial Studies Reader*, London and New York: Routledge.

Ashcroft, Bill, Griffiths, Gareth and Tiffin, Helen (1998) *Key Concepts in Post-Colonial Studies*, London and New York: Routledge.

Attwell, David (1993) *J. M. Coetzee: South Africa and the Politics of Writing*, Berkeley, CA: University of California Press.

Atwood, Margaret (1972) *Survival: A Thematic Guide to Canadian Literature*, Toronto: Anansi.

Azodo, Ada Uzoamaka and Wilentz, Gay (eds) (1999) *Emerging Perspectives on Ama Ata Aidoo*, Trenton, NJ: Africa World Press.

Bakhtin, Mikhail (1965) *Rabelais and His World*, trans. Helene Iswolsky, Cambridge, MA and London: MIT Press.

Bakhtin, Mikhail (1994) *The Bakhtin Reader: Selected Writings of Bakhtin, Medvedev, Voloshinov*, ed. Pam Morris, London: Edward Arnold.

Balfour, Sebastian ([1990] 1995) *Castro: Profiles in Power*, revised 2nd edn, Harlow: Longman.

Balutansky, Kathleen M. and Sourieau, Marie-Agnes (eds) (1998) *Caribbean Creolization: Reflections on the Cultural Dynamics of Language, Literature, and Identity*, Gainesville, FL: University Press of Florida; Cave Hill, Barbados: University of the West Indies Press.

Banham, Martin, Hill, Errol and Woodyard, George (eds) (1994) *The Cambridge Guide to African and Caribbean Theatre*, Cambridge: Cambridge University Press.

Barfoot, C. C. and D'haen, Theo (eds) (1998) *Oriental Prospects: Western Literature and the Lure of the East*, Amsterdam and Atlanta, GA: Rodopi.

Barker, Francis, Hulme, Peter and Iversen, Margaret (eds) (1994) *Colonial Discourse/Postcolonial Theory*, Manchester and New York: Manchester University Press.

Barker, Francis, Hulme, Peter and Iversen, Margaret (eds) (1998) *Cannibalism and the Colonial World*, Cambridge: Cambridge University Press.

Barnett, Ursula A. (1976) *Ezekiel Mphahlele*, Boston: Twayne.

Barr, Michael D. (2000) *Lee Kuan Yew: The Beliefs behind the Man*, Washington, DC: Georgetown University Press.

Barrett, Leonard E. (1988) *Rastafarianism: Sounds of Cultural Dissonance*, Boston: Beacon Press.

Barrow, Steve and Dalton, Peter ([1997] 2001) *The Rough Guide to Reggae: The Definitive Guide to Jamaican Music, from Ska through Roots to Ragga*, 2nd edn, London: Rough Guides.

Bassnett, Susan and Trivedi, Harish (eds) (1999) *Post-Colonial Translation: Theory and Practice*, London and New York: Routledge.

Baugh, Edward (ed.) (1978) *Critics on Caribbean Literature*, London: Allen and Unwin.

Bebey, Francis (1975) *African Music: A People's Art*, London: Harrap.

Bell-Villada, Gene H. (1990) *García Márquez: The Man and His Work*, Chapel Hill, NC: University of North Carolina Press.

Bell-Villada, Gene H. (ed.) (2001) *Gabriel García Márquez's 'One Hundred Years of Solitude': A Casebook*, New York: Oxford University Press.

Bennett, Bruce and Strauss, Jennifer (eds) (1998) *The Oxford Literary History of Australia*, Melbourne: Oxford University Press.

Benson, Eugene and Connolly, Lloyd W. (eds) (1994) *The Routledge Encyclopedia of Post-Colonial Literatures in English*, 2 vols, London and New York: Routledge.

Bernabé, Jean, Chamoiseau, Patrick and Confiant, Raphaël (1989) *Éloge de la créolité*, bilingual edn, trans. M. B. Taleb-Khyar, Paris: Gallimard.

Bhabha, Homi K. (ed.) (1990) *Nation and Narration*, London and New York: Routledge.

Bhabha, Homi K. (1994) *The Location of Culture*, London and New York: Routledge.

Bickerton, Derek (1975) *Dynamics of a Creole System*, Cambridge: Cambridge University Press.

Birmingham, David (1999) *Kwame Nkrumah: The Father of African Nationalism*, revised edn, Athens, OH: Ohio University Press.

Bissoondath, Neil (1994) *Selling Illusions: The Cult of Multiculturalism in Canada*, Toronto: Penguin.

Bloom, Harold (1973) *The Anxiety of Influence: A Theory of Reading*, New York: Oxford University Press.

Blumberg, Marcia and Walder, Dennis (eds) (1999) *South African Theatre as/and Intervention*, Amsterdam and Atlanta, GA: Rodopi.

Boehmer, Elleke (1995) *Colonial and Postcolonial Literature: Migrant Metaphors*, Oxford and New York: Oxford University Press.

Bolt, Christine (1971) *Victorian Attitudes to Race*, London: Routledge.

Booth, James (1981) *Writers and Politics in Nigeria*, London: Hodder and Stoughton.

Boxer, David (1985) 'Edna Manley: Sculptor', *Jamaica Journal* 18.1: 25–40.

Brathwaite, (Edward) Kamau (1971) *The Development of Creole Society in Jamaica, 1770–1820*, Oxford: Clarendon Press.

Brathwaite, (Edward) Kamau ([1970] 1981) *Folk Culture of the Slaves in Jamaica*, revised edn, London and Port of Spain: New Beacon.

Brathwaite, (Edward) Kamau (1984) *History of the Voice: The Development of Nation Language in Anglophone Caribbean Poetry*, London and Port of Spain, Trinidad: New Beacon.

Brathwaite, (Edward) Kamau (1993) *Roots*, Ann Arbor, MI: University of Michigan Press.

Breiner, Laurence A. (1998) *An Introduction to the Study of West Indian Poetry*, Cambridge: Cambridge University Press.

Brennan, Timothy (1989) *Salman Rushdie and the Third World*, London: Macmillan.

Brewer, Anthony (1980) *Marxist Theories of Imperialism: A Critical Survey*, London: Routledge and Kegan Paul.

Britton, Celia (1999) *Edouard Glissant and Postcolonial Theory*, Charlottesville, VA: University of Virginia Press.

Brodber, Erna (1983) 'Oral Sources and the Creation of a Social History of the Caribbean', *Jamaica Journal* 16.4: 2–11.

Brotton, Jerry (1998) '"This Tunis, sir, was Carthage": Contesting Colonialism in *The Tempest*', in Loomba, Ania and Orkin, Martin (eds), *Post-Colonial Shakespeares*, London and New York: Routledge, 23–42.

Brown, Lloyd W. (1978) *West Indian Poetry*, Boston: Twayne.

Brown, Lloyd W. (1981) *Women Writers in Black Africa*, Westport, CT: Greenwood Press.

Brown, Wayne (1975) *Edna Manley: The Private Years, 1900–1938*, London: André Deutsch.

Brydon, Diana and Tiffin, Helen (eds) (1992) *Decolonising Fictions*, Mundelstrup, Denmark: Dangaroo Press.

Burnett, Paula (ed.) (1986) *The Penguin Book of Caribbean Verse in English*, Harmondsworth: Penguin.

Burnett, Paula (2001) *Derek Walcott: Politics and Poetics*, Gainesville, FL: University Press of Florida.

Butcher, Maggie (ed.) (1983) *The Eye of the Beholder: Indian Writing in English*, London: Commonwealth Institute.

Campbell, Horace (1987) *Rasta and Resistance: From Marcus Garvey to Walter Rodney*, Trenton, NJ: Africa World Press.

Carr, Helen (1996) *Jean Rhys*, Plymouth: Northcote House/British Council.

Cartelli, Thomas (1999) *Repositioning Shakespeare: National Formations, Postcolonial Appropriations*, London and New York: Routledge.

Caute, David (1970) *Frantz Fanon*, New York: Viking.

Chakrabarty, Dipesh (2002) *Habitations of Modernity: Essays in the Wake of Subaltern Studies*, Chicago: University of Chicago Press.

Chamberlin, J. Edward (1993) *Come Back to Me My Language: Poetry and the West Indies*, Toronto: McClelland & Stewart.

Chaudhuri, Nirad [1960] n.d. *A Passage to England*, New Delhi: Orient Paperbacks.

Chaudhuri, Nirad (1987) *Thy Hand, Great Anarch! India 1921–1952*, London: Chatto and Windus.

Chauhan, Pradyumna S. (ed.) (2001) *Salman Rushdie Interviews: A Sourcebook of His Ideas*, Westport, CT: Greenwood Press.

Chinweizu, Jemie Onwuchekwa, and Madubuike, Ihechuckwu (1980) *Towards the Decolonization of African Literature*, Enugu, Nigeria: Fourth Dimension.

Chow, Rey (1993) *Writing Diaspora: Tactics of Intervention in Contemporary Cultural Studies*, Bloomington, IN: Indiana University Press.

Clark, Maureen (2001) 'Unmasking Mudrooroo', *Kunapipi* 23.2: 48–62.

Clarke, Sebastian (1980) *Jah Music: The Evolution of the Popular Jamaican Song*, London: Heinemann.

Clifford, James (1988) *The Predicament of Culture: Twentieth-Century Literature, Ethnography and Art*, Cambridge, MA: Harvard University Press.

Clifford, James (1997) *Routes: Travel and Translation in the Late Twentieth Century*, Cambridge, MA: Harvard University Press.

Clingman, Stephen (1986) *The Novels of Nadine Gordimer: History from the Inside*, London: Allen and Unwin.

Coetzee, J. M. (1988) *White Writing: On the Culture of Letters in South Africa*, Johannesburg: Radix.

Cooke, Michael G. (1993) 'V. S. Reid', in Lindfors, Bernth and Sander, Reinhard (eds), *Twentieth-Century Caribbean and Black African Writers*, Second Series (Dictionary of Literary Biography, vol. 125), Detroit: Gale Research, 256–60.

Cooper, Carolyn (1990) 'Afro-Jamaican Folk Elements in Brodber's *Jane and Louisa Will Soon Come Home*', in Davies, Carole Boyce and Fido, Elaine (eds), *Out of the Kumbla: Caribbean Womanist Perspectives on Caribbean Literature*, Trenton, NJ: Africa World Press, 279–88.

Cooper, Carolyn (1995) *Noises in the Blood: Orality, Gender and the Vulgar Body of Jamaican Popular Culture*, Durham, NC: Duke University Press.

Cosentino, Donald J. (ed.) (1995) *The Sacred Arts of Haitian Vodou*, Los Angeles: UCLA Fowler Museum of Cultural Arts.

Cowasjee, Saros (1977) So *Many Freedoms: A Study of the Major Fiction of Mulk Raj Anand*, Delhi: Oxford University Press.

Crane, Ralph J. (ed.) (1998) *Nayantara Sahgal's India: Passion, Politics and History*, New Delhi: Sterling.

Crystal, David (1997) *English as a Global Language*, Cambridge: Cambridge University Press.

Cundy, Catherine, (1996) *Salman Rushdie*, Manchester and New York: Manchester University Press.

Dabydeen, David and Samaroo, Brinsley (eds) (1987) *India in the Caribbean*, London: Hansib.

Dance, Daryl Cumber (ed.) (1986) *Fifty Caribbean Writers*, Westport, CT: Greenwood Press.

Dash, Michael (1995) *Edouard Glissant*, Cambridge: Cambridge University Press.

Datta, Sangeeta (2002) *Shyam Benegal*, London: British Film Institute.

Davidson, Basil (1973) *Black Star: A View of the Life and Times of Kwame Nkrumah*, London: Allen Lane.

Davies, Carole Boyce and Fido, Elaine (eds) (1990) *Out of the Kumbla: Caribbean Womanist Perspectives on Caribbean Literature*, Trenton, NJ: Africa World Press.

Davies, Carole Boyce and Graves, Anne Adams (eds) (1986) *Ngambika: Studies of Women in African Literature*, Trenton, NJ: Africa World Press.

Davis, Gregson (1997) *Aimé Césaire*, Cambridge: Cambridge University Press.

Davis, Jack and Hodge, Bob (eds) (1985) *Aboriginal Writing Today*, Canberra: Australian Institute of Aboriginal Studies.

Dawes, Kwame (1999) *Natural Mysticism: Towards a New Reggae Aesthetic in Caribbean Writing*, Leeds: Peepal Tree Press.

D'Costa, Jean (1978) *Roger Mais: 'The Hills Were Joyful Together' and 'Brother Man'*, London: Longman.

DeCamp, David (1961) 'Social and Geographic Factors in Jamaican Dialects', in Le Page, R. B. (ed.), *Creole Language Studies*, London: Macmillan 61–84.

Deleuze, Gilles and Guattari, Félix ([1980] 1987) *A Thousand Plateaus: Capitalism and Schizophrenia*, trans. Brian Massumi, Minneapolis: University of Minneapolis Press.

Deren, Maya (1953) *Divine Horsemen: The Living Gods of Haiti*, London: Thames and Hudson.

Desai, Anita (1983) 'Indian Women Writers', in Butcher, Maggie (ed.), *The Eye of the Beholder: Indian Writing in English*, London: Commonwealth Institute, 54–8.

Desai, Anita (1994) 'Re-reading Tagore', *Journal of Commonwealth Literature* 29.1: 5–13.

Devy, G. N. (1992) *After Amnesia: Tradition and Change in Indian Literary Criticism*, London: Sangam.

D'haen, Theo (ed.) (1998) *(Un)Writing Empire*, Amsterdam and Atlanta, GA: Rodopi.

Dhawan, R. K. and Kapadia, Novy (eds) (1996) *The Novels of Bapsi Sidhwa*, New Delhi: Prestige.

Dodd, Philip (ed.) (1982) *The Art of Travel: Essays on Travel Writing*, London: Frank Cass.

Donnell, Alison (ed.) (2001) *Companion to Contemporary Black British Culture*, London and New York: Routledge.

Donnell, Alison and Lawson Welsh, Sarah (eds) (1996) *The Routledge Reader in Caribbean Literature*, London and New York: Routledge.

Driver, Dorothy, Dry, Ann, MacKenzie, Craig and Read, John (1993) *Nadine Gordimer: A Bibliography of Primary and Secondary Sources, 1937–1992*, London: Hans Zell.

Dunton, Chris (1992) *Make Man Talk True: Nigerian Drama in English since 1970*, London: Hans Zell.

Durosimi-Jones, Eldred (1998) 'Childhood before and after Birth', *African Literature Today* 21: 1–8.

Dymkowski, Christine (ed.) (2000) *Shakespeare in Production: 'The Tempest'*, Cambridge: Cambridge University Press.

Eagleton, Terry (1983) *Literary Theory: An Introduction*, Oxford: Blackwell.

Edwards, Paul and Rewt, Polly (eds) (1994) *The Letters of Ignatius Sancho*, Edinburgh: Edinburgh University Press.

Ee Tiang Hong (1997) *Responsibility and Commitment: The Poetry of Edwin Thumboo*, Singapore: National University of Singapore/Singapore University Press.

Ezenwa-Ohaeto (1997) *Chinua Achebe: A Biography*, Oxford: James Currey; Bloomington, IN: Indiana University Press.

Fanon, Frantz ([1963] 1968a) *The Wretched of the Earth*, trans. Constance Farrington, New York: Grove Press.

Fanon, Frantz ([1952] 1968b) *Black Skin, White Masks*, trans. Charles Lam Markmann, London: MacGibbon and Kee.

Fanon, Frantz ([1965] 1970) *A Dying Colonialism*, trans. Haakon Chevalier, Harmondsworth: Penguin.

Femia, Joseph (1981) *Gramsci's Political Thought: Hegemony, Consciousness and the Revolutionary Process*, Oxford: Clarendon Press.

Figueroa, John (1989) 'The Flaming Faith of These First Years: *Caribbean Voices*', in Butcher, Maggie (ed.), *Tibisiri: Caribbean Writers and Critics*, Mundelstrup, Denmark: Dangaroo Press, 59–80.

Finn, Julio (1988) *Voices of Négritude*, London: Quarto.

Finnegan, Ruth (1970) *Oral Literature in Africa*, Oxford: Clarendon Press.

Fletcher, D. M. (ed.) (1994) *Reading Rushdie: Perspectives on the Fiction of Salman Rushdie*, Amsterdam and Atlanta, GA: Rodopi.

Foucault, Michel (1972) *The Archaeology of Knowledge and the Discourse on Language*, trans. A. M. Sheridan Smith, New York: Pantheon.

Foucault, Michel (1980) *Power, Knowledge: Selected Interviews and Other Writings*, Brighton: Harvester.

Fraser, Robert (1980) *Ayi Kwei Armah: A Study in Polemical Fiction*, London: Heinemann.

Frye, Northrop (1971) *The Bush Garden: Essays on the Canadian Imagination*, Toronto: Anansi.

Fuchs, Anne (2002) *Playing the Market: The Market Theatre, Johannesburg*, revised edn, Amsterdam and New York: Rodopi.

Gandhi, Leela (1998) *Postcolonial Theory: An Introduction*, Edinburgh: Edinburgh University Press.

Gates, Henry Louis, Jr (ed.) (1984) *Black Literature and Literary Theory*, New York: Methuen.

Gates, Henry Louis, Jr (ed.) (1986) *'Race', Writing and Difference*, Chicago and London: University of Chicago Press.

Gates, Henry Louis, Jr (1988) *The Signifying Monkey: A Theory of African-American Literary Criticism*, New York: Oxford University Press.

Gellner, Ernest (1983) *Nations and Nationalism*, Ithaca, NY: Cornell University Press.

George, Rosemary Marangoly (1996) *The Politics of Home: Postcolonial Relocations and Twentieth-Century Fiction*, Cambridge: Cambridge University Press.

Gérard, Albert (1986) *European-Language Writing in Sub-Saharan Africa*, 2 vols, Budapest: Akadémia Kiadó.

Ghosh, Amitav ([1992] 1994) *In an Antique Land*, London: Granta.

Gibson, Ross (1984) *The Diminishing Paradise: Changing Literary Perceptions of Australia*, Sydney: Angus and Robertson.

Gikandi, Simon (1987) *Reading the African Novel*, London: James Currey.

Gilbert, Helen (ed.) (2001) *Postcolonial Plays: An Anthology*, London and New York: Routledge.

Gilbert, Helen and Johnston, Anna (eds) (2002) *In Transit: Travel, Text, Empire*, Bern: Peter Lang.

Gilbert, Sandra M. and Gubar, Susan ([1979] 1984) *The Madwoman in the Attic*, New Haven, CT, and London: Yale University Press.

Gilkes, Michael (1975) *Wilson Harris and the Caribbean Novel*, London: Longman Caribbean.

Gilkes, Michael (1981) *The West Indian Novel*, Boston: Twayne.

Gilroy, Paul (1987) *'There Ain't No Black in the Union Jack': The Cultural Politics of Race and Nation*, London: Hutchinson.

Gilroy, Paul (1993) *The Black Atlantic: Modernity and Double Consciousness*, London: Verso.

Glissant, Édouard (1989) *Caribbean Discourse: Selected Essays*, trans. Michael Dash, Charlottesville, VA: University of Virginia Press.

Goff, Martin (ed.) (1989) *Prize Writing: An Original Collection of Writings by Past Winners to Celebrate 21 Years of the Booker Prize*, London: Hodder and Stoughton.

Gooneratne, Yasmine (1983) *Silence, Exile and Cunning: The Fiction of Ruth Prawer Jhabvala*, Hyderabad: Orient Longman.

Gordon, Hayim (1990) *Naguib Mahfouz's Egypt: Existential Themes in His Writing*, New York: Greenwood Press.

Grant, Kevin (ed.) (1997) *The Art of David Dabydeen*, Leeds: Peepal Tree Press.

Greet, Annie, Harrex, Syd and Hosking, Susan (eds) (1992) *Raj Nostalgia: Some Literary and Critical Implications*, Adelaide: Centre for Research in the New Literatures in English.

Griffiths, Trevor R. (1983) '"This Island's Mine": Caliban and colonialism', *Yearbook of English Studies* 13: 159–80.

Guha, Ranajit *et al.* (eds) (1982–99) *Subaltern Studies: Writings on South Asian History and Society*, 10 vols, Delhi: Oxford University Press.

Habekost, Christian (ed.) (1986) *Dub Poetry: 19 Poets from England and Jamaica*, Neustadt, Germany: Michael Schwinn.

Habekost, Christian (1993) *Verbal Riddim: The Politics and Aesthetics of African-Caribbean Dub Poetry*, Amsterdam and Atlanta, GA: Rodopi.

Hamner, Robert D. (ed.) (1977) *Critical Perspectives on V. S. Naipaul*, Washington, DC: Three Continents Press.

Hamner, Robert D. (ed.) (1993) *Critical Perspectives on Derek Walcott*, Washington, DC: Three Continents Press.

Haq, Kaiser (ed.) (1990) *Contemporary Indian Poetry*, Columbus, OH: Ohio State University Press.

Hardt, Michael and Negri, Antonio (2000) *Empire*, Cambridge, MA: Harvard University Press.

Harrex, S. C. (1978) *The Fire and the Offering: The English Language Novel of India 1935–1970*, 2 vols, Calcutta: Writers' Workshop.

Harrex, S. C. and O'Sullivan, Vincent (eds) (1986) *Kamala Das: A Selection with Essays on Her Work*, Adelaide: Centre for Research in the New Literatures in English.

Harris, Wilson (1967) *Tradition, the Writer and Society: Critical Essays*, London and Port of Spain, Trinidad: New Beacon.

Harris, Wilson (1981) *Explorations: A Selection of Talks and Articles 1966–1981*, ed. Hena Maes-Jelinek, Mundelstrup, Denmark: Dangaroo Press.

Harris, Wilson (1999) *Selected Essays of Wilson Harris: The Unfinished Genesis of the Imagination*, ed. Andrew Bundy, London and New York: Routledge.

Harrow, Kenneth W. (ed.) (1994) *Thresholds of Change in African Literature: The Emergence of a Tradition*, London: James Currey.

Hayward, Helen (2002) *The Enigma of V. S. Naipaul: Sources and Contexts*, Basingstoke: Palgrave Macmillan.

Head, Dominic (1994) *Nadine Gordimer*, Cambridge: Cambridge University Press.

Head, Dominic (1998) *J. M. Coetzee*, Cambridge: Cambridge University Press.

Hergenhan, Laurie (1983) *Unnatural Lives: Studies in Australian Fiction about the Convicts, from James Tucker to Patrick White*, St Lucia, Queensland: University of Queensland Press.

Heron, George (1976) *The Poetry of Okot p'Bitek*, New York: Africana; London: Heinemann.

Hill, Errol (1972) *The Trinidad Carnival: Mandate for a National Theatre*, Austin, TX: University of Texas Press.

Hodge, Bob and Mishra, Vijay (1991) *Dark Side of the Dream: Australian Literature and the Postcolonial Mind*, North Sydney: Allen and Unwin.

Holm, John (2000) *An Introduction to Pidgins and Creoles*, Cambridge: Cambridge University Press.

Holquist, Michael (1990) *Dialogism: Bakhtin and His World*, London and New York: Routledge.

hooks, bell (1990) *Yearning: Race, Gender, and Cultural Politics*, Boston: South End Press.

Howells, Coral Ann (1991) *Jean Rhys*, London: Harvester Wheatsheaf.

Hubel, Teresa (1996) *Whose India? The Independence Struggle in British and Indian Fiction and History*, Durham, NC: Duke University Press.

Huggan, Graham (1994) *Territorial Disputes: Maps and Mapping Strategies in Contemporary Canadian and Australian Fiction*, Toronto: University of Toronto Press.

Huggan, Graham (2001) *The Postcolonial Exotic: Marketing the Margins*, London and New York: Routledge.

Huggan, Graham and Watson, Stephen (eds) (1995) *Critical Perspectives on J. M. Coetzee*, New York: St Martin's Press.

Hughes, Robert (1987) *The Fatal Shore: A History of the Transportation of Convicts to Australia, 1787–1868*, London: Collins Harvill.

Hulme, Peter and Sherman, William H. (2000) *'The Tempest' and Its Travels*, London: Reaktion.

Hutcheon, Linda (1988) *The Canadian Postmodern: A Study of Contemporary English-Canadian Fiction*, Toronto: Oxford University Press.

Hutcheon, Linda (1989) *The Politics of Postmodernism*, London and New York: Routledge.

Ilmberger, Francis and Robinson, Alan (eds) (2002) *Globalisation* (SPELL, Swiss Papers in English Language and Literature, 15), Tübingen: Gunter Narr.

Innes, C. L. (1990) *Chinua Achebe*, Cambridge: Cambridge University Press.

Innes, C. L. (2002) *A History of Black and Asian Writers in Britain, 1700–2000*, Cambridge: Cambridge University Press.

Ivory, James (comp.) (1975) *Autobiography of a Princess: Also Being the Adventures of an American Film Director in the Land of the Maharajas*, New York: Harper and Row.

Iyengar, K. R. Srinivasa ([1962] 1973) *Indian Writing in English*, 2nd edn, Bombay: Asia Publishing House.

Jahn, Jahnheinz ([1966] 1968) *A History of Neo-African Literature: Writing in Two Continents*, trans. Oliver Coburn and Ursula Lehrburger, London: Faber.

James, C. L. R (1938) *The Black Jacobins: Toussaint L'Ouverture and the San Domingo Revolution*, London: Secker & Warburg.

James, Louis (ed.) (1968) *The Islands in Between: Essays on West Indian Literature*, London: Oxford University Press.

James, Louis (1999) *Caribbean Literature in English*, London: Longman.

Jameson, Fredric (1986) 'Third World Literature in the Era of Multinational Capitalism', *Social Text* 15: 65–88.

Jankowski, James P. (2001) *Nasser's Egypt, Arab Nationalism, and the United Arab Republic*, Boulder, CO: Lynne Rienner.

JanMohamed, Abdul R. (1983) *Manichean Aesthetics: The Politics of Literature in Colonial Africa*, Amherst, MA: University of Massachusetts Press.

JanMohamed, Abdul R. (1986) 'The Economy of Manichean Allegory: The Function of Racial Difference in Colonialist Literature', *Critical Inquiry* 12.1 [1985]: 59–87; reprinted in Gates, Henry Louis, Jr (ed.), *'Race', Writing and Difference*, Chicago and London: University of Chicago Press, 78–106.

Jarrett-Macauley, Delia (1998) *The Life of Una Marson, 1905–65*, Manchester and New York: Manchester University Press.

Jefferson, Albertina (ed.) (1998) *Rex Nettleford and His Works: An Annotated Bibliography*, Mona, Jamaica: University of the West Indies Press.

Jekyll, Walter (comp. and ed.) ([1907] 1966) *Jamaican Song and Story*, New York: Dover.

Jones, Dorothy (1994) 'Fabricating Texts of Empire', *Kunapipi* 16.3: 1–16.

Jordan, David M. (1994) *New World Regionalism: Literature in the Americas*, Toronto: University of Toronto Press.

Judd, Denis (1996) *Empire: The British Imperial Experience from 1765 to the Present*, London: HarperCollins.

Jung, Carl G. *et al.* (1964) *Man and His Symbols*, London: Aldus.

Kain, Geoffrey (ed.) (1993) *R. K. Narayan: Contemporary Critical Essays*, East Lansing, MI: Michigan State University Press.

Kanneh, Kadiatu (1998) *African Identities: Race, Nation and Culture in Ethnography, Pan-Africanism and Black Literatures*, London and New York: Routledge.

Keith, W. J. (ed.) (1981) *A Voice in the Land: Essays by and about Rudy Wiebe*, Edmonton: NeWest Press.

Kermode, Frank (1954) 'Introduction', in *The Tempest* (Arden Shakespeare), 2nd edn, London: Methuen.

Khair, Tabish (2001) *Babu Fictions: Alienation in Contemporary Indian English Novels*, New Delhi: Oxford.

Khair, Tabish (ed.) (2003) *Amitav Ghosh: A Critical Companion*, New Delhi: Permanent Black.

Killam, Douglas and Rowe, Ruth (eds) (2000) *The Companion to African Literatures*, Oxford: James Currey; Bloomington, IN: Indiana University Press.

King, Bruce (1992a) *Modern Indian Poetry in English*, Delhi: Oxford University Press.

King, Bruce (ed.) (1992b) *Post-Colonial English Drama*, Basingstoke: Macmillan.

King, Bruce (1993) *V. S. Naipaul*, London: Macmillan.

King, Bruce (1995a) *Derek Walcott and West Indian Drama: 'Not Only a Playwright But a Company': The Trinidad Theatre Workshop 1959–1993*, Oxford: Clarendon Press.

King, Bruce (ed.) ([1979] 1995b) *West Indian Literature*, 2nd edn, London: Macmillan.

King, Bruce (2000) *Derek Walcott: A Caribbean Life*, Oxford: Oxford University Press.

Kirpal, Viney (ed.) (1996) *The Postmodern Indian English Novel: Interrogating the 1980s and 1990s*, Bombay: Allied Publishers.

Knight, Vere W. (ed.) (1975) *French Caribbean Literature*, Toronto: Black Images.

Knowles, Owen and Moore, Gene M. (2000) *Oxford Reader's Companion to Conrad*, Oxford: Oxford University Press.

Koch, C. J. (1985) *The Doubleman*, London: Chatto and Windus.

Koch, C. J. (1987) *Crossing the Gap: A Novelist's Essays*, London: Chatto and Windus.

Kuortti, Joel (comp.) (1997) *The Salman Rushdie Bibliography: A Bibliography of Salman Rushdie's Work and Rushdie Criticism*, Bern: Peter Lang.

Kurtz, J. Roger (1998) *Urban Obsessions, Urban Fears: The Postcolonial Kenyan Novel*, Oxford: James Currey; Trenton, NJ: Africa World Press.

La Guerre, John G. (ed.) ([1974] 1985) *Calcutta to Caroni: The East Indians in Trinidad*, 2nd edn, St Augustine, Trinidad: University of the West Indies.

Lal, Malashri (1995) *The Law of the Threshold: Women Writers in Indian English*, Simla: Indian Institute of Advanced Study.

Lamming, George (1953) *In the Castle of My Skin*, London: Michael Joseph.

Lamming, George (1960) *The Pleasures of Exile*, London: Michael Joseph.

Landry, Donna and MacLean, Gerald (eds) (1996) *The Spivak Reader: Selected Works of Gayatri Chakravorty Spivak*, London and New York: Routledge.

Lansbury, Coral (1970) *Arcady in Australia: The Evocation of Australia in Nineteenth-Century English Literature*, Carlton: Melbourne University Press.

Lawrence, Peter (1964) *Road Belong Cargo: A Study of the Cargo Movement in the Southern Madang District, New Guinea*, Manchester: Manchester University Press.

Lazarus, Neil (1990) *Resistance in Postcolonial African Fiction*, New Haven, CT: Yale University Press.

Lazarus, Neil (1999) *Nationalism and Cultural Practice in the Postcolonial World*, Cambridge: Cambridge University Press.

Lechner, Frank and Boli, John (eds) (1999) *The Globalization Reader*, Oxford: Blackwell.

Ledent, Bénédicte (2002) *Caryl Phillips*, Manchester and New York: Manchester University Press.

Le Gassick, Trevor (ed.) (1991) *Critical Perspectives on Naguib Mahfouz*, Washington, DC: Three Continents Press.

Levi, Darrell E., (1990) *Michael Manley: The Making of a Leader*, Athens, GA: University of Georgia Press.

Lévi-Strauss, Claude ([1962] 1966) *The Savage Mind*, trans. George Weidenfeld, London: Weidenfeld and Nicolson.

Lewis, Gordon K. (1968) *The Growth of the Modern West Indies*, London: MacGibbon and Kee.

Leyburn, George (1941) *The Haitian People*, New Haven, CT: Yale University Press.

Lindfors, Bernth (ed.) (1975) *Critical Perspectives on Amos Tutuola*, Washington, DC: Three Continents Press.

Lindfors, Bernth (1993) 'Okot p'Bitek', in Lindfors, Bernth and Sander, Reinhard (eds), *Twentieth-Century Caribbean and Black African Writers*, Second Series (Dictionary of Literary Biography, vol. 125), Detroit: Gale Research, 225–37.

Lindfors, Bernth (1994) *Comparative Approaches to African Literatures*, Amsterdam and Atlanta, GA: Rodopi.

Lindfors, Bernth and Sander, Reinhard (eds) (1993) *Twentieth-Century Caribbean and Black African Writers*, Second Series (Dictionary of Literary Biography, vol. 125), Detroit: Gale Research.

Long, Robert Emmet (1997) *The Films of Merchant Ivory*, revised edn, New York: Harry N. Abrams.

Loomba, Ania (1998a) *Colonialism/Postcolonialism*, London and New York: Routledge.

Loomba, Ania (1998b) '"Local-manufacture made-in-India Othello fellows": Issues of Race, Hybridity and Location in Post-Colonial Shakespeares', in Loomba, Ania and Orkin, Martin (eds) *Post-Colonial Shakespeares*, London and New York: Routledge, 143–63.

Loomba, Ania and Orkin, Martin (eds) (1998) *Post-Colonial Shakespeares*, London and New York: Routledge.

Macey, David (2001) *Frantz Fanon: A Life*, London: Granta.

McArthur, Tom (ed.) (1992) *The Oxford Companion to the English Language*, Oxford and New York: Oxford University Press.

McClintock, Anne (1995) *Imperial Leather: Race, Gender and Sexuality in the Colonial Contest*, London and New York: Routledge.

McClintock, Anne, Mufti, Aamir and Shohat, Ella (eds) (1997) *Dangerous Liaisons: Gender, Nation, and Postcolonial Perspectives*, Minneapolis: University of Minnesota Press.

MacKenzie, Craig (1999) *Bessie Head*, New York: Twayne.

McLeod, A. L. (ed.) (1994) *R. K. Narayan: Critical Perspectives*, New Delhi: Sterling.

McLeod, John (2000) *Beginning Postcolonialism*, Manchester and New York: Manchester University Press.

Maes-Jelinek, Hena (1971) 'The Myth of El Dorado in the Caribbean Novel', *Journal of Commonwealth Literature* 6.1: 113–28.

Maes-Jelinek, Hena (1982) *Wilson Harris*, Boston: Twayne.

Maes-Jelinek, Hena (ed.) (1998) *Wilson Harris: The Uncompromising Imagination*, Mundelstrup, Denmark: Dangaroo Press.

Maes-Jelinek, Hena and Ledent, Bénédicte (eds) (2002) *Theatre of the Arts: Wilson Harris and the Caribbean*, Amsterdam and New York: Rodopi.

Maes-Jelinek, Hena, Petersen, Kirsten Holst and Rutherford, Anna (eds) (1989) *A Shaping of Connections: Commonwealth Literature Studies – Then and Now*, Mundelstrup, Denmark: Dangaroo Press.

Maja-Pearce, Adewale (ed.) (1994) *Wole Soyinka: An Appraisal*, Oxford: Heinemann.

Majumdar, Margaret A. (ed.) (2002) *Francophone Studies: The Essential Glossary*, London: Arnold.

Malik, Kenan (1996) *The Meaning of Race: Race, History and Culture in Western Society*, London: Macmillan.

Mallaby, Sebastian (1992) *After Apartheid: The Future of South Africa*, London: Faber.

Mandela, Nelson (1994) *Long Walk to Freedom*, Boston: Little Brown.

Manley, Michael (1975) *A Voice at the Workplace*, London: André Deutsch.

Mannoni, Octave (1956) *Prospero and Caliban: The Psychology of Colonization*, trans. P. Powesland, London: Methuen.

Massey, Doreen (1994) *Space, Place and Gender*, Cambridge: Polity Press.

Memmi, Albert (1965) *The Colonizer and the Colonized*, trans. Howard Greenfeld, New York: Orion Press.

Mendelsohn, Oliver and Vicziany, Marika (1998) *The Untouchables: Subordination, Poverty and the State in Modern India*, Cambridge: Cambridge University Press.

Meredith, Martin (1988) *In the Name of Apartheid: South Africa in the Postwar Era*, London: Hamish Hamilton.

Meredith, Martin (1997) *Nelson Mandela: A Biography*, London: Hamish Hamilton.

Minh-ha, Trinh T. (1989) *Woman, Native, Other: Writing Postcoloniality and Feminism*, Bloomington, IN: Indiana University Press.

Mishra, Sudesh (1995) *Preparing Faces: Modernism and Indian Poetry in English*, Suva and Adelaide: University of the South Pacific and CRNLE/Flinders University of South Australia.

Mishra, Vijay and Hodge, Bob (1991) 'What is Post(-)Colonialism', *Textual Practice* 5.3: 399–414.

Mittelman, James H. (2000) *The Globalization Syndrome: Transformation and Resistance*, Princeton, NJ: Princeton University Press.

Mohanty, Chandra Talpade and Alexander, M. Jacqui (eds) (1997) *Feminist Genealogies, Colonial Legacies, Democratic Futures*, London and New York: Routledge.

Mohanty, Chandra Talpade, Torres, Lourdes and Russo, Ann (eds) (1991) *Third World Women and the Politics of Feminism*, Bloomington, IN: Indiana University Press.

Mongia, Padmini (ed.) (1996) *Contemporary Postcolonial Theory: A Reader*, London and New York: Arnold.

Moore-Gilbert, Bart (1996) *Writing India 1757–1990: The Literature of British India*, Manchester and New York: Manchester University Press.

Moore-Gilbert, Bart (1997) *Postcolonial Theory: Contexts, Practices, Politics*, London: Verso.

Moore-Gilbert, Bart (2001) *Hanif Kureishi*, Manchester and New York: Manchester University Press.

Morey, Peter (2000) *Fictions of India: Narrative and Power*, Edinburgh: Edinburgh University Press.

Morrison, Toni (1992) *Playing in the Dark: Whiteness and the Literary Imagination*, Cambridge, MA: Harvard University Press.

Mphahlele, Ezekiel (Es'kia) ([1962] 1974) *The African Image*, revised edn, London: Faber.

Mudrooroo (1994) *Aboriginal Mythology: An A-Z Spanning the History of Aboriginal Mythology from the Earliest Legends to the Present Day*, London: Aquarian.

Mukherjee, Meenakshi (ed.) (1999) *Rushdie's 'Midnight's Children': A Book of Readings*, Delhi: Pencraft.

Mukherjee, Meenakshi ([1971] 2001) *The Twice Born Fiction: Themes and Techniques of the Indian Novel in English*, 2nd edn, Delhi: Pencraft.

Mukherjee, Sujit (1994) *Translation as Discovery*, London: Sangam.

Mullaney, Julie (2002) *Arundhati Roy's 'The God of Small Things': A Reader's Guide*, London and New York: Continuum.

Naik, M. K. (1972) *Raja Rao*, Boston: Twayne.

Naik, M. K. (1982) *A History of Indian English Literature*, New Delhi: Sahitya Akademi.

Naik, M. K. (1983) *The Ironic Vision: A Study of the Fiction of R. K. Narayan*, New Delhi: Sterling.

Naik, M. K. and Narayan, Shyamala A. (2001) *Indian English Literature: 1980–2000 – A Critical Survey*, Delhi: Pencraft.

Naipaul, V. S. (1962) *The Middle Passage: The Caribbean Revisited*, London: André Deutsch.

Naipaul, V. S. (1964) *An Area of Darkness*, London: André Deutsch.

Naipaul, V. S. (1967) *The Mimic Men*, London: André Deutsch.

Naipaul, V. S. (1972) *The Overcrowded Barracoon*, London: André Deutsch.

Naipaul, V. S. (1977) *India: A Wounded Civilization*, London: André Deutsch.

Naipaul, V. S. (1980) *The Return of Eva Perón with the Killings in Trinidad*, London: André Deutsch.

Nandy, Ashis (1993) *The Intimate Enemy: Loss and Recovery of Self under Colonialism*, Delhi: Oxford University Press.

Nanton, Phillip (1998) 'What Does Mr Swanzy Want? Shaping or Reflecting? An Assessment of Henry Swanzy's Contribution to the Development of Caribbean Literature', *Kunapipi* 20.1: 11–20.

Narasimhaiah, C. D. (1991) *N for Nobody: Autobiography of an English Teacher*, New Delhi: D. K. Publishers.

Nasta, Susheila (ed.) (1988) *Critical Perspectives on Sam Selvon*, Washington, DC: Three Continents Press.

Nasta, Susheila (2002) *Home Truths: Fictions of the South Asian Diaspora in Britain*, Basingstoke: Palgrave.

Nettleford, Rex (1970) *Mirror, Mirror: Race, Identity and Protest in Jamaica*, Kingston: William Collins and Sangster.

Newell, Stephanie (2000) *Ghanaian Popular Fiction: 'Thrilling Discoveries in Conjugal Life' & Other Tales*, Oxford: James Currey; Athens, OH: Ohio University Press.

Newman, Judie (1988) *Nadine Gordimer*, London and New York: Routledge.

Ngugi wa Thiong'o (1986) *Decolonising the Mind: The Politics of Language in African Literature*, London: James Currey; Portsmouth, NH: Heinemann.

Niven, Alastair (1981) *Elechi Amadi's 'The Concubine': A Critical View*, London: Rex Collings/British Council.

Nixon, Rob (1992) *London Calling: V. S. Naipaul, Postcolonial Mandarin*, New York: Oxford University Press.

Nkrumah, Kwame (1965) *Neo-Colonialism: The Last Stage of Imperialism*, London: Nelson.

Nnaemeka, Obioma (ed.) (1997) *The Politics of (M)Othering: Womanhood, Identity and Resistance in African Literature*, London and New York: Routledge.

Nunley, John W. and Bettelheim, Judith (eds) (1988) *Caribbean Festival Arts*, Seattle: University of Washington Press.

Obiechina, Emmanuel (ed.) (1972) *Onitsha Market Literature*, London: Heinemann.

Obiechina, Emmanuel (1973) *An African Popular Literature: A Study of Onitsha Market Literature*, Cambridge: Cambridge University Press.

O'Callaghan, Evelyn (1983) 'Rediscovering the Natives of My Person', *Jamaica Journal* 16.3: 61–4.

O'Callaghan, Evelyn (1993) 'Historical Fiction and Fictional History: Caryl Phillips's *Cambridge*', *Journal of Commonwealth Literature* 28.2: 34–47.

Offord, Malcolm, Ibnlfassi, Laïla, Hitchcott, Nicki, Haigh, Sam and Chapman, Rosemary (2001) *Francophone Literatures: A Literary and Linguistic Companion*, London and New York: Routledge.

Ogude, James (1999) *Ngugi's Novels and African History: Narrating the Nation*, London: Pluto Press.

Ogunba, Oyin and Irele, Abiloa (eds) (1978) *Theatre in Africa*, Ibadan, Nigeria: Ibadan University Press.

Olson, David R. and Torrance, Nancy (eds) (1991) *Literacy and Orality*, Cambridge: Cambridge University Press.

O'Meara, Patrick, Mehlinger, Howard D. and Krain, Matthew (eds) (2000) *Globalization and the Challenges of the New Century: A Reader*, Bloomington, IN: Indiana University Press.

Ondaatje, Michael (1982) *Running in the Family*, Toronto: McClelland & Stewart.

Ong, Walter (1982) *Orality and Literacy: The Technologizing of the Word*, London and New York: Routledge.

Orkin, Martin (1998) 'Whose *Muti* in the Web of It? Seeking "Post"-Colonial Shakespeare', *Journal of Commonwealth Literature* 33.2: 15–37.

Ormerod, Beverley (1985) *An Introduction to the French Caribbean Novel*, London: Heinemann.

Owomoyela, Oyekan (1999) *Amos Tutuola Revisited*, New York: Twayne.

Pakenham, Thomas (1991) *The Scramble for Africa, 1876–1912*, London: Weidenfeld and Nicolson.

Palmer, David (1965) *The Rise of English Studies: An Account of the Study of English Language and Literature from Its Origins to the Making of the Oxford English School*, London: University of Hull/Oxford University Press.

Palmer, Vance (1954) *The Australian Legend*, Melbourne: Melbourne University Press.

Panton, David (1993) *Jamaica's Michael Manley: The Great Transformation (1972–92)*, Kingston: Kingston Publishers.

Paquet, Sandra Pouchet (1982) *The Novels of George Lamming*, London: Heinemann.

Paranjape, Makarand (ed.) (2001) *In-Diaspora: Theories, Histories, Texts*, New Delhi: Indialog.

Parekh, Bhikhu (1987) *Gandhi's Political Philosophy: A Critical Examination*, Basingstoke: Macmillan.

Parekh, Bhikhu (2000) *Rethinking Multiculturalism: Cultural Diversity and Political Theory*, Basingstoke: Macmillan.

Patteson, Richard F. (1998) *Caribbean Passages: A Critical Perspective on New Fiction from the West Indies*, Boulder, CO: Lynne Rienner.

Petersen, Kirsten Holst and Rutherford, Anna (eds) (1990) *Kunapipi* 12.2 (Chinua Achebe special issue).

Petty, Sheila (ed.) (1996) *A Call to Action: The Films of Ousmane Sembene*, Westport, CT: Praeger.

Pfaff, Françoise (1984) *The Cinema of Ousmane Sembene: A Pioneer of African Film*, Westport, CT: Greenwood Press.

Pfaff, Françoise (ed.) (1996) *Conversations with Maryse Condé*, Lincoln, NE: University of Nebraska Press.

Phillips, Caryl ([1987] 1993) *The European Tribe*, London and Basingstoke: Picador.

Phillips, Caryl (ed.) (1997) *Extravagant Strangers: A Literature of Belonging*, London: Faber.

Phillips, Caryl ([1997] 1998) *The Nature of Blood*, London: Faber.

Phillips, Caryl (2000) *The Atlantic Sound*, New York: Knopf.

Phillips, Mike and Phillips, Trevor (1998) *Windrush: The Irresistible Rise of Multi-Racial Britain*, London: HarperCollins.

Pratt, Mary Louise (1992) *Imperial Eyes: Travel Writing and Transculturation*, London and New York: Routledge.

Price, Richard (ed.) ([1973] 1996) *Maroon Societies: Rebel Slave Communities in the Americas*, 3rd edn, Baltimore: Johns Hopkins University Press.

Primorac, Ranka (2001) 'Crossing into the Space-Time of Memory: Borderline Identities in novels by Yvonne Vera', *Journal of Commonwealth Literature* 36.2: 77–93.

Procter, James (ed.) (2000) *Writing Black Britain 1948–1998: An Interdisciplinary Anthology*, Manchester and New York: Manchester University Press.

Pym, John (1983) *The Wandering Company: Twenty-One Years of Merchant Ivory Films*, London: British Film Institute; New York: Museum of Modern Art.

Quayson, Ato (1999) *Postcolonialism, Theory, Practice or Process?* Oxford: Polity Press.

Quayum, Mohammad A. and Wicks, Peter C. (eds) (2001) *Malaysian Literature in English: A Critical Reader*, Kuala Lumpur: Longman Malaysia.

Quayum, Mohammad A. and Wicks, Peter C. (eds) (2002) *Singaporean Literature in English: A Critical Reader*, Serdang: Universiti Putra Malaysia Press.

Radin, Paul (1956) *The Trickster: A Study in American Indian Mythology*, New York: Schocken Books.

Ram, Susan and Ram, N. (1996) *R. K. Narayan, The Early Years: 1906–1945*, New Delhi: Viking.

Ramchand, Kenneth ([1970] 1983) *The West Indian Novel and Its Background*, London: Heinemann.

Rao, R. Raj (2000) *Nissim Ezekiel: The Authorized Biography*, New Delhi: Viking Penguin India.

Ray, Satyajit (1976) *Our Films, Their Films*, New Delhi: Orient Longman.

Reder, Michael R. (ed.) (2000) *Conversation with Salman Rushdie*, Jackson, MS: University Press of Mississippi.

Robinson, Andrew (1989) *Satyajit Ray: The Inner Eye*, London: André Deutsch.

Rodney, Walter (1972) *How Europe Underdeveloped Africa*, London: Bogle-L'Ouverture.

Rogerson, Margaret (1998) 'Reading the Patchworks in *Alias Grace*', *Journal of Commonwealth Literature* 33.1: 5–22.

Rohlehr, Gordon (1981) *Pathfinder: Black Awakening in 'The Arrivants' of Edward Kamau Brathwaite*, Port of Spain, Trinidad: privately published.

Rohlehr, Gordon (1990) *Calypso and Society in Pre-Independence Trinidad*, Port of Spain, Trinidad: privately published.

Rushdie, Salman (1982a) *A Tall Story: How Salman Rushdie Pickled All India*, BBC2 television, 22 March.

Rushdie, Salman (1982b) 'The Empire Writes Back with a Vengeance', *The Times*, 3 July: 8.

Rushdie, Salman (1991) *Imaginary Homelands: Essays and Criticism*, 1981–1991, London: Verso.

Rutherford, Anna (ed.) (1988) *Aboriginal Culture Today*, Mundelstrup, Denmark: Dangaroo Press / *Kunapipi* 10: 1–2.

Rutherford, Anna (ed.) (1992) *From Commonwealth to Post-Colonial*, Mundelstrup, Denmark: Dangaroo Press.

Ruthven, Malise (1990) *A Satanic Affair: Salman Rushdie and the Rage of Islam*, London: Chatto and Windus.

Sahgal, Nayantara (1982) *Indira Gandhi: Her Road to Power*, New York: Frederick Ungar.

Said, Edward (1984) *The World, the Text and the Critic*, London: Faber.

Said, Edward ([1978] 1985) *Orientalism: Western Conceptions of the Orient*, Harmondsworth: Penguin.

Said, Edward ([1993] 1994) *Culture and Imperialism*, London: Vintage.

St Jorre, John (1972) *The Nigerian Civil War*, London: Hodder and Stoughton.

Sander, Reinhard W. (comp.) (1973) *An Index to BIM*, St Augustine, Trinidad: University of the West Indies Extra-Mural Studies Unit.

Sander, Reinhard W. (ed.) (1978) *From Trinidad: An Anthology of Early West Indian Writing*, London: Hodder and Stoughton.

Sander, Reinhard W. (1995) *The Trinidad Awakening: West Indian Literature of the Nineteen-Thirties*, Westport, CT: Greenwood Press.

Saro-Wiwa, Ken (1989) *On a Darkling Plain: An Account of the Nigerian Civil War*, London: Saros.

Sartre, Jean-Paul ([1964] 2001) *Colonialism and Neo-Colonialism*, trans. Azzedine Haddour, Brewer Steve, and McWilliams Terry, London and New York: Routledge.

Schipper, Mineke (1999) *Imagining Insiders: Africa and the Question of Belonging*, London and New York: Cassell.

Seacole, Mary ([1857] 1984) *Wonderful Adventures of Mrs Seacole in Many Lands*, reprinted 2nd edn, ed. Ziggi Alexander and Audrey Dewjee, Bristol: Falling Wall Press.

Senior, Olive (1983) *A–Z of Jamaican Heritage*, Kingston: Heinemann (Caribbean)/ The Gleaner.

Senn, Werner and Capone, Giovanna (eds) (1992) *The Making of a Pluralist Australia*, Bern: Peter Lang.

Serle, Geoffrey (1973) *From Deserts the Prophets Come: The Creative Spirit in Australia, 1788–1970*, Melbourne: Heinemann.

Sethi, Rumina (1999) *Myths of the Nation: National Identity and Literary Representation*, Oxford: Clarendon Press.

Shankar, Ravi (1997) *Raga Mala: The Autobiography of Ravi Shankar*, Guildford, Surrey: Genesis Publications.

Sharpley-Whiting, T. Denean (1997) *Frantz Fanon: Conflicts and Feminisms*, Lanham, MD: Rowman and Littlefield.

Sharrad, Paul (ed.) (1993) *Readings in Pacific Literature*, Wollongong, NSW: University of Wollongong.

Showalter, Elaine (1991) *Sister's Choice: Tradition and Change in American Women's Writing*, Oxford: Oxford University Press.

Silverberg, Robert ([1967] 1996) *The Golden Dream: Seekers of El Dorado*, Athens, OH: Ohio University Press.

Sistren, with Honor Ford-Smith (ed.) (1986) *Lionheart Gal: Life Stories of Jamaican Women*, London: Women's Press.

Slemon, Stephen (1987) 'Monuments of Empire: Allegory/Counter-Discourse/Post-Colonial Writing', *Kunapipi* 9.3: 1–16.

Slemon, Stephen (1988) 'Post-Colonial Allegory and the Transformation of History', *Journal of Commonwealth Literature* 23.1: 157–68.

Slemon, Stephen and Tiffin, Helen (eds) (1989) *After Europe: Critical Theory and Post-Colonial Writing*, Mundelstrup, Denmark: Dangaroo Press.

Smythe, Karen (ed.) (1994) *ECW: Essays on Canadian Writing* 53 (Michael Ondaatje special issue).

Soja, Edward (1989) *Postmodern Geographies: The Reassertion of Space in Critical Social Theory*, London: Verso.

Sougu, Omar (2002) *Writing Across Cultures: Gender Politics and Difference in the Fiction of Buchi Emecheta*, Amsterdam and New York: Rodopi.

Soyinka, Wole (1969) 'The Writer in a Modern African State', in Wästberg, Per (ed.), *The Writer in Modern Africa*, New York: Africana, 14–21.

Soyinka, Wole (1976) *Myth, Literature and the African World*, Cambridge: Cambridge University Press.

Spass, Lieve and Stimpson, Brian (eds) (1996) *Robinson Crusoe: Myths and Metamorphoses*, Basingstoke: Macmillan.

Spivak, Gayatri Chakravorty (1985) 'Three Women's Texts and a Critique of Imperialism', *Critical Inquiry* 18.4: 756–69.

Spivak, Gayatri Chakravorty (1988a) *In Other Worlds: Essays in Cultural Politics*, London: Routledge.

Spivak, Gayatri Chakravorty (1988b) 'Can the Subaltern Speak?' in Nelson, Cary and Grossberg, Lawrence (eds), *Marxism and The Interpretation of Culture*, Urbana and Chicago: University of Illinois Press, 271–313; reprinted in Williams, Patrick and

Chrisman, Laura (eds), *Colonial Discourse and Post-Colonial Theory: A Reader*, Hemel Hempstead: Harvester Wheatsheaf, 66–111.

Spivak, Gayatri Chakravorty (1990) *The Post-Colonial Critic: Interviews, Strategies, Dialogues*, ed. Sarah Harasym, London and New York: Routledge.

Spivak, Gayatri Chakravorty (1993) *Outside in the Teaching Machine*, London and New York: Routledge.

Spivak, Gayatri Chakravorty (1999) *A Critique of Postcolonial Reason: Toward a History of the Vanishing Present*, Cambridge, MA: Harvard University Press.

Sprinker, Michael (ed.) (1992) *Edward Said: A Critical Reader*, Oxford: Blackwell.

Srivastava, Pramila (ed.) (2001) *The Non-Aligned Movement: Extending Frontiers*, New Delhi: Kanishka.

Stone, Judy S. J. (1994) *Studies in West Indian Literature: Theatre*, London and Basingstoke: Macmillan.

Strathern, Oona (1994) *Traveller's Literary Companion to Africa*, Brighton: In Print.

Stratton, Florence (1994) *Contemporary African Literature and the Politics of Gender*, London and New York: Routledge.

Subramani (1985) *South Pacific Literature: From Myth to Fabulation*, Suva: University of the South Pacific Press.

Suk, Jeannie (2001) *Postcolonial Paradoxes in French Caribbean Writing: Césaire, Glissant, Condé*, Oxford: Clarendon Press.

Suleri, Sara (1992) *The Rhetoric of English India*, Chicago: University of Chicago Press.

Taussig, Michael (1987) *Shamanism, Colonialism, and the Wild Man: A Study in Terror and Healing*, Chicago: University of Chicago Press.

Terada, Rei (1992) *Derek Walcott's Poetry: American Mimesis*, Boston: Northeastern University Press.

Terdiman, Richard (1985) *Discourse/Counter-Discourse: The Theory and Practice of Symbolic Resistance in Nineteenth-Century France*, Ithaca, NY and London: Cornell University Press.

Tharu, Susie and Lalita, K. (eds) (1991) *Women Writing in India: 600 BC to the Present*, New York: Feminist Press at the City University of New York.

Theroux, Paul (1998) *Sir Vidia's Shadow: A Friendship across Five Continents*, Boston: Houghton Mifflin.

Thieme, John (1987) *The Web of Tradition: Uses of Allusion in V. S. Naipaul's Fiction*, Mundelstrup, Denmark: Dangaroo Press; London: Hansib.

Thieme, John (ed.) (1996) *The Arnold Anthology of Post-Colonial Literatures in English*, London and New York: Arnold.

Thieme, John (1997) 'After Greenwich: Crossing Meridians in Post-Colonial Literatures', in Delrez, Marc and Ledent, Bénédicte (eds), *The Contact and the Culmination: Essays in Honour of Hena Maes-Jelinek*, Liège: University of Liège, 353–63.

Thieme, John (1999) *Derek Walcott*, Manchester and New York: Manchester University Press.

Thieme, John (2001) *Postcolonial Con-Texts: Writing Back to the Canon*, London and New York: Continuum.

Thomas, Sue (1999) *The Worlding of Jean Rhys*, Westport, CT: Greenwood Press.

Tiffin, Chris and Lawson, Alan (eds) (1994) *De-Scribing Empire*, London and New York: Routledge.

Tiffin, Helen (1987) 'Post-Colonial Literatures and Counter-Discourse', *Kunapipi* 9.3: 17–34.

Todd, Loreto ([1974] 1990) *Pidgins and Creoles*, 2nd edn, London and New York: Routledge.

Tong Chee Kiong, Pakir, Anne, Ban Kah Choon and Goh, Robbie H. (eds) (2001) *Ariels: Essays for Edwin Thumboo*, Singapore: Oxford University Press.

Torres-Saillant, Silvio (1997) *Caribbean Poetics: Towards an Aesthetic of West Indian Literature*, Cambridge: Cambridge University Press.

Trivedi, Harish (1993) *Colonial Transactions*, Calcutta: Papyrus.

Turner, Victor (1967) *The Forest of Symbols: Aspects of Ndembu Ritual*, Ithaca, NY: Cornell University Press.

Uslar Pietri, Arturo (1972) 'The Mestizo Experience and the New World', in Seymour, A. J. (ed.), *New Writing in the Caribbean*, Georgetown, Guyana: Guyana Lithographic, 172–8.

Van Gennep, Arnold (1960) *The Rites of Passage*, London: Routledge.

Vaughan, Alden T. and Vaughan, Virginia Mason (1991) *Shakespeare's Caliban: A Cultural History*, Cambridge: Cambridge University Press.

Veeser, H. Aram (ed.) (1989) *The New Historicism*, New York: Routledge.

Veit-Wild, Flora and Chennels, Anthony J. (eds) (1999) *Emerging Perspectives on Dambudzo Marechera*, Trenton, NJ: Africa World Press.

Visweswaran, Kamala (1994) *Fictions of Feminist Ethnography*, Minneapolis: University of Minnesota Press.

Walcott, Derek (1965) *The Castaway and Other Poems*, London: Jonathan Cape.

Walcott, Derek (1970) *Dream on Monkey Mountain and Other Plays*, New York: Farrar, Straus and Giroux.

Walcott, Derek (1990) *Omeros*, New York: Farrar, Straus and Giroux; London: Faber.

Walcott, Derek (1998) *What the Twilight Says: Essays*, New York: Farrar, Straus and Giroux; London: Faber.

Walder, Dennis (ed.) (1990) *Literature and the Modern World: Critical Essays and Documents*, Oxford: Oxford University Press in association with the Open University.

Walder, Dennis (1998) *Post-Colonial Literatures in English: History, Language, Theory*, Oxford: Blackwell.

Walder, Dennis (2002) *Athol Fugard*, Plymouth: Northcote House/British Council.

Walmsley, Anne (comp.) (1990) *Guyana Dreaming: The Art of Aubrey Williams*, Mundelstrup, Denmark: Dangaroo Press.

Walmsley, Anne (1992) *The Caribbean Artists Movement 1966–1972: A Literary and Cultural History*, London: New Beacon.

Wambu, Onyekachi (ed.) (1998) *Empire Windrush: Fifty Years of Writing about Black Britain*, London: Victor Gollancz.

Ward, Russel (1958) *The Australian Legend*, Melbourne: Oxford University Press.

Warner, Keith (1982) *The Trinidad Calypso: A Study of the Calypso as Oral Literature*, Washington, DC: Three Continents Press.

Warner, Keith (ed.) (1988) *Critical Perspectives on Léon-Gontran Damas*, Washington, DC: Three Continents Press.

Watt, Ian ([1957] 1963) *The Rise of the Novel*, Harmondsworth: Penguin.

Webby, Elizabeth (2000) *The Cambridge Companion to Australian Literature*, Cambridge: Cambridge University Press.

Weiner, Annette B. and Schneider, Jane (eds) (1989) *Cloth and the Human Experience*, Washington, DC: Smithsonian Institution Press.

Weiss, Timothy (1992) *On the Margins: The Art of Exile in V. S. Naipaul*, Amherst, MA: University of Massachusetts Press.

White, Hayden (1973) *Metahistory: The Historical Imagination in Nineteenth-Century Europe*, Baltimore: Johns Hopkins University Press.

White, Hayden (1978) *Tropics of Discourse: Essays in Cultural Criticism*, Baltimore: Johns Hopkins University Press.

White, Landeg (1975) *V. S. Naipaul: A Critical Introduction*, London: Macmillan.

White, Richard (1981) *Inventing Australia: Images and Identity, 1688–1980*, Sydney: Allen and Unwin.

White, Timothy ([1983] 1998) *Catch a Fire: The Life of Bob Marley*, revised edn, New York: Henry Holt.

Whitehead, Neil L. (ed.) (1997) *The Discoverie of the Large, Rich and Bewtiful Empyre of Guiana by Sir Walter Ralegh*, Manchester and New York: Manchester University Press.

Wilde, William H., Hooton, Joy and Andrews, Barry (1985) *The Oxford Companion to Australian Literature*, Melbourne: Oxford University Press.

Williams, Patrick (1999) *Ngugi wa Thiong'o*, Manchester and New York: Manchester University Press.

Williams, Patrick and Chrisman, Laura (eds) (1993) *Colonial Discourse and Post-Colonial Theory: A Reader*, Hemel Hempstead: Harvester Wheatsheaf.

Williams, Raymond L. (1984) *Gabriel García Márquez*, Boston: Twayne.

Wilson-Tagoe, Nana (1998) *Historical Thought and Literary Representation in West Indian Literature*, Gainesville, FL: University Press of Florida.

Wintz, Cary D. (ed.) (1996) *The Emergence of the Harlem Renaissance (The Harlem Renaissance 1920–1940)*, New York: Garland.

Worsley, Peter M. (1957) *The Trumpet Shall Sound: A Study of 'Cargo' Cults in Melanesia*, London: MacGibbon and Kee.

Wright, Derek (1989) *Ayi Kwei Armah's Africa*, London: Hans Zell.

Wright, Derek (ed.) (1992) *Critical Perspectives on Ayi Kwei Armah*, Washington, DC: Three Continents Press.

Wright, Derek (1993) *Wole Soyinka Revisited*, New York: Twayne.

Wright, Derek (1994) *The Novels of Nuruddin Farah*, Bayreuth: University of Bayreuth.

Wright, Derek (1997) *New Directions in African Fiction*, New York: Twayne.

Wylie, Dan (2000) *Savage Delight: White Myths of Shaka*, Pietermaritzburg: University of Natal Press.

Young, Robert (1990) *White Mythologies: Writing History and the West*, London and New York: Routledge.

Young, Robert (1995) *Colonial Desire: Hybridity in Theory, Culture and Race*, London and New York: Routledge.

Young, Robert (2001) *Postcolonialism: An Historical Introduction*, Oxford: Blackwell.

Yousaf, Nahem (2001) *Alex La Guma: Politics and Resistance*, Portsmouth, NH: Heinemann.

Zamora, Lois Parkinson and Faris, Wendy B. (eds) (1995) *Magic Realism: Theory, History, Community*, Durham, NC: Duke University Press.

Zehnder, Martin (ed.) (2003) *Something Rich and Strange: Selected Essays on Sam Selvon*, Leeds: Peepal Tree Press.